D1203849

GOVERNING *the* AMERICAN LAKE

GOVERNING *the* AMERICAN LAKE

THE US DEFENSE *and* ADMINISTRATION *of* the PACIFIC, 1945–1947

HAL M. FRIEDMAN

MICHIGAN STATE UNIVERSITY PRESS · EAST LANSING

⊛ The paper used in this publication meets the minimum requirements of ANSI/NISO
Z39.48-1992 (R 1997) (Permanence of Paper).

 Michigan State University Press
East Lansing, Michigan 48823-5245
www.msupress.msu.edu

Printed and bound in the United States of America.

13 12 11 10 09 08 07   1 2 3 4 5 6 7 8 9 10

LIBRARY OF CONGRESS CATALOGING-IN-PUBLICATION DATA
Friedman, Hal M., 1965–
Governing the American Lake : U.S. defense and administration of the Pacific Basin,
19451947 / Hal M. Friedman.
p. cm.
Includes bibliographical references and index.
ISBN 978-0-87013-794-5 (hardcover : alk. paper) 1. Pacific Islands (Trust Territory)—
Strategic aspects. 2. Pacific Islands (Trust Territory)—Politics and government. 3. Pacific
Area—Defenses. 4. Pacific Area—Strategic aspects. 5. United States—Military policy.
6. Pacific Area—Foreign relations—United States. 7. United States—Foreign relations—
Pacific Area. 8. United States—Foreign relations—1945–1953. 9. Imperialism—History—
20th century. 10. Cold War. I. Title.
UA876.P165F754 2006
355'.0330182309044—dc22
2006100329

Cover and book design by Sharp Des!gns, Lansing, Michigan

g green Michigan State University Press is a member of the Green Press Initiative
press and is committed to developing and encouraging ecologically responsible
INITIATIVE
publishing practices. For more information about the Green Press Initiative and the use
of recycled paper in book publishing, please visit *www.greenpressinitiative.org.*

Visit Michigan State University Press on the World Wide Web at *www.msupress.msu.edu*

To my wife, Lisa,
whose love and support
made our life together,
and this book, possible.

Contents

Figures and Maps

■ Figures

■ Maps

Acknowledgments

I have incurred many debts in the process of producing this monograph. None of the individuals or organizations mentioned here are in any way responsible for the opinions asserted in this work. Any accountability for interpretations or errors is mine alone. However, each of the people cited assisted me in a very significant way and deserve thanks for that assistance.

This book is dedicated to my wife, Lisa. I cannot imagine what life would be like without her. In every sense of the word, she has been the humanizing factor of my life. Lisa has not only been my soul mate in terms of our life together, but she has been the most active supporter of career aspirations that any spouse could ask for. This support has come while she has pursued her own career and has taken the central part in raising our son. I simply do not know what I would have done without her during all these years of personal and professional life. I would have truly been lost without her.

My son Jeffrey is now a teenager and is growing into quite a remarkable young man. My hope is that this work will add further to his appreciation of studying the past. More exactly, I hope this work will further demonstrate to him what his great-grandparents' and grandparents' generations did for the benefit of our country, and even what mistakes they made. Finally, I hope that this gives him some idea of what I did during all of those hours in front of the computer, and what contributions I am trying to make to my profession.

My parents, Irving and Elaine Friedman, continue to be my personal connection with the past. It has been several years since my father's death, something that everyone in my family is still deeply affected by. Yet for me, studying 1940s American Pacific policy brings my father back to life, if only momentarily and in certain dimensions. Given his wartime service, studying the 1940s Pacific brings me closer to my father and helps me bring this era a bit more to life for my students. Unfortunately, my mother died just as this book was in the final stages of production. Up to her death, she continued to read my material and constantly asked why historians do certain things in certain ways. Whenever she asked me about research and writing techniques, I became even more convinced that she would have made a good English Literature teacher. In all kinds of ways such as these, my parents' absence in my life will be particularly felt as I write additional monographs in the years to come.

My parents-in-law, Ronald and Carolyn Sampsell, hold a special place in the creation of this book, as they did with my first book and my thesis and dissertation. They provided my wife and me with various kinds of support during graduate school. Since then, they have been the best and most intense kind of inspiration to our son. I am glad that he has been able to grow up in close physical proximity to at least one set of grandparents, as I did. They have also provided us with many historical lessons as well, as they were part of the last sizable generation to grow up on farms in the United States. For me, they continue to be my advisers on professional career matters, as they were throughout the 1990s.

I continue to benefit from my interaction with my siblings. My sisters Karen and Nancy have been an inspiration to me with their hard work in their careers and their attention to professionalism and detail. I especially thank Nancy for encouragement in pursuing a college education when I was young and I thank my sister Margaret for continuing to give me career advice even as she transitioned to a new career herself. I also want to thank my brother Alan for introducing me to the now late Professor John Bowditch, former Chair of the History Department at the University of Michigan, and for always listening when I talked about how difficult it is to publish professionally while teaching full-time at a community college. This book would also not have been possible without the generosity of my sister Phyllis and my brother-in-law Mark in giving their support, which included lodging while I was conducting research at the MacArthur Memorial Archives in Norfolk, Virginia, in the 1990s. The best, however, was when my niece Sarah reacted to the publication of my first book with "Uncle Hal's an author; for real?" For real, Sarah.

Two individuals who should have been thanked for helping me with my first book, but were not because of my own oversight, were my godparents, my great-aunt and great-uncle, Rose and Mac Carp. They have, like my parents, particularly inspired me to pursue a career as a historian. Both are now, unfortunately, deceased, but they provided me with financial support through my undergraduate years as well as moral support since then. My Uncle Mac came to Canada from Imperial Russia in 1913, so with his thick accent, his ability to converse in several languages, and his constant interest in historical and political affairs, he always reminded me of the typical, or perhaps stereotypical, European intellectual, living in the United

States. He was, in fact, the intellectual of our family. Similarly, my Aunt Rose, raised in a Jewish farming colony in Bad Axe, Michigan, and then educated as a school librarian, was the teacher of the family. She constantly encouraged us to read as children, she was always interested in what we were reading, and she was forever focused on our careers and aspirations. As a cousin of mine said, every family should have an Uncle Mac and Aunt Rose, and I sincerely think that my interest in becoming an historian was, at least in part, because of their example as I grew up.

I must also thank many colleagues at Henry Ford Community College. Now retired President Andrew Mazarra, now retired Interim President Sally Barnett, now retired Vice President/Dean of Academic Education Edward Chielens, former Social Science Associate Dean Henry Bowers, and John McDonald, President of the Henry Ford Community College Federation of Teachers (American Federation of Teachers Local 1650) stand out. In particular, I must thank Dr. Mazarra, Dr. Chielens, and Dr. Bowers, as well as the Sabbatical Review Committee, for approving my Fall 2003 sabbatical request, during which time I was able to complete the rough draft of this manuscript. John McDonald is deserving of a special thanks since he negotiated sabbaticals as a contractual right with the College and has been a champion of faculty contractual access to professional development opportunities. The Executive Board and rank and file of Local 1650 have also gone far in creating numerous sources of funding for instructors to pursue research for professional development, especially by presenting papers at conferences. Vice President/Controller Marjorie Swan and now retired Vice President/Dean of Student Services Michael Meade have generously approved several of my requests for such funding, during which ideas for this book were presented and refined. I have also received helpful hints and ideas from our college library staff, especially Kathy Cunningham, Pat Doline, Dan Harrison, Terrence Potvin, and Nancy Widman. A special thanks goes to Kathy and Terry for tracking down several volumes of the *United States Government Manual* and the *Biographic Register of the Department of State* from the 1940s so that I could copy personnel lists for various agencies from that time period.

Maggie Anderson, Rodney Barnhart, John Burks, Rob Butler, Derek Croxton, Mario Di Ponio, Michael Johns, Saeed Khan, Richard Marquis, Devissi Muhammad, Wendy Osthaus, Sam Plaza, Pamela Sayre, Bill Secrest, Ken Shepherd, Michael Swope, Reginald Witherspoon, and Sue Zimmerman, as well as my retired colleagues Virginia Caruso, Bill Hackett, Bob Spiro, Morris Taber, the late Art Thomas, and the late Armen Ovhanesian, have gone even further in fostering this type of professional environment. Whether they realize it or not, they have created and sustained a history department at Henry Ford Community College that is the most conducive environment to unencumbered exchange about pedagogy, research, writing, and historiography that I have ever encountered in the field. I value our comradeship more than I can express in words, and I hope it continues for a very long time. I have to particularly thank Pamela Sayre, not only for editing and indexing this work, but for taking on much of the day-to-day departmental administration that is so typical in small colleges. Her willingness to take on these tasks freed much of the time I needed to write this book. To the list of HFCC historians must be added the names of four now-retired HFCC political scientists: Brian Coyer, Tom Payette, John Smith, and Barbara Suhay. In particular, my conversations with Brian about the literature on bureaucratic rivalry were quite useful, and John encouraged me — and still does — about the importance of publishing as a community college scholar. In addition, I have to acknowledge several colleagues with whom I have had general conversations about political and international affairs, which have added to this monograph — especially Nabeel Abraham, Pete Cravens, Tarek Joseph, Dan Kearney, Greg Osowski, Tony Perry, Kim Schopmeyer, and Brian Smith.

Numerous acknowledgments are due to the staffs of archives and libraries throughout the country. I would like to thank James Zobel and Edward Boone of the MacArthur Memorial Archives in Norfolk, especially Jim Zobel for trying to find out about 1940s Army officers serving in the Pacific. Michael Hussey, Sally Kuisel, Kathy Nicostra, Matthew Olsen, Jimmy Rush, Joseph Schwartz, and John Vandereedt of the National Archives' Civilian Records Branch are due thanks for helping me find material on the State and Interior Departments, especially organizational charts. Also at the National Archives, Dave Giordano, Wilbert Mahoney, Tim Nenninger, Patrick Osborn, and Kenneth Schlessinger of the Modern Military Records Branch all indulged my numerous questions about Army personnel in the Western Pacific in the 1940s, and I have to thank John Haynes of the Library of Congress Manuscript Division for doing the same regarding Interior Department personnel. In addition, the staff at the Halle Library at Eastern Michigan University was particularly helpful in finding biographical information on 1940s US Government officials as was the staff at the Government Documents section of the University of Michigan's Hatcher Graduate Library, especially Grace York, Documents Librarian. Ruth Carr and David Smith from the New York Public Library also helped in attempting to find biographical information on several individuals mentioned in the book. I particularly want to thank Patricia Sayre McCoy, Head of Cataloging for the D'Angelo Law Library at the University of Chicago, who helped me with copyright issues concerning GPO publications.

Thanks also go to David Hogan from the US Army's Center of Military History for help on copyright matters concerning Army and AAF organization charts. Providing similar assistance about copyright and senior officers in the 1940s AAF was Herman Wolk from the Office of Air Force History. Melinda Torres and Thomas Buffenbarger of the US Army's Military History Institute in Carlisle, Pennsylvania, were particularly helpful with tracking down general officers from US Army Forces, Pacific in the 1940s. Similarly insightful in obtaining information on civilian and military personnel associated with US Pacific policy in the 1940s was the staff at the National Personnel Records Center in St. Louis, Missouri — especially Alvis Poe,

Archives Technician. Archie DeFante, Joe Caver, Lynn Gamma, Marcie Green, Essie Roberts, Air Force Reserve Major Ken Tilley, and Anthony Wise at the Air Force Historical Research Agency, Maxwell Air Force Base, Montgomery, Alabama, were extraordinarily professional in their assistance even as their archive was enduring some of the worst budget cuts it has ever seen. A special thanks to Mrs. Green and Major Tilley for researching the biographies of several AAF officers for me. Richard Geselbracht and the entire staff of the Harry S. Truman Library were wonderful—especially Randy Sowell, who has probably taken a million little research requests of mine and always produced answers for me in record time. Similarly, the staff of the Dwight D. Eisenhower Library, especially Jim Leyerzapf, has put in duty above and beyond the norm in answering my questions about Army and AAF personnel in the 1940s Pacific.

Numerous people at the US Naval Historical Center in Washington, D.C., helped me get a start on this project in the 1980s and 1990s and continued to help me finish it in the early twenty-first century. These individuals include Dr. Dean Allard, Bernard Cavalcante, and Kathy Roar. More particularly with this project, I must thank Kathy Lloyd, Head of Operational Archives, for her flexibility in providing me with research facilities. Included also would be Regina Akers, John Hodges, Ken Johnson, Allen Knechtmann, Tim Pettit, and Mike Walker, all of whom made my last research excursion to the Operational Archives so successful. In addition, this last research trip would not have been very successful if it were not for Senior Historian Ed Marolda, Head of the Contemporary History Branch Gary Weir, and Contemporary Branch historians Jeff Barlow, Randy Papadopoulos, and John Sherwood. I especially have to thank the Contemporary Branch folks for helping a technological novice figure out how to work a digital camera!

The staff at the US Naval War College also helped, in particular with the photocopied maps and organizational charts in this book. Thanks go first to Edward Miller for generously establishing the Edward S. Miller Research Fellowship in Naval History. That award allowed me to travel to Newport, Rhode Island, in October 2003 and obtain the materials noted above. Thanks must also go to Rear Admiral Joseph Strasser, USN (RET), President of the Naval War College Foundation, and to John Hattendorf, the Ernest J. King Professor of Maritime History and Chair of the Maritime History Department, for coordination of the award and especially for encouragement in my research efforts. Professor Hattendorf was particularly helpful in the logistics of administrative support, as was his Assistant, Patricia Cormier, who did more photocopying than I had a right to ask of her. Putting in an equally wonderful effort during the week when I was in Newport were Evelyn Cherpak, Curator of the War College's Naval Historical Collection, and Teresa Clements, Archival Technician, both of whom pulled numerous records for me as I raced against the research clock. At subsequent meetings and conferences, Dr. Cherpak has been very supportive of my work, especially in regard to future planned monographs.

Individually, the following scholars also have to be acknowledged for their continued help in my quest to research the United States' role in the mid-1940s Pacific Basin. These individuals include Dirk Ballendorf of the University of Guam, Marc Gallicchio of Villanova University, and Heather Staines of Greenwood Press. Dirk again served as a reviewer for this manuscript, as he did on the first one, and Marc continued to evoke an interest in the importance of the US military in the twentieth-century Pacific that is sadly lacking among most American military and diplomatic historians today. Heather saw my first monograph to publication and was eager to publish this one before a policy change at the Greenwood Group precluded it. In spite of that policy change, she has been very supportive of my subsequent activities by being steadfast in getting historiography on the United States in the Pacific published. To Bob Miller of Southwest Missouri State University, I still owe a debt for providing me with the main title for my first article by suggesting that the immediate postwar Pacific Basin was a paradise that was being trampled on by a beast, in this case the United States. That quick suggestion in 1993 has helped me write and title several publications on the same and related subjects. To Kay Reist of the University of Pittsburgh-Johnstown, I am grateful for comments on the Navy chapter in connection with the Northern Great Plains History Conference. Kay not only gave me very useful feedback but also expressed confidence in the manuscript at a time when mine was lacking. To Joe Fitzharris of the University of St. Thomas, I am indebted for organizing the Great Plains History Conference, providing feedback to me on the AAF, and creating an atmosphere both friendly and fruitful to national-security-policy historians.

At Michigan State University and the University of Michigan, a number of people again need to be mentioned. To Don Lammers, thanks are again due for being such a professional example, not only as a dissertation director but as a teacher, scholar, and colleague as I embarked on this second book and my own tenured teaching career. To John Shy at the University of Michigan, I still have to thank you for helping me get my career off the ground, even though you don't want to be thanked. In the end, suffice it to say that you continue to inspire me with your example as a scholar, and that I am paying you back by "paying it forward." Other individuals were also key to this study being completed. Chris Hamel taught me what being a historian is all about. He not only instructed me in how and why historians analyze and write the way they do, but his help in classifying my first monograph into strategic and bureaucratic dimensions was the starting point for this book. Our long conversations about these matters were a basic building block upon which this work flourished, and his assistance during graduate school and since has been vital to the beginning of my career. I still have to thank Michael Lewis for forcing me to think about enlarging my initial, narrow study from Navy policy concerning Micronesia to US strategic policy, broadly conceived, for the entire Pacific Basin. That, too, was a significant step in turning a doctoral dissertation into what will eventually be three historical monographs. I would also again like to acknowledge Michael Unsworth, History Bibliographer at Michigan State University, who has assisted me for nearly twenty years in finding government sources, and in general has been my East Lansing military-history connection.

My professors at Eastern Michigan University, my undergraduate alma mater, are perhaps even more central to this study since they first introduced me to serious historical studies and taught me that college teachers can also be first-rate scholars. I must thank the late Richard Abbott for first discussing the idea of the United States in the 1940s Pacific with me during the 1980s, and for continuing to discuss this project with me as I pursued it in graduate school and as he scuba-dived in Micronesia. I find it ironic and more than a bit sad that I have now taught his course on US military history on an occasional basis, but I am trying to follow in his footsteps as much as possible. He is greatly missed. I must also thank Don Briggs, George Cassar, Robert Grady, Jim Johnson, Roger King, Karen Linderman, Jim Magee, Walter Moss, Joe Ohren, James Pfister, Leonis Sabaliunas, Janice Terry, Jiu Upshur, and Reinhard Wittke for instilling in me the professionalism and high standards that I was able to hone in graduate school and am now able to impart to students at Henry Ford Community College. The History and Political Science Departments at Eastern Michigan in the 1980s were the most encouraging environments I can think of in which a first-generation college student from a working-class background could get started in the profession. Similarly, I have to thank several individuals from the current EMU History and Philosophy Department who have been instrumental in my graduate education, my career as an instructor, and my development as a professional historian. These include, but are not limited to, Marsha Ackerman, Kathy Chamberlain, Mark Higbee, Richard Nation, Gersham Nelson, and Philip Schmitz. Especially helpful in these matters has been Michael Homel. Mike's advice to me about the travails of graduate school were like charts in rough waters and his EMU History Reader's Group has been a wonderful outlet of professional activity for me and a magnificent release from the rigors of teaching. Most especially at EMU, I have to thank Rob Citino. Rob and I have become close colleagues in the last few years, and he has become a professional model for me to emulate. In just over twenty years of teaching, always with heavy classroom and administrative loads, Rob has managed to publish seven monographs, is working on additional ones, and has become a recognized specialist in his area, all while maintaining an extraordinary reputation for teaching excellence in the classroom. I'll never catch up, Rob, but I am sure going to try!

I would also like to acknowledge the assistance I received from my membership in the War Studies Group at the University of Michigan's Department of History. Since I joined that informal weekly group in January 1991, WSG has been a forum for communicating my ideas, my hopes, and my fears about professional life in general. Special thanks go to past and present members Saiful Islam Abdul-Ahad,

Keith Arbor, Bill Boardman, Tom Collier, David Fitzpatrick, Paul Forage, Jim and Chris Holoka, Bob Jefferson, Doron Lamm, Gerald Lindermann, Jonathan Marwil, Dennis Ringle, Mike Riordon, Ken Slepyan, and Jack Sherzer for constantly providing me with new perspectives on military history and strategic thought.

In addition, the Metro Detroit Historians Collegium has been another outlet for my professional activities. A group of historians from small two-year and four-year college history departments in the Detroit area, the Collegium has become a local forum for history instructors at institutions that have minimal resources for professional development. The Collegium was kind enough to hear a presentation on my first book, and continues to be significant to my professional development. Within the Collegium, I especially have to thank Jayne Morris-Crowther from Madonna University and Oakland University; Tom Klug from Marygrove College; Shawn Dry, Ed Gallagher, Marilynn Kokoszka, and Tim Koerner from Oakland Community College; Evan Garrett and Steve Berg from Schoolcraft College; and Roy Finkenbine from the University of Detroit–Mercy. In addition, I have to thank my colleagues from HFCC who helped start the Collegium—namely, John Burks, Virginia Caruso, Mario Di Ponio, Michael Johns, Richard Marquis, Devissi Muhammad, Pamela Sayre, Bill Secrest, Ken Shepherd, Bob Spiro, and Wendy Osthaus.

Finally, I must thank Julie Loehr, Assistant Editor and Editor in Chief; Martha Bates, Acquisitions Editor; Kristine Blakeslee, Project Editor; Bonnie Cobb, Copy Editor; Annette Tanner, Production Manager; and Julie Reaume, Marketing & Sales Manager at Michigan State University Press for getting this book into publication. Martha, in particular, was very encouraging about this manuscript, even when I was doubtful about publishing traditional policy history in an era of bottom-up social and cultural historiography. I especially have to thank Kristine, Bonnie, and Julie for putting up with my ignorance on editing and marketing.

■ Permissions

Trusteeship, 1945–1947," *ISLA: A Journal of Micronesian Studies* 3, no. 2 (Dry Season 1995): 339–370.

"Modified Mahanism: Pearl Harbor, the Pacific War, and Changes to U.S. National Security Strategy in the Pacific Basin, 1945–1947," *The Hawaiian Journal of History* 31 (1997): 179–204.

"The 'Bear' in the Pacific? U.S. Intelligence Perceptions of Soviet Strategic Power Projection in the Pacific Basin and East Asia, 1945–1947," *Intelligence and National Security* 12 (October 1997): 75–101 [reprinted from *Intelligence and National Security* 12, no. 4, with permission of Frank Cass & Co.].

"'Americanism' and Strategic Security: The Pacific Basin, 1943–1947," in *American Diplomacy* 2, no. 3 (1997) [electronic journal cited October–December 1997], available from http://www.unc.edu/depts/diplomat/AD_Issues/amdipl_5/ friedman.html.

Creating an American Lake: United States Imperialism and Strategic Security in the Pacific Basin, 1945–1947, © 2001 by Hal M. Friedman, reproduced with permission of Greenwood Publishing Group, Inc., Westport, Conn.

"Civil versus Military Administration: The Interior Department's Position on US Pacific Territories, 1945–1947," *Pacific Studies* 29, no. 1/2 (March–June 2006).

Acronyms

AAA	Anti-Aircraft Artillery
AAF	Army Air Forces
ACAS	Assistant Chief of Air Staff
ACNO	Assistant Chief of Naval Operations
ACS	Assistant Chief of Staff
AFMIDPAC	US Army Forces, Middle Pacific
AFHRA	Air Force Historical Research Agency
AFPAC	US Army Forces, Pacific
AFSHRC	Albert F. Simpson Historical Research Center
AFWESPAC	US Army Forces, Western Pacific
AGF	Army Ground Forces
ALCOM	Alaskan Command
ASF	Army Service Forces
ASW	Anti-Submarine Warfare
ATC	Air Transport Command
ATS	Army Transport Service
CAA	Civil Aeronautics Administration
CAF	Continental Air Forces
CARIBSEAFRON	Caribbean Sea Frontier
CCC	Civilian Conservation Corps
CCS	Combined Chiefs of Staff
CG	Commanding General
CINCAFPAC	Commander-in-Chief, Army Forces, Pacific
CINCAL	Commander-in-Chief, Alaskan Command

CINCFE	Commander-in-Chief, Far East Command
CINCNAVFE	Commander-in-Chief, Naval Forces, Far East
CINCPAC	Commander-in-Chief, Pacific Command
CINCPACFLT	Commander-in-Chief, Pacific Fleet
CINCPOA	Commander-in-Chief, Pacific Ocean Areas
CINCSWPA	Commander-in-Chief, Southwest Pacific Area
CNO	Chief of Naval Operations
CO	Commanding Officer
COMADIV	Commander, [Numbered] Air Division
COMAF	Commanding Officer, [Numbered] Air Force
COMALSEAFRON	Commander, Alaskan Sea Frontier
COMGENAIR	Commanding General, Army Air Forces
COMINCH	Commander-in-Chief, US Fleet
COMMARIANAS	Commander, Marianas Area
COMNAVJAP	Commander, Naval Activities, Japan
COMNAVFORWESPAC	Commander, Naval Forces, Western Pacific
COMNORPAC	Commander, Northern Pacific
COMPHIBSPAC	Commander, Amphibious Forces, Pacific Fleet
CP	Division of Commercial Policy
CSA	Chief of Staff, United States Army
C SPGAR USA	Chief, Special Purposes Garrison, US Army
DA	Dependent Area Affairs Division
DCAS	Deputy Chief of Air Staff
DCNO	Deputy Chief of Naval Operations
DCS	Deputy Chief of Staff
DCSA	Deputy Chief of Staff, United States Army
DDEL	Dwight D. Eisenhower Library
DOD	Department of Defense
EUR	Office of European Affairs
FE	Office of Far Eastern Affairs
FEAF	Far East Air Forces
FECOM	Far East Command
FMF	Fleet Marine Forces
FRUS	*Foreign Relations of the United States*
FY	Fiscal Year
GHQ	General Headquarters
GP	General Purpose
GPO	Government Printing Office
HSTL	Harry S. Truman Library
IS	Division of International Security Affairs
JA	Division of Japanese Affairs

JAAF	Japanese Army Air Force
JAG	Judge Advocate General's Office
JCS	Joint Chiefs of Staff
JPS	Joint Staff Planners
JNAF	Japanese Naval Air Force
MARBO	Marianas-Bonins Command
MED	Manhattan Engineer District
MG	Military Government
MI	Military Intelligence
MP	Military Police
MSC	Military Staff Committee
MTB	Motor Torpedo Boat
NA	National Archives, Washington, D.C.
NA II	National Archives, College Park, Maryland
NAF	Naval Air Facility
NAS	Naval Air Station
NATS	Naval Air Transport Service
NAVFE	Naval Forces, Far East
NAVFORPHIL	Naval Forces, Philippines
NHC	US Naval Historical Center
OA	Operational Archives
OFD	Office of Financial and Development Policy
OINC	Officer-in-Charge
OPD	Operations and Plans Division
OPNAV	Office of the Chief of Naval Operations
P&O	Plans and Operations
PAC DIV ATC	Pacific Division, Air Transport Command
PACOM	Pacific Command
PACFLT	US Pacific Fleet
PACUSA	Pacific Air Command, United States Army
Pan Am	Pan American World Airlines
PASC	Pacific Air Service Command
PHILRYCOM	Philippines-Ryukyus Command
PI	Division of Philippine Affairs
POA	Pacific Ocean Areas
POW	Prisoner of War
PWD	Post-War Division
PPS	Policy Planning Staff
PS	Philippine Scouts
PSF	President's Secretary's Files
RCT	Regimental Combat Team

RFC	Reconstruction Finance Corporation
RG	Record Group
SAC	Strategic Air Command
SANACC	State-Army-Navy-Air Force Coordinating Committee
SC	Supply Corps
SCAP	Supreme Commander for the Allied Powers in Japan
SOPACBACOM	South Pacific Base Command
SPA	Office of Special Political Affairs
SWNCC	State-War-Navy Coordinating Committee
SWPA	Southwest Pacific Area
TTPI	Trust Territory of the Pacific Islands
UN	United Nations
USAFIK	United States Army Forces in Korea
USAFNC	United States Army Forces, New Caledonia
USCC	United States Commercial Company
USNIP	*United States Naval Institute Proceedings*
USASTAF	United States Army Strategic Air Forces
VCNO	Vice Chief of the Naval Operations
VHB	Very Heavy Bomber
WDGS	War Department General Staff
WHCF	White House Central Files
WHOF	White House Official Files
WPBC	Western Pacific Base Command
XTS	Radiograms Outgoing Radios
ZI	Zone of the Interior

Introduction

Between 1945 and 1947, the United States set out to turn the Pacific Basin, especially north of the equator, into an exclusive strategic sphere.[1] It largely succeeded in doing so. The reason the United States sought to turn the Pacific Basin into an "American lake" has much to do with American policymakers', planners', and strategic thinkers' historical perceptions of interwar events, wartime crises, and potential future international engagements. American misperceptions that Japan had turned the Western Pacific into a Japanese lake by fortifying their Micronesian Mandate before leaving the League of Nations in 1934 fueled a suspicion of Japan that was obviously stoked by the strike on Pearl Harbor. Added to the interwar suspicions of Japan and the horror of Pearl Harbor were the defeats dealt to the United States by Japan in the first six months of 1942. In addition, the bloody campaigns the United States fought against Japan throughout the Pacific Basin between June 1942 and August 1945 had a telling effect. Specifically, the battles to liberate the Gilberts and Micronesia, and then to conquer the Bonins, the Volcanoes, and the Ryukyus convinced many Americans, especially those in power, that the United States should never again have to endure operations like these.[2] Further adding to the impetus to create an American lake in the Pacific Basin were rising tensions with the Soviet Union. At a time of rapid postwar US military demobilization and perceived Soviet aggression, US policymakers, planners, and analysts sought to secure the United States' rear area against any kind of "future Pearl Harbor."[3] While in 1945 most American strategists who thought about the Pacific did so in terms of policing a potentially resurgent Japan, by 1946 and 1947 the potential enemy in the Pacific and East Asia had become a Soviet Union that appeared to be a "Red" version of Hitler's Germany.[4]

Clearly, the Pacific Basin was not to be the United States' primary theater of operations in any future war against the Soviet Union. The Atlantic, the Mediterranean, and Europe would be the primary theaters of operation. Moreover, the Persian Gulf and the Middle East were assumed to be a secondary theater, with perhaps East Asia, especially the area neighboring China and Japan, as a tertiary theater.[5] So why study US policy toward the Pacific Basin during the first two years after the end of World War II? For a number of reasons, US policy to defend the Pacific Basin and administer the new Pacific territories is important to historical study. First, the Pacific was the second most important area of military operations to the United States in World War II and, it could be argued, the primary theater for the United States Navy, the United States Marine Corps, and the American public.[6] Thus, a study of US policy in the Pacific Basin in the first two years of the postwar period is, to a great extent, a study of how a great power carries out reconstruction in a major theater of operations that became a vast, war-torn region by the end of the conflict. In addition, the Pacific Basin is important as a focus of study for US policy because the Pacific was the region of the world where the United States most clearly violated its traditional rhetoric about being anti-colonial and anti-imperial. In the same time period that European empires were beginning to encounter decolonization as a political reality, sometimes because of US actions, the United States was turning the Pacific Basin into an American lake by a process that many critics at the time called "security imperialism."[7] While the reasons for this phenomenon have been covered in great detail in my first book,[8] it is important here to study how the United States planned to defend the Pacific Basin and integrate its new territories into the American polity.

Furthermore, a close study of US policy tells us a great deal about how the US Government operates. The main focus of this monograph is not interservice and interdepartmental rivalry over Pacific policy. However, I found it necessary to delve into those phenomena enough to illustrate that the Executive Departments responsible for defending and administering this new Pacific empire—the War, Navy, State, and Interior Departments—all took their various positions on policy toward the Pacific Basin, in part at least, because of bureaucratic competition with each other. This reality may be passé to historians and political scientists, but as I write this book, significant proportions of Americans assume that the US Government operates by a series of conspiracy theories. Perhaps a study like this may help to inject some historical reality into the picture, since the primary sources show that the US Government did not operate in the 1940s by conspiracy, but by competition over real and imagined hopes, fears, and interests. Accordingly, I am hoping that this study suggests to contemporary Americans that the US Government does not operate in a radically different way now than it did in the 1940s.

Finally, there are several other reasons for studying US policy toward the Pacific in the immediate postwar period. While the United States never did fight a third world war in the Pacific Islands, and while the Pacific Basin itself remained a "backwater" during the Cold War, it was an important backwater. The Pacific Basin became a significant strategic base complex for the United States' projection of power toward East Asia during its two main "hot" conflicts of the Cold War: the Korean War and the Vietnam War. Not only did Kwajalein Atoll become the central missile testing ground in the Pacific for the United States, but Guam became one of the United States' primary bomber bases. Strategic Air Command (SAC) bombers not only flew from Guam on patrol missions against the USSR, but Guam was one of the main bases for B-52 operations in support of American forces throughout the Vietnam War.[9] Furthermore, the Philippines and Japan became major base complexes for the Navy, the Marine Corps, and the Air Force, probably to the point that the United States would not have been able to project its military power into Asia without these Pacific Basin facilities. Thus, this study should illustrate not only how the United States started to reconstruct a war-torn area, but also how the country began to transform that region into a supporting base system for its future strategic use.

Beyond the issues of postwar reconstruction, imperial defense and administration, and interdepartmental rivalry, a study of the Pacific Basin is important because it was a "backwater" that has been neglected by historians. The notion that only "important" or primary areas of operation or policy should be studied seems, to me, to be ahistoric. The Pacific Basin may not have been uppermost in American strategic policymakers' minds between 1945 and 1947, but it was clearly on their minds because of the ghosts of Pearl Harbor, their fears for the future security of the Republic, and their idea that the Pacific Islands could be a showcase of American democracy and capitalism for the postwar world. Moreover, I think quite a bit can be learned from history even by studying supposedly minor events and people. While the notion that "all of history" is vital can be taken to an extreme, US policy toward the "backwater" Pacific can reveal a great deal about the US Government during the crucial two years between the end of the war and the formulation of the Containment Doctrine.

A final word about the concept of "useable history" is necessary. A cultural-history term from the 1990s, it refers to historical actors' use or abuse of the past in order to justify their actions, policies, or suggestions. In regard to US Pacific policy in the immediate postwar period, the event of great note is, of course, the Pacific War. Some military historians, most notably Carol Reardon, have begun to employ the concept of useable history in order to study how military services and institutions react to wars. Very few historians of the United States in the Pacific Islands, however, have so far done this, with the exception of David Hanlon.[10] By employing this concept, it is hoped that this study will add to the discourse about the idea, the methodology, and the place of useable history in the historiography, especially since I think that these concepts are vitally important for those of us who study the various meanings of past actions.

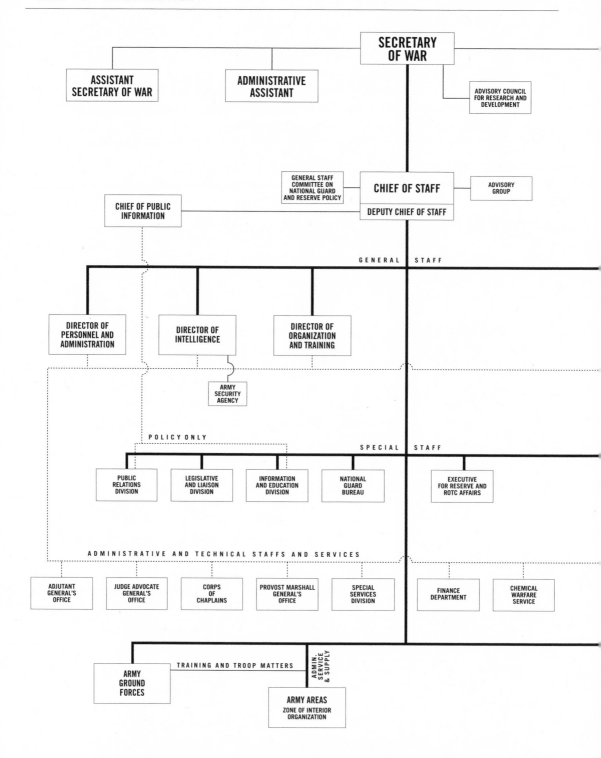

Figure 1. Organization of the War Department, 11 June 1946. (Reprinted from *Root to McNamara: Army Organization and Administration, 1900–1963,* courtesy of the US Army Center of Military History.)

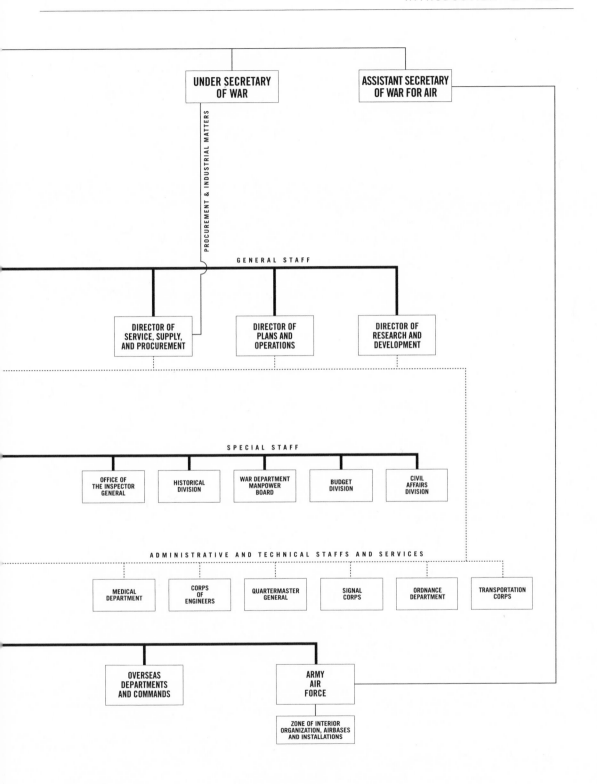

∎ Synopsis

The book's first chapter will explore how the Army Ground Forces (AGF) planned to deal with demobilization, basing issues, and a possible war with the USSR in East Asia or the Pacific Basin. Most of this primary-source material focuses around the correspondence of General of the Army Dwight Eisenhower, Chief of Staff of the Army (CSA), and General of the Army Douglas MacArthur, Commander-in-Chief of US Army Forces, Pacific (CINCAFPAC), rather than the Army's planning apparatus. These two senior officers were central enough to the immediate postwar Army planning process for the reader to obtain a picture of what Pacific war planning must have been like as most of the Army's wartime force was disappearing into civilian life and Army officers were beginning to focus most of their attention on the Soviet enemy in Europe. Probably more importantly, any study of the AGF during this time period will begin to fill a historiographical gap in the literature, since most discussions of postwar US defense policy have heretofore been dominated by studies of the Army Air Forces (AAF) and the Navy.[11]

The study of the various military services' perspectives on Pacific policy continues in the next two chapters. The second chapter will explore in detail how the AAF employed a useable history from the Pacific War to argue that land-based strategic airpower was the future first line of defense for the United States. This chapter will also illustrate the difficulties the AAF had in carrying out its planned deployments in the Pacific because of postwar demobilization and budget cuts. Finally, this chapter will demonstrate the degree to which interservice rivalry could cloud judgment by illustrating the sometimes vociferous animosity toward the Navy exhibited by some senior AAF officers. The third chapter will study the Navy from the same perspectives. Especially pertinent here will be the Navy's plans for defending the postwar Pacific Basin in the context of demobilization and major budget cuts. Also important was the Navy's employment of a useable history of the Pacific War to argue, many times disingenuously, that carrier-based naval aviation was the mainstay of US victory in the war. This second point tied directly into the Navy's hopes that Pacific War history would justify allowing the Navy to remain as the acknowledged first line of American defense in the postwar Pacific and the postwar world.

Studies of the policies put forth by the civilian Executive Departments comprise the remainder of the monograph. The fourth chapter entails a narrative of the State Department's position on US "strategic trusteeship" over the former Japanese Mandated Islands and the other territories taken from Japan by the United States during and after the war. In addition, the chapter gives a more detailed perspective on the United States' position in the United Nations (UN) negotiations of 1945–1947 than most accounts of early trusteeship diplomacy provide. In particular, the chapter outlines the lengths to which State Department officers had to go in order to obtain virtual control over these Pacific Island groups for the United States without making that control appear to be too colonial or imperial.[12] The fifth chapter looks in detail at one example of US Pacific policy by exploring some of the issues that had to be dealt with by the State Department in regard to obtaining base facilities in the Philippines. In particular, this chapter looks at State Department policy vis-à-vis the needs and desires of the US military, American and global public opinion about the US presence in the Philippines, and the political goals that Filipino elites had set for themselves with their newly won independence. All of this occurred, of course, in the context of rising tensions with the USSR, and the issues arising from the United States granting independence to a former colony at the dawn of European decolonization.

The book concludes with a chapter on the Interior Department's position concerning civil versus military administration over Micronesia, as well as that department's ideas for administering the prewar US territories of Guam and American Samoa. Certainly, the Army and the Navy argued over which service was to be the first line of American defense in the region. In addition, the military services disagreed with the State Department about a trusteeship administration of Micronesia since they favored outright annexation. Nevertheless, all three of those departments agreed to a great extent that the Interior Department should not be assigned the mission of carrying out the civil administration of the Trust Territory of the Pacific Islands (TTPI), Guam, or American Samoa. Interestingly enough, the Interior Department employed its own useable history of US territorial administration to try to convince President Harry Truman—unsuccessfully in the short term but more successfully in the long term—that Interior had the expertise to administer the populations of the TTPI, Guam, and American Samoa toward full integration into the US polity.

CHAPTER 1

Ground Power in Paradise

The Army Ground Forces' Conception of Pacific Basin Defense

etween the early fall of 1945 and the summer of 1947, United States Army officers attempted to determine their postwar force deployments for the Pacific Basin in a context of rapid demobilization, drastic budget cuts, and the specter of Pearl Harbor. These deployments first and foremost entailed carrying out the occupations of Japan and Korea. However, many of these officers assumed a rather short occupation of these East Asian positions and thus saw an eventual contracted defense perimeter based on Alaska, the Ryukyus, the Philippines, the Marianas, and Hawaii. In addition, there were a significant number of differences among senior officers about where the emphasis of limited force deployments should be placed, where military commitments ended and political commitments began, and how diplomatic negotiations for base sites could impact on the postwar force deployments. Accordingly, the primary sources cited below make clear basic differences between some of these officers as to how they would have fought a future conflict in the region.

■ Army Ground Forces Dispositions for the Pacific Basin

Part of the conception for postwar Army defense in the Pacific was made apparent in late September 1945. General of the Army George Marshall, CSA, stated in a radio message to General MacArthur, CINCAFPAC, that he agreed with an early estimate by MacArthur that 400,000 soldiers would be needed in the region, minus Alaska. Marshall also agreed with MacArthur that 200,000 of those personnel should be stationed in Japan and Korea, with an AAF strength of 174,000 for the

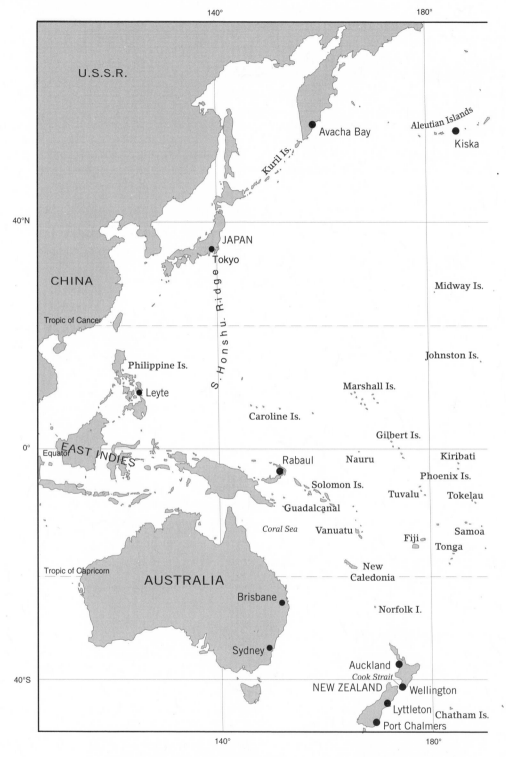

Map 1. Pacific Ocean Orientation Chart, 1945. (Courtesy of the Naval Historical Collection, US Naval War College, Newport, Rhode Island.)

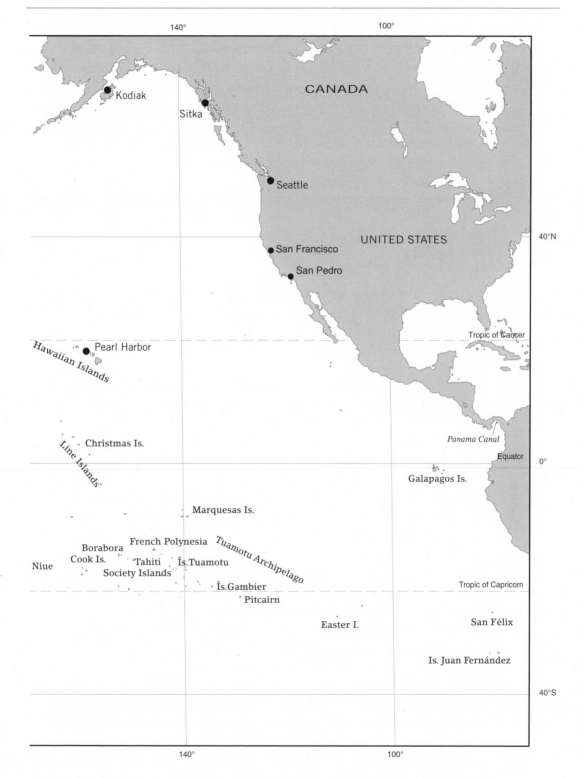

region. Marshall, however, saw no need for AGF units in Hawaii, the Ryukyus, or the other Pacific Islands at all, and estimated only about 20,000 to 40,000 Army Service Forces (ASF) personnel in the Pacific, outside of Japan. Marshall ended the message with a request that MacArthur confirm these estimates.[1] MacArthur replied later that day. Reiterating that the postwar US Army in the Pacific would need to number 400,000, MacArthur envisioned about 200,000 personnel in Japan and Korea, including about 30,000 AAF personnel. He also contemplated that AAF personnel would comprise another 120,000 soldiers, outside of Japan, while ASF units would comprise another 50,000 personnel for the entire region. MacArthur, however, saw the need for one ground-combat regiment each for the Ryukyus and the Marianas, in addition to anti-aircraft artillery (AAA) and combat-support units. He did not foresee the need for any ground-combat garrisons for Hawaii, except for AAA and support units, until occupation forces were withdrawn from Japan and Korea.[2] These dispositions speak strongly to senior Army officers' ideas about postwar duties in the Pacific Basin. More importantly, they indicate the degree to which Army leaders saw a quick end to the postwar occupations of Japan and Korea, since both officers were discussing these withdrawals as matters of fact.[3]

MacArthur continued with more details about his ideas for the Pacific Basin in early November 1945. At that time, he called for a postwar Pacific deployment that provided for an "active defense" of long-range, land-based airpower, emphasizing initial readiness, flexibility, rapid concentration and expansion, and economy. He again assumed an eventual withdrawal of US occupation forces from Japan and Korea, and a defense-in-depth line consisting of the Marianas, the Philippines, the Ryukyus, and the Aleutians. Hawaii, he thought, would be developed as the major logistical-support center so that operational forces could be massed for offensive purposes in the front-line areas. MacArthur went on to state that the initial garrisons of these bases should be Very Heavy Bomber (VHB), long-range fighter, and reconnaissance units, all for offensive purposes, along with the ground and service elements that were necessary for security and support. MacArthur also saw the need to develop these Pacific Island bases during the occupation of Japan and Korea so that the facilities would be ready when US forces withdrew from the East Asian positions. He also wanted to develop facilities at these locations for American naval forces, even implying Army control of Navy forces when he stated that these establishments in US possessions would be "secured" by the Army in accordance with the capabilities and missions "normally" assigned by joint Army and Navy action. Further, MacArthur thought that while all of the elements of this active defense organization were in place, except for the construction of rearward bases, the construction should proceed as ground and air occupation forces retired from Japan and Korea. He said it would be "uneconomical to contemplate a deployment of Marine ground forces and Naval air land-based forces on the rearward or ultimate line while occupation forces are in place." MacArthur further stated

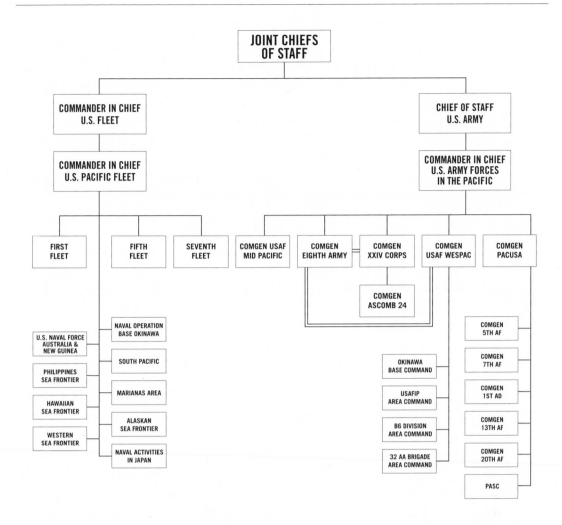

Figure 2. Command Chart, Pacific Area, 1945–1946. (Reprinted from the *Annotated Guide to Documents in the USAF Historical Research Center Relating to United States Armed Forces in the Pacific, August 1950–June 1950,* courtesy of the US Air Force Historical Research Agency, Maxwell Air Force Base, Montgomery, Alabama.)

that these front-line units should be Army units. He did not concur with the suggestion that ground and air striking forces be other than Army elements, and he only saw a need for Navy land-based air in terms of search planes needed for fleet operations. Likewise, ground elements should be Army units since those were organized, trained, and equipped to be "self-supporting" and "self-sustaining" in ground, amphibious, or ground-air operations. In addition, he thought that command responsibility in the Marianas should be vested in the Army to permit that service the fulfillment of its "normal" functions of the defense of land areas and the conduct of all phases of land warfare, including land-based air operations. The

Navy, on the other hand, should be given command jurisdiction over functions that it had been trained, organized, and equipped for—namely, sea warfare. Accordingly, MacArthur wanted AGF units in the Marianas to consist of one infantry division on Guam, and staging facilities for one infantry division on Saipan. In terms of AAF units, he thought Guam should be able to handle facilities for an air head-quarters and depot, an air-transport command terminal, two VHB groups, a light-bomber group, a fighter-bomber group, a troop-carrier group, and four separate squadrons. On Saipan, he wanted facilities for a very-long-range fighter group and two separate squadrons, while Tinian was to have facilities for the maintenance of existing airfields in standby condition for staging purposes.[4]

An even clearer idea about Army dispositions in the Pacific was made in late November 1945 by MacArthur's headquarters. Put forth by Major General Richard Marshall, CINCAFPAC Deputy Chief of Staff (DCS), the study, called "Relevant," was a postwar base-development program for the Philippines and Okinawa. The study, while taking into account an early US military withdrawal from Japan and Korea, apparently considered Okinawa as an entity separate from Japan proper. "Relevant" was to determine the permanent installations for US Army garrison forces in these island groups. It was also meant to determine any necessary expansion of facilities for staging and mounting expeditionary striking forces in order to uphold "any" national policy in the Far East. "Relevant" saw potential centers of "disturbance" to be the areas north, west, and south of the Philippines, and the plan asserted that this threat was not naval. In fact, the threat was seen as primarily from the north and limited to air attacks. An enemy being able to accumulate sufficient naval power to threaten Okinawa and the Philippines was seen as a long-range issue, supposedly long-range enough to allow time for a "readjustment" of US power in the Pacific and thus keep the current threat to one of enemy airpower. The study saw major air units in Okinawa and the Philippines having the primary responsibility of reconnaissance and "prompt" offensive missions, and the secondary missions of securing the bases and supplying the necessary air support to US expeditionary forces in East Asia. Ground forces on Okinawa were perceived as having an essential base-security mission, while those in the Philippines would have a primary responsibility of strike preparedness in the direction of East Asia. The plan clearly pointed out that the bases in the Philippines and Okinawa were not merely defensive outposts, but were offensive staging and mounting bases toward East Asia, and that they should have integrated facilities for air, ground, and naval forces. In the Philippines, local security was to be provided by the Philippine military, but US installations and forces were to be provided for with maximum accessibility, and with due consideration for surprise attack from the sea and air. The plan envisioned creating these forces and installations from surplus materials and forces stationed in other areas of the Pacific. The plan also called for consideration of joint Army and Navy facilities as much as possible. Most of the remaining plan outlined in significant detail the types and strengths of air, ground, and naval units to be deployed, as well as the base facilities and installations that were needed for these deployments. "Relevant" was also careful to delineate the Army commands that would provide for logistical requirements for Army units in the Philippines and Okinawa, namely, the Commanding General (CG) of US Army Forces, Western Pacific (AFWESPAC), and the Navy commands that would be responsible for supplying US naval forces in the region, namely, those of the Commander-in-Chief of the US Pacific Fleet and the Pacific Ocean Areas (CINCPAC-CINCPOA).[5]

Army deployments in the Pacific, as well as elsewhere in the world, were also the subject of January 1946 testimony before the House of Representatives' Committee on Military Affairs by General Eisenhower, General Marshall's successor as CSA. Eisenhower pointed out to the Representatives that Army deployment in the Pacific in 1946, excluding Alaska, would include seven divisions and nineteen air groups. A few months later, Eisenhower made it even clearer to the House of Representatives' Committee on Appropriations that the units he had outlined in January were necessary for American national security in terms of a "cordon of bases" from which these forces could intercept attacking enemy forces and launch counterblows. In his testimony, Eisenhower focused on the value of mobile forces conducting offensives as the primary means of defense. Eisenhower further cautioned that the bases themselves were not to become the object of defense and thus tie the mobile forces to a static defense. Accordingly, Eisenhower was concerned that the United States only garrison these bases in a minimal way while building the base facilities, and have the bases ready for quick reinforcement in times of need. Later in the testimony, Eisenhower was engaged by Representative Albert Engel of Michigan about island bases in the Atlantic and Pacific that were thought necessary for future US defense plans. This engagement occurred in a way that clearly demonstrated the impact of the Pearl Harbor defeat on American strategic concerns—concerns that were voiced at various times by both uniformed officers and civilian officials. For instance, arguing that US national security required the acquisition and retention of certain island bases, Engel asked if the United States was acquiring those locations, especially in the Pacific, and how they would be divided between the Army and Navy. Eisenhower answered that both services would have bases, with the Navy's mainly being anchorages and the Army's mainly being bases for land-based airpower. Engel later asked if arrangements had been made between the Army and Navy through the Joint Chiefs of Staff (JCS) for defining spheres of operations for the two services, or if there were going to be divided operations—which Engel thought had helped lead to Pearl Harbor. Eisenhower answered that it was a concrete problem that had not yet been solved in terms of "coordination." Engel went on to insist that coordination needed to be achieved so that functions such as those of the Committee on Military Affairs were not duplicated by naval functions such as those of the House's Naval Appropriations Subcommittee. He also argued that the President and the JCS had to achieve this coordination, especially in terms of the operation of land-based planes, since US military spheres of operation were expanding. Eisenhower agreed with Engel in all of these matters.[6]

This kind of questioning about Army policy toward the Pacific may explain some statements made by Eisenhower in a January 1946 letter to MacArthur. Eisenhower first explained to MacArthur that as CSA he was trying to hold off public pressure, or what he called a "hysteria," for a fast and major demobilization of US Army forces. Eisenhower specifically told MacArthur about instances where he had used MacArthur's statements before Congress to link American prestige, interests, and even safety in the Pacific to levels of military strength. He continued that "so far no one has openly questioned our estimates for actual occupational duties in any area, including Korea, Japan and Germany. All other places have been under the most tremendous attack, including the Philippines and Okinawa." Eisenhower complained, however, that in spite of support from the President, the Secretary of War, and the principal civilian assistants, "logic" and "good sense" were being ignored in favor of emotionalism. Eisenhower ended the message by saying that he would battle "to the death," especially for the occupation forces, and he claimed that true happiness would come from getting completely out of official life, and shouting from the rooftops about the dangers the United States was creating for itself in the international world![7]

In a speech to women's magazine writers in June 1946, Eisenhower elaborated on his ideas for a global system of US bases, including Pacific locations. He emphasized the United States' need for the "maintenance" of key points in places such as the Panama Canal and Alaska, as well as the need for air bases along the approaches to the United States. He reinforced this statement with the idea that the United States needed to retain physical control of these bases, especially in regard to its future UN duties. Moreover, he pointed out that a few strongly held, distant bases would not be sufficient to withstand a strong enemy assault, and that many bases would be needed for purposes of dispersing US forces. He did not see a ring of "impregnable" fortresses as the key to US security, but instead thought in terms of bases for mobile offensive forces in Panama, Newfoundland, Alaska, Hawaii, the Marianas, and the Philippines, supplemented by communication links and outposts.[8] Of course, it should also be pointed out that Eisenhower's remarks to this group were in contrast to most of the internal planning documents cited in this chapter, including statements made by Eisenhower himself. In most cases, Army officers saw the need to reduce the number of bases to a bare minimum in order to put the maximum amount of scarce resources into maintaining mobile offensive forces by which to defend entire regions such as the Pacific Basin. Still, his statement about avoiding too heavy of an investment in a *few* impregnable fortresses was consistent with American strategic thought at this time.

Deployments were also the subject of a radio message between Lieutenant General John Hull, Commanding General of US Army Forces, Middle Pacific (AFMIDPAC), and General MacArthur in July 1946. Hull wanted units being scheduled for deployment to Iwo Jima to be canceled, and to have that island's garrison reduced to caretaker status. Contrary to Eisenhower's ideas about dispersing forces in the Pacific, Hull argued that although Iwo Jima was one of the islands thought necessary for long-term US control and Pacific Basin defense, he did not think that this defense justified permanent air and ground forces at a time of budget reductions. He further thought that there was a clear need to concentrate the reduced forces at a few select points. Assuming, unlike MacArthur, that US forces would be occupying Japan for some time, Hull nevertheless thought Iwo Jima was necessary merely as an emergency landing field, not as a fighter base or early warning center for the Marianas. Hull also pointed out how expensive Iwo Jima was to support in terms of base facilities, and even basic necessities such as drinking water. Therefore, he thought that reducing Iwo's garrison to a token size would permit the island to be supplied by air from Saipan. In addition, Hull argued that in times of need, Iwo could quickly be augmented by air from the Marianas, especially from Saipan or Guam. However, Lieutenant General Ennis Whitehead, Commanding General of Pacific Air Command, United States Army (PACUSA), when informed about this matter by a different radio message, countered that withdrawal or occupation of Iwo Jima was an AAF issue, and that PACUSA could not fulfill its mission in the region without a larger garrison on the island. Still, Hull ended the series of messages with a reiteration of his idea that Iwo Jima be garrisoned by only one hundred men, and that all of the remaining air and ground units be withdrawn to the Marianas. According to Hull, the smaller garrison could provide emergency landing-field service, communications, and air-warning facilities, operate minimum airfield and supply facilities, and maintain the cemeteries on the famous island.[9]

Later in the month, MacArthur also began communicating details of a War Department plan called "Arouse" to General Whitehead, General Hull, and Major General James Christiansen, Acting Commanding General of AFWESPAC. This deployment planning was to be the basis for detailed annexes. One annex was to outline post-Occupation PACUSA deployments by individual station, with detailed troop lists for these individual stations being forwarded later. Another annex indicated principal ground units and troop ceilings for AFMIDPAC and AFWESPAC deployments. MacArthur told his commanders that the disposition of divisions had been set by the War Department. He also included his ideas for probable War Department revisions in the future. The last annex included the revision and preparation of "Arouse" budget estimates. As to AGF and ASF units, all forces in Hawaii were planned at 70 percent strength except for the infantry division, which was to be at 80 percent strength. There was also to be an AAA group consisting of two automatic-weapons battalions, two gun battalions, and a searchlight battalion in the US Territory. Hawaii was additionally to have "overhead" associated with AFMID-PAC Headquarters, and civilian personnel as needed. In the Marianas, units that were to be kept at 70 percent strength included an AAA group consisting of two automatic-weapons battalions, two gun battalions, and a searchlight battalion. Any additional overhead was to be supplied by PACUSA. The Volcanoes were to have an AAA group consisting of one automatic-weapons battalion, a gun battalion, and a searchlight battery. Any additional personnel were here again to be supplied by PACUSA. A combat division was planned for the Philippines at 80 percent strength. Other units were also to be at this strength, though US Army Forces, Pacific (AFPAC) Headquarters was apparently only to be kept at 35 percent strength. Provisions were made here for additional military and civilian supporting personnel as well. In the Ryukyus, it was planned to keep an infantry regiment at 80 percent strength in being, with a field-artillery battalion at 70 percent strength. Other units were listed at varying strengths, with allowance also made for Military Government (MG) units. "Arouse" did not change anything for small island garrisons, but MacArthur did tell his subordinate commanders that the plan's annexes would include priorities for base construction. MacArthur also told the three generals to confer about priorities, but he made it clear that PACUSA had the highest priority. He also told them that he would decide from Tokyo about final priorities and budgets.[10]

Another War Department plan for overseas bases, this time for the post-Occupation period, was issued on 6 August 1946, with a cover letter from Major General Edward Witsell, War Department Adjutant General. The purpose of the plan was to outline guidance for each major global postwar theater in terms of ground and air combat units, missions, the preparation of base facilities, budgetary estimates, and especially wartime expansion plans. In addition, the plan listed the desired officer, warrant-officer, enlisted, and civilian personnel strength desired for each base facility, though it recognized that the budget would not allow for 100 percent strength. Witsell talked about the plan, outlining each major base's function within a theater-wide integrated plan, but he also pointed out that the allotment of personnel could not be completely decided upon until the post-Occupation command structure in the Pacific had been determined.[11]

The plan itself broke the bases down into categories of Primary, Secondary, Subsidiary, and Minor. Primary Base areas were strategically located ones constituting the foundation of the US postwar security system, especially in terms of the projection of US military power. Secondary Bases were those essential for the protection of the Primary Bases, while Subsidiary ones increased the flexibility of the system of Primary and Secondary Bases. Minor Bases, probably ones in the South Pacific at this point, were merely ones needed for things such as military transit rights. All categories of bases were also broken down and classified in various ways as Operational, Reserve Operational, and Non-Operational. Not surprisingly, Primary Operational Bases for the Pacific included Hawaii, the Marianas, the Philippines, and the Ryukyus.

Secondary Bases included the Bonins and the Volcanoes; Wake, Midway, Johnston, and Canton Islands; Kwajalein Atoll; Marcus Island; American Samoa; Manus Island; and Truk, with most of the latter being Reserve or Non-Operational. Subsidiary Bases included Eniwetok Atoll, Tarawa, Yap-Ulithi, Peleliu, Funa Futi, Palmyra Island, and Majuro Atoll, all of these being classified as Non-Operational. Minor bases included Christmas Island, Morotai, Biak-Woendi, Guadalcanal, Tulagi, Espiritu Santo, New Caledonia, Fiji, and British Samoa, all in a Non-Operational status. Clearly, the majority of resources were going to be put into the Northern Pacific chains of the Ryukyus, the Philippines, the Marianas, and Hawaii. While most of the rest of the plan was devoted to delineating in great detail the table of organization of each existing peacetime unit with personnel strength outlined, the peacetime missions and wartime requirements of these Army bases make clear what the Army envisioned in terms of immediate postwar Pacific Island deployments in the event of war with "any hostile power" in the region. For instance, the units in Hawaii were to defend those islands from air, sea, and amphibious attack; serve as a Primary Base denying the mid-Pacific to any hostile power; assist in the defense of the West Coast of the United States; and facilitate movement of US forces between the Zone of the Interior or ZI (the Continental United States) and the Western Pacific. Moreover, these units were to assist in the control and security of mid-Pacific and trans-Pacific air and sea routes, as well as to prepare base facilities for wartime expansion to two reinforced divisions and three air groups. Finally, the plan provided for Hawaii to be prepared for wartime transit and mounting of various air and ground units up to at least two divisions to any location in the Pacific within ninety days from the "date of warning" order.[12]

Units in the Philippines had the mission of defending those islands against air, sea, and amphibious attack. These units were also to provide for the denial of base sites or military installations within the radius of air action by which enemy powers might threaten US military installations or lines of communication. The Philippines were also to serve as a base for the projection of air and amphibious operations into contiguous areas. In addition, units in the Philippines were to assist in the defense of the western approaches to the Central Pacific Ocean, and assist in the defense of the lines of communication between the Philippines and Asia on the one hand and the Philippines and US bases to the south and east on the other. Further, the Philippines was to house the headquarters of AFPAC as well as PACUSA, have training facilities for one division (as was Hawaii), and be able to expand in wartime to a garrison of two reinforced divisions and nine air groups, including three VHB groups. Finally, the Philippines was to be ready on 120 days' notice to mount out three additional reinforced divisions, and to transit through two squadrons of any type of aircraft on an average day with a maximum backlog of three days. The Ryukyus units also had a similar mission to defend the islands from air, sea, and amphibious attack; deny hostile powers the military installations in the islands; and assist in maintaining the control and security of the lines of communication in the

Ryukyus. The Ryukyus units were also to assist in the defense of the northwestern approaches from Asia to the Western and Middle Pacific, assist in the defense of the northern approaches to the Philippines, and serve as a base for the projection and support of air or amphibious offensive operations into contiguous areas. The Ryukyus' wartime mission was slightly different, providing advanced headquarters for AFPAC and PACUSA, along with one reinforced division; seven air groups, including three VHB groups; and separate squadrons.[13]

The Marianas units were to defend those islands from similar types of attacks and to deny base sites or installations to any hostile power in the western portion of the Middle Pacific, including by operating in conjunction with Iwo Jima and Marcus Island. They were also to serve as an offensive springboard into the Western Pacific, logistically support bases in the eastern portion of the Western Pacific (such as Palau, Iwo Jima, and Marcus), and assist in the control and security of air and sea lines of communication between the mid-Pacific bases and the Western Pacific. The Marianas were to further assist in maintaining a peacetime system of outlying US Army bases, including one operational airfield on Iwo, a reserve transient airfield on Marcus, and a wartime garrison in the Marianas consisting of a reinforced division and six air groups. The Marianas were also to maintain an air garrison of two search squadrons at Iwo Jima, and even provide for a wartime potential of Iwo housing a division and two air groups, though none of these latter were to be VHB units. Finally, the Marianas were to be able to mount out an additional two reinforced divisions on ninety days' notice, as well as flow two squadrons through per day on a maximum backlog of three days.[14]

The Bonins-Volcanoes units figured in much the same way, assisting in the defense of the region from air, sea, and amphibious attack as well as helping to deny any hostile power base sites in the western portion of the Middle Pacific. They also were to assist in offensive power projection into contiguous areas of the Western Pacific, and assist in the control of air and sea communications in the mid-Pacific and Western Pacific. Midway, Wake, Johnston, and Marcus Islands; Kwajalein Atoll; and Canton Island were to assist in their own defense as their garrisons allowed, as well as to help in maintaining the security of trans-Pacific lines of communication, trans-Pacific air and sea routes, and the approaches to US Pacific bases. Their abilities to expand into large wartime bases were limited. For instance, Midway and Wake were each envisioned as expanding their wartime ground-force garrisons, but only to one infantry regiment each. The other atolls and islands were to provide transient airfields and various support facilities. The remainder of the islands mentioned at the beginning of the plan were listed as Non-Operational, and in the event of war were also to assist in maintaining trans-Pacific lines of communication, the security of trans-Pacific air and sea routes, and the security approaches to US Pacific bases. Wartime expansion would entail creating transient airfields and emergency airfields for air transport operations.[15]

Several themes explored in this chapter were also demonstrated in a late October 1946 presentation about projections of the Army's postwar strength and organization that was prepared for President Truman by Major General Lauris Norstad, War Department General Staff (WDGS) Director of Operations and Plans (OPD). Norstad outlined for Truman the Army's basic tasks in both the Occupation period and the immediate aftermath. For one thing, he assumed that a majority of AGF units would be in the Pacific and East Asia, rather than Europe or even the Continental United States. The US mainland, as of 1 July 1947, was to have four divisions based in it, along with one regiment in Panama, and one division, two regimental combat teams (RCTs), and ten construction regiments in Central Europe. Alaska was only to have two infantry battalions, but Micronesia was to have one and two-thirds divisions, while Japan and Korea combined were to have six divisions stationed on their soil. Once the German, Austrian, Japanese, and Korean Occupations were over, Norstad assumed that there would be a major redeployment of American ground power. There were no American ground units envisioned for Europe or East Asia in the post-Occupation period, although there was to be one regimental combat team in Alaska, two and one-third divisions in Micronesia, one division in Panama, and seven and one-third divisions in the Continental United States. Not only did the Army envision a quick end to its occupation duties in Central Europe and East Asia, but Micronesia was to play host to the largest deployment of US ground units other than the Continental United States once the other occupations were completed.[16]

"Relevant," "Arouse," and OPD's conceptions aside, however, budgetary restrictions and rapid demobilization were wreaking havoc with such detailed deployment planning. Moreover, senior Army officers did not always agree with each other about the best way to deploy their limited resources. Late November 1946 witnessed one of these deployment disagreements between Eisenhower and MacArthur. On 25 November, MacArthur sent a message to Eisenhower about the role and level of occupation forces in Japan. MacArthur thought that Eisenhower's office had a mistaken conception of the role played by the Supreme Commander of the Allied Powers in Japan (SCAP) as well as CINCAFPAC's role in Korea. In particular, MacArthur thought it mistaken for the War Department to believe it could continue to maintain an occupation in these areas no matter how low troop levels dropped. He thought that at some point, policies in these occupied areas would have to change if troop levels dipped too much. MacArthur disagreed that lower troop levels merely meant partial fulfillment of the occupation policies laid out by the Potsdam Agreement, since he took these aims to either be fully carried out or not carried out at all. In his opinion, if troop levels dropped too far, "the only recourse would be to abandon the concept of long-range occupation and democratization and thereby lose the peace." If troop levels were reduced too greatly, MacArthur thought it would signal to the Japanese and Koreans that the United States lacked the will to quell opposition to

US policies, or to follow through on the United States' stated commitments. In particular, MacArthur was convinced that it took a certain amount of US military force to support Japanese and Korean reformers who were willing to cooperate with US Military Government units against "hostile elements and ideologies" in their countries. MacArthur stated that the War Department had been "advised" by him about the minimum numbers of US Army forces needed—essentially four divisions in Japan and two in Korea—and that this minimum level of troops had been reached on 1 July 1946. "Further cuts involving reduction in the occupation forces will destroy the whole and inevitably prematurely terminate the occupation." In that case, MacArthur found it difficult to see how the War Department could support the foreign-policy national objectives created by the State Department and other governmental agencies. Nor did he see how the occupation of the rest of the Pacific Islands could be maintained if military forces in the region were cut "to the bone" by the War Department. MacArthur saw Pacific Basin forces being reduced to such an extent that he thought that significant proportions of the Pacific might have to be militarily abandoned in peacetime. "If these outposts are abandoned and war comes to the Pacific, the results might be disastrous." MacArthur concluded that in other areas of the Pacific, these reductions might not amount to much if a war did not occur. But in Japan and Korea, occupation had to be, in his opinion, "all or nothing."[17]

Meanwhile, planning went forward based on the Army having greatly reduced resources at its disposal. In December 1946, Hull informed MacArthur that even though AAF units had a primary interest in base planning for Iwo Jima, Wake, and Midway, his headquarters planned to carry out a "Master Construction Plan" for ground-force facilities at those three islands. In addition, he was going to have Brigadier General Willard Irvine's Western Pacific Base Command (WPBC) on Saipan coordinate ground-facility construction with the Twentieth Air Force for more effective inclusion of the AGF into AAF plans at Wake and Iwo Jima. He told MacArthur that his headquarters would also directly coordinate with the Seventh Air Force for ground-unit facilities at Midway so that the Seventh Air Force would enjoy the same type of close inclusion of AGF facilities with AAF plans.[18] A few days later, Lieutenant General Hull also informed MacArthur that Army ground support for the AAF's Air Transport Command (ATC) on Kwajalein had ended as of 3 December 1946, that all property transfers had been completed, and that the remaining personnel would be transferred to Oahu by 14 December. He made it clear, however, that AFMIDPAC logistical support to the docks at Kwajalein would continue, no doubt to finish closing out equipment and surplus materials, but perhaps also related to the construction program noted above.[19]

Army deployment plans continued to be outlined in the New Year within the context of a new, unified command system. In early February 1947, Major General Francis Griswold, Commanding General of the Marianas-Bonins Command (MARBO), stated to MacArthur, now Commander-in-Chief of the Far East Command (CINCFE), his idea of having the bulk of AAF Pacific units stationed on Guam and Tinian, having a small force on Iwo Jima, and having an infantry division (less one RCT) on Saipan.[20] This idea was followed by a message a few days later proposing the placement of the bulk of AAF forces on Guam, another 1,700 AAF personnel on Iwo Jima, a caretaker detachment on Tinian, and an airdrome squadron on Saipan. Griswold continued to recommend an infantry division on Saipan. No explanation was given in the message for the change in deployment ideas for the AAF units, but it was probably somehow related to the cost of additional facilities at this time of retrenchment.[21] Apparently, MacArthur had difficulties with this deployment concept. MacArthur wanted the placement of AGF units reconsidered if Guam was where the majority of the air and naval assets were going to be. If these AGF units were to be the reduced infantry division in question, MacArthur thought the division should be on Guam. He thought stationing the infantry division on Saipan could only be justified for logistical reasons, since putting AGF units on Saipan would entail having to place Marine ground units on Guam in order to guard the air and naval bases there. These Marine forces would have to be under the command of the senior officer charged with defending the Marianas, a naval officer.[22] However, the idea of a naval officer being responsible for the ground defense of the Marianas was a controversy still being worked out by the services in early 1947.

Eisenhower's ideas for a postwar defense in the Pacific, as well as other areas of the world, within a context of limited resources came out again in February 1947 in testimony before the House Subcommittee on Military Appropriations. At this time, Eisenhower spoke about the need for overseas bases that provided for a "cushion of distance" and that had to be adequately supported if they were not to give hostile nations an "illusion" about US security.[23] A few days later, at a reception of the St. Louis Chamber of Commerce, Eisenhower talked about "reasonable security" requiring air, ground, and sea forces, but "efficiently" organized into a force capable of holding "key outer bases" on the periphery of American defenses. He also talked about forces that were ready at all times to establish immediate defenses against air or surface attacks. In addition, these forces needed to be powerful enough to either seize or destroy the sources of the attack.[24] That budget cuts were leading to consolidations can also be determined by another radio message from MacArthur to Griswold in late May 1947. The subject of the message was the need by Griswold's command for Japanese prisoners of war (POWs) to load surplus property for shipment to Korea. In the message, MacArthur also talked about an upcoming command conference that was to deal with a probable consolidation of AGF and AAF activities on Iwo Jima, no doubt with the majority of the remaining units being AAF.[25]

A look at consolidated AGF dispositions and deployments by the summer of 1947 is also provided by the final report from the Joint Marianas On-Site Board, a base planning body composed of both Army and Navy officers and co-chaired by

Vice Admiral Daniel Barbey, Commandant of the Tenth Naval District and Commander of the Caribbean Sea Frontier (CARIBSEAFRON), as Senior Naval Member, and Major General Grandison Gardner, AAF Deputy Assistant Chief of Air Staff for Materiel, as Senior Army Member. The Board spent several months touring the Marianas in order to best determine base sites, installations, and especially the divisions of responsibility between the Army and Navy. Concentrating mainly on Guam, Saipan, and Tinian because of the "physical aspects" and military importance of these three islands, the Board made final determinations by 1 June about where American forces should be stationed in this strategic group.[26] In one of its appendices, the Board elaborated that AGF units would primarily consist of an Army division (less one RCT and a tank battalion). The main mission of this unit would be the ground defense of the Marianas base area, and the Board determined that this division should be stationed on Guam. In determining this deployment, it was influenced by the mission of the division and by considerations of economy. Since the only "reasonable" training area in the Marianas was on Guam, this dictated the location of the division. In addition, it had been decided to locate the major air and naval bases and principal communication centers of the Western Pacific and East Asia on Guam. Since the AGF division was there to protect these bases and communication centers, the Board determined that it should be based there.[27] The Navy had suggested stationing the division on Saipan in order to guard against that base falling into enemy hands, but such a deployment, to the Board, would have necessitated an increase of service troops, housing, and utilities. The Board also thought that there would have been an increased cost of supplies due to divided shipping and warehousing. In addition, the Board argued that this would have thrown off the construction schedule and the utilization of "common use" facilities between the services. This delay in turn would have caused an increase in harbor and port facilities without reducing those facilities on Guam. The Board also believed that any division of the AGF unit between the two islands would have caused similar disadvantages from a perspective of "economy" and that these problems would have led to additional disadvantages in training and administration.[28] The Board further asserted that Guam was going to house the majority of the naval and air installations. These facilities would comprise "most vital" target areas for enemy aircraft, as would Isley Field on Saipan, since the latter was going to be kept operational for the use of carrier air groups and Army fighters in emergency situations. Moreover, Tanapag Harbor and a naval air base were going to be kept operational on Saipan. Given these deployments, the initial plan of deployment that called for just two battalions of AAA would see both of those units deployed on Guam. However, if the AAA units were able to expand to eight battalions, as was hoped for in the future, six battalions would be retained on Guam and two on Saipan. Since Guam was to base the majority of the AGF and AAF units, the Board also thought that Guam should house the majority of the ASF forces in the Marianas.[29]

Finally, in July 1947 hearings before the Senate Foreign Relations Committee over the proposed agreement for the TTPI, Eisenhower answered rhetorical questions about why the United States needed control over the former Japanese Mandates since those areas were of such great strategic importance to postwar US security. In particular, Eisenhower stated that the lessons of World War II should have been foreseen as early as the Spanish-American War. He described an environment that consisted of great powers that were increasingly capable of transferring military forces to different regions of the world and striking "in any direction." In this kind of environment, he thought that the United States should have anticipated the need for bases in the areas from which such strikes might be launched. He therefore thought that since World War I, at least, the United States should have begun to acquire base sites in the Pacific. In a form of questionable historical hindsight, but one which was quite common in the US national security establishment by 1947, Eisenhower even asserted that if the United States had acquired those base sites at that time, "I know that the costs of this latest war would have been far reduced, and possibly the war at least in the Pacific would not have occurred."[30]

Eisenhower's conclusions are interesting from a number of perspectives. First, Pacific Island bases, with exceptions like Guam and American Samoa, had not been acquired by the United States before 1945 because there had never been a consensus in the American Government about such acquisitions. In 1898, 1919, and 1922, the Navy wanted to acquire base sites in Micronesia, but the Army was opposed on grounds of having to defend those locations. Moreover, the State Department was opposed to such actions, based on American "traditions" against acquiring territory in situations that smacked of Great Power imperialism. Most importantly, President Woodrow Wilson was opposed in 1919 because US annexations would have so obviously contradicted his Fourteen Points, and President Warren Harding did not want these territorial questions to interfere with the 1921–1922 Washington Naval Conference.[31] It was not until 1945 that there was anything approaching a consensus within the US national-security establishment about the United States obtaining full control of Pacific Basin sites, and then much of this consensus was built on dubious historical conclusions about how the Pearl Harbor disaster could have been prevented. Eisenhower might have been subscribing to this post–Pearl Harbor mythology in his testimony, but there is no credible evidence that prewar US acquisition of base sites in locations such as Micronesia would have prevented Japan from successfully attacking Pearl Harbor, or pursuing its war in China and Southeast Asia.[32]

■ The Philippine Base Issue

Difficulties that the Army had in carrying out its postwar deployments included problems with the Philippine Government during base site negotiations about whether or not US bases would be allowed in the vicinity of Manila. Some planners' recommendations included staying in and around prewar US bases near Manila, but others pointed to the need to build new facilities some distance from the capital city because of Filipino anger over the atrocious conduct of US military personnel there. In a mid-October 1946 radio message to MacArthur, Major General Christiansen, Acting Commanding General of AFWESPAC, also speculated that the Philippine Government may have started a publicity campaign to convince the Filipino people of the value of the United States vacating military bases near Manila. He further thought that some of this pressure was coming from the Philippine Congress and the Philippine press.[33] In addition, Christiansen argued that a new supply system on Bataan with road and rail networks was not worth the expense. The minimum he thought the Army would need in the Manila area was the prewar Army Port Area South Manila Harbor, and the retention of Fort McKinley and Nichols Field. Military reservations outside of these areas would not be required, but he thought that Nichols Field itself was essential for air operations. He also thought that all headquarters, hospitals, and overhead installations could be moved to Clark Field. He believed it desirable, however, to keep the General Headquarters (GHQ), PACUSA Headquarters, and US Naval Forces, Philippines (NAVFORPHIL) at Fort McKinley because of its close proximity to Philippine Government agencies and Philippine Army Headquarters. Christiansen asserted that the latter would help improve relations between the military forces of the two nations so that the base agreements could be more effectively carried out. Most of the rest of the message outlined what Christiansen thought would be desirable versus necessary facilities, particularly various warehousing, repair, and supporting activities. He concluded the message by reiterating his introductory assertions about the attitudes of the Philippine negotiators toward these facilities.[34]

The Philippines as a potential basing problem for the Army came up again in early November 1946. Major General Norstad, OPD Director, in a memo to Brigadier General George Lincoln, Chief of OPD's Plans and Policy Group, asserted that the current difficulty with the Philippine Government "on the question of bases and other subjects relating to the presence of American troops in the Philippines is only the beginning of the trouble we expect as long as we are located in that country." Norstad speculated that part of this trouble stemmed from Filipino perceptions that the United States had to have the bases in these areas, and that the Filipinos were being forced to bargain with the United States. Norstad also communicated to Lincoln that in recent meetings with State Department representatives, he had made the suggestion that the alternative to getting "reasonable" base sites was for the United States to get out of the Philippines entirely. However, he had told State that this alternative was not practical at the time because of the United States' strategic requirements in the region. He therefore charged Lincoln's group with studying two subjects. First, he wanted to know what might happen if the United States evacuated the Philippine area entirely if it had desired rights in the Pacific Islands, including the Ryukyus. Second, he wanted to know the implications if the United States had to vacate the Philippines and the Ryukyus, but had desired rights in the former Japanese Mandates.[35]

Eisenhower expressed his doubts about the value of the Philippine bases in a radio message to MacArthur just one day later. He said that for some time, the question as to the "real value" of permanent Army bases in the Philippines had been troubling him. To Eisenhower, past history demonstrated that peacetime Army garrisons could never be manned in sufficient numbers to ensure that the Philippines would be secured in the event of future Pacific hostilities. Therefore, he thought that in the event of an emergency the bases would have no value, and in peacetime they would be a drain on expenditures and resources. Eisenhower thought that if the Filipinos could be counted on to have a solid, peacetime military-preparedness program and be ready as a loyal ally for a future attack, "the picture might be different." However, Eisenhower thought that this situation was beyond the "expectation of logic," at the very least because of the fiscal state of the new Philippine Republic. Eisenhower then went on to assert that the presence of US personnel in the Philippines would only engender friction, intensify bad feeling, and "keep us constantly in hot water." He thought that financially and materially the cost did not justify the strategic advantages, but he admitted not yet having discussed the matter with the Navy or any other agency, including the State Department. Saying that this was merely something that had been on his mind for some time, Eisenhower asked for MacArthur's ideas because of the General's long acquaintanceship with East Asia. Eisenhower wanted to clarify this position on a strictly military basis so that he could have "sound advice" when called upon.[36]

Eisenhower instead obtained feedback from Fleet Admiral Chester Nimitz, the Chief of Naval Operations (CNO), on 12 November. In Nimitz's opinion, there would be an "indefinite" need for American naval forces in the Western Pacific. Part of the function of these bases would be shore facilities for hospitalization, recreation, and the housing of naval dependents, but Nimitz also saw the need for a Naval Operating Base at Subic Bay in order to support Pacific Fleet submarines and to provide service to vessels transiting the region. In addition, he thought the Navy would need a Naval Air Station (NAS) at Sangley Point on Luzon, that it should have the right to use the Leyte-Samar area, and that the Tawi-Tawi anchorage area in the Sulu Archipelago should be available when needed. However, Nimitz also stated his intention of inactivating and disestablishing all other US naval bases in the Philippines. He thought, however, that this was a bare minimum, and he did not advocate any further reduction in US naval facilities in the new republic. Nimitz said he would be willing to have the Marines provide the local security for these bases and even to withdraw from the bases if a hostile strategic situation should so dictate. Therefore, he agreed with Eisenhower's conclusion that Army troops were not needed to defend the Navy bases remaining in the Philippines.[37]

Eisenhower communicated his ideas to the JCS a few days later. Arguing that objections by the Filipino people to a large concentration of US troops and installations in the Manila area had forced the War Department to reduce its strategic requirements, he claimed that he had subsequently rethought the strategic and political importance of the bases in the Philippines. The acrimony of ongoing base negotiations also changed the situation, he said. Apparently, US strategy originally envisioned not only the defense of the Philippines in a new Pacific war, but the archipelago's use as a staging and mounting area for large numbers of US air and ground forces. Eisenhower now claimed that the reduction of Army facilities demanded by the Filipinos called that second mission into question. In fact, he said that he had now rethought the entire deployment of US Army forces worldwide based on withdrawal from the Philippines. On the one hand, he saw a withdrawal of US Army forces from the Philippines to be potentially signaling a decreased US interest in East Asia, including China. This might, he thought, prejudice US interests in Japan and Korea, and be, to some Filipinos, an act of desertion. Moreover, Eisenhower said that the United States had to ensure that there was not a military vacuum in East Asia in the future. On the other hand, he thought that all of these needs were met by keeping US naval forces in the Philippines, especially as the Navy planned to retain bases in the Philippines after negotiations were completed with the Philippine Government. Of even greater concern to Eisenhower was the "good faith" that currently existed between "the United States and all weaker nations, and the Philippine nation in particular." If US Army base rights were obtained in acrimonious negotiations, they would be of minimal value in keeping relations warm between the two nations. He was especially concerned about jeopardizing the sense that Philippine independence resulted from the common actions of the two peoples since he believed that this relationship in and of itself was important to the security of the world. Eisenhower, accordingly, thought that any base agreements without the full and complete cooperation of the Filipino people would be of very limited value. In view of these factors, Eisenhower, on behalf of the Army, proposed that all US Army forces be withdrawn from the Philippines on an orderly basis. He understood that the Philippine Government might want some US military forces to remain for reasons of political and military security, and if the Philippine Government and the Department of State pressed this matter, Eisenhower thought that a very limited force—basically one composite air group and a small ground contingent—could be retained. If all Army forces were withdrawn, the Army would merely ask for air transit rights. As long as other members of the JCS did not object, Eisenhower proposed to obtain higher authorization for this action.[38]

A few days later, Secretary of War Robert Patterson, agreeing with Eisenhower's idea, sent Secretary of State James Byrnes a letter about withdrawing US Army forces from the Philippines. Patterson began with Eisenhower's points about the Philippine Government's and Philippine population's resistance to US Army bases near Manila, and the need to rethink US strategic policy for the region. Patterson agreed with Eisenhower's recommendations to withdraw all Army forces or keep a small force there for a limited amount of time. He then pointed out to Byrnes that Eisenhower's idea about the military importance of the Philippines was of lesser weight in US national interests than future good relations, and that retention of US Army forces might be detrimental to the latter. Patterson also pointed out that in the event of the Philippine Government asking that all US Army forces be moved from the Manila area, the United States would incur quite an expense in building new facilities if large US forces were to be maintained in the Philippines. Patterson was quite clear that this was an expense the War Department could not afford. He reiterated to Byrnes that War Department responsibilities should not be greater than its resources entailed; that commitments in occupied areas such as Germany, Austria, Italy, Japan, and Korea would take practically all of the War Department's resources for the foreseeable future; and that these commitments were of primary importance. "We cannot afford, in my opinion, to waste our strength by maintenance of a force of any considerable size in the Philippines." Finally, Patterson called for orderly and timely preparations to be made, whatever action was decided on. Therefore, he requested notice from the State Department as soon as possible as to whether or not the War Department was to withdraw all Army forces from the archipelago or maintain some token force, and he suggested that he and Eisenhower meet with Byrnes to iron out any difficulties.[39]

In early December, the State Department was heard from concerning the subject of US Army withdrawal from the Philippines. In a memo to Acting Secretary of State Dean Acheson, Byrnes agreed with Eisenhower that the United States should withdraw its Army forces from the Philippines. Byrnes went on to say that if the Philippine Government urged that a force be retained, the United States should grant the request and keep a limited force in the new republic for a limited period of time, but make it clear to the Philippine Government that it would be gradually reduced and then withdrawn.[40] Acheson then sent a memo to President Truman that there was concurrence between the War, Navy, and State Departments about the withdrawal of US Army forces from the Philippines. Acheson reiterated that if the Philippine Government pressed the issue that some sort of force remain in the new republic, the departments concerned thought that the force in question should be small and that it should be withdrawn after a period of time. Acheson also forwarded supporting memos for this policy from Byrnes, Patterson, Eisenhower, and Nimitz.[41]

By the middle of the month, General Thomas Handy, Deputy Chief of Staff of the Army (DCSA), informed Eisenhower about the timing of the communication with the Philippine Government over this matter. Handy thought that Eisenhower's proposals concerning Army forces in the Philippines had been submitted to the President and that Byrnes wanted to announce these intentions publicly, but that the Secretary of State refrained after Secretary of War Patterson suggested that the

Philippine Government be informed first. Apparently that task was being left to Paul McNutt, US Ambassador to the Philippines. As of the writing of this letter, Handy did not think that the Filipinos had been informed, but he did not know of any opposition to Eisenhower's idea on the US side.[42] The issue of US Army withdrawal from the Philippines, however, continued to be a subject of discussion into late December 1946. In a memo to Fleet Admiral William Leahy, Chief of Staff to the Commander-in-Chief of the Army and Navy, Handy, now Acting CSA, returned a copy of a State Department memo on the subject that Leahy had sent to him. Handy stated that Secretary of War Patterson had no objection to how the memo was worded, and that it could be dispatched to the President. Handy, however, wanted the President warned that the small force and defense installations now being planned for the Philippines might not be sufficient for the defense of the archipelago in the future. Therefore, Handy thought the United States should avoid any kind of mutual defense agreement in which the United States was responsible for guaranteeing the security of the Philippines.[43]

The day before Christmas also brought a memo from Acting Secretary of State Acheson to Truman that summarized for the President the suggestion to withdraw US Army forces from the Philippines. The memo stated that any forces remaining by request of the Philippines would be small in number, and that the President had approved this policy. In addition, the memo referred to Ambassador McNutt being in the process of communicating this policy to the Philippine Government. By this time, the State Department also informed Truman that McNutt had been told by Philippine President Manuel Roxas that some US military bases in the Philippines were desired, and that the Philippine Government would like US troops necessary for the maintenance of those bases to remain. Roxas cited previous agreements in which the United States and the Philippines pledged to take measures necessary for the mutual protection of the two nations. Roxas more specifically asserted that this was part of Philippine law, and that he had made previous public commitments about US military bases being maintained in the postwar Philippines.[44] In spite of these protestations by the Philippine Government, Admiral Leahy was willing to suggest a more complete withdrawal of American troops from the archipelago. In a memo dated 30 December, Leahy noted that there were currently 30,000 Philippine Scouts in the new republic who were in the pay of the US Army. Leahy was concerned that the United States might be committed by this current action to maintaining the Scouts with American funding into the future. He then noted that he did not think that it was "wise in the interest of economy to make any commitment whatever as to the maintenance of American troops in the islands." Thus, Truman's principal military adviser thought it better to completely withdraw from the Philippines, though his reference to "American troops" makes it unclear if he only meant Army forces being withdrawn, or if he was referring to Navy and Marine Corps units as well.[45]

Acheson told Truman that in light of the memo approved by Truman to withdraw Army forces from the Philippines, the War Department was now requesting a special directive from Truman calling for token US Army units to be maintained in the new republic. Acheson thought such a request was in order and attached a directive draft to this memo. This draft addressed the War Department withdrawing its forces from the Philippine Republic, especially in and around the Manila area, with the exception of the troops necessary for the maintenance of the remaining US bases being negotiated between the two governments. This documentation was then provided by Admiral Leahy to General Handy with a cover letter dated 31 December 1946.[46] Handy communicated all of this to Eisenhower early in January 1947. Specifically, he notified Eisenhower that Leahy had provided Handy with materials indicating that troops remaining in the Philippines would be maintained because of Roxas's request and that the area around Manila would be vacated as much as possible, but that the numbers of remaining troops had not yet been determined. Handy told Eisenhower that his staff was working on this latter problem, and that his intention was to ensure that the remaining force be token in size. Handy also wanted the Philippine Government to be certain that remaining US Army forces in the Philippines were not to be taken as a signal that the United States was pledging itself to the mutual defense of the two nations in the event of hostilities.[47] Later that month, Truman replied to the State Department's memo of 24 December 1946 with a memo of his own that clearly stated his position on the matter, but also clearly followed the line of advice from Acheson and Eisenhower.[48] More specifically, Truman confirmed for Patterson and communicated to Byrnes that the information received by McNutt about the Philippine Government's wishes should be considered as an expression of the desires of the Filipino people. A significant part of the rationale were the public statements Roxas had made to the Filipino people, as well as resolutions from the Philippine Congress about US forces remaining in some strength in the new republic. Accordingly, Truman ordered that the War Department withdraw the major portion of its forces from the Philippines as rapidly as possible, especially from the metropolitan area of Manila. However, he ordered that minimal Army forces be retained, as agreed upon in the final military-base treaty being negotiated by the two governments.[49]

■ The South Pacific

Part of the Army's deployment in the postwar Pacific also entailed a fairly complete, though somewhat hesitant, withdrawal from the island bases south of the equator. Reluctance to completely withdraw US Army forces from the South Pacific stemmed from concern that the lack of a US military presence would preclude the United States from having any base access rights to islands controlled by Australia and

New Zealand in the event of a resurgent Japan, or more likely, an expansionist Soviet Union. Any situation that might threaten US lines of communication with the South Pacific in a manner similar to Japan's advances of 1941–1942 was obviously considered anathema to American planners.[50]

In this context, Lieutenant General Hull radioed MacArthur about the South Pacific garrisons in early August 1946. Hull reported that on 1 September there would still be about five hundred Army personnel on six widely separated islands, but that there was little to no surplus materiel left on these islands. According to Hull, these forces were essentially limited to taking care of themselves, but the islands represented potential bases for the United States. Hull knew from JCS plans, and probably War Department plans as well, that the bases were desired as part of the postwar system, but he thought that weather personnel would be the only US Army personnel stationed there. He also pointed out that supplying these garrisons was difficult because of a shortage of planes and navigational aids. Because of these supply problems, he suggested that Penrhyn Island be turned over to New Zealand and that the garrison of ten men be withdrawn, but that one Army officer be retained there to represent US interests in "residual base rights." Aitutaki Island had been eliminated from the JCS base list, but Guadalcanal still had thirty-five men on it, largely involved in communications and weather operations as well as representing US base interests. Espiritu Santo only had eleven Army personnel left on it, and here again he suggested turning the island facilities over to a foreign government while leaving one US representative. New Caledonia still had four hundred Army personnel on the island, but the War Department required that the Army operate weather facilities on the island. Hull, however, hoped that the equipment could be turned over to the Oceanic Institute of French New Caledonia, and that Pan American World Airways (Pan Am) and the US Government's Civil Aeronautics Administration (CAA) could operate the weather facilities so that Army forces could be completely withdrawn. Finally, seventy-four men were operating communications equipment on Fiji, but that equipment was scheduled for transfer to Pan Am. Since Pan Am was thinking of operating weather stations from another location, Hull thought the Army facility should be turned over to "a foreign government" and the troops withdrawn. Hull thought that the paucity of information about final transfers of equipment made it virtually impossible to plan for withdrawals, so he was asking the concerned succeeding organizations for firm data regarding the dates by which they could assume their duties. He also needed more information about what role these South Pacific Islands would play in the JCS's Post-Hostilities Mapping Program. He understood that US troops and representatives on the islands would facilitate the bases' use in the mapping program, but he needed more data on timetables, reductions, and withdrawals. He ended the long radio message with a request that early consideration be accorded to reduce these garrisons wherever possible so that this "uneconomical" deployment of Army personnel in the South Pacific could be concluded.[51]

The need to evacuate Army personnel from the South Pacific was again the subject of a message a few days later between Hull and Christiansen. Hull told Christiansen that it was still paramount to reduce personnel wherever possible in order to meet the Army's higher-priority missions. These missions were the Japanese and Korean Occupations, as well as the orientation of postwar bases and mobile striking forces toward the Philippines, the Marianas, the Ryukyus, Hawaii, and the Aleutians. In addition, Hull reminded Christiansen that the Army still had to fulfill these roles while meeting its obligations toward demobilization and accommodating the budget cuts coming from Washington. Thus, Hull reiterated to Christiansen his desire to evacuate certain South Pacific bases as soon as possible. Hull said that the amount of surplus materiel there was negligible, but that Army personnel had to be maintained as long as there was some surplus property to be disposed of. He also pointed out that surplus materiel and personnel on Iwo Jima were being transferred to bases in the Marianas, and that garrisons had to be maintained at New Caledonia, Guadalcanal, Espiritu Santo, Penrhyn, Aitutaki, Fiji, Christmas and Canton Islands, Tarawa, and Kwajalein Atoll for the time being. However, he thought that it was desirable to relieve these posts as soon as possible.[52]

In early September, MacArthur sent a message to Hull about the personnel in the South Pacific. He made sure that Hull was apprised of the secret nature of this information as it involved base-rights negotiations with foreign allied powers. In essence, MacArthur told Hull that withdrawing American forces that were in "excess" of operational requirements at Biak and Morotai would not adversely affect future base-rights negotiations at those locations. Accordingly, those troops could be withdrawn in the same manner as personnel from islands on which the Army had no future base interests. MacArthur then directed Hull to reduce to token size the garrisons at Funa Futi, Nandi, Tarawa, Espiritu Santo, Upolu, Guadalcanal-Tulagi, Canton and Christmas Islands, and Tontoutt as soon as allowed for by the completion of their current missions. However, he emphasized that complete withdrawal was not to happen without prior War Department approval. He ended the communication by saying that Bora Bora, Aitutaki, and Penrhyn had been stricken from the JCS list of bases, and that these locations no longer needed garrisons on them.[53] In late September, Hull sent a message to the Chief of the Special Purposes Garrison, US Army (C SPGAR USA) that indicated that he was still interested in reducing the South Pacific garrisons as much as possible, but the lack of surface transportation, its excessive cost, and American airline companies' limited space led Hull to call for the continuation of the ATC routes between Hickam, Canton Island, Nandi, and Tontoutt. He also wanted the Pan American contract to be extended. Hull supplied C SPGAR USA with information on flights, passengers, and cargo weight, information that had also been provided to Brigadier General Bob Nowland, Commanding General of the Air Transport Command's Pacific Division (PAC DIV ATC), and he recommended that necessary action be taken to provide airlifts for October, November, and December.[54]

In mid-October, Hull informed MacArthur that withdrawal of the garrisons from New Caledonia and possibly Fiji was not planned, but he needed to negotiate certain contractual services from Pan Am, as well as obtain base-rights negotiation information from the State Department about airfield operation, communications, and weather service. He was also concerned that complete withdrawal of the garrisons might complicate reentry of the Thirtieth Engineering Base Topographical Battalion, the unit that would be conducting the JCS's Post-Hostilities Mapping Program in the area.[55] He was still concerned about this issue a few days later when it came to informing MacArthur about the impending withdrawal of the garrisons at Guadalcanal and Espiritu Santo.[56] Nonetheless, withdrawal from the South Pacific bases continued to be planned for later that same month. A radio message from Hull to Colonel John Harry, the Commanding Officer of US Army Forces, New Caledonia (CO USAFNC), ordered the latter officer to withdraw all Army forces from Guadalcanal, Espiritu Santo, and Fiji no later than 1 December 1946, and from New Caledonia no later than 15 December 1946. All military personnel were to be returned by air or water as determined by the New Caledonia command, civilian employees were to be "disposed of" as required by employment agreements, and Chinese and Formosan POWs of the Japanese were to be returned to Oahu for repatriation. The garrisons at the first three locations were to be discontinued concurrent with withdrawal. USAFNC Headquarters was to be kept active for an additional two weeks on Oahu in order to finish administrative work, though Hull wanted recommendations about how small that reduced administrative structure should be. The rest of the message outlined the equipment that would be returned to Hawaii, the equipment that was to be declared surplus, and the transportation details of how to return personnel to their respective destinations. Interestingly enough, there was no longer any mention of keeping officers on the islands in order to represent US residual interests in base rights.[57]

Still, bases in the South Pacific continued to figure in Army planning documents into the winter of 1946–1947. According to Hull in an early December 1946 message to MacArthur, the War Department's "Plan For Peacetime Overseas Bases," which assigned missions and requirements to AAF units, included the "Master Construction Plan" that called for facilities at Johnston, Eniwetok and Majuro Atolls, Canton Island, Tarawa, Christmas Island, Kwajalein, Yap-Ulithi, Guadalcanal-Tulagi, Marcus Island, Peleliu, Espiritu Santo, American Samoa, Funa Futi, New Caledonia, Truk, Palmyra, Viti Levu, Fiji, and Upolu![58] In addition, one document written a few months later, revealed some Army units still in the South Pacific and some interest in maintaining them in the region. In May 1947, Major General Griswold, Commanding General of

MARBO, reported to MacArthur that 179 men—the Army Garrison Force, Manus, consisting of postal, engineering, medical, transportation, and supply personnel— would be stationed on Manus to support the JCS's Post-Hostilities Mapping Program.[59] While the mapping program is a clear explanation as to why some Army personnel were still in these locations this late in the period covered by this study, the possibility also remains that Army planners wanted to maintain some sort of postwar US presence in the South Pacific. The exact reason is a bit of mystery to this author, given the Army leadership's ease in deciding to withdraw its forces from a key location such as the Philippines. Still, differences in land area, population size, and the history of US relations with civilian populations might have encouraged Army planners to count on postwar base facilities south of the equator in case of future hostilities in the region even while they were discounting them in the Philippines. Only strained US relations with Australia and New Zealand over this issue would have obviated the acquisition of South Pacific bases.[60]

■ Unity of Command

The process of planning for Army postwar force dispositions in the Pacific was tied in very heavily with the whole issue of postwar American defense reorganization. Between 1945 and 1950, the US armed services fought a bureaucratic battle over which service—the Army, the Navy, or the newly independent Air Force—would become the nation's first line of defense, with commensurate political clout and budgetary authority going to the service that was so designated. What eventually resulted between an Army that wanted a unified national department of defense, and a Navy that merely wanted stronger coordination between the services was the National Security Act of 1947. This legislation provided for a central department of defense, with the services supposedly being unified under a secretary of defense. In reality, however, each service was able to exercise a significant amount of autonomy.[61]

The United States' postwar defense of the Pacific Basin came into this fight specifically through the issue of "unity of command," or the idea that there should be one theater commander in the Pacific who had a joint staff of subordinate air, ground, and naval commanders. Command arrangements in the Pacific, which had never been worked out to the satisfaction of either service during the war, were a major hurdle to truly unified commands, and of some urgency because of the Japanese and Korean Occupations. One major disagreement was that the Army wanted general unity of command of forces, while the Navy wanted unity of command of forces in specific geographic areas such as the Central Pacific or Western Pacific.[62] MacArthur went further than the rest of the Army and wanted to command all US forces in the entire Pacific Basin. The Army, and MacArthur in particular, lobbied for such a situation on the grounds that the Pacific was an integrated strategic theater, and that divided command was a recipe for disaster—or at least "uneconomical" fighting such as occurred, the Army argued, during the Pacific War. To solve the problem, the Army and Navy created numerous interservice boards. However, the issue did not begin to be solved until July 1946, when Vice Admiral Forrest Sherman, Deputy Chief of Naval Operations (DCNO) for Operations, and Major General Norstad, OPD Director, were assigned the task of drafting a unification plan.[63]

What Sherman and Norstad developed was a global series of unified commands in which a theater commander, responsible to the JCS, would have a joint staff and three service commanders under him. The JCS would exercise strategic direction of the entire unified command in terms of missions and tasks, while each subordinate service commander would report back to his own service for purposes of administration, supply, training, finance, and construction. The CSA, the CNO, and the AAF Commanding General (COMGENAIR) would be the JCS's "Executive Agents" for the various forces deployed globally within the unified commands. The major problem occurred when the JCS decided to turn the newly formed Strategic Air Command (SAC) into a "specified command" directly under JCS control from Washington. There had been a wartime precedent for this kind of command arrangement when the Twentieth Air Force on Guam was put under JCS control, and General of the Army Henry Arnold, COMGENAIR, acted as the JCS's Executive Agent. The arrangement, however, was not at all popular with the Navy. Now desired by the AAF on a global scale, specified commands were anathema to the Navy, which had assumed that all overseas-based forces would be under unified commanders and that there would not be any specified commands. Regardless of this disagreement, the unified command plan, along with the SAC specified command, was approved by President Truman in December 1946, went into effect on 1 January 1947, and was fully implemented by December 1947. For the Pacific, this meant the creation of a Far East Command (FECOM), a Pacific Command (PACOM), and an Alaskan Command (ALCOM) instead of various service commands such as the US Pacific Fleet or US Army Forces, Pacific.[64]

A central part of the AGF's conception for force deployments in the postwar Pacific, in fact, was intertwined with the unity-of-command issue long before the National Security Act of 1947. In August 1945, Lieutenant General Robert Richardson, Hull's predecessor as Commanding General of AFMIDPAC, complained to General MacArthur that Admiral Nimitz was violating the spirit, if not the letter, of an Executive Order having to do with service control of a sister service's forces in the Hawaiian Area.[65] More specifically, Richardson asked that peacetime control of Army forces in the Hawaiian Area be returned to him now that hostilities with Japan were coming to a close. During the war, an Executive Order had put Army forces in Hawaii under Navy control. With the end of the fighting, that same Executive Order gave Nimitz the ability "to determine the use of the personnel and resources of the Army." Richardson could find no justification after Japan's surrender for Nimitz's continued control over Army forces in Hawaii. Therefore, he asked MacArthur to intervene with the JCS so that US forces in Hawaii could be reorganized on the same basis as in the Ryukyus—namely, "that the Army Forces come exclusively, both administratively and operationally, under the control of CINCAFPAC." One day later, MacArthur concurred with Richardson's recommendations and forwarded them to General Marshall.[66]

Later in the month, MacArthur again told Marshall that since hostilities had ended, there was now need for a "complete restudy" of the command arrangements over the United States' Pacific forces, and that all Army forces in the Pacific should be placed under their own commander. MacArthur saw a "sound" Army organization in the Pacific to be "essential" prior to Congressional consideration of postwar military organization. More specifically, MacArthur wanted Hawaii, the Philippines, and the Ryukyus under his command, with Guam, Manus, and other atolls retained for fleet support under Navy control with Marine Corps garrisons. In addition, MacArthur thought it important to establish the principle that garrisons for various Pacific bases should come from the service that predominated in the area. He wanted forces that were domiciled in an area that was under another service to be given "exempted status" so that the commander had operational autonomy except when the area commander needed to coordinate operations for purposes of local defense.[67] In the latter instance, MacArthur was no doubt referring to the Twentieth Air Force's situation on Guam, where those AAF units had been in Nimitz's operational area but had been under direct JCS control from Washington, D.C.[68]

In early October 1945, MacArthur sent a message to Marshall about certain jurisdictional issues concerning Nimitz's control over Army forces in the Pacific Islands. Specifically, MacArthur wanted clarification of Nimitz's operational and administrative control of ASF units in Hawaii and the South Pacific. MacArthur pointed out that the Navy had control over ASF forces in the Marianas because of unity of command, just as MacArthur had operational control of Marine Corps units in Japan. The release of the ASF units in the Marianas, about 60,000 personnel, was the subject of an upcoming Guam conference, but MacArthur believed that the Navy was intent on retaining control of the majority of Army units in the Pacific. According to MacArthur, such a situation would not allow the Army in the Pacific to demobilize according to War Department directives, nor to reorganize as necessary in order for the Army to continue to fulfill its mission in that theater as its numbers were reduced.[69] Part of the unity-of-command issue in the Pacific was also heavily, if not centrally, tied in with another issue: Congress's report on the Pearl Harbor attack. In late July 1946, Secretary of War Patterson told MacArthur that the principal recommendations of the report were to ensure unity of command at all outposts, and that Army and Navy intelligence functions were to be integrated. Patterson hoped—in vain—that Congress would "go the whole distance" and insist on unity of command throughout the US Government. Congress did not go that far, so Patterson was at a loss as to how effective unity of command was to be achieved if it did not begin in Washington. The letter ends with Patterson asking for MacArthur's views on the subject.[70]

The command situation was the object of another long radio message from Eisenhower to MacArthur a few months later. Eisenhower spoke about the effort that had been going on "for some months" to solve both near- and long-term command issues in the Pacific. He said that the War Department had run into basic differences of conception and made no real progress, though he claimed that the Department had attempted to reflect MacArthur's ideas. Eisenhower thought that for the long-term future, unification of the services was the best solution. He then pointed out an example of the conceptual differences that had arisen with the Navy when Admiral John Towers, the current CINCPAC-CINCPOA, had asked for the mission of transporting Marines to Tsingtao, China, covering these operations, and establishing and exercising control over the Yellow Sea and Sea of Japan. Eisenhower had indicated to the Navy that this was not acceptable since it would have provided for a divided operational command in the Western Pacific, but the Army could not prevent the matter from being discussed since the JCS had not yet fully determined overall geographic-command issues. Because the JCS had not yet made final decisions, Towers was empowered to discuss these matters with MacArthur on a planning level. Thus, because of JCS inaction, Eisenhower asserted that the Navy envisioned an operational situation in the Western Pacific under which Navy and Army forces would act in the same geographic region, but under divided command. Eisenhower told MacArthur that the situation demanded urgent action since he thought the arrangement was completely unsound from an operational standpoint. More specifically, Eisenhower thought that the command situation should conform more closely to MacArthur's ideas of operations in the Japanese area, in which the AGF led the effort with support by the AAF and the Navy. He reiterated the first recommendation from Congress's Joint Committee on the Investigation of the Pearl Harbor Attack, which was that unity of command should prevail in all military and naval outposts. Eisenhower thought that the unity-of-command issues in the Pacific would, therefore, become an important matter in the reconvened Congress in light of the report and the lack of JCS action.[71]

In this same vein, Secretary Patterson urged that in advance of any additional Congressional pressure, the President be contacted about creating a truly unified command in which a single commander had a joint staff and exercised control through ground, air, and naval subordinate commanders in a given strategic area. In the Western Pacific, Eisenhower thought the operational issue was obviously the support of occupation forces in Japan and Korea. In light of the Navy's attitude, Eisenhower urged a "sound" unified-command arrangement for the Western Pacific, with the Navy's Seventh Fleet coming under MacArthur's planning and operational control in case of emergencies. He was certain that comparable arrangements would be established for the rest of the Pacific. He did not think, however, that MacArthur's idea of having one commander for the entire Pacific—in this case MacArthur, commanding all US forces in the Pacific west of San Francisco from his headquarters in Tokyo—would be "practical." Eisenhower thought it more likely that under the final arrangement, one officer would become the commander for the Central Pacific—probably a naval officer with a joint staff representing subordinate ground and air commanders. MacArthur would then be the principal commander in the Western Pacific, with planning control over naval and air units as well as operational control in an emergency. Eisenhower was quick to point out that if this plan had to go to the President, it had to be done with a "reasoned, cooperative, conciliatory attitude absolutely free of any implication of service jealousy. Otherwise we may find ourselves forced to apply a solution far short of our minimum requirements."[72]

MacArthur replied on 31 July 1946, stating that his views on the command situation in the Pacific were unchanged. He wanted to see "true" unity of command in the Pacific, with all land, sea, and air forces under one command, and he thought that the recent proposals divided the Pacific into two commands. MacArthur claimed that the proposal to create two commands would leave the forward area without operational depth and place major bomber-supporting bases under the charge of a rear-area commander. He further claimed that it would result in a "potentially disastrous discontinuity of supply responsibility, with the outposts under one commander and the supporting bases under another." MacArthur added that any command situation had to be predicated on the primary mission of occupation, with modifications being made for the post-Occupation period. He thought that for the Occupation period, the ideal position, geographically and psychologically, for the commander in the Pacific was Tokyo. When the Occupation was over, the general headquarters could be relocated. He reiterated that the protection of the Pacific Basin rested on the "proper" application of land-based airpower that was under unified command and located in the Western Pacific—including the Marianas and Volcanoes—and "poised to strike at the source of any possible future aggression." According to MacArthur, with no enemy naval forces existent in the area, naval forces could only play a secondary role in the Pacific. He therefore thought it was inconceivable that the Pacific should be partitioned under independent commanders, or divided into Army and Navy spheres. Such a division, he argued, would only "scramble" functions, surrender fundamental War Department concepts of command, and retreat to the "unsatisfactory" system that had existed in the Pacific prior to World War II. MacArthur denied that he held the slightest idea of service rivalry. He argued that his conclusions were based on the belief that sound, basic principles had to be applied without compromise or there would be some sort of disaster. He recognized that until the final legislative enactment of postwar defense organization took place, unity of command in the Pacific might be unattainable. But he preferred that if there were any division in the Pacific, it not be geographical, but by service between the Army and Navy. By retaining merely a service division, MacArthur asserted that true unity of command could be had by simple orders from above. A geographical division would make operations more difficult, making defense in the Pacific and the furtherance of US interests in East Asia more difficult.[73]

In early August 1946, MacArthur made his views known to Patterson. He had not yet seen Congress's Pearl Harbor report, but claimed he did not need to in order to comment on unity of command in the Pacific. MacArthur began by arguing that since command flowed from the top down, not vice versa, no commander could control his subordinate commands if they were responsible to separate authorities or if differences of military opinion could not be settled by one authority. Basic decisions, as well as physical resources and intelligence, had to flow from Washington. MacArthur went on to argue that the Pacific was "properly" a single integrated theater where the concept of future military operations had to "necessarily" be primarily dependent on land-based airpower, with that airpower being fully supported by the other services. He maintained, as he had during the war, that the division of the Pacific into geographical areas was faulty, and that it made unity of command impossible. In addition, he again stated that unity of command in the Pacific would be impossible if it did not start in Washington. He acknowledged that the present system, in which the Army and Navy each operated under its own command with overall control being achieved by coordination through the two commanders, was far from ideal but much sounder than a division into entirely independent areas, which would preclude any kind of theater-wide unification. He therefore thought that the present system of coordination would do until true unification came about. His criticism of pending Congressional legislation on these lines was that the legislation did not go "far enough." He agreed with Patterson that effective unity of command at the outposts depended on abolishing the division of command in Washington, D.C.[74]

Later in the month, Eisenhower sent MacArthur more information on the Pacific command situation. He said that MacArthur's views on the problem had been considered with great care, that MacArthur's views were essentially in line with the War Department's, and that the War Department was fully committed to supporting MacArthur in his main mission of governing Japan. However, he also said that the Army was now faced with the report by the Congressional Joint Committee, and the clamoring of the press and public for the two services to solve any problems that might lead to another Pearl Harbor–type catastrophe. Eisenhower stated that recent planning instructions from Nimitz to Towers implied a divided authority within MacArthur's area, creating problems for MacArthur in any attempt to carry out emergency missions. However, Eisenhower said that any agreement would have to be approved by the President, and that in the absence of such agreement between the Army and Navy, the Army and Navy leadership had to be aggressive in getting the two service Secretaries to refer the matter to the President. He also said that although he had discussed matters with Admiral Nimitz, no agreement would come about if both sides stuck rigidly to their original positions. However, he did think that an agreement on several broad principles could be reached if both services made some concessions. The first principle that Eisenhower put forth was that MacArthur, as the theater commander in the Western Pacific, would exercise command—now and in emergencies—over all forces allocated to him by the JCS, including command of Pacific-based AAF strategic elements, i.e., VHBs and escorting fighters. Operational control over all forces in this area would also include the Seventh Fleet. MacArthur's missions would continue to be the occupation of Japan and Korea, the provision of military support for US policy in China and other areas of East Asia, and the conduct of operations in and defense of the Western Pacific—the latter comprising Japan, Korea, the Ryukyus, and the Philippines. MacArthur was also to make plans for the safety of US forces in China and Korea, oppose enemy advances, and militarily secure Japan, the Ryukyus, and the Philippines. Eisenhower additionally said that there would be a theater commander for the Central Pacific whose responsibility would include supporting MacArthur in his missions, protecting sea and air communications in the Pacific (unless otherwise assigned), and securing US island positions in the Pacific (unless otherwise assigned). The Central Pacific commander was also to support the defense of Alaska, including the Aleutians, and make plans for carrying out these operations in an emergency. Eisenhower further proposed that unified command would take place in each theater, that each theater commander would have a joint staff, and that the commanders of component forces would communicate directly with their appropriate service headquarters on matters of administration, training, and supply—none of the latter being the responsibility of the joint commander. The assignment of forces and any significant changes would be by order of the JCS. To Eisenhower, this proposed plan achieved unified command in the Pacific, gave MacArthur direct control over all of the forces he needed to carry out his missions, and gave each commander control over all of the forces that they would need for wartime or other emergency operations assigned to them by the JCS. Eisenhower ended the message by asking MacArthur for his views, but he also made it clear that negotiations with the Navy entailed command-and-control arrangements for worldwide US military operations, not just those in the Pacific Basin.[75]

Two days later, MacArthur responded to Eisenhower. He first stated that his views had not changed, and that the arrangement was militarily unsound. According to MacArthur, it failed to achieve unity in the Pacific, and it formalized disunity in an emergency. It also, he argued, perpetuated the Pearl Harbor concept of divided authority, but on a broader and more dangerous scale. Further, he thought it sacrificed military principles to temporary expediency. He repeated that the Pacific Theater should be one theater under one commander; to MacArthur, the Pacific was a single theater and would remain so even after the end of the Japanese and Korean Occupations. Additionally, given limited US resources for the Occupation and post-Occupation periods, he thought dividing an integrated theater into two commands was "inimical to the fulfillment of current missions." For MacArthur, the post-Occupation period in the Pacific, even more than the Occupation period itself, required an integrated strategic theater with a single commander, and both the Occupation and post-Occupation periods needed a Pacific Basin defended by highly mobile, long-range, land-based airpower operating from and along a corridor of mutually supporting bases. He did not agree with Eisenhower that the Navy was sacrificing its concept for the sake of agreement. He saw the Navy perspective as one that divided the Pacific, and thought the entire question transcended individuals or services and was a question vital to the defense of the nation. In addition, MacArthur was confident that the arguments for a unified Pacific command were so sound that the Army need not have fear of US Congressional or public censure if it made clear that the reasons for doing so were to achieve complete unity of command and action for all of the armed forces engaged in the area. "If the problem is properly presented to the President and congress [*sic*] they cannot fail to see that the defense of vital areas, under the conditions of warfare as they are developing, depends initially on long range offensive action by air forces." MacArthur continued that in order to launch this type of effort, maintain it, and follow it up with coordinated military force, the full resources of the Pacific had to be mobilized under a single commander. MacArthur concluded that he thought Eisenhower's plan allowed for each of the Pacific commanders to call on the JCS for the allocation of resources, and that this situation would create a division of strength, exactly as MacArthur claimed occurred during most of the Pacific War. He then requested that his views be placed before the Secretary of War and the President before any "negative" decisions were made. He concluded by saying that none of the messages sent to him included any arguments against his ideas about a single Pacific commander, except the inability to obtain the concurrence of the Navy. Therefore, he thought that there was a need to seek a decision from a higher authority.[76]

Eisenhower responded with a long radio message a few days later. He assured MacArthur that the General's views would be made known to the President before any final decision was made, but he also sought to inform MacArthur about the logic in Washington, D.C., concerning the proposed division of the Pacific command arrangements. First, Eisenhower described the Pacific Basin as essentially a large ocean area over which a power would need offensive and defensive control of the ocean's surface until heavy shipping was no longer an essential part of warfare. Even if airpower could ship modern military forces, Eisenhower thought that control of the Pacific would be needed into the foreseeable future in order to forward-deploy land-based bombers attacking targets in the Northern Hemisphere. He also stated that, from the United States' standpoint, every Pacific Island over which the

United States retained an exclusive control was part of a great outpost system based on the US West Coast and the main US base in Hawaii. Eisenhower argued that for the entire outpost system to be linked effectively, it had to be linked through surface shipping. In addition, he stated that the United States did not know which Pacific Island locations would be available to it, and would not know for some time until "political international maneuvering" and the budget crystallized.[77]

Eisenhower then stated that flanking the great Pacific area was another northern region that was becoming more important in US strategic calculations: Alaska and its contiguous islands. Although Eisenhower admitted that Alaska was an area in which ground forces and land-based airpower would fulfill most of the operational requirements, the area had to be supplied from the south by the Navy. Eisenhower also envisioned that the Pacific Basin would operate as a supporting area for operations in Alaska and Northwest Asia, which is where he thought the major ground and air action would take place in the next Pacific conflict. Thus, from a long-range perspective, Eisenhower thought that the entire Pacific should be organized as an outpost and supporting system—first to ensure the protection of the Continental United States, and then as an area supporting US military operations in the theaters bordering the Pacific Ocean. Eisenhower argued that even if Washington was to give one theater commander all of the forces and jurisdiction which that commander would need, a single commander would always be dependent on naval support for convoying his personnel and supplies. This officer would have naval forces operating under his control, but Eisenhower thought the Central Pacific, as an outpost and supporting area, should be commanded in the long-term by an officer directly responsible to the JCS. Eisenhower then said that he did not think any single officer should command the entire Pacific Theater or retain personal control over any one service operating in it. Instead, Eisenhower wanted a separate top commander, named by the JCS, and then subordinate ground, air, and sea commanders for particular areas of the Pacific such as Hawaii and the Marianas.[78] Though not explicitly stated by Eisenhower, it seems he saw the need for two theaters in the Central and Western Pacific in order to support a third, Alaska, and he did not think one officer could command the entire Pacific Basin structure.

Addressing more immediate problems, Eisenhower turned to the Japanese and Korean Occupations. Pointing out that the majority of US ground and air forces were tied up with these occupations, he wanted to plan for completing these missions, as well as for dealing with any "emergencies" that might arise. As Eisenhower saw it, there was not a clear and established system of single authority in the Western Pacific for dealing with emergencies. In particular, Eisenhower thought that unless MacArthur commanded everything in the Western Pacific, the Navy would devise its own plans and merely cooperate with MacArthur. Eisenhower thought this might work, but he also thought that everything that could operate by land, sea, or air in the Western Pacific should be under MacArthur's command. Eisenhower envisioned a situation in which the areas of the Pacific to the rear of MacArthur's forces would be classified as supporting areas, would be placed under the JCS, and would be used to do everything that needed to be done for MacArthur to carry out the Occupation and address any other contingencies. He envisioned possible operations that would involve MacArthur on his immediate front, but also potentially in Alaska, and he thought the line of demarcation between operating and supporting areas would have to be delineated. Eisenhower did not agree with MacArthur that the line of demarcation went all the way back to San Francisco. He saw the area east of the Marianas becoming momentarily critical, but he did not "see how anyone engaged in a major campaign, possibly battling for his life in the Japanese Island Area, could give special and specific attention to operations either in Alaska or in some particular position of this supporting area." He admitted that these were complex problems, but in his view, all overseas areas of US military operations should be organized under commanders reporting directly back to the JCS, though he admitted that even that situation would not end all of the conflicts with the Navy. Eisenhower concluded by telling MacArthur that these were his ideas about the Pacific command problem, and that he would not place the problem before the President or the Secretary of War before outlining MacArthur's differing viewpoints in detail. He also said he appreciated any ideas MacArthur had on the subject, that he valued MacArthur's opinions because of the General's vast experience in the region, and that he was trying to the best of his ability to obtain a legal organization for the military that would assure singular responsibility and authority for overseas strategic commanders.[79]

Three days later, a longer message went from MacArthur to Eisenhower, the former putting in greater detail than ever before his ideas about how to defend the Pacific Basin in time of war. This time he also put forth his ideas about defending Alaska as it related to the rest of the Pacific. He said he appreciated the opportunity to touch on this subject for the first time, but he then said that the idea of Hawaii and the Marianas being the supporting area for the southern flank of Alaska was faulty. He thought the key was having a single theater commander who could deal with the "source of the threat that emanated toward Alaska." Hawaii and the Marianas, he thought, were sure to be active battlegrounds and actual defense positions. If the enemy advanced from the north, MacArthur saw the Pacific area lying on the enemy's southern flank, and the entire power of the Pacific area being used strategically from the south. If the enemy drove from the west, however, the Pacific Islands would be integral sections of the battlefront. MacArthur thought that to deprive the Pacific Theater commander of his jurisdictional disposition would deprive him of his actual campaign localities. MacArthur said that the commander would not have any depth of position and would hold nothing but a thin line of outposts that would be thrown back into the supporting area. In short, MacArthur thought that the entire Pacific area should be used to support the Alaskan Theater, but to deprive the Pacific

Theater of its depth might not only destroy it but also limit the extent to which the Pacific Theater could support Alaska. The solution, he argued, was not in a lateral compartmentalization of the Pacific, but in a radial division from the United States between Alaska and the Pacific, with unified command for each. He also thought that the Alaskan Theater was of such importance that it should not be "intermingled" with the Pacific Theater. MacArthur further noted that San Francisco had been the main base area for the proposed invasion of Japan. He assumed that San Francisco and the Continental United States would again be the main base area in any future operations in the Western Pacific. Yet, if Hawaii were taken from a general Pacific Command, that command would be deprived of its intermediate base. Nothing, MacArthur thought, could be fraught with greater peril. He said he shared Eisenhower's views on the importance of the sea lanes, but thought that the control of sea lanes rested with airpower, not naval power—especially airpower employed by one commander in full exploitation of mobility and flexibility. MacArthur said that he was unclear about Eisenhower's reference to JCS control. To him, under any system of command, the JCS would exercise complete control of the Pacific and any other theater, and he assumed that the JCS could exercise that complete control through the field commander. He claimed he had repeatedly advocated for one overall commander under the JCS. MacArthur also claimed appreciation of the difficulties Eisenhower was having, and he admitted that the problem was complex. However, he thought it was simply a matter of principle, and that if the basic structure was decided on, the details would fall into place. "We gain nothing towards the defense of the United States and of its interests by compromise. Rather we lose the opportunity to achieve the unity for which we have all been striving for so long."[80]

A few weeks later, Eisenhower wrote again to MacArthur about matters in the Pacific, including command organization. He complained to MacArthur that this matter "has dragged on and on," but he thought that in the "highest circles" there was a determination to achieve an organization that would allow the President to say that a unified command structure was being constructed in every one of the United States' important outposts. Eisenhower said that he had visited Truman and asked that Truman read MacArthur's comments before making a final decision. He also said that Admiral Leahy had read all of MacArthur's estimates of the Pacific situation. Eisenhower now specifically asked MacArthur to write Leahy if there was anything further to add on this matter, since the Admiral "occupies a key position in these struggles and is a devoted admirer and friend of yours. He will take very seriously anything you might have to say." Eisenhower estimated that "final actions" would entail some sort of defense reorganization, and that the Navy would bitterly fight having the Marines in the Pacific placed under MacArthur's command, but that the Army would not agree with the alternative.[81]

In December 1946, General Handy sent a memo to Eisenhower about the command situation in the Pacific, as well as the issue of Army forces in the Philippines, in which he specifically spoke to the issue of the newly unified commands that were about to take effect. Handy said that the JCS had approved of the command paper almost as Eisenhower wanted it. He noted that a covering memo to the President pointed out MacArthur's divergent views, and that these additional perspectives from MacArthur would be given to Admiral Leahy for presentation to Truman. He also stated that the JCS had approved the new command relationship in the Pacific, which divided command between MacArthur, Towers, and Major General Howard Craig, Commanding General of the Army's Alaskan Department. Handy went on to inform Eisenhower that a press release had been prepared, but that there must have been a leak since an article appeared by Hanson Baldwin, Military Editor of the *New York Times*, in that morning's newspaper. Handy and Admiral Nimitz therefore stressed fast action by the President, but Leahy said the matter could not be pressed further. Handy appeared most concerned that MacArthur and Towers were hearing about the new command arrangement from the *New York Times*, rather than from official channels.[82]

The final outcome of this communication controversy is unknown. However, AGF missions within the new command structure became clearer when they were communicated early in the New Year. On 2 January 1947, Lieutenant General Hull sent a message to Colonel Harry, also the Commander of the South Pacific Base Command (SOPACBACOM) delineating the mission for Army Ground Forces, Pacific (AGFPAC). AGFPAC, which had been Army Ground Forces, Middle Pacific, was ordered to maintain defense forces for the Pacific Islands as directed, to continue to maintain postwar bases as staging facilities for mounting strike forces, and to continue to close out wartime installations as directed by the JCS. The command was also to conduct necessary training of AGF personnel, particularly in terms of preparing these units for joint operations. The radio message then detailed which commands were to report to whom in a manner that was fairly complex and reflective of the nature of these newly unified commands. For instance, AGFPAC comprised the ground forces of what had been Army Forces, Middle Pacific, except for those that had been located in the Western Pacific Base Command. Ground-force units in Hawaii were assigned to AGFPAC for joint training operations, but AGFPAC units stationed in the Pacific Islands outside of the Hawaiian Area would report to various subordinate ground-force commanders, who in turn reported to overall unified commanders. The Commanding Officer of AGF Tarawa, for instance, would report to Commodore George Seitz, the Commander of the Marshalls-Gilberts Sub-Area, a naval officer, while Colonel Harry, as the Commanding Officer of US Army Forces, New Caledonia, would report to Captain Harold Houser, the Commander of the South Pacific Area and the Commandant of Naval Station Tutuila, American Samoa.[83]

What appears to be a very complicated and confusing situation in terms of officers from various services commanding forces from other services was, in fact, a partial continuation of what had occurred during the Pacific War between

MacArthur, then Commander-in-Chief of the Southwest Pacific Area (CINCSWPA) and Admiral Nimitz, then CINCPAC-CINCPOA. This phenomenon was also the beginning of what would become truly unified and joint commands in the late Cold War.[84] In the 1940s, however, unified command meant the establishment of "objective" control of all forces and elements concerned in an operational area under a single commander. This unity of forces could mean the organization of task forces, task groups, or task units; the assignment of missions; the designation of objectives; and the coordination necessary to achieve the objectives. It did not include the administration, discipline, internal organization, or training of the units, which broke down to the senior officer of a particular branch in each geographic area—with the exception of any joint-forces training that needed to be conducted. For example, Lieutenant General Hull told Colonel Harry that on matters of administration, logistics, supply, and construction projects, AGFPAC units would report to Hull even if they were stationed outside of PACOM.[85]

■ Conclusion

AGF deployments between 1945 and 1947 clearly reflected the stringent constrictions placed on AFPAC, PACOM, and FECOM by rapid demobilization and budget cuts. Even though the Army continued to place some interest in residual base rights in the South Pacific bases well into 1947, it was clear that the deployments would really be restricted to the Pacific Islands north of the equator, in part because of personnel and fiscal shortages, but also because of deployment strategies which emphasized a limited number of bases supporting mobile defensive and offensive striking forces. In addition, it is important to remember how strongly some of these AGF officers, especially MacArthur, had taken on land-based strategic airpower as the new mantra for the Army. Since a shift to airpower of any kind would not have been surprising in the wake of the Second World War, it is nevertheless of key interest that senior officers such as Eisenhower and MacArthur disagreed so strongly on how to allocate their limited resources. Of particular note were ideas of a frontline war against the Soviets beginning in Japan and Korea, as MacArthur envisioned matters, versus a focus on Alaska—almost to the abandonment of the rest of the Pacific Basin—as argued by Eisenhower. Finally, these two officers are a microcosm by which to study a much larger issue concerning Pacific Basin defense, as well as postwar global American military organization and deployments. The unity-of-command issue was not only a matter of disagreement between the services. It wound up demonstrating internal fissures within the Army, epitomized by the disagreements between Eisenhower and MacArthur, over the creation of one theater command in the Pacific versus the continuation of two theaters. The unity-of-command issue also brought out another question. The postwar American military establishment was larger than any peacetime military the United States had ever had, though it was drastically smaller than what had been fielded during World War II. In spite of increased peacetime size, however, budgetary restrictions dictated that the American military decide how it could carry out US defense policy in a radical new foreign-policy environment as the United States began to engage in a cold war with the Soviet Union. The AAF and the Navy thought they had the answers, just as the AGF did.

CHAPTER 2

Air-Power War in Paradise

The Army Air Forces and the Defense of the Pacific Basin

An even larger part of the postwar conflict between the US armed services than the unity-of-command controversy was the fight over service roles and missions. Given the demobilization of the major portion of the services after 1945 in the context of President Truman's postwar focus on fiscal conservancy, each service sought to demonstrate that its particular form of postwar defense was the most effective and economical for the United States. The service that could demonstrate this expertise to a greater extent would not only become the nation's "first line of defense," but would accordingly command the lion's share of the now leaner postwar defense budget. Tied in with this fight over roles and missions were disagreements over the administrative unification of the military. AAF support for a unification of the services into a "department of national defense" focused around the idea of the AAF as a separate service that would become the new, more cost-effective first line of defense for the postwar United States. Navy opposition to unification coalesced around the idea that a separate air force could not fulfill postwar mission requirements, even if the AAF tried through public-relations campaigns to convince the President, Congress, and the public that it could provide for the national security on its own. Not surprisingly, the Pacific Basin became a geographic arena for conflict between the AAF and the Navy over these bureaucratic conflicts.

Most interesting, from this author's perspective, is that the AAF employed a "useable history" to justify its recent past and its future. Employing the history of the Pacific War, the AAF attempted to demonstrate that land-based airpower was the primary weapon that had won the war, and that therefore, land-based airpower should be the first line of defense for the postwar United States. While AAF officers were, at times, willing to acknowledge the contributions of the other services, the majority of their historical material was oriented toward proving their case that land-based airpower was central, and that all other units were merely support. What this author has found so fascinating is that the discourse in the primary documents was so bellicose. More specifically, AAF officers employed a discourse of war in their references to the US Navy, almost as if the Navy were an enemy power rather than just a bureaucratic rival. Ironically, at the same time that the United States perceived its future foreign enemies as a potentially resurgent Japan and an increasingly threatening Soviet Union, the AAF was discussing its primary domestic rival in terms typically reserved for international-relations opponents.

∎ Context

One of the most interesting aspects of the AAF's argument concerning the defense of the Pacific Basin, both during and after the war, was the essential similarity to Navy arguments about the region. To be sure, the Navy and the AAF had widely disparate strategic and intellectual views of the efficacy of carrier-based airpower versus land-based airpower as the most effective and economical means of postwar defense. Nevertheless, Navy and AAF postwar strategies for the Pacific, though kept secret from each other until 1945, were remarkably similar.

For example, in broad strategic terms between 1943 and 1945, both Navy and AAF planning officers seemed to subscribe to President Franklin Roosevelt's idea about the "Big Four" (the United States, Great Britain, the Soviet Union, and China) policing the postwar world. Just like early naval planners, AAF planning officers during the war assigned exclusive strategic spheres to the United States in the Western Hemisphere and the Pacific Ocean Areas (POA), while leaving Europe, the Middle East, and South and Southeast Asia to be "policed" by Great Britain, the Soviet Union, and China.[1] Not surprisingly, most AAF planners up to 1945 saw a resurgent Japan as the primary enemy in the postwar Pacific, and still saw the Soviet Union as a cooperative postwar ally.[2] Although previous historiography has demonstrated that a few AAF intelligence officers perceived the USSR as an immediate potential postwar enemy, their conclusions were either never communicated to AAF planning bodies, or were rejected by those officers. In fact, even the AAF's Air Intelligence Division did not become very alarmist about the Soviet Union until the winter of 1946–1947.[3] On the contrary, just as naval officers prior to 1945 denied the potential of the USSR as a significant threat because of its lack of a large, blue-water navy, so AAF planners saw potential future enemies only where large strategic-bombing air forces were in existence or were considered possible. Not only did AAF planners and key officers such as General Arnold dismiss the Soviets as a short-term potential enemy, they actually had such an overt disdain for Soviet aviation technology that they did not think the Soviets could become a threat to the United States sooner than twenty years after the end of the war.[4]

There were other similarities between early Navy and early AAF postwar plans for the Pacific Basin that again are rather startling, considering the degree to which the two services took different paths in their strategic thinking after the end of the war. Both services, for instance, discussed "policing" the region within the context of a "United Nations International Police Force." While AAF officers seemed to subscribe much more seriously to this idea than did naval officers, both services' planning documents in 1943 and 1944 were replete with references to an "International Police Force," and both services explored the possibility of their respective branches fulfilling the majority of these "police" functions for the UN in the postwar Pacific.[5] Two other major similarities between Navy and AAF plans deserve mention. One similarity had to do with the mutual use of Mahanian doctrine. Clearly, the Navy subscribed to Rear Admiral Alfred Mahan's turn-of-the-century ideas about using a concentrated battle fleet to destroy enemy naval forces, gain command of the sea, and police an American empire for the strategic benefit of the United States. By the 1940s, any differences within the Navy over the use of Mahanian doctrine had to do with substituting carrier forces for battleships, not the employment of the doctrine itself.[6] The AAF likewise applied Mahanian doctrine to the use of an American strategic air force during and after World War II. Calling the doctrine "Modified Mahan," one historian has convincingly argued that AAF planners merely substituted the strategic bomber for the capital ship, and saw the end goal as the destruction of an enemy's air force and industrial potential for command of the air rather than the obliteration of enemy naval forces for command of the sea. Similar to Mahanian naval officers who called for a "concentrated battle fleet," the AAF planners also consistently argued for a concentrated strategic air force to fulfill its mission properly. Like naval officers who ignored the implications of new technologies such as submarines and naval airpower, so the AAF planners ignored new technologies that created "problems" for their ideology, such as high-speed fighter aircraft that could disrupt bombing formations. Like the interwar and wartime Navy, the AAF planners even called for a large number of overseas bases from which their strategic assets—bombers in this case—could police various regions of the world and ensure postwar American security.[7]

This similarity of outlook with respect to the use of mobile strategic power takes on importance once again when it is realized that the two services, with supposedly such wide divergence in strategies and methods, were really quite close in outlook with regard to the need for mobile forces and overseas bases in the postwar Pacific. Like the Navy, the wartime AAF at first saw a need to blanket the entire Pacific with American bases as a support system for the forces policing a possibly resurgent Japan.[8] Overseas bases fulfilled certain requirements for the postwar AAF, as they did for the Navy. Strategically speaking, a large number of bases were significant for the AAF since it subscribed to the idea of constant postwar preparation in order to repel a future Pearl Harbor–style attack. This preparation included an emphasis on immediate retaliation, preemptive strikes, and even preventive war under certain conditions. Additionally, both services sought to strategically deny possible base sites to any potential enemy power by having the US obtain political control over these islands, even if US military facilities were not to be maintained at those locations.[9] As with the Navy, advocating a large number of bases was also an AAF bureaucratic tactic for securing a policing role in a large geographic area that would justify a large postwar strategic force, and thus the lion's share of postwar defense appropriations from a budget-conscious President and Congress.[10] The ambition to gain control of a large number of bases throughout the Pacific Basin for bureaucratic as well as strategic reasons goes far in explaining American defense plans for the region, no matter which service was carrying out the planning.

■ A Useable History

The AAF used the history of the Pacific War to justify its call for a postwar unified national defense department, an independent air force, and the employment of unified theater commands in overseas regions. This use, or abuse, of history can be seen at least as early as November 1944 in a speech to the Army-Navy Staff College by then Brigadier General Lauris Norstad, an AAF Deputy Chief of Air Staff (DCAS) and the US Twentieth Air Force Chief of Staff. In the address, Norstad related the Twentieth Air Force's Marianas-based strategic-bombing operations against Japan up to that point in time. By doing so, Norstad also outlined the AAF's postwar position for the future of the service and the future of US defense policy. Norstad did this by first focusing on the great advantage of range in the B-29 Superfortress bomber, pointing out that the bomber had been "thoroughly battle tested" by carrying out operations from bases that were located 1,500 miles from Japan. Thus, Norstad thought that the control of base areas such as the Marianas was absolutely necessary for the conclusion of the war, as were bases in the Philippines and an "island base or staging area considerably closer to the prime target areas in Japan"—no doubt Okinawa. Norstad, like the AAF leadership at this time, also emphasized the need for unity-of-command in the region. To Norstad, unity-of-command was "a primary requirement," which was why, he argued, the JCS created the Twentieth Air Force as a strategic unit operating directly under the JCS and having General Arnold as the Joint Chiefs' implementing Executive Agent. Claiming that the capacity of the B-29 in the Pacific was improving daily, as strategic air forces in the European Theater had allegedly done, Norstad further emphasized the development of what he called "depot groups," which could be placed at advanced bases so that the Twentieth Air Force could be as mobile as possible.[11] This point about operational mobility would return in the early postwar period as a major part of the AAF's argument for independence from the Army and Navy, and it probably was meant at this time to counter Navy arguments that land-based bomber groups could never be as mobile as carrier-based ones.

The interwar and wartime belief that land-based airpower could defeat an enemy by destroying its industrial capability and civilian morale was an additional part of Norstad's argument. The "progressive destruction and dislocation" of the Japanese industrial and economic infrastructure, and the undermining of civilian morale to the point of "decisively" weakening the Japanese capacity for war were the emphasized goals. For instance, he pointed out that with units operating from the Marianas, most of Japan's aircraft industry was now in B-29 range. However, Norstad did not neglect the tactical operations that the AAF could perform in the theater. Thus, he recognized a "secondary but important" mission of the Twentieth Air Force as supporting "Pacific operations," presumably the operations of the other services.[12] This issue of the AAF supporting the other services to the point that it was carrying those services in the war would also come up in later documentation. Later in the speech, Norstad returned to the notion that unified command was absolutely necessary, asserting that the Pacific War showed that dispersed headquarters could not effectively direct operations along the entire strategic continuum. He also returned to the importance of forward-based aviation forces in areas such as the Marianas, not only to emphasize the obvious advantages of having such basing areas for wartime operations, but also implying the need for the United States to retain general control over the region in the postwar period. Finally, he asserted that the bases would prove of utmost importance for the AAF in demonstrating its mobility as a "proven" method for land-based bombers to put more ordnance on target than could the other services.[13] Finally, the Marianas, to Norstad, were the key to winning the war by having a large complex of bases that could accommodate VHBs with long runways, provide these planes with larger bomb loads because of their geographic proximity to Japanese Home Island targets, increase the rate of operations, and thus help to bring the war to a faster conclusion. While Norstad acknowledged the need for a great deal of shipping to provide for Twentieth Air Force operations against Japan, his bare mention of it in the rest of the speech and his emphasis on future aircraft with greater range clearly indicated that airpower was supposedly the key to mobile power, independent of ground or naval forces.[14]

The more public the medium, however, the more balanced Norstad's approach became. In a February 1945 talk on NBC entitled "Pacific Story," Norstad gave more credit to the Navy, the AGF, and the ASF for helping to win the war against Japan. Calling actions against Japan "an almost perfect example of cooperation between our armed services," Norstad gave partial credit to the Navy's Seabee units and the

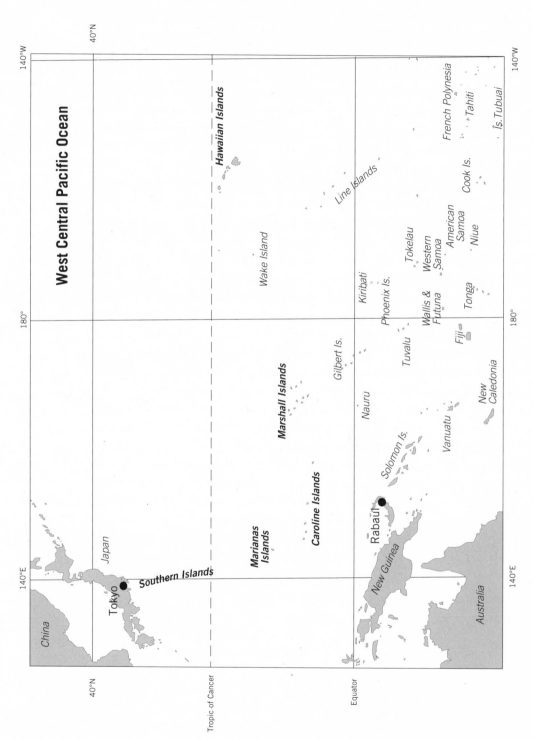

Map 2. West-Central Pacific Ocean Sub-Orientation Chart, 1945. (Courtesy of the Naval Historical Collection, US Naval War College, Newport, Rhode Island.)

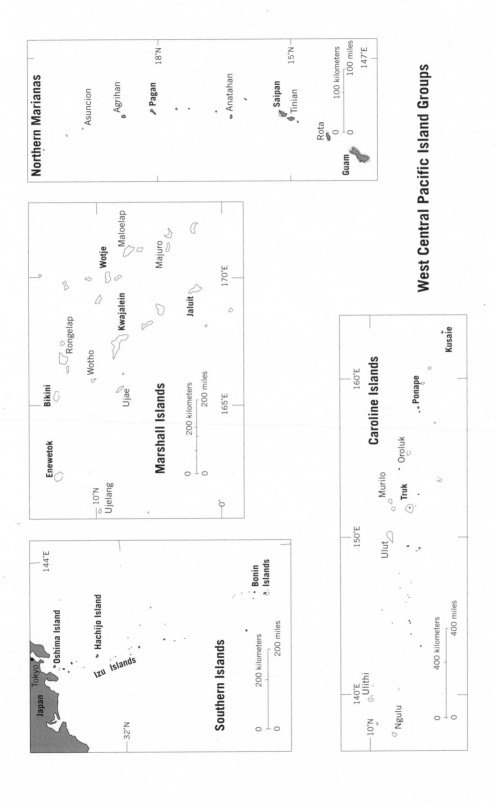

West Central Pacific Island Groups

Northern Marianas

Asuncion

Agrihan

Pagan   18°N

Anatahan

Saipan   15°N
Tinian

Rota

Guam

0   100 kilometers
0   100 miles

147°E

Marshall Islands

Enewetok

Bikini

Rongelap

Wotho

Ujae

Wotje

Maloelap

Kwajalein

Majuro

Jaluit

Ujelang   10°N

0   200 kilometers
0   200 miles

165°E   170°E   0°

Southern Islands

Japan

Tokyo

Oshima Island

Hachijo Island

Izu Islands

Bonin
Islands

144°E

32°N

0   200 kilometers
0   200 miles

Caroline Islands

Ngulu

Ulithi

Ulut

Murilo

Truk

Oroluk

Ponape

Kusaie

140°E   150°E   160°E

10°N

0   400 kilometers
0   400 miles

Army's combat engineers for the AAF's use of Saipan as a key base. In addition, he predicted that Japan would be brought down by a "well-established team of land, sea and air forces." However, the majority of the broadcast was still specifically about the AAF. In fact, Norstad spent the majority of the broadcast discussing the same major points as in his Staff College address. First, he focused on the ideal location and status of Saipan and the entire Marianas group as a "perfect base" for land-based airpower. Norstad pointed out to his radio audience that US acquisition of this island group had two roles to play. The most obvious one was continued prosecution of the war against Japan. The second was the Marianas' great potential as a series of strategic air bases designed to help "insure the peace." Unity-of-command and its "absolute necessity" was again stressed, supposedly because of the Twentieth Air Force having an operational area that overlapped a number of theaters and commands. This creation of a specified command under the JCS was the opportunity for Norstad to introduce the audience to the idea of an administratively independent, globally capable American air force that could fulfill its mission as America's first line of postwar defense by being unfettered by traditional ties to the Army and Navy. Finally, Norstad, like many AAF proponents, emphasized Pacific geography and its great distances as a reason for having long-range bombers, like the B-29 and its successors, at advanced base sites in the region. Norstad was correct that distances made the Pacific an entirely different kind of war, and he did admit that the B-29 was not going to win the war by itself. He even said that its operations were a preparation for an "ultimate decision" by combined forces.[15] Nonetheless, in a broadcast as broadly titled as "Pacific Story," Norstad's admission of the need for combined-arms forces did not go so far as to mention carrier-based ones. In fact, carrier forces proved to be much more effective than high-level, land-based strategic bombers in the vastness of Pacific geography, as evidenced by how early in the war they were used against Japanese bases and how much more accurate they were in the bombing of Japanese fleet units.[16] These points were not mentioned in Norstad's broadcast.

Norstad's points, however, were repeated in a report by General Arnold to Secretary of War Henry Stimson later in the same month. Arnold laid out the importance of "large, fully equipped, strategically located bases." He also asserted that air operations were already global, that bases had to be forward so that airpower could overpower the aggressor's air threat as soon as possible, and that US air forces must be able to operate in all conditions and climates. Like Norstad, he stressed Pacific geography as a unique factor in "aerial offensives." While admitting the burden on organization from this geography, and the need for ground and naval forces in blockading Japan, his call for air bases even closer to Japan was a precursor to even heavier bombing. Arnold thought that if a "maximum amount" of airpower was brought against Japan, it could be defeated with a minimum loss of American lives.[17] It is unclear if naval air forces were to be part of this noose around Japan's neck, but given Arnold's past and current positions on an independent air force, it can be assumed that he was suggesting that the final defeat of Japan could be carried out by land-based airpower alone.[18]

The need to impress the media was also seen in another presentation given by General Norstad. In early March 1945, he talked to the Aviation Writers Association about the AAF's role in the Pacific War. He was emphatically told that the Navy had already done this, and that the AAF should do likewise. He was also ordered to be as discreet and off-the-record as possible.[19] In this talk, Norstad emphasized the speed with which the AAF was able to begin bombing attacks on Japan after the capture of Saipan: "just 5 months and 10 days." He also emphasized numbers of bombing missions, with progress apparently being measured by a greater number of missions rather than the effectiveness of those missions. In addition, Norstad gave all kinds of facts and figures about various military and industrial targets damaged or destroyed after AAF raids, again emphasizing the "off the record" nature of this information to the writers. Finally, he claimed—again off the record—that cooperation with the Navy was complete. He asserted, for instance, that carrier planes and land-based units took turns going in first to clear out Japanese fighter and flak opposition, that the Navy focused on low-level dive bombing and strafing runs by agreement with the AAF, and that the AAF emphasized the high-altitude bombing of industrial targets. When it came to the future, Norstad waxed eloquent about land-based air's role in keeping the peace. He said he was "particularly impressed" with the B-29, and was convinced that it and the "sky giants" following it would be able to keep the peace. To Norstad, the experiment in unity of command whereby the Twentieth Air Force in the Pacific was controlled by the JCS from Washington, D.C., was a blueprint for the future by which the "sky giants" were to become "instruments of top policy and with top control." The VHB airplanes were, he asserted, a "truly global air weapon." Norstad also argued that Pacific operations demonstrated that "We have perfected the *organization* to control far-flung long-range planes from the nation's capital, employable in any direction" (emphasis in original). He also said that the AAF was "perfecting" the airplane so that it could not only be centrally controlled, but employed anywhere on the globe for policing purposes. Apparently, with base locations on both US coastlines, "the Superfort can fly in a matter of a few hours to any trouble spot on earth, in force and with great bomb tonnages." To Norstad, this was the "perfect" peacetime vehicle by which to ensure the peace.[20] Of course, Norstad then pulled back, saying that it had still been necessary for the Marines to go in and physically take islands such as Iwo Jima despite heavy AAF bombing, and that there would have to be a land-sea-air team to occupy Japan before the current war was over. In spite of this last admission, the statements above—all off the record—leave a clear idea as to which service Norstad and his superiors thought was to be the first line of postwar defense in the Pacific and elsewhere.

In August 1945, Norstad, still the Twentieth Air Force Chief of Staff but now also a Major General serving as the AAF Assistant Chief of Air Staff (ACAS) for Plans, enunciated another strong statement about the AAF's role in the war. Claiming that airpower could carry the battle to the enemy anywhere on the globe, he also stated that airpower could "destroy, at its source, the enemy's ability to wage war." Recognizing the strength of this statement and that it might be considered in the realm of the visionary, Norstad claimed that wartime operations in theaters like the Pacific that were "fully recorded by the historian" were now actual experiences. In addition, with the ability of planes that could fly from Japan to Washington non-stop, Norstad argued that VHB forces were now available to guard air routes over both the Pacific and Atlantic, as well as those over the Arctic. Norstad also envisioned aircraft getting larger, longer-ranged, and more capable of transporting troops, equipment, and supplies. While he was correct in this, he was incorrect to assume that air transportation would replace sea transportation as the primary means of mobility for military forces intending to stay in an overseas area for long periods of time. Still, claiming that in the next generation planes would exist that could transport entire armies, Norstad's bottom line was that the United States had to maintain adequate airpower in order to stop or prevent future wars. He further thought that possessing this airpower entailed creating fear of retaliation in a potential enemy in order for the United States to truly enjoy postwar security.[21]

Along similar lines, in August 1945 Lieutenant General Whitehead, at that time Commander of the Fifth Air Force (COMAF 5), wrote to General George Kenney, then Commanding General of the Far East Air Forces (FEAF), about the development of airborne forces for the postwar US military. Like Arnold and Norstad, Whitehead also used the Pacific War as a justification for his ideas. His vision of the use of airborne forces indicates his belief that airpower was the key to the United States' strategic position in the postwar world. His ideas about airpower, in turn, were fairly reflective of the AAF's belief in the efficacy of postwar land-based airpower over that of carrier-based or combined-arms forces. Whitehead thought that although airborne operations were limited in the Pacific War, the postwar era would bring a great expansion in size, tactical capability, and strategic potential. By strategic operations, Whitehead meant the ability of airborne forces to be dropped, supplied, and relieved by air so that they could take significant proportions of enemy territory and hold them for long periods of time. Whitehead thought that these seizures of enemy territory could continue for "an indefinite period of time," but he also thought it imperative that the United States develop an airplane that could carry "armies" and all of their equipment, and then be able to supply these forces until "slower moving" forces caught up. Given Whitehead's support of a postwar air force that would dominate the military establishment, it is not surprising that he then told Kenney that there was need for a unified "Department of National Defense," and that both air and ground components of theater forces should be placed under the command of one officer. Though not stated, it can be assumed that Whitehead thought that this theater commander should be an air officer. Moreover, he thought that the use of airborne forces for a new type of strategic operation required a postwar air force that could achieve not only air superiority but absolute destruction of enemy air forces, and air domination of the region in question. To Whitehead, the advantages of "strategic air" were obvious and should be exploited to the fullest. He was firmly convinced that the test case was the use of airborne forces in limited strategic operations during the Pacific War.[22]

The Pacific War as useable history again came into play in late October 1945. At that time, Lieutenant General Barney Giles, Commanding General of US Army Strategic Air Forces (USASTAF) Pacific, invited Norstad to visit him and see the destruction wrought by the B-29s on Tokyo in the final months of the war. Claiming that the AAF had underestimated the damage done to the city by 30 percent— though not giving any evidence for this numerical claim—Giles asserted that it was AAF airpower that caused him to be so confident in the last months of the war about the war's outcome. In a postscript to Norstad, he emphasized this confidence when he said that he was sending Norstad "a Jap sword and pistol. I consider you one of the main B-29 operators and you fully deserve a sample of the weapons that the B-29's put out of commission." Seemingly, Giles was a firm believer that it was strategic airpower, even short of the atomic bombings of Hiroshima and Nagasaki, that finally ended the war with the Japanese Empire.[23]

General Carl Spaatz, soon to be Arnold's successor as COMGENAIR, also used the Pacific War to argue AAF ideas to the Senate Military Affairs Committee during November 1945 hearings. Asserting that Pearl Harbor was the penalty the United States paid for "self-satisfied and easy-going optimism," Spaatz then discussed the United States' luck in having time after Pearl Harbor to prepare for future operations because of the bulwark of friendly nations that absorbed the first Japanese strikes. He then argued that this cushion of time that had been enjoyed during both of the world wars was gone forever because of airpower. To Spaatz, Pearl Harbor was also irrefutable evidence of the necessity of unity-of-command. To maintain what he and many others perceived as disunity and confusion in the nation's security apparatus was to invite a "much more dangerous Pearl Harbor in the future, a Pearl Harbor without a time lag." The Pearl Harbor strike and the Pacific War also figured heavily when he discussed future attacks on the United States coming across the Atlantic, the Pacific, and the Arctic to inflict a "future Pearl Harbor" against Washington, Chicago, Detroit, or Pittsburgh. In the end, he warned the Committee that there could be "only one defense: invincible Air Supremacy in this hemisphere, and along the air approaches thereto." In conclusion, Spaatz claimed that arguments about the Navy handling defense matters over the ocean while the Army defended ground territory no longer took the reality of modern military technology or tactical geography into account since the "air medium" existed over both land and sea.[24]

At about the same time, Lieutenant General James Doolittle, leader of the famous 1942 raid on Tokyo, and COMAF 8 when the war ended, supported these remarks about Pearl Harbor and the AAF's desired course for American national-security policy. In a statement prepared for the Senate Military Affairs Committee, Doolittle claimed that Japan lost the war as soon as it lost control of the air. Doolittle also argued that naval and ground forces had the power to make the invasion of Japan successful, but that B-29 bombardment made that unnecessary. Even without taking the atomic bomb into account, Doolittle asserted that heavy bombardment of Japan, like the operations over Germany, was the great lesson of the war in terms of postwar American national defense. Doolittle even went so far as to say that the previous, "visionary" idea of "air invasion" was now a reality, and that the United States needed to concentrate to the utmost on its postwar air defense.[25] The way to do this, of course, was aerial striking power that was not "fettered" by land or sea. Long-ranging, massed airpower was, to Doolittle, the key since the Pacific War taught him that "[Y]ou can't lose a war if you have command of the air and you can't win a war if you haven't." He concluded by stating that four B-29s had just flown nonstop from Japan to Washington, and that the AAF had a bomber on the drawing board that had twice the range of the B-29. Of course, nothing in Doolittle's remarks took into account the US Navy's submarine blockade of Japan, the threat of land invasion, or the atomic bomb itself as factors that might have helped bring about the Japanese surrender.[26]

Numbers also mattered in these arguments. Later in the same month when Spaatz and Doolittle gave their testimony, Colonel William Fisher, Assistant for Special Projects in the Requirements Division of the Office of the Assistant Chief of Air Staff for Operations and Training, sent a memo to Spaatz detailing Marianas-based B-29 operations that were conducted in support of the Navy from March to July 1945. Apparently, the memo was meant to demonstrate how valuable the AAF was to naval operations, or perhaps how badly the Navy needed assistance from the AAF in the final months of the war against Japan. These missions entailed, in particular, mine-laying operations against the Japanese Home Islands and tactical bombing operations against Kyushu airfields in support of the invasion of Okinawa. Fisher detailed the dates of the operations, the numbers of aircraft involved, the numbers of missions, the aircraft lost, and the tons of bombs on target. Fisher went to great lengths to show that a substantial proportion of B-29 missions during this period were either tactical or mine-laying operations rather than strategic bombing missions. According to Fisher, 22 percent of all of the B-29 missions flown from the Marianas at this time were in support of the Navy in one way or the other, and they were carried out at a cost of fifty-four B-29s, or 16 percent of all of the Twenty-First Bomber Command's combat losses.[27] The figures, if accurate, must have been grist for the AAF's campaign to demonstrate that the Navy needed a great deal of support from the AAF and was not at all self-sufficient. Moreover, with such figures, the AAF could argue that the Navy needed assistance that required the diversion of scarce resources from the strategic-bombing campaign against Japanese cities, a campaign that was supposedly the key to ending the war quickly.

The issue of the most appropriate use of strategic bombers aside, the AAF was consistent in its argument that the Pacific War dictated a new style of fighting for the next conflict. In a speech before the Aero Club of Philadelphia, Pennsylvania, in January 1946, Norstad again invoked Pearl Harbor as the lesson for the next war's strategy and tactics. Asserting that the last war started for the United States with bombs falling on Pearl Harbor and ended with "a single B-29 over Hiroshima," Norstad went on to argue that the next war would "inevitably" be more of an air war than the last one. He even speculated that the next war might be exclusively an air war. Unlike previous periods of US history when enemies had to come by sea, and even then could only reach geographically marginal areas, Norstad warned of an aerial enemy that could now strike at the US heartland. To Norstad, our "frontiers are no longer on the sea; they are in the air."[28]

The Pacific War figured again in the AAF's ideas about unity of command in the same month as Norstad's presentation in Philadelphia when General Kenney, now COMGENAIR Representative for the JCS to the UN Security Council's Military Staff Committee (MSC), stated his ideas about unified command in the postwar period to the Senate Military Affairs Committee. Employing the history of General MacArthur's Southwest Pacific campaigns, Kenney asserted that only the command of sea, air, and ground forces under MacArthur's unified command allowed for the "high premium on flexibility and close coordination" that resulted in successful battles for the United States from Port Moresby to the liberation of the Philippines. Criticizing the "committee type" of command organization allegedly practiced by the JCS during the war, Kenney claimed that even Admiral Nimitz as CNO had supported unified theater command until the issue became entangled in postwar Army-Navy disputes over service roles, missions, and unification.[29] Kenney also invoked Pearl Harbor in a September 1946 address to the Spokane, Washington, Chamber of Commerce. By this time the first Commanding General of SAC, Kenney devoted most of his speech to the need to have a military that had absorbed the atomic lessons of Hiroshima and Nagasaki, and for the nation to keep "eternal vigilance" in light of both world wars and potential future aggressors. Also spending quite a bit of time on the need for a unified military structure and overseas bases from which to deter potential aggressors, Kenney called for an end to further commissions, hearings, and debates about these matters. To Kenney, "[D]elay can bring the apathetic frame of mind which led us to the brink of disaster at Pearl Harbor. Another Pearl Harbor might well be this nation's last."[30]

In November 1946, the Pacific War was again invoked in a document entitled "Statement of Army Air Forces Position regarding Pacific Island Bases." In addition to being an example of useable history, the document was also politically sensitive because of the strategic and bureaucratic implications of the policies being suggested. With rising tensions vis-à-vis the USSR and the bureaucratic conflict between the Army and the Navy in mind, Colonel Harold Bowman, the AAF's Deputy Director of Information, specifically noted in the cover letter to Lieutenant General Ira Eaker, AAF Deputy Commander and Chief of Air Staff, that he did not think that publicity on this document would be "appropriate" at the present time. Most of Bowman's study was devoted to the USSR being the new enemy in the Pacific, the deployment of AAF forces in a "strategic triangle" based on the Marianas, the Philippines, and the Ryukyus, and concern that AAF bases not be too far to the "rear" of the Pacific Basin. In addition, Bowman discussed the post–World War II period in East Asia as being a time of power vacuum of "post–World War I dimensions," which the USSR would fill unless the United States prevented this and thus stopped inviting the repetition of events in East Asia circa 1920–1941. According to Bowman, the "predominant factor in preventing such a vacuum . . . is the presence in the area of strong Air Power. Such Air Power must be present, not at rearward bases, but forward near the areas from which expansionist activity could take place." Bowman concluded with concerns that the Navy was planning a postwar system of entrenched defense in the region based on depth instead of mobility. Fully admitting the need for naval bases in the postwar Pacific, Bowman saw the number and location of the proposed bases as an indication that the Navy was preparing to fight "the last war" in which a large number of naval bases were needed to defeat a "first class" naval power. Supposedly, the need for so many naval bases in the Pacific was the institutional justification of "elaborate" naval forces, including Marine Corps divisions and significant shore installations. Instead, Bowman was convinced that the "tremendous" effect of land-based air forces in defeating Japan had introduced a new element in postwar defense planning for the region that would result in a cheaper but still effective policy. Claiming that the AAF only needed seven island bases in the region, Bowman asserted that the "deployment of very heavy bombers to these bases will enable the U.S. to utilize Air Power consistent with the military mission in the Pacific and the economic temper of the nation."[31]

In the same month, Major General Norstad, by this time serving as OPD Director, again used the history of the Second World War to argue to officers at the National War College about the necessity of new thinking for the new age. Starting out by asserting that nations which survive are those that "proceed most intelligently from the lessons of history," Norstad went on to argue that "it is a mortal danger to cling for security in a next war to those things which made for security in a last war." Norstad then focused on the importance of US control of both the Atlantic and Pacific approaches to the Western Hemisphere, asserting that the United States "has gone further in defining its interests by fighting two world wars against aggressive powers threatening us from across the Atlantic, or from too close range in the Pacific." Norstad was concerned that this line of thinking might continue with the idea "that another war . . . [can] be won by the U.S. with the weapons, and the types and balance of combat forces, employed in the last war." He was fairly certain, however, that "no one" would now agree with that notion. While Norstad's conclusion was that the American home front was actually the key to victory in World War II and would be so in the next war as well, his focus on airpower and transportation again left a clear message about which service he thought should be the first line of American defense in the postwar world.[32]

At times, this AAF useable history was enunciated in tangential ways. In a long memorandum for General Eisenhower in February 1947 on the need for a postwar global American military communications net, Edward Bowles, Consultant to the Secretary of War and Special Consultant to COMGENAIR, talked about the need for more accurate weather forecasting for strategic and tactical operations. The historical examples used to demonstrate this need were B-29 operations in the Saipan-Tokyo area in 1944–1945. Apparently, those weather forecasts were obtained from mainland Asian bases, including some in the Soviet Union, as well as US intercepts of Japanese weather transmissions. This data was then transmitted to the Twentieth Air Force on Guam. Based on this historical experience, Bowles thought that a more unified global weather-forecasting system would make future air operations more efficient. In addition, he thought that a unified global communications net would improve "interconnections" between air force headquarters and subordinate air forces as they were established in areas such as the postwar Pacific.[33]

Finally, a study by Brigadier General George McDonald, AAF Assistant Chief of Air Staff for Intelligence, in August 1947 employed the useable history of the Second World War to argue that the next war would be entirely different. According to McDonald, "World War III will resemble no other war in history." He concluded that the United States would be "undoubtedly" attacked in force from the air, but that if this initial air offensive failed, the world's greatest naval power, the United States, would be facing the world's greatest land power, the USSR. McDonald assumed that in "classical times," stalemate would have ensued from this type of confrontation. McDonald, however, now assumed that World War III would move into a new medium of war: a type of air war in which, effectively, civilians as a separate category of participants would cease to exist since production facilities and workers would become the enemy's prime target. McDonald thought that in this scenario, a "pattern for the next war is thus nominated."[34]

■ AAF Deployment Concepts

The AAF's reading of Pacific War history helped translate into the service's post-1945 thought that the Pacific was one of the regions best suited to supporting land-based airpower. By the 1945–1947 period, rising tensions with the Soviet Union in Europe, the Middle East, and East Asia convinced many AAF officers that Stalin was another Hitler, and that the Soviet Union was, like Nazi Germany and Imperial Japan, a nation bent on global conquest, or at least domination of Eurasia.[35] It follows that AAF officers began to argue that the Soviet Union was indeed the new enemy, and that, of course, land-based airpower was the most effective and economical first line of defense for the United States. Interestingly, the AAF's early postwar argument was again similar to one provided by a senior naval officer, Admiral Towers, who strongly urged a postwar Pacific defense based on mobile carrier power.[36] General Arnold merely substituted strategic bombers for aircraft carriers with his idea of an integrated, mobile AAF capable of long-range attack as the best means by which to defend the United States and its Pacific possessions. Given that worst-case scenarios of Soviet invasions of Western Europe, the Middle East, and East Asia were practically identical to the actual Axis victories of 1939–1942, it was assumed by the AAF that air bases in many of these regions would not be secure. Yet AAF bombers, for all of their strategic abilities, needed forward bases since range limitations of the aircraft still prevented staging attacks from the Continental United States. Therefore, in 1946 and 1947, the AAF deployed strategic-bombing units to Great Britain, Alaska, and the Western Pacific in order to determine the best bases from which to deliver attacks on the USSR. Obviously, bases in Western Europe were the most ideal for access to European Russia, and these areas became major NATO airfields after 1949. At the time, however, the AAF was greatly concerned about the vulnerability of these bases to Soviet attack. Alaska was considered secure, but due to a lack of Arctic training for AAF personnel, the state of current technology, and harsh weather conditions, AAF deployments to the Northern Pacific were unduly hazardous, unproductive, and impractical.[37]

The Western Pacific was different. It had the disadvantage of being too far removed from targets in European Russia, but it was still close enough to strike at targets in the Soviet Maritime Provinces in East Asia. In addition, many of the primary sources cited above and below indicate that AAF planners assumed they would have longer-range bombers at their disposal in the near future. Moreover, bases in Micronesia, the Philippines, and the Ryukyus were considered by the AAF to be secure from the possibility of Soviet attack, at least in the first few years after the end of the war. Unilateral American control or predominant influence over these areas also precluded the possibility of having to deal with nations that were reluctant to host American military bases, a repeated occurrence in Europe and the Middle East during the early Cold War. Furthermore, General Kenney, Commanding General of SAC, and his Deputy Commanders in 1946 and 1947, Major Generals St. Clair Streett and Clements McMullen, respectively, had all served in the Pacific during the war and apparently considered the region more critical to American interests than Europe.[38] Accordingly, these generals and AAF planners strongly cited operational experiences in bombing Japan from bases in Micronesia in 1944–1945 as evidence for the efficacy of AAF bases in the postwar Pacific.[39] Given all of these factors, the AAF saw Micronesia and other island groups as a complex of "permanent aircraft carriers" in the Pacific. The AAF could claim that the major value of Micronesia, the Ryukyus, and the Philippines lay in their potential as a system of advanced bomber bases that could be used to repel Soviet assaults from East Asia into the Pacific Littoral. More proactively, however, these bases could also be used to launch retaliatory or preemptive strikes against targets in the Soviet Union itself. If they were used for offensive purposes against the USSR by the AAF, the Pacific bases could also help undermine the Navy's arguments that postwar deterrence in this "most naval" of regions had to be based on carrier groups. Thus, the AAF emphasized Pacific operations to some extent in its training deployments in 1946–1947. By deploying VHB units from the Continental United States to Guam, Okinawa, the Philippines, and Japan with minimal logistical support from the Navy, the AAF was suggesting that naval support was largely unnecessary for the AAF to project American power toward the Asian periphery.[40] The AAF could use its wartime and immediate postwar operational experiences to undermine the Navy's arguments by suggesting that an expensive mobile fleet was not only an obsolete force with which to defend the United States' strategic sphere in the postwar Pacific, but a redundant waste of scarce national resources as well. Like the Navy, the AAF was also being selective and less than forthright about both its wartime record and its claims for the postwar world.[41] Strategic airpower did not win the war against Japan by itself, and AAF pilots had a less than admirable record against naval and merchant shipping during much of the war.[42] Nor was the AAF any more logistically self-sufficient than the Navy. But neither service was searching for strategic or intellectual accuracy. They were searching for a postwar mission.

Part of the AAF's assumption about what it needed for the postwar world, also arising from its Pacific War experiences, was US control of outlying Pacific bases so that VHB units capable of delivering an atomic bomb could be forward-deployed, and the AAF could continue to be the primary American means of atomic delivery in the postwar world. This establishment of bases was a "must" according to the Spaatz Board Report, an October 1945 report by General Spaatz; Lieutenant General Hoyt Vandenberg, AAF ACAS for Operations and Training; and Major General Norstad, at this time the ACAS for Plans and Twentieth Air Force Chief of Staff. The report concluded with polar projection maps that had shaded areas showing the operating radii of the B-29 and the new B-36 bomber. The largest shaded areas of operating radii emanated from bases in the Pacific—possibly because of geographic realities, but also possibly because of the volume of bomber attacks the AAF expected to launch from that area.[43] Some of the earliest AAF ideas for force dispositions in the postwar Pacific, as well as some of the limitations on those dispositions, were also made apparent in late January 1946 by General Whitehead, by this time Commanding General of PACUSA. In light of force reductions necessitated by budgetary constraints, Whitehead outlined to General MacArthur the necessity of withdrawing AAF tactical units from Iwo Jima, Saipan, and Tinian in order to support the forward basing of strategic strike units. In step with his earlier idea of promoting the strategic use of airborne and airlifted forces, Whitehead also saw another major problem related to withdrawal from these forward bases. With only one troop-carrier squadron in the region—and that one primarily being used for courier service—Whitehead argued that PACUSA would have no airborne troop capability, either strategic or tactical, for the near future. PACUSA therefore would not be able to support the Japanese Occupation with an airlift capability of one battalion, as he had previously assumed. Further emphasizing to MacArthur his concerns about personnel reductions impacting on his ability to maintain both occupation forces in Japan and strike forces for use against the USSR, Whitehead saw it as absolutely necessary to maintain Okinawa as a base in full strike status, even if it meant reducing support forces in the Marianas, support forces elsewhere in the Ryukyus, and some VHB units in Hawaii. In fact, Whitehead told MacArthur that he was specifically reducing headquarters units at various PACUSA deployment sites so as to devote scarce personnel and resources to the mobile strategic and tactical strike units. It was clear, however, that although he thought his units were all under-strength, Whitehead, like other senior AAF officers, definitely saw forward deployment as the key to this aspect of the AAF's postwar strategy in the region.[44]

AAF strategy also became a little clearer in March 1946 in a radio interview between Richard Harkness, NBC Washington Correspondent, and General Spaatz, now COMGENAIR. Asked by Harkness about the deployment of air units to bases outside the United States, such as in the Pacific, Spaatz answered that this was necessary in order to meet any potential future threats to the United States' national security. Specifically, Spaatz argued that the United States must have an offensive force "poised well within reach of the war potential of any possible enemy." However, he also asserted that the number of units could be kept to a minimum by a system of rotation between a strong, mobile striking force in the Continental United States and those units needed overseas in Pacific Basin locations such as Hawaii, Guam, the Philippines, Okinawa, and the Aleutians.[45] Similarly, AAF dispositions in the Pacific Basin came into play in an official history of SAC. In the first volume of this history, the world was strategically divided into three theaters: the North Atlantic, which included Greenland, Iceland, Newfoundland, and Labrador; the North Pacific, which included Alaska and the Aleutians; and the Far East, which included the Philippines, the Ryukyus, and Guam. Personnel were to be rotated in and out of these theaters on four months' temporary duty, with the major part of SAC, the "Strategic Striking Force," being held in reserve in the Zone of the Interior (ZI). The economic and political advantages of these deployment practices were emphasized. Since the majority of SAC units were already at established bases in the Zone of the Interior, economic advantages would be realized, as there would be no need to send dependents to overseas theaters since personnel would not be deployed for extended periods of time. Political advantages also accrued since the majority of SAC's proposed bases were in the Continental United States, and since a significant number of the overseas bases were in US territories or US occupied areas, especially in the Pacific Basin.[46]

Whitehead gave significant detail to AAF Pacific dispositions in a long letter to General Kenney in mid-March. Based on a "minimum mission" for the Ryukyus, Whitehead told Kenney that about 6,000 AAF troops would be needed there. Reminding the Commanding General of SAC that PACUSA had to perform all of its maintenance as well as carry out its operations, he informed Kenney that the aircraft warning system alone took up almost 800 personnel. Whitehead also organized the units so that each one was a "composite" wing or task force that was self-sufficient, with its own supply squadron. These composite wings also consisted of VHB squadrons detached from the group in the Philippines. These squadrons were to carry out long-range reconnaissance from the Ryukyus, and Whitehead envisioned a rotation of PACUSA VHB squadrons so that units from the Philippines could gradually be trained in this mission. Whitehead was also going to rotate troop-carrier squadrons from the Philippines to the Ryukyus for the same purpose, but he emphasized that 6,000 AAF troops for the Ryukyus was a minimum, and that the Ryukyus would be a very poor staging area with this kind of limitation.[47]

Moving on to the Marianas-Bonins Area, Whitehead emphasized the idea that Japan would be "wide open" to the "Reds" once the United States withdrew from Japan and Korea. Given that defense forces in the Marianas-Bonins were therefore vital, Whitehead assigned two fighter groups and two night fighter groups there in addition to a VHB squadron for long-range reconnaissance. He also assigned weather, emergency-rescue, liaison, and troop-carrier squadrons. In addition, Whitehead said that if he were commanding this operation, he "would garrison Iwo Jima by rotating the personnel of the station complement squadron and Airdrome Squadron which form the permanent garrison." Whitehead included in this rotation of units a fighter squadron from his six currently available ones, as well as one-half of a night fighter squadron from his two currently available units. Whitehead further planned on the Marianas-Bonins Area having emergency-rescue services provided by rotated planes from his rescue squadron. Given all of the staging and rotation of units, he additionally needed two troop-carrier squadrons, and he told Kenney that the Marianas was going to have quite a bit of transient traffic if AAF units were going to be deployed from the United States. In order to support all of his B-29s, for instance, Whitehead said he needed a VHB Air Service Group. To service all of the airdromes from Iwo Jima to Guam, including about 150,000 tons of bombs, he also requested the "necessary colored" utility, engineer, and service units—about 2,800 African-American soldiers in all. In addition, Whitehead told Kenney that he had about $750,000 worth of AAF supplies at Guam, so he was establishing a Base Headquarters and Air Base Squadron there, as well as an Air Repair and Supply detachment to manage those supplies.[48]

As to other areas, Whitehead outlined some aspects of deployments to Hawaii, other bases in the mid-Pacific, and the Philippines. He thought that base forces at Wake, Midway, Kwajalein, and Johnston might be too small to run operations as well as billet, feed, and transport AAF detachments coming across the Pacific. Given the small size of the base forces, Whitehead told Kenney that "they will [have to] operate everything from cold storage plants and bull-dozers to type-writers and pots and pans." Whitehead therefore thought that these personnel should be rotated every two to three months. This rotation could apparently be accomplished by placing these smaller bases under the Seventh Air Force in Hawaii. Concerning Hawaii itself, he had reduced the VHB Group there to two squadrons, so that a VHB squadron could be deployed to the Marianas-Bonins Area for long-range reconnaissance. He also envisioned almost entirely "civilianizing" the Hawaiian Air Depot, as it required 11,000 personnel that were needed elsewhere. As regarded the Philippines, while he had not worked out details about deployments due to lack of time, Whitehead did think that a "strong" Air Service Command organization was necessary. In addition, he wanted an aircraft warning service, a minimum of three fighter groups, and a VHB group. He also thought that the Philippines needed two attack groups, a troop-carrier group, a long-range photo squadron, and a tactical-reconnaissance squadron. He rounded out this deployment with an emergency-rescue squadron, two night fighter squadrons, a weather squadron, and two liaison squadrons. Adding in PAC-USA Headquarters and the Pacific Air Service Command (PASC), Whitehead thought that about 22,000 to 25,000 AAF troops would be needed in the Philippines.[49] Dispositions, this time in the Philippines and Japan, figured again with Whitehead in June 1946. Writing to Spaatz, Whitehead claimed all that he had heretofore heard about future air-defense plans for the Western Pacific indicated that there would not be any air bases in Japan. Whitehead, however, thought that Japan and the Philippines were both vital for the deployment of major air forces, since he thought those two locations were the only land masses large enough to support VHB forces. If Japan was not retained as a location of postwar air bases, then the Philippines, he believed, became even more important. In fact, Whitehead thought that "[A]ir bases in Japan with Okinawa, the Philippines, the Mariannas [sic], and Hawaii held lightly, mean control of all the north Pacific by air power. The Aleutians would no longer be a vulnerable salient." Whitehead thought that the Japanese would go along with the United States in this strategic deployment plan and even provide ground, service, and financial support for US air forces based in Japan, since he believed that the Japanese feared the Russians even more than they disliked the Americans![50]

July 1946 SAC documents added to the picture of AAF deployments in the post-war Pacific. In that month, Major General Streett, SAC Deputy Commander, outlined for Spaatz the SAC proposal for the operational training and strategic employment of its units. Again dividing the world into the three operational areas of the North Atlantic, the North Pacific, and the Far East, the plan called for SAC units to be able to carry out offensive operations either in cooperation with land and sea forces, or independently. For this operational status to be reached, SAC units had to be trained *"to operate from, to or through* each of these three principle areas" (emphasis in original). Streett then went into great detail about which types of units were to be deployed and how they were to be trained. He again emphasized that the AAF could provide the most economical national defense for the United States, with SAC becoming a "highly mobile strategic strike force" trained in all potential areas of operations, capable of "immediate" deployment to any part of the world, and able to provide "maximum protection at the least expense."[51] Streett continually emphasized that land-based airpower could defeat the enemy by destroying industrial resources and capacity. He also consistently focused on the creation of "air-mobile" tactical units that were streamlined down to the bare minimum so as to be as self-contained as possible in terms of support and service functions. These self-sufficient mobile air units could then be deployed from the Zone of the Interior to outpost areas such as the Northern Pacific and East Asia, and rotated back and forth to the Continental United States. According to Streett, air mobility of these tactical units was the "primary factor" in SAC's proposed structure and organization.[52]

On the same day, MacArthur sent Whitehead, Hull, and Christiansen a long radio message about their command's roles in the War Department's plan "Arouse." PACUSA dispositions for the various parts of the Pacific Basin indicated a VHB group at Barbers Point, Hawaii, as well as an emergency-rescue squadron, a day fighter squadron, and one half of an all-weather fighter squadron at that airfield. Hickam Field was also to have an air depot and a transport group (less one squadron). Wheeler Field was to host an air-force headquarters and a possible new fighter base in the future. In the Marianas, Guam was to base a VHB group, a long-range reconnaissance squadron, a long-range weather squadron, a day fighter group, an all-weather fighter group, and an emergency-rescue squadron. Guam was also to have a transport squadron, an air depot, and an air-force headquarters. The Volcanoes was to base one day fighter squadron, an all-weather fighter flight, and an emergency-rescue flight, with all of these units being located on Iwo Jima. The Philippines would be responsible for basing a VHB group at Clark Field, along with a long-range weather-group headquarters and squadron, an emergency-rescue squadron (less two flights), and an air-force headquarters. The AAF field at Florida Blanca was going to base two day fighter groups (less one squadron), a tactical reconnaissance group, a liaison squadron, and an all-weather fighter group (less two squadrons). Mactan Field would host a long-range reconnaissance group (less two squadrons) and two light-bomb groups (less one squadron). There would also be an additional emergency-rescue flight, a transport group (less one squadron), and an air depot at Nichols Field, while Fort McKinley would house PACUSA Headquarters.

In the Ryukyus, Kadena Field on Okinawa would host a light-bomb squadron, a long-range weather flight, a long-range reconnaissance squadron, an emergency-rescue flight, one-half of an all-weather fighter squadron, and an air-division head-quarters. Futema would host a day fighter group (less one squadron), and Naha Field would have a transport squadron and an air depot.[53]

Atomic weaponry also continued to be central to AAF thinking about these de-ployed forces and overseas bases. In a September 1946 talk given to the War Depart-ment Atomic Energy Group, General Norstad stated that the Second World War demonstrated that the most effective defense for a nation was one that was "beyond its frontiers" because of the atomic bomb. Forward bases from which attacks could be intercepted were vital, as were bases from which retaliatory strikes could be car-ried out by the United States. Norstad also talked about balanced air, naval, and ground forces, but in light of AAF thinking at the time, his emphasis was obviously on land-based atomic airpower.[54] Related to this idea of forward-deployed, atomic-capable B-29 units was a communication the next month from Kenney to White-head regarding information on a flight of thirty-three B-29s that was scheduled to fly around the world. Partially an attempt to train bomber crews in long-range flight and to increase the operational capability of the AAF, these exercises were also ways to demonstrate that the AAF could be just as mobile as the Navy. Kenney told Whitehead that the B-29s would leave Camp Dix, New Jersey, on 15 November 1946, route through Germany, Egypt, and India, and then proceed to the Philippines. From there, the flight would head to the United States by way of Guam, Hawaii, San Francisco, and Washington. Kenney thought that the first part of the route might change, but not the Pacific segment. Kenney also told Whitehead that when the flight reached Clark Field in the Philippines, all of the aircraft would probably need a 100-hour inspection and some maintenance. Hoping that the maintenance would be minor, Kenney said he would appreciate any help PACUSA could provide. He assumed that the services of about 150 B-29 specialists and mechanics would be re-quired. He also told Whitehead that eleven C-54s would accompany the flight part of the way, five of these transport aircraft coming into Clark with the group and continuing on to the Zone of the Interior to provide transportation for extra main-tenance personnel and the press. Kenney told Whitehead that these planes might also need maintenance, and that one of Kenney's officers would give Whitehead the "dope" about the matter. Kenney concluded by reiterating to Whitehead that he would appreciate any assistance PACUSA could provide in this operation.[55]

At this time, the War Department itself also started planning on post-Occupation AAF deployments. Since US postwar occupations were assumed to be relatively short commitments, Norstad and his OPD planners also envisioned a major redeployment of AAF units, just as they had for the AGF. During the German, Austrian, Japanese, and Korean Occupations, for instance, it was seen as necessary for the AAF to have eleven air groups stationed in Central Europe; two each in Alaska, Iceland, and Panama;

thirty-one in the Continental United States; a total of six in Japan and Korea; and sixteen in Micronesia. Once the Occupations were completed, however, there would be forty-two air groups in the mainland United States, four in Iceland, three in Panama, six in Alaska, and fifteen in Micronesia. Just as all AGF units were to have been withdrawn from Central Europe and mainland East Asia by this time, so too were all AAF forces to be withdrawn from these forward areas. Micronesia would then become the major overseas basing area for AAF assets, just as it would be for the AGF.[56]

In December 1946, Major General McMullen, COMAF 8, described to Whitehead in greater detail the process of training units between the Pacific and the Zone of the Interior, a process relating back to the whole notion of mobile air units. McMullen stated that a squadron of six B-29s, along with a C-54 loaded with spare parts and supplies, would proceed to Japan by way of the Aleutians. He then illustrated how this unit would operate with PACUSA for one month out of Japan, Okinawa, or any other location that Whitehead determined. Training alongside Whitehead's regular forces, this unit would take part in operations that would prepare it for bombing runs against the Soviet Union in a time of war. This squadron would then proceed back to the Zone of the Interior by way of Guam and Hawaii. The emphasis was to be on the unit's self-sufficiency, and the ability of the AAF to quickly rotate squadrons back and forth on an almost continuous basis between the Pacific Basin and the Zone of the Interior. In fact, McMullen sent the letter in order to find out the degree to which Whitehead agreed with these plans, the exact length of time Whitehead thought was appropriate for the training deployments, and whether or not he thought these rotations could begin as soon as March 1947.[57] The idea of rotational B-29 deployments as an argument for increased strategic emphasis on land-based airpower was further elucidated in an April 1947 letter by McMullen, by this time SAC Deputy Commander, to Whitehead. This letter gave some additional details on changes to the B-29 flights, i.e., routing the bombers to Tokyo through Hawaii and Guam instead of the Aleutians. McMullen specifically asked Whitehead to ensure that the equipment packages that were the key to B-29 mobility were tested. He also hoped that Whitehead would experiment with this new deployment concept as much as possible. Additionally, McMullen said that it was now assumed as part of the planning process that Whitehead's command would always have one of these B-29 units present for one-month periods of time, and that hopefully these squadrons would return to the Zone of the Interior with heightened knowledge of forward-deployed B-29 operations.[58]

By early May 1947, a VHB unit had arrived in Whitehead's theater. General Kenney proposed the rotation of similar units to FEAF—PACUSA's post-1 January 1947 unified command designation—on a thirty-day basis at the rate of one unit per month, starting approximately the first of each month, until all units of SAC had rotated through the Pacific for training. The SAC Commanding General ended with a request that Whitehead acknowledge this operational plan and provide

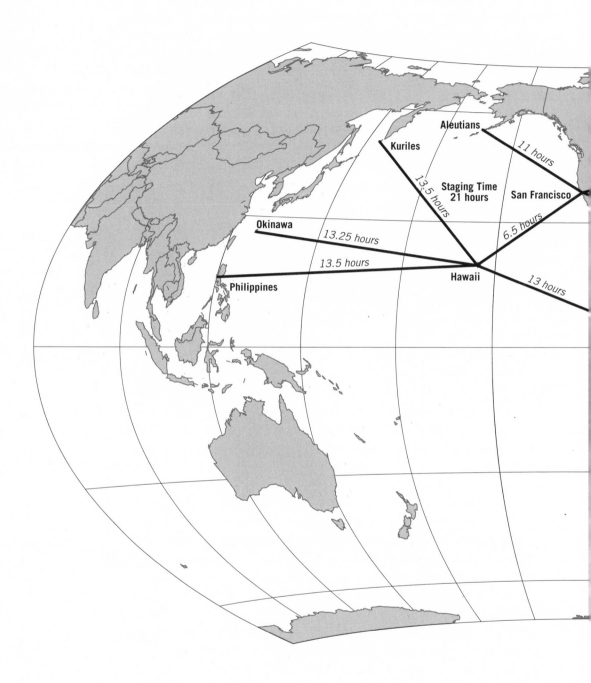

Map 3. B-36 Flying Time between Major US Installations, 1947. (Courtesy of the Bureau of Archives, MacArthur Memorial, Norfolk, Virginia.)

timetables for the aviation fuel, oil, and ordnance that were to be supplied to these flights.[59] Whitehead concurred in this request two days later, agreeing to supply all necessary items that the "self-supporting" units could not.[60] Further plans for additional flights were described by Whitehead to Spaatz later in May. This outline was mainly concerned with the actual units to be deployed, the types and numbers of personnel involved, and the distances that could be traveled on fuel allowances with various crew and passenger loads. Whitehead also pointed out that SAC should airlift the personnel from the Zone of the Interior to Hawaii and back again after the deployment, but that FEAF would handle all airlifting from Hawaii to points further west in the Pacific, such as Guam or Okinawa.[61]

A final analysis of AAF deployments and the budgetary constraints on them in the time period covered by this study can be seen from the 1 June 1947 report by the Joint Marianas On-Site Board. After some deliberation, the Board decided that the three Army airfields on Guam had adequate runway facilities for contemplated deployments, and were more susceptible to "economic" expansion for use by larger types of aircraft that were projected for the future than were the airstrips on Saipan or Tinian. The Board also asserted that operational characteristics made the use of any one field by all types of aircraft "undesirable." Guam, however, offered the most "practicable" solution to segregation by types in one locale. The alternative was to divide the AAF between several islands within the Marianas, which the Board thought would result in the duplication of logistical and utility facilities. It did, however, want North Field on Saipan maintained on a "caretaker" basis, as well as Isley Field on Saipan kept operational to permit rapid expansion in emergencies. In addition, the Board cited that funds were already available for permanent construction on Guam, and contracts had already been let. Moreover, some of this permanent construction had already begun, and interim housing for dependents had already been concentrated on the island. The Board also wanted the AAF's Air Material Depot located as near to its primary operations as possible, since locating the bulk of the AAF on another island would have necessitated a costly change in the Depot's location. While some of the air-warning facilities and units had been stationed on Saipan, the majority were on Guam in accordance with AAF's desires that the bulk of the AAF units be stationed on Guam. In the end, the Board thought that this was the most economical and practicable peacetime deployment.[62]

■ Operational and Logistical Difficulties in AAF Deployments

PACUSA, and then FEAF, faced a number of operational and logistical difficulties in trying to implement this strategy. These difficulties became apparent at least as early as March 1946, if not before. In mid-March, Whitehead told Kenney about the various missions that PACUSA had responsibility for that were interfering with operational capability. He told Kenney, for instance, that PACUSA was charged with the maintenance of its airdromes, the upkeep of the interior roads on its air bases, and the operation of its ammunition depots. In addition, Whitehead's command had to construct and maintain its telephone and road communications facilities, haul its supplies from dockside, and billet, feed, and transport weather, ATC, and other detachments in the Pacific. While Whitehead thought that PACUSA should provide these services for reasons of economy, doing so was having an operational impact on the unit.[63] PACUSA, while enduring the problems brought about by rapid demobilization, also had a top priority of ferrying excess B-29s back to the United States. This mission, called the Sunset Project, was having an obvious impact on crew training, unit efficiency, and operational capability. According to Colonel Woodbury Burgess, PACUSA Assistant Chief of Staff for Intelligence, the Eighth Air Force VHB Group, for instance, was thought to be about 40 percent operational at this time, and most other PACUSA units had similar or worse ratings.[64]

About two months later, Whitehead was more upbeat about PACUSA capabilities, but he still made it clear that his command was not near wartime capability. In another letter to Kenney, Whitehead told the SAC Commanding General that PACUSA was "on its way up," but that it had hit its "low" in February and March when it had had "virtually" nothing in commission. Now, the Fifth Air Force had six out of twelve fighter squadrons operational, as well as three out of six light-bomber squadrons. Whitehead also had one out of two reconnaissance squadrons operational, as well as two out of four troop-carrier squadrons. He also cited the Thirteenth Air Force as having two out of six fighter squadrons operational, and predicted that it would have an entire fighter group operational by the end of the month. He further told Kenney that the training of B-29 crews was behind schedule, but that he expected good progress to be made in July and August. In addition, he noted that his air-sea rescue squadrons were 50 percent operational.[65] On 5 June 1946, Whitehead also told Brigadier General Thomas White, COMAF 7, that he concurred with certain recommendations that White had given concerning the Sunset Project. Whitehead thought that the program had gone "unbelievably" well, but he wanted to terminate it, probably because of the personnel resources it consumed. He told White that the Seventh Air Force, the Twentieth Air Force, and the Hawaiian Air Depot had done a "splendid" job, but that the "excess B-29s were a 'rock around our necks.' Once we are rid of them, the combat availability of B-29s will increase."[66] About one month later, though, Whitehead was singing praises about the program, or at least the way it was completed, to another one of his subordinate commanders. Whitehead noted the completion of the Sunset Project in a congratulatory note to Brigadier General Patrick Timberlake, Commander of the First Air Division (COMADIV 1) on Okinawa, whose unit carried out much of the mission. According to

Whitehead, the departure of the last two Superfortresses from Oahu marked the end of Sunset. Whitehead noted to Timberlake that the project would have been a significant undertaking at any time, but that it was particularly so at this time since PACUSA was in the middle of demobilization and reorganization. Attributing the successful completion of the operation to the manner in which it was carried out by Timberlake's "highly trained" personnel, Whitehead also noted the safety record and commended the First Air Division for a job well done: "Through your efforts a large number of fine aircraft have been saved for future use and our VHB Groups have been given the opportunity to devote maximum effort towards increasing their combat potential." To Whitehead, all of this added to PACUSA's overall effectiveness and efficiency.[67]

Basing issues were another major problem that the AAF had to take into account. In mid-October 1946, Whitehead sent a long radio message to MacArthur about the difficulties that PACUSA was encountering in establishing "minimum" bases in the Philippines by way of the United States' negotiations with the Philippine Government. Whitehead had moved his headquarters to Tokyo for the remainder of the Japanese Occupation, but once the Occupation was over he assumed that PACUSA would again be headquartered near Manila, and that a large proportion of its forces would also be stationed on Luzon.[68] The negotiations for future base sites were taking place between the two governments, however, just as significant problems ensued, specifically with Filipinos in the Manila area being victimized in various ways by US troops based around the capital city.[69] Ignoring this context until the end of the message, Whitehead began by telling MacArthur that further concessions on base sites must not be made. For instance, he thought that US withdrawal from the port facilities in the Manila Harbor area would be financially prohibitive and would make the United States' position at Nichols Field "untenable." He also thought that post-Occupation movement of PACUSA's headquarters sites from the Manila area was impractical and a "major" psychological blunder. Furthermore, he believed that additional repair and storage facilities at Nichols were necessary. He reiterated to MacArthur that all of these requirements were based on his assessment of the AAF's mission in the postwar Pacific. Whitehead then emphasized to MacArthur that the Philippines' importance to US security could not be denied. In particular, he thought that the Philippines, because of its large land area, was "the one area in the Western Pacific from which we can mount and stage and deploy adequate forces to forward areas to forestall aggression." He also thought that the Philippines was the one area that would allow the United States to employ airpower alone to control the vital sea lanes of the South China Sea west to Singapore, as well as strike the "vast" land areas of Southeast Asia.[70]

Whitehead also told MacArthur that he had considered some 500 sites for airfields in the Philippines, and that he had eliminated all but twelve. Of these twelve, he further reduced the list to only three: Clark, Nichols, and Florida Blanca.

He claimed that these three airfields were the only ones that could support operations by modern aircraft. The other nine, he assumed, would have to be "completely" rebuilt before they were of use for other than emergency purposes. Thus, Whitehead thought that if the United States was forced to withdraw to the three major airfields because of the base negotiations, it would mean that the United States' situation was so "untenable" that the Army should completely withdraw AAF personnel from the archipelago.

Whitehead also thought that with the advent of Philippine independence, it was more essential than ever that he be permitted to establish his headquarters in the Manila area. Arguing that performance of his mission would entail "favorable" support by the Philippine Government and adequate port, communication, road, and rail facilities, he asserted that only by the closest personal contact between his headquarters and the Philippine Government could he carry out his assignment. He followed up this statement by outlining additional base requirements, telling MacArthur that in addition to Nichols Field, he needed 50 percent of the site west of the field so as to extend the base to the Manila Bay shore. Not only did he think that this was the only "suitable" land for AAF personnel housing, but he said that in US hands, this land would assure US military access to docking facilities and logistical support for air-depot operations. Whitehead did not think that either rail or road facilities were developed enough in the Philippines to permit continuous overland transport of aircraft supplies and equipment. Having to develop port facilities on the Bataan Peninsula would also make land deliveries of heavy equipment impractical because of increased distances. Whitehead continued by saying that PACUSA had considered all of the possibilities for major air bases in the Philippines, but that the United States had put "millions" into Clark, Nichols, and Florida Blanca. Therefore, he thought that the United States "cannot give them up."[71]

Whitehead then proceeded to reduce the list further. He told MacArthur that PACUSA had at one time thought that the Florida Blanca field might be a VHB base site, but that tests had proved the approaches to be too hazardous. In particular, the Bataan Mountains obscured these approaches, and the mountains themselves were continually shrouded in clouds during certain periods of the year. Whitehead claimed that the Philippine Government wanted the AAF to put its air depot fifteen to twenty miles closer to this mountain range, which he thought was an impractical solution. The bottom line was that he thought the United States needed its air depot on Luzon, and that the only "suitable" site was Nichols Field. Whitehead also told MacArthur that he had information indicating that the majority of property owners on the site west of Nichols Field expressed "informal" consent to sell their property, but that the Philippine Government wanted to establish Manila as the major civil air terminal in the region. As Whitehead saw it, Philippine control of Nichols Field would obviously prevent the AAF from establishing its postwar facility there and be a major step in allowing the Philippines to turn that base into "the major terminal of commercial air lines of all nations with interests in the Orient." Whitehead further thought, however, that recent friction between US military personnel and Filipinos could be "quickly" corrected once the United States became more "stabilized" in the newly independent republic. He even thought that this friction was less intense between US military personnel and Filipinos on the one hand than between different factions of Filipinos on the other, and he recommended "vigorous" and "immediate" State Department negotiation with the Philippine Government for these base sites. He concluded by stating that PACUSA representatives at the Philippine Base Agreement conferences had been given maximum latitude up to the point where further concessions would "seriously endanger" the AAF's position in the Philippines. In Whitehead's opinion, the United States had reached that point "and must now operate on a take all or nothing basis. We must stand firm on the Air Forces requirements in the Philippines as they have been presented above."[72]

Other logistical problems ensued in late October 1946. In a message to Spaatz, Whitehead pointed out problems in PACUSA's relations with commercial airlines, as well as with the Department of Commerce. More specifically, conflicts were becoming apparent between PACUSA, the Commerce Department's Civil Aeronautics Administration (CAA), and various commercial airlines over which organization should provide airfield, air navigation, and servicing facilities. Whitehead said that there were issues of safety aids, search-and-rescue operations, flight control, and coordination of air traffic across US, occupied, and foreign air space that also needed to be solved. While Whitehead thought that the air routes across the entire Pacific Basin were military in nature, he did not want to harm the future of American aviation in the region through "government heavy handedness." Thus, he was asking Spaatz for "high-level" policy guidance about a successful integration of military, government, and private aviation interests, especially any "additional info which will keep the Army in the clear on this matter."[73]

By late December 1946, with the change to unified commands slated for the first of the year, other difficulties started to surface since there would now be theater-wide (as opposed to service-wide) commanders having control over air, ground, and naval forces. Whitehead told MacArthur that he had no interest in having administrative control or responsibility for any AAF units that were not physically located in PACUSA's theater unless those units were under the control of the theater commander whom Whitehead reported to. Specifically, he did not want any administrative responsibility for the Seventh Air Force, which was going to be part of Admiral Tower's PACOM in Hawaii rather than General MacArthur's FECOM in Japan. Because the Pacific Command's senior officer was a naval officer, because Hawaii was closer to Washington than to Tokyo, and because of the need for additional supply and administrative personnel, Whitehead thought it would be best to let COMGENAIR or some subordinate unit in the Zone of the Interior handle administrative matters for the Seventh Air Force.[74] Whitehead received an answer to this question about the division of command responsibilities in the Pacific in early January 1947 from General Spaatz. Spaatz told Whitehead that there had been considerable discussion of command responsibilities in the Pacific due to the JCS's assignment of unified commands. Spaatz thought it was a "good idea" that Whitehead exercise administrative control over all of the AAF units in the Pacific, in spite of the fact that they were tactically divided between MacArthur in Japan and Towers in Hawaii. Still, he understood Whitehead's reasons for not wanting to do so, and AAF units under Towers were to report to the Admiral for operational purposes but to Spaatz for administrative purposes. Spaatz also further explained the unified-command concept. Under the new JCS regime, troops of a respective service in the Pacific would report to their branch chief, except during tactical emergencies. In Hawaii, for instance, Admiral Towers would have overall tactical control of all forces during emergencies, but the naval forces would report to Admiral Nimitz for administrative and logistical purposes, the ground forces would report to General Eisenhower for the same reasons, and the AAF units would report to Spaatz. Spaatz ultimately felt it would be a better situation if all forces under a theater commander that were not from that commander's parent service were handled in this manner.[75] It is also apparent from the primary sources that well into 1947 a shortage of personnel continued to have a major impact on operational readiness and capability. FEAF continued the mission of ferrying excess bombers back to the Zone of the Interior, probably for use by SAC, but at a cost of operational readiness that was noted in early March 1947 when Whitehead specifically talked about "rolling up" bases as quickly as possible so that the few trained technicians he had available could be better employed.[76]

■ The AAF and Interservice Rivalry

The AAF's goal for this operational training and regional deployment was, of course, to be recognized and rewarded as the nation's most economical and, therefore, first line of defense. Demonstrating this status took good public relations, such as breaking records in areas of aviation like long-range flights. The Pacific Basin was a key area for this activity because of its size. This idea can be seen in late October 1945, when Norstad, as Assistant Chief of Air Staff for Plans and Twentieth Air Force Chief of Staff, received a letter from Lieutenant General Giles, Commanding General of United States Army Strategic Air Forces Pacific, detailing the employment of one B-29 with extra fuel tanks to break the world's long-distance flight record and achieve a flight of 11,500 miles. Giles stated his need for personnel to carry out this assignment in the context of early postwar demobilization. Touching on one of the other major issues between the Army and the Navy, Giles also informed Norstad that he was headed to Tokyo to discuss postwar command organization in the Pacific with General MacArthur. Giles specifically mentioned his intention to discuss alleged plans he had heard about that would separate Army and Navy logistical arrangements in the region. Moreover, Giles planned on telling MacArthur of his preference for one overall air-force command in the Pacific with a primary mission of supporting MacArthur in the Japanese Occupation.[77] B-29 record-breaking flights across the Pacific coalesced with the AAF coming into conflict with the Navy over another issue as well: the control of island airstrips suitable for the Superfortress. The beginnings of this specific conflict were first found by this author in a February 1946 letter by Whitehead to MacArthur. In the letter, Whitehead asked MacArthur to obtain the use of the Barbers Point Naval Airdrome in Hawaii for the AAF as a refueling stop for B-29s returning to the Zone of the Interior. Whitehead argued that the John Rogers Airdrome was too close to a heavily populated area of Oahu for B-29s with heavy fuel loads to risk landings. He also said that Hickam Field was too close to heavy population concentrations, and that the Mokuleia Airdrome was too poorly surfaced.[78] He therefore asked for Barbers Point for fear of peacetime crashes that would have to be explained by the AAF.[79]

The intensity of interservice conflicts can also be seen in other sources. In March 1946, Whitehead went after the Navy in a letter to General Kenney. After saying that the AAF needed the "three important pieces of real estate" of the Philippines, the Marianas-Bonins, and the Ryukyus, Whitehead went on to discuss which service—the AAF or the Navy—was to provide the air defense for these areas. Whitehead "naturally [felt] . . . that the Army Air Forces should do it." He told Kenney that he was "certain that unless we do it, the Navy will go into land based [*sic*] air force units on a large scale." He was further convinced that once "the Navy does that, we are sunk—rather I should say, once we put ourselves in a position of forcing the Navy to do that . . . the end of Army Air Forces is in sight." The budget cuts of the immediate postwar era were also evident, as each service was forced to carry out its missions with minimal forces, and each service proactively tried to carry out those missions in a way that demonstrated service efficiency. Thus, much of this letter focused on Whitehead's outline to Kenney of the minimal unit and personnel dispositions needed in the postwar Pacific. In discussing these dispositions, the Navy again figured prominently, with Whitehead proposing "a minimum force for doing the job. If we cannot do it that way, then we better turn the job over to the Navy."[80] Whitehead also assumed—like many other high-ranking American officers at this time—that the US occupation of Japan and Korea would be a temporary matter of three to five years. From an AAF perspective, Whitehead thought that such a situation was a negative for the military development of the region since it entailed the Navy having large air bases in the Pacific that might preempt the AAF's role of land-based airpower in the region. For instance, he surmised that "[O]nce we get out of Japan and Korea, in view of the large naval bases which are being built on Guam and Saipan, I feel that we should provide this minimum defense or we 'force' the Navy into land based [*sic*] air operations." He also thought that the Navy wanted "our big airdromes all over the Pacific and they mean to get them if we give them the slightest entering wedge." He reminded Kenney that "[Y]ou know better than I how quickly the Navy would grab the opportunity." If the AAF was properly organized, led, and motivated, however, Whitehead was confident about ultimate success, believing "that we are just as good as they are."[81] General officer assignments were also discussed by Whitehead in this interservice context. For instance, when discussing the possible assignment of Major General Streett as COMAF 7 on Oahu, Whitehead talked about Streett knowing how to "look after Army Air Forces [*sic*] interests . . . in that hot-bed of naval intrigue." Whitehead's idea that the AAF's postwar dispositions in the Pacific not only had to "sell" the AAF but also had to defeat the Navy in its postwar plans were again apparent in his concluding paragraph to Kenney. Apologizing to Kenney about the length of his letter, he stated that "I know how you feel about our major enemy, the Navy. You and I both know that there can be no compromise with those people." Whitehead then proceeded to describe the Navy as having reached a "fork" in the road, one branch of which left it "top dog" and in control of postwar American military airpower, and the other of which left it as an adjunct to land-based AAF forces. The bottom line for Whitehead was that "[T]he fight to save the Navy will eliminate us if it succeeds."[82]

Similarly, Whitehead's ideas about the AAF's need for Pacific bases had an interservice dimension to them. In early April 1946, he wrote to Spaatz to request that the AAF be given Guam as its major bomber base in the Marianas instead of Saipan or Tinian. Whitehead cited the length of the runways on the various islands as one reason for the request. The fact that Guam already had shops and warehouses capable of supporting combat units, while the other two islands did not, also bolstered his argument—though for some reason he did not explain what had happened to the base infrastructure that had supported AAF operations on Tinian in 1944–1945. Still, the Navy was again the enemy, since, to Whitehead, the large naval development on Guam was the reason that the AAF should be in Guam "in force" in order to protect "its" installations. Air defense also came back into the equation. "The air defense of land areas is a traditional Army Air Force [*sic*] mission. Unless we retain air bases and provide the fighter defense for naval installations we 'force' the Navy to operate land based [*sic*] air force units."[83] These difficulties over issues with the Navy, such as the air-defense responsibilities in regions like the Marianas, were made worse by a lack of clarification from higher authorities as to which service held the various responsibilities in these island groups. While the AAF charged the Twentieth Air Force with the air defense of the Marianas, the JCS had assigned the same responsibility to naval forces in the area! Although the discrepancy had been brought to the attention of higher headquarters, the Twentieth Air Force was merely instructed to devise the best plan it could envision.[84] In spite of this lack of clarification from the

JCS, Whitehead continued to enunciate his ideas that airpower was the main line of defense in the postwar Pacific. In a letter to General MacArthur about the pay of Philippine Air Force pilots, Whitehead asserted that since the Philippines was composed of "isolated" land masses, "an Air Force is the only military arm which can operate expeditiously within any part of the Philippine nation. It appears, therefore, that an Air Force should be given top priority in building up the military organization of the Commonwealth."[85]

By July 1946, Whitehead also was communicating to now Major General White, COMAF 7, saying that he still did not have a final decision from Washington about the assignment of Barbers Point, Hawaii, to the AAF. He pointed out to White the problems that this delay was causing with AAF deployments in other areas of the Pacific. Recognizing that "COMGENAIR is having considerable difficulty in forcing a decision since it has both the War Department and the Navy Department to contend with," he told White that he was preparing a report "which I hope will give COMGENAIR additional ammunition to force a decision on Barbers Point."[86] This theme of publicity vis-à-vis the Navy also continued, with October 1946 documentation once more pertaining to record-breaking flights of B-29s. Whitehead advised his subordinate commanders to be ready to send a flight of B-29s across the Pacific via the Philippines, Guam, and Hawaii as part of a world-wide demonstration flight. Though the flight was not yet approved, PACUSA was to prepare this flight, including a dozen C-54 transport aircraft to carry the necessary supplies and maintenance personnel. Again, the objective was not only for this flight to carry out an around-the-world mission, but also to demonstrate that the operation was largely free of both Navy and Army ground and supply support. Apparently, this planning continued, since a radio communiqué later in the month detailed the routes, the units involved, and even the communication frequencies for the sortie.[87]

In December 1946, Major General McMullen, COMAF 8, sent a letter to Whitehead asking for feedback about B-29 rotations. This feedback was meant to further clarify AAF regional operational-training plans that were intended to emphasize the service's dynamic qualities in the context of interservice debates, defense unification, and declining budgets. Discussions with General Kenney, for example, emphasized the "mobility of our Air Force. General Kenney is very eager for us to demonstrate this mobility as soon as we are organized and operating." This latter reference was to the impending reorganization of US overseas commands into unified commands on 1 January 1947, as well as the creation of an independent Air Force, which was scheduled to occur in September 1947.[88] In this context, by early 1947 Whitehead again had specific ideas for countering Navy claims that land-based bombers could not successfully engage naval vessels at sea because of the vessels' mobility and land-based bombers' range limitations. In a communication to Spaatz, Whitehead stated the idea that the way to counter naval vessels, such as highly mobile carrier groups, was to develop attack bombers with low-level capability. No doubt based on his experiences in the Pacific War, he thought "that the attack bomber definitely has a place in air warfare as presently conceived." Along these lines, he also thought that ships, "airdromes and troops all 'curl up' when a deck level bomber attack is driven home. I feel the attack bomber must be capable of carrying the A-bomb." Continuing more specifically about future naval threats—including, no doubt, the US Navy as a bureaucratic opponent—Whitehead thought that future Air Force attack bombers had to be "capable of carrying a large enough GP [general purpose] bomb to sink any vessel which exists 10 years from now and [it] must be radar equipped for low level [sic] attacks under instrument conditions."[89] In a later document, he admitted to General Kenney that low-level techniques, rather than the high-level ones normally emphasized by strategic-bombing advocates, were the key, and that these attack bombers needed to carry big enough bombs not only to attack any vessel but to sink the vessel in question with just one device. In the same letter, Whitehead also touched on another issue that illustrated the degree of competition between the two services over these issues. Specifically, the AAF and the Navy were arguing over which service sank the Japanese battleship *Haruna* in the summer of 1945. While most sources credit Admiral William Halsey's Third Fleet with doing so, the AAF initially claimed that Army bombers had taken this ship out. In this context, Colonel Clarence Irvine, FEAF Deputy Chief of Staff (DCS), had interrogated Japanese naval officers about the sinking soon after the end of the war, and Whitehead told Kenney that his staff had done a study on the subject. Wartime experiences, the interrogations, and the study, however, probably convinced Whitehead that the Navy had, indeed, sunk the Japanese battleship since he was now advocating low-level bombing to Kenney, a tactic not normally argued for by high-ranking AAF officers after the war.[90]

In a matter related to this bitter example of interservice rivalry in early March 1947 Whitehead cautioned General Spaatz about the need to prevent public disclosure of internal AAF disagreements over the future of the service branch and its operations. "I would feel very bad to have any Air Force arguments get outside Air Force channels. There are some in AGF and in the Navy who are just waiting for that."[91] In another memo to Spaatz later in April 1947, Whitehead also went into great detail delineating Army and Navy facilities on postwar Pacific bases such as Iwo Jima. Specifically, he wanted signs installed to show "the areas in which the U.S. Navy has property and facilities. I want to be certain visitors do not confuse these areas with AAF or AGF installations."[92] Also, concerning the issue of publicity for the newly emerging US Air Force, Whitehead acknowledged FEAF's continued support to Spaatz in helping to carry out the JCS's Post-Hostilities Mapping Program. Whitehead wanted as much publicity as possible about this operation, "within the limits of justifiable classification," in order to emphasize the theme of airpower employed for the benefit of neighboring nations, mariners, and aviators. With FEAF carrying out the Pacific and Far East portions of the program, Whitehead was concerned about the entire operation being classified as "Secret" and precluding "any public releases regarding this program in my area." If Spaatz and the War Department could agree to declassify some of the material, Whitehead thought he could put it to good public-relations use for the new Air Force.[93] Spaatz replied a couple of weeks later, saying that he agreed with Whitehead about the release of information, but that Major General Stephen Chamberlin, War Department General Staff Director of Intelligence, did not. Spaatz, however, thought there would be no harm in declassifying some of the material on the Japanese Home Islands, the former Japanese Mandates, and the Philippines. He concluded by telling Whitehead that he would try again on the other aspects of the mapping program and let him know about a final War Department decision.[94]

In early June, Whitehead sent another memo to Spaatz that further delineated what types of threats he saw to the postwar Pacific Basin, and how land-based airpower could counter those threats. Whitehead thought that the area "can most economically be controlled by air power." He thought this since "bases can be attacked only from the air or by an amphibious force," and since "[no] amphibious force can attack successfully unless our air has been destroyed." Whitehead also thought that "[one] atomic bomb would defeat an amphibious force." He went on to say that, in his judgment, "the greatest threats are an airborne invasion or the destruction of our bases by air bombardment or submarine launched projectiles." Far from being tied to bases, Whitehead thought that both the tactical and strategic mobility of units must be maintained in peace, or the AAF would be "fixed" to its bases and destroyed piecemeal. However, Whitehead argued that if FEAF could maintain its mobility, it could defend the Pacific Basin, at least until the time came when the enemy had developed "airborne atomic bombs," submarine-borne atomic weapons, or an air force massed on mainland Asia or Japan.[95] This focus on land-based airpower for both strategic and bureaucratic reasons came up again a few days later in a letter from Whitehead to Kenney. Whitehead asserted that General MacArthur thought the United States' military policy was "horse and buggy," that fewer men under arms in traditional areas of the military were necessary in order to sustain more airpower, and that the leading military officials had "missed the boat" by overvaluing areas that were less strategic than the development of modern airpower. Arguing from hearsay by British and Australian military-aviation officers, Whitehead asserted that most British leaders were also focusing too heavily on infantry and warships, not airpower. Along these lines, he added that Field Marshal Sir Bernard Montgomery, Chief of the British Imperial General Staff, was quoted as saying that US Army and Navy leaders were complacent and "mentally unready" to wage "air power war."[96]

Interservice rivalry manifested itself again in late July. With the passage of the 1947 National Security Act that month, the AAF was slated to become a newly independent US Air Force in September as part of a Department of Defense. Many

feathers had been ruffled in getting to this point, and much still needed to be decided between the new services. Still, Whitehead sent a message to Spaatz congrat-
ulating him for the fine work he had done in getting the Air Force into a position of
"equality" with the Army and Navy, and getting the new service recognized as the
nation's "first line of defense." The last point, however, was not something the National Security Act of 1947 actually defined.[97] This assertive statement may have
been the reason for Spaatz sending Whitehead a radio message, dated the same
day, in which the Air Force's parity with the Army and Navy was made clear. Spaatz
stated that the Air Force was not claiming "first line of defense" status. In addition,
he spent the majority of the message detailing the need for Air Force personnel to
maintain cordial relations with the personnel of the other services—so that the numerous problems ahead could be solved, and so that the Air Force could prove its
"capacity to carry our share of the responsibility for national defense."[98] Additional
perspectives in contexts of both inter- and intraservice rivalry also surfaced in a
letter from Whitehead to Kenney in early November 1947. Again discussing general
officer assignments in the Pacific, Whitehead told Kenney that it was fine with him
if he remained in the Pacific as long as General MacArthur thought he should stay.
Whitehead confidentially told Kenney that MacArthur "plans to take Army and
Navy troops out of Japan first—wants AF to remain since it is the real defense any-
how." Whitehead continued that "Spaatz' headquarters wants to pull air out. I feel
that USAF is making a mistake in bucking MacA. He is the best friend the USAF has
outside its own men." Whitehead also communicated another fear that was indicative of this time period and these bureaucratic issues. Along with Major General
William Kepner, Chief of the Air Force's Atomic Energy Division and Special
Weapons Group, Whitehead was concerned that the Air Force was "'losing its shirt'
and pants too" in the interservice disagreements with the Army and Navy. Vice Admiral Sherman, DCNO for Operations; Lieutenant General Albert Wedemeyer, Director of the Department of the Army's Plans and Operations (P&O) Division; and
newly promoted Lieutenant General Norstad, now the Air Force Deputy Chief of
Staff (DCS) for Operations, had been tasked by the JCS with solving the problems
ensuing from defense reorganization and unification. Whitehead and Kepner were
fearful that Norstad, as the junior of these three-star officers, was being "dominated" to the detriment of Air Force interests.[99]

■ Army Intraservice Rivalry

As some of the previous documents suggest, there appeared to be intraservice issues within the Army as well. For example, in an April 1946 letter, Whitehead assured Spaatz that all of PACUSA's commanders had been briefed on the necessity
of "harmonious relations" between PACUSA units, as well as between AAF, AGF,

and ASF units in the Pacific.[100] This effort may have been an attempt to insure against any bad publicity vis-à-vis the Navy as interservice roles and missions were being debated in Washington. The statement also, however, may have been an indication of the intensification of existing internal problems as Army budgets got leaner. The idea that the AAF should have priority over both the Navy and the AGF became apparent in another document from July 1946. At that time, Whitehead sent a radio message to MacArthur marked "Urgent" in which he stated satisfaction with the number of Japanese POWs that had been furnished to his units in the Philippines. He claimed, however, that he only received a fraction of the number requested for labor duties on Guam and Okinawa. More specifically, Whitehead recommended that on Okinawa "the Air Forces [sic] receive a more proportionate share of available POW labor there." He also urged "that on Guam all POWs received from Truk be allocated to the Guam Air Depot and that the balance of POWs in the Marianas . . . be divided among Army, Navy and Air Forces [sic] in proportion to their troop strength."[101] However, "in proportion to troop strength" was not sufficient for Lieutenant General Hull, Commanding General of AFMIDPAC. Hull complained that service and supply agencies should have priority over tactical units since service and supply units usually performed more technical, logistical, and construction projects than tactical units.[102] In addition, Major General Christiansen, Acting Commanding General of AFWESPAC, suggested to Whitehead a few days later that the AAF units on Okinawa already had the higher proportion of POWs since the projects that the POWs were being employed on were of benefit to both AAF and AGF units, something Whitehead had not previously mentioned. Still, Christiansen stated that he would divert more prisoners to the AAF units "if and when they can be removed from Ground Force projects of less importance and lower priority than Air Force projects." A few days later, however, he more directly told MacArthur that further allocation of POWs to the AAF was unjustifiable since POWs had already been assigned to AAF projects, and since the AAF units were also benefiting from the work done by prisoners who had been assigned to the AGF projects.[103] MacArthur was convinced that no changes should be made. His headquarters had had a conference with Whitehead's representatives concerning POW allocation on Okinawa and Guam at which it was decided "by both parties" that no further action needed to be taken.[104] Still, this did not prevent Hull from complaining that AAF projects were considered more important than AGF projects. Hull argued that AGF projects equated to overall island-garrison efficiency, both for the operation of the AAF unit facilities and the improved efficacy in AGF operations. Hull therefore wanted prisoners withdrawn on a percentage basis from all agencies and projects in the Marianas, not just from projects that would favor the AAF.[105]

The issue of unity of command in this context of intraservice rivalry was also communicated in an August 1946 letter to Whitehead from Hull. Hull was concerned about the question of command throughout the Pacific as it affected air, ground, and naval forces. With MacArthur asking his commanders for their recommendations on this issue, Hull told Whitehead that he thought current arrangements were not satisfactory. He argued that for an organization designed to fight a war, reduced peacetime funding would not suffice, and he thought the Army in the postwar Pacific had to achieve greater integration in order to avoid waste and duplication. Given the Army's hopes for a merger of the services with unified command from Washington, D.C., down the entire chain of command, Hull thought it appropriate that the Army in the Pacific effect a merger between Army Ground Forces and Army Air Forces, no matter the outcome of the unification controversy in Washington. For one thing, Hull thought that command unification of Army forces in the Pacific made sense from a military viewpoint, regardless of the political and media pressures on the service. However, he also recognized the military and public relations aspects of this, stating that "[I]f we don't effect a sound organization, we are in a weak position to defend whatever organization we have."[106]

Hull further elaborated on current problems. Taking the Marianas as an example, he painted a portrait of competition for funds, space, and supplies between AGF and AAF units that were separately commanded. Admitting that there would never be enough resources for both groups, Hull admired how the Navy had unified its command arrangements in the Marianas: all American naval forces in the Marianas, for instance, were commanded by an admiral, at this time Rear Admiral Charles Pownall, Commander of the Marianas Area (COMMARIANAS). Hull particularly pointed out the weakness of having Army commands without a higher headquarters in the Marianas, which had to deal separately with the Navy commands in that island group. Hull therefore thought that there should be "one top Army man" in the Marianas and Bonins who could deal with the Navy on an "equal footing," and that the officer in question should eventually be an air officer because of the key importance of the Marianas as a postwar air-base complex. This officer, whom Hull called "Commander, U.S. Army Forces Marianas," would be the senior Army officer in that area, with command of all Army forces in the region. Yet the arrangement was more complex than it at first seemed. Hull saw the Marianas commanded operationally by an air officer, but logistically and administratively he saw forces in the Marianas reporting to him on Hawaii. He also saw his command as responsible for ground defense, while air defense and combat units would remain with the air officer. Hull further complicated matters at the end of his letter. Asserting that he in no way wanted tactical or strategic control over AAF units, he nevertheless thought that the defense of Hawaii should be his entirely, both in a ground and air sense. So, without wanting any command over AAF units, he wanted command of some of those units in order to affect a unified defense of the Hawaiian Islands and the Middle Pacific![107]

Whitehead responded with a letter to Hull on 29 August. Not surprisingly, his ideas, while at times in agreement, essentially countered Hull's thoughts. Agreeing that unified command was the key to the deployment of postwar AAF units in the Pacific, he strongly reiterated that "air power in the Pacific should not be divided. The Pacific is one air area." Whitehead said that he was sold on the idea of unified command throughout because of his observations of the General Headquarters (GHQ) Air Force that was created in the 1930s by MacArthur when the latter was Chief of Staff of the Army. Whitehead emphasized that centralized control of air transportation, weather services, supply, and technical functions were also vital to the proper operation of postwar Pacific airpower. He then disagreed with Hull that the creation of a Commander of US Army Forces, Marianas would increase administrative efficiency and, in fact, he thought it would have the opposite effect. Contradicting earlier statements in which he asserted visceral feelings about Navy dispositions in the postwar Pacific, Whitehead now argued that he did not see conflicts with the Navy about Admiral Pownall's jurisdiction over Army forces, nor did he see competition between AAF and AGF units over space, funding, or supplies! Any conflicts that did occur, he assumed, would be solved by MacArthur as CINCAFPAC, just as MacArthur had supposedly done during the war as CINC-SWPA. As to the local defense of the Marianas and Hawaii, MacArthur's headquarters had carried on a wartime policy of coordinating air operations with ground, naval, and foreign forces. Again contradicting earlier statements in which he called for "true" unification instead of just coordination, Whitehead now saw no reason why this kind of coordination could not continue in peacetime. Whitehead again voiced his resistance to any "limited concept" of local area defense that might inhibit AAF deployments or his control over those units. Clearly thinking, even if Hull did not, that air forces would be the main line of Army defense in the region, and that these forces would be forward-deployed, Whitehead envisioned Hawaii and the Marianas being defended by air forces in Japan, Okinawa, and the Philippines. As he had in other documents, he also emphasized the deployment of most of the AAF units to the forward areas, including places like Iwo Jima. In conclusion, Whitehead stated to Hull that the latter's ideas ran counter to Whitehead's conceptions about the employment of airpower. Whitehead did not want to take over any AGF units, since he did not have the personnel or shipping to handle this administration and since he only wanted to deal with air forces. As he stated to Hull concerning the AAF, airplanes "are our business." Belying previous AAF rhetoric about a true unification of US forces throughout the world, Whitehead now talked about "coordination" between air, ground, and naval commanders over plans, training, and operations, especially in areas of anti-aircraft defense. Accordingly, he saw no reason for his assumption of direct command over ground or naval units.[108]

The flavor of this intraservice rivalry can also be detected in an October 1946 letter from Whitehead to Spaatz that further communicates the, at times, depth and intensity of this bitter competition. In the letter, Whitehead congratulated Spaatz on being able to get guided-missile development in the War Department put under AAF control. Not only did Whitehead invoke his thinking that guided-missile development "belonged" with the AAF, but he also told Spaatz that "[some] of us who have been around for a long time can well appreciate the great effort and the intelligent logic which was required to obtain a change in a basic War Department decision." He continued in the paragraph by asserting that General MacArthur, to his knowledge, was the only AGF officer who favored the decision. He then concluded the letter by stating that the decision to house guided-missile development in the AAF was "the greatest forward step since the day the Japanese surrendered at the ceremony which you attended, without the necessity of invasion."[109] In another swipe at the AGF and ASF in April 1947, Major General McMullen, SAC Deputy Commander, also complained about the new Air Force high command becoming too economy-minded, as well as taking in too many ground officers from the AGF. In McMullen's opinion, "[W]e are accumulating a large percentage of non-flying officers who will eventually take away the dash and glamour of the Air Forces as we knew it." McMullen went on to say that this infusion of ground officers would make the Air Force "into a precedent ridden lifeless activity similar to our pre-war Quartermaster Corps. Apparently there can be little done since decisions have already been made."[110] Later in the same month, Whitehead came back to his intraservice theme of the AAF being the Army's primary force in the postwar Pacific. He said that all Army activities on Iwo Jima should be consolidated under an AAF officer, something he thought would cut duplication and save the Army both men and money. Along similar lines, he thought all supply areas should be consolidated under AAF control as it "makes no sense to have AGF scattered all over the Island. That costs money and therefore effort." Even more specifically, Whitehead said that the "AGF must provide the personnel for their mission which is to support AAF on Iwo." Whitehead became even more forthright when he told Kenney that AGF support of the AAF was "*now unsatisfactory*." He concluded by telling Kenney that he "need not add that I want *action* on the above" (emphasis in original).[111]

■ Conclusion

Several phenomena can be seen in this discourse over the AAF's position on defending the postwar Pacific Basin. First, the AAF employed, or attempted to employ, a useable history from the Pacific War to justify its position as the main defense force in the region. This useable history, at times, included giving credit to the other services for their roles in defeating Japan, but usually in a back-handed or slighting way. In most of the documents, not surprisingly, the lion's share of the credit for defeating Japan was given to the AAF, and the war itself was used to justify postwar appropriations, force compositions, and deployments. Second, the documents make it clear that the Pacific War had an enormous impact on AAF officers, and even on some AGF officers, in that they saw land-based airpower as the basis for the postwar defense of the region, and even saw the region as one "integrated strategic physical complex," as the JCS began to refer to East Asia and the Pacific in 1945.[112] The idea that the postwar defense of the region should be focused on fixed bases had been put aside in favor of a mobile defense based on airpower that rotated between the Continental United States and the Pacific Basin itself. Moreover, AAF deployments were to be as far forward or westward as possible, so that Hawaii was a rear area supporting Alaska, Japan, Korea, the Philippines, and Micronesia. When US forces were withdrawn from Korea, Japan, and the Ryukyus, AAF officers thought that the Philippines, the Aleutians, and Micronesia would become even more important as the forward deployment areas. Last, there is clear evidence that numerous problems presented themselves in terms of the AAF carrying out these deployments. Not the least of these problems stemmed from personnel and equipment shortages due to rapid postwar demobilization and budget cuts. In addition, the interservice rivalry, which was endemic between 1945 and 1947 throughout the entire military establishment, definitely reared its head in the Pacific commands. It was intriguing for this author to discover how intense the interservice rivalry was, with some AAF officers employing a discourse of war to describe their naval counterparts. Probably even more interesting is the degree to which intraservice rivalry between the AAF on the one hand and the AGF and ASF on the other hand took place. To be sure, the AAF's conception of defending the United States' strategic sphere in the postwar Pacific Basin was a complex fabric of wartime lessons, speculation about the future, and bureaucratic rivalry.

CHAPTER 3

Sea-Air Power in Paradise

The Navy Position on the Defense of the Pacific Basin

S oon after the Japanese surrender on 2 September 1945, the JCS outlined a policy which they hoped would be adopted as the postwar American military
strategy. The Joint Chiefs argued for the maintenance of a highly trained and
equipped military deployed on a global basis as the guarantor of American national
interests. Supporting such a force would be overseas bases, a centralized intelligence
and warning system, and the peacetime stockpiling of strategic materials. One of the
key components of this force would be mobile striking units capable of instant and
sustained action against potentially hostile nations.[1] Navy officials agreed with this
concept of mobile striking power. According to Vice Admiral Richard Edwards,
Deputy Chief of Naval Operations and Deputy Commander-in-Chief of the US Fleet
(Deputy CNO-Deputy COMINCH), and Rear Admiral Donald Duncan, COMINCH
Assistant Chief of Staff for Plans, postwar policing responsibilities in the Pacific
Basin over a potentially resurgent Japan, and then an increasingly confrontational
Soviet Union, would inevitably come under their service's jurisdiction. In fact, during
wartime planning for the postwar Pacific, Edwards and Duncan assumed that because of the maritime nature of the region, postwar control of the Pacific was a particularly "naval" problem, and that postwar base requirements, such as those in
Micronesia, would be based on naval needs that met naval requirements.[2] The Navy
also had fairly clear ideas about the best way to provide for the postwar defense of
the Pacific. Taking into account the fast tempo of operations during the Pacific War,
naval officers echoed the Joint Chiefs' emphasis on highly alert and mobile forces
ready for instantaneous action. The Navy's postwar planners then emphasized that
these mobile forces needed to be predominantly naval in composition. For example,
a January 1945 memorandum on postwar base requirements from Admiral Frederick

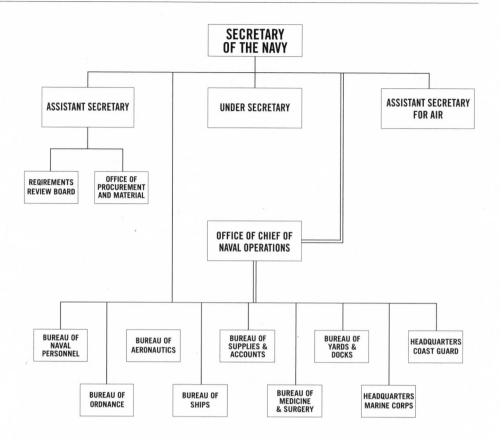

Figure 3. Secretary of the Navy Organization, 1946–1947. (Courtesy of the Naval Historical Collection, US Naval War College, Newport, Rhode Island.)

Horne, Vice Chief of Naval Operations (VCNO), to Secretary of the Navy James Forrestal urged tailoring the minimum shore bases to the needs of a highly mobile fleet. In a statement which clearly reflected the Navy's interwar and wartime experiences, Horne asserted that an overabundant number of bases would tie a mobile force to base defense and negate the mobility that the Pacific War had demonstrated was necessary for successful military operations. According to Horne, an emphasis should be placed on floating bases and support facilities to the greatest degree possible in order to support a mobile fleet.[3]

Equally important was the fact that concentrating Navy assets on a mobile fleet instead of static bases could be a powerful counter to AAF charges that the Navy was obsolete and a waste of scarce postwar national resources. In fact, Navy statements emphasized mobile fleets, de-emphasized shore bases, and conveniently ignored how heavily the Navy itself had to rely on island bases between 1942 and 1945. Moreover, the Navy charged the AAF with being significantly dependent on Navy operational and logistical assistance against Japan in 1944–1945. The Navy, of course, did not acknowledge its need for AAF assistance against Japan at various points during the war since its argument was part of an offensive against the AAF that entailed accusing the air service of an overdependence on island bases for its operations in the wartime and postwar Pacific. However, not every naval officer was immediately sold on the idea of the postwar fleet being built around carrier air-power. In fact, there was a great deal of friction both during and immediately after the Pacific War between naval aviators and surface officers over the future force structure of the Navy.[4] The superior qualities of naval airpower as the central element of postwar American naval power were not subscribed to by every officer, even after Pearl Harbor. This fact was evident in at least one wartime planning document dealing with the postwar world. In March 1943, Admiral Arthur Hepburn, Chairman of the Navy's General Board, writing about postwar base requirements, only belatedly and hesitantly added air bases for an international police force, and tended to discuss facilities for surface ships before those of naval or land-based aviation. This was consistent with one historian's conclusion that American naval planning before the summer of 1944 continued to see the postwar world in interwar terms, and saw the Navy as essentially a surface police force in the Pacific, with a general ignorance of the growing importance of naval aviation.[5] Even as late as 1947, Fleet Admiral Nimitz, CNO, was still writing about postwar control of the Pacific Basin in terms of a "balanced" fleet comprised of a variety of ship types. This viewpoint was consistent with Admiral John Towers's wartime complaints against Nimitz that the latter used aircraft carriers in an overly conservative fashion because of lack of conviction about carrier airpower.[6]

After the summer of 1944, however, when Secretary Forrestal was able to assert his control over the Navy's planning and policymaking bureaucracy, Navy officials began to use the pattern of Pacific War operations to assert that the Navy was not a conservative and obsolete service, but was practicing cutting-edge naval strategy by relying heavily on carrier airpower. In fact, Forrestal was undoubtedly one of the most powerful civilian advocates for the Navy in this context. Diary entries, as well as numerous statements before Congress, illustrate that the pattern of the Pacific War in 1944–1945 and the geographic nature of the region allowed him to argue for a reliance on carrier airpower as the foundation for postwar Pacific Basin defense in particular, and global American naval strategy in general.[7] Forrestal's vision for a postwar defense in the Pacific, in part derived from the JCS, entailed the Navy forming what he called a "defensive wedge" based on "sea-air power."[8] This defensive wedge in the postwar Pacific would supposedly guarantee not only the "freedom" of the Pacific but also American security against any future attacks from East Asia. This security was seen by Forrestal and others as necessary against either a possibly resurgent Japan or a potentially hostile Soviet Union, the latter usually referred to as "any other power" that might oppose US interests in the Pacific and East Asia.[9] Forrestal answered the charge that carrier airpower was vulnerable to land-based air forces by arguing that carrier operations in the Pacific had "overwhelmed" numerous Japanese land-based forces on a number of occasions, even when the Japanese had prior warning of the attacks.[10] Forrestal also used Pacific War events to deflect criticism that the Navy would be useless against a continental enemy like the Soviet Union. For example, Forrestal asserted that the last winter of the Pacific War saw the carrier-based fleet being used more often as a close air-support and defense force for amphibious operations in the Philippines, the Volcanoes, and the Ryukyus. He further pointed out that the fleet regularly struck targets in Japan itself after the Imperial Fleet was destroyed or immobilized. Forrestal used these operations to argue that a naval force could be used against non-naval enemy forces. In doing so, he helped solve wartime planning officers' intellectual dilemmas about American naval forces being employed to project power toward continental peripheries. In addition, he created a mission for the Navy vis-à-vis the Soviet Union, and answered charges that land-based airpower had made navies obsolete.[11]

Navy officials used other aspects of Pacific operations to argue that their service was ideally suited to fulfill the mission of postwar defense in the Pacific Basin. They asserted that carrier airpower in the Pacific was the only means of providing the United States with a mobile tactical air force close to the Eurasian continent.[12] Moreover, the Navy argued that it could carry out vital strategic missions in the Pacific that the AAF could not because of the inherent limitations of land-based aircraft. Navy officials and officers, for instance, believed that a heavy maritime lift capability and a continual presence on the world's oceans guaranteed maritime supremacy to the United States and that maritime supremacy was absolutely necessary for American national security and economic prosperity. Therefore, the physical limitations of land-based airpower in these categories provided evidence for the Navy to argue that the AAF could not fulfill the necessary strategic roles in the postwar Pacific.[13] In addition, the Navy and some of its Congressional allies claimed it had been the only service able to operate "reliable" systems of supply, communications, and surface transportation on a scale necessary to win the Pacific War. The Navy thus believed it would be the only service capable of carrying out these functions and keeping the peace in the Pacific in the future.[14]

Micronesia would play an important role in Forrestal's mobile defensive perimeter concept.[15] Throughout World War II and the Early Cold War, Navy officials and officers, along with those from the other services, argued that Micronesia had to be retained unconditionally by the United States in order to "neutralize" its potential use by any other hostile power. The Navy even implied that the Japanese attack on Pearl Harbor would not have occurred if Micronesia had been under American control.[16] Yet, the Navy's ideas about Micronesia went beyond mere neutralization and defense. As early as 1943 and into the late 1940s, Navy officials and officers claimed that the islands would be absolutely necessary as logistical-support bases for offensive carrier-based forces, which would ensure Japanese acquiescence to postwar American control and contain the Soviet Union in East Asia.[17] Just as

Micronesian bases had been used as fleet anchorages, dry dock and repair facilities, and recreational havens for the wartime Pacific Fleet, so would the tiny islands fulfill the same basic support role for the Navy in the postwar world. Naval Reserve Commander Harold Stassen, Third Fleet Flag Secretary, Aide, and Assistant Chief of Staff for Administration, as well as a US Delegate to the inaugural UN Conference in San Francisco, even argued that bases were as essential for the postwar fleet as guns and ships.[18]

Stassen's statement, of course, has to be tempered with views put forth by more senior figures, such as Forrestal or Towers, who for strategic and fiscal reasons did not want to develop a large number of bases, but wanted to keep shore facilities in the Pacific to a minimum.[19] Other than developing a few bases throughout the Pacific, officials and officers like Forrestal and Towers wanted to devote scarce resources to a mobile carrier fleet and thus illustrate that the Navy was not nearly as dependent on shore support as was the AAF.[20] Still, Stassen's statement about the bases being important does have to be taken into account, even if he exaggerated what the admirals were saying. Moreover, in spite of some of these differences of opinion about emphasis in the postwar naval defense of the Pacific, Navy officials and officers uniformly asserted that their service was ideally suited to patrol the vast expanse of the Pacific Basin in the postwar era because of its familiarity with the region, the area's obvious maritime nature, and the Navy's alleged ability to conduct sustained, mobile operations at sea with minimal shore base support. The Navy was not being entirely honest, of course, in its assertions about strategic or logistical independence. The Pacific War is replete with examples of senior naval officers showing significant reluctance to expose naval forces, especially aircraft carriers, to concentrations of land-based enemy air forces for long periods of time. In addition, the Navy needed quite a large shore establishment to support its operations. Nevertheless, the Navy hoped that it had constructed a sufficient strategic argument to oppose the one put forward by the AAF.[21]

■ A Useable History

Like the AAF, the Navy searched for a useable history by which to justify its postwar position. As numerous primary sources indicate, the Pacific War served as this useable history. Notations from Secretary Forrestal's diaries in November 1944 illuminate wartime issues between the two services that were used by the Navy to justify its position on the postwar defense of the Pacific Basin. Looking at some of the reasons for the Japanese success at Pearl Harbor, for example, Forrestal focused to some extent on the lack of unity of command in Oahu, especially the failure to hold daily meetings even during days of rising tensions. He was willing to blame the Navy for failing to study the British carrier strike on the Italian Fleet at

Taranto in 1940, as well as what was (in his opinion) the focus of then CNO Admiral Harold Stark on "excessive detail," to the detriment of a larger picture of the events. He was even willing to admit that the Navy had been skeptical about the Japanese being able to carry out such a strike in the first place. Forrestal then noted what he thought was the main point in the Pearl Harbor controversy: the superior ability of carrier forces to strike land targets. In an argument that would become almost formulaic immediately after the war, Forrestal argued that the mobility of carrier forces was the key to avoiding detection, surprising the enemy, and even defeating an enemy that had detected the carrier force. Employing a useable history very similar to the AAF's—with the exception of replacing carrier-based forces with land-based ones—Forrestal asserted that "this war has proved that any carrier strike when pressed home with resolution is almost impossible to deflect." He further emphasized "our carrier operations in the Pacific, particularly Admiral Mitscher's strikes in the Marianas last winter when he was picked up 24 hours before reaching his target."[22]

Forrestal continued this line of thinking in another diary entry in January 1945. He noted his belief that the Army conception of strategy was "conditioned" by operations on land, and that the Army did not view operations from the same "global" perspective as did the Navy. In addition, he did not think that the Army understood the extent to which naval operations were dictated by distance, long sea lines of communication, and the vulnerability of those lines of communication to enemy attack. This rather "limited" perspective on the part of the Army supposedly came into play during the attack on Guadalcanal. Asserting that Guadalcanal was the pivotal battle of the entire Pacific War, Forrestal intimated that the Navy had had to insist on the attack because of the Army's limited understanding of naval operations.[23] Along this same line of thought about the naval predominance of the Pacific War, in April 1945, Forrestal returned to the theme that the Navy was the key determinant of power in the postwar Pacific. Answering questions from Representative Albert Thomas of Texas during House hearings on Fiscal Year (FY) 1946 Navy appropriations, Forrestal pointed out that the United States would "wind up this war with the greatest aggregation of naval power, and naval power is the determinant of Pacific power."[24] In similar appropriations hearings before the Senate, Forrestal again elaborated on Pacific War events to demonstrate the postwar efficacy of carrier airpower. Asking the rhetorical question of whether or not "sea-air power" could cope with land-based airpower, Forrestal asserted that the answer was "obvious," that carrier-based airpower could "cope" with land-based air and would be able to defeat it into the near future. Speaking in May 1945 as the final campaigns of the Pacific War still raged, Forrestal also claimed that although land-based Japanese airpower had not yet been defeated, the Navy was "literally fighting the Japanese land-based air force for superiority in the air over Japan's islands," that American carrier-based airpower had specifically been used to "knock out or pin down" Japanese land-based airpower around American targets, and that this use of naval airpower was "unique" in the history of war. More specifically, Forrestal said that up to this point in the Pacific War, the United States had not controlled sufficient land areas to deploy a large land-based air force. To Forrestal, therefore, because of the necessity of Pacific Basin geography, the campaign became one of American carrier-based airpower versus Japanese land-based airpower. Forrestal thought that the proof was in the pudding as he recalled that in both the Marianas and Philippine campaigns—as well as earlier ones—American carrier forces had to go up against large Japanese land-based air forces and "beat" them down before each amphibious landing began. It was, in Forrestal's thinking, the carrier-based forces that caused so much destruction and loss to Japanese air forces, and it was clear to him that the US Navy won "this battle of sea-based air against land-based air."[25]

The Pacific War also was used significantly by John Sullivan, Assistant Secretary of the Navy for Air, in a radio broadcast in late August 1945. Sullivan, speaking on a show entitled "Navy Hour," said that the major striking force of the fleet was the carrier force, and that every "major fleet engagement in the Pacific was fought almost exclusively by carrier aircraft." Sullivan then went into detail about the number of Japanese ships and planes destroyed by American carrier aircraft in the Pacific War. Sullivan was quick to point out that he was not "unmindful" of the "obvious" contributions by the non-aviation branches of the Navy, as well as the Army and Army Air Forces, in defeating Japan. Still, he thought "it must be obvious that without Naval Aviation our fleet would not be in Tokyo Bay tonight or our Army of occupation landing in Japan this week." Thinking about the postwar period, he asserted that America must realize that to dominate the Pacific in the interests of peace, an ever-alert, highly mobile naval force had to be maintained. This well-maintained, powerful, mobile American naval task force, he thought, would be the best and least expensive way to keep the postwar peace.[26]

A few weeks later, in another radio address that was clearly intended to downplay the role of land-based atomic airpower as the nation's future defense, Sullivan emphasized the combined-arms aspects of the US defeat of Japan. However, he was quick to note that the "giant bombers" of the Army Air Forces were only able to pound Japan because the Army, Navy, Marines, and Coast Guard took islands in the Marianas, the Volcanoes, and the Ryukyus that could be turned into air bases. His emphasis on "teamwork" in taking control of air and naval bases closer to Japan was most likely meant to dissuade the public from accepting the AAF's idea that land-based airpower had single-handedly ended the war in the United States' favor. Sullivan then directed attention to the Navy's "big gun," the aircraft carrier. Reemphasizing its high degree of mobility and denying the idea that land-based airpower had made the aircraft carrier obsolete, Sullivan went into a long rendition of how the "Japs" had quite a few "unsinkable" aircraft carriers, i.e., island bases, in places such as Truk, Rabaul, and Formosa. However, he pointed out that the Japanese soon discovered that because of mobile carrier airpower, those unsinkable but also immobile island bases could be highly vulnerable to attack, invasion, or neutralization. Sullivan was willing to admit that in a future war, the carrier, or what he called the "head man" of the Pacific War, might not have the leading role. But he wanted it noted that in the Pacific War, the aircraft carrier was definitely the deciding factor because of the geographical limitations on land-based airpower and because of logistics. Sullivan spoke of the day when aircraft could conquer the distances of Pacific geography in the same way that carrier airpower had done, but he wanted the audience to understand that that day had not yet arrived, and that carrier-based airpower in places like the Pacific Basin was not yet finished. Again returning to the idea that no one knew what the future would bring, Sullivan argued that the Pacific War was a guide to the future. He was willing to talk about combined-arms warfare, such as the contributions of the battleships in the Battle of Leyte Gulf, the need for well-trained ground forces, the achievements of the AAF's "huge bombers," and the technological and logistical aspects of the war such as radar, the atomic bomb, and oil. In his final paragraph, however, Sullivan returned to naval aviation, especially carrier-based aviation, as one key to victory. To Sullivan, the Pacific War "proved" that the United States "could build carrier-based planes which could whip anything the Japs could put into the air." Interestingly, he also changed his focus toward the end of the speech when he asserted that the talent of American naval personnel in the Pacific War was the true key to victory. To Sullivan, "the thing which really made it possible for the Navy to establish its remarkable record in the air was the American Youth whose magnificent courage, skill and belief in himself proved more than the Japs could overcome."[27]

Not surprisingly, the House Committee on Naval Affairs echoed these ideas about the Navy and the Pacific Basin. In hearings that were included in the August 1945 report by the Committee's Subcommittee on Pacific Bases, Representative Carl Vinson of Georgia, Chairman of the Committee, supported Navy positions on taking the lead in postwar Pacific Basin defense by asserting that the Pacific War was "predominantly naval." While Vinson was willing to give some credit to the other Allied Powers, the Army, and the AAF, it was clear to him, just as it was to Sullivan, that the "defeat of Japan was predominantly an American Navy victory." In fact, in a tactic highly similar to AAF claims that the Japanese surrender came about primarily because of strategic bombing, Vinson claimed American naval power had brought Japan "to its knees" and made an invasion of the Japanese Home Islands unnecessary. Additionally warning that the "noble intentions" of international charters and treaties could not keep the peace, Vinson asserted that a strong postwar US Navy was needed. Vinson then quoted several senior American naval officers, including Admiral William Halsey, Commander of the Third Fleet; Admiral Raymond Spruance, Commander of the Fifth Fleet; Admiral Richmond Turner, Commander of

Pacific Fleet Amphibious Forces (COMPHIBSPAC); and the late Admiral John Mc-Cain, wartime Commander of the Second Fast Carrier Task Force, Pacific, all of whom thanked the Committee for the "tremendous" appropriations that were given to the Navy by Congress during the war and that allowed the Navy to defeat Japan.[28] In speaking to the same Committee, Forrestal also reiterated familiar themes about the need for a combined-arms naval force in the postwar world that would consist of air, surface, subsurface, and amphibious forces. However, carrier-based airpower came in for special attention. Again using the Pacific War as his example, Forrestal claimed that the carrier task forces were the "spearheads" of the attack against Japan. Asserting that the carrier task forces were a unique creation of the United States, he argued that their special mobility and striking reach could ensure the postwar peace in the Pacific and elsewhere, especially if backed by the other elements of the nation's maritime forces.[29]

At times, professional naval journals also communicated ideas about the Navy's postwar position in the Pacific, and how the Pacific War justified various concepts about naval developments. The United States Naval Institute's journal *Proceedings*, while not an official Navy Department document, had nevertheless been a semi-official outlet for the Navy since the journal's inception in the 1870s. In October 1945, former Navy Commander Harry Knox, as well as retired Rear Admirals Frederic Harris and Husband Kimmel, all focused on points that Forrestal and Sullivan had discussed. According to these officers, the war demonstrated that it was not possible to provide for land-based defenses that could withstand the concentrated power of a modern fleet, especially given the mobility of modern fleets. Knox, Harris, and Kimmel then stressed how vital air coverage for the Pacific Island landings had been in the war, and how obviously important carrier airpower had been in providing this coverage for extended periods of time until land-based airfields had been established. No doubt, this history demonstrated to these officers that even with longer-range bombers, the need for naval bases in the Pacific Islands would continue, and carrier airpower would not be made obsolete because of Pacific Basin geographical distances. While Knox, Harris, and Kimmel did not think that all of the islands conquered from Japan or used as bases during the war should be made into postwar bases, they did argue that there had to be a sufficient number to support mobile fleet forces and the afloat supply train. The rest, they thought, should be occupied so as to be denied to potential enemy powers.[30]

Along similar lines, Assistant Secretary Sullivan again gave the Navy the lion's share of victory in the Pacific War in an October 1945 Navy Day speech to the District of Columbia Council of the Navy League. Sullivan first talked about the war as the "greatest naval struggle in the history of mankind." By talking about the Pacific War, and even World War II in general, as a predominantly sea-power conflict and then asserting that victory rested with the Navy, Sullivan was returning to his earlier theme that the Navy was the key service in the conflict. Again paying compliments

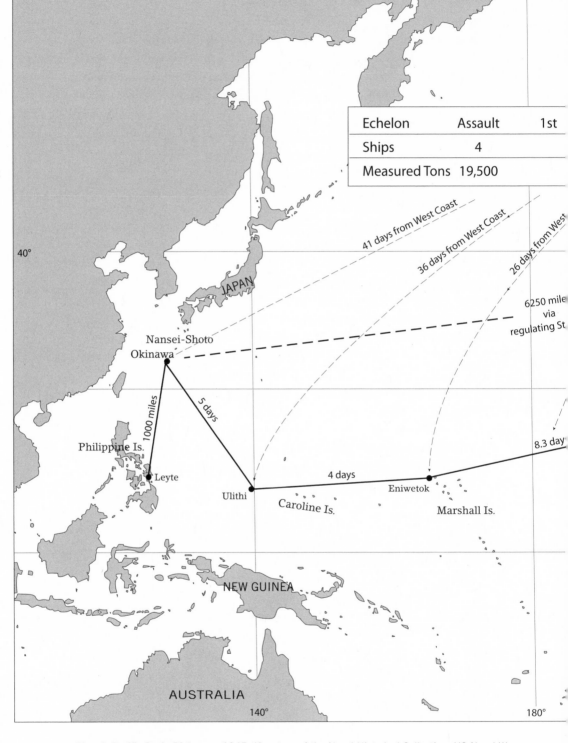

Echelon	Assault	1st
Ships	4	
Measured Tons	19,500	

40°

41 days from West Coast

36 days from West Coast

26 days from West

6250 mile
via
regulating St

JAPAN

Nansei-Shoto
Okinawa

1000 miles

5 days

Philippine Is.

Leyte

Ulithi

Caroline Is.

4 days

Eniwetok

8.3 day

Marshall Is.

NEW GUINEA

AUSTRALIA

140°

180°

Map 4. Pacific Basin Distances, 1945. (Courtesy of the Naval Historical Collection, US Naval War College, Newport, Rhode Island.)

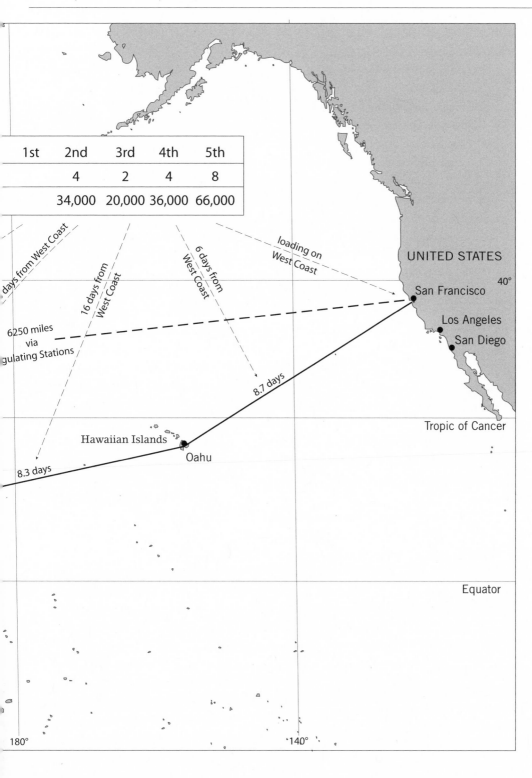

1st	2nd	3rd	4th	5th
4	2	4	8
	34,000	20,000	36,000	66,000

to Navy personnel as the "real" secret weapon of the US arsenal, Sullivan did pay tribute to the Army as the Navy's "partner" in victory over Japan, though this tribute did not come until the second page of the speech, well after the thesis about the Navy was clearly stated. Sullivan also paid tribute to the various branches within the Navy, mentioning naval aviation first, then surface and subsurface forces, and finally the Marines and Coast Guard. While he was willing to see victory in the Pacific as one of combined-arms naval warfare, he nevertheless asserted his thought that the Pacific War victory was essentially one of naval airpower. Apparently, all others were merely support. Along this line of thought, Sullivan saw carrier forces as the key force component, from the Japanese strike on Pearl Harbor to the decisive Battle of Midway and then the island-hopping campaign across the Pacific. Supposedly, it was carrier airpower that finished the Japanese base at Rabaul, flanked New Guinea, helped set the stage for the invasion of the Philippines, and made the Japanese so vulnerable to eventual land invasion in the Central and Western Pacific. For this reason, Sullivan thought the future of the Navy would continue to be embodied by what he called "air-sea power." Nor did Sullivan see the atomic bomb or "push button" warfare replacing the Navy or creating a radically different kind of mechanized warfare in the near future. According to Sullivan, even an atomic bomb–laden plane or guided missile must launch from some platform. The implication here was that the platform, in a Pacific Basin setting, must either be a carrier, a surface ship protected by carrier airpower, or an island made secure by a roving, mobile carrier fleet. Moreover, he was absolutely opposed to the idea of a unified department of national defense because of the alleged lack of ability of one officer from any of the services to be able to command combined-arms ground, air, and naval forces. In addition, Sullivan thought that World War II demonstrated that the Army should be reduced in size—as it had always been after a major war—and that the Navy would continue to be the nation's first line of defense. Moreover, he thought that the interwar period had demonstrated that "peace at any price" was an illusion, that enjoying peace meant being prepared for war, and that peace for the United States meant having a Navy that would be "capable of snuffing out any threat against the just and enduring peace for which the entire world yearns."[31]

Retired Captain Kenneth McIntosh, Officer-in-Charge (OINC) of Navy Supply Corps School–Boston, also used Pacific War history in a November 1945 *Proceedings* article to argue against creating a separate air force. Like so many of his fellow naval officers, McIntosh talked about coordination rather than unification between the armed services as a way to achieve a more efficient unity of command. He claimed that postwar unification, by "pulling" the air forces out of both the Army and Navy, was unnecessary since the war had "demonstrated" that coordination was successfully implemented by the senior officers in each service. McIntosh further claimed that withdrawing airpower from each service to create a third branch would create an air force that knew little to nothing about ground and sea operations. In addition, he thought that such a situation would create an Army and Navy bereft of air-operations expertise. His wartime example was that ground, air, and naval forces had all been present at the British base at Singapore, but that since there was no coordination of command, the Japanese invasion had not been stopped. McIntosh also asserted that "real" historical evidence could be found in the Japanese success in sinking HMS *Prince of Wales* and HMS *Repulse* because of a lack of Allied air cover for these capital ships.[32] Of course, what McIntosh failed to mention is that *Prince of Wales* and *Repulse* were sunk by land-based Japanese "Betty" bombers, not the carrier airpower that McIntosh thought was so vital!

In November 1945, Captain Arleigh Burke, Director of Research and Development in the Navy's Bureau of Ordnance, also employed a useable history of the Pacific War, though with a less parochial emphasis than the interservice rivalry focused on by such figures as Forrestal and Sullivan. Burke communicated his ideas about Navy cooperation with universities for postwar research to Dr. Merle Tuve, Director of the Applied Physics Laboratory at Johns Hopkins University. Burke talked about the Navy's recognition that "wars occur fast and without warning." "Looking back at the war just completed," Burke asserted that there had been many warnings and indications of the beginning of the war. However, he thought that the United States was "notoriously" slow in recognizing what he called the "symptoms" of war, and that the United States had twice been saved from "catastrophe" by its allies. Moreover, Burke was sure that the next war would be much like the last one, in which the Navy had had to fight with whatever weapons it had at the beginning of the war. He pointed out that "[the] Japanese were stopped and turned back with weapons developed before the war by the armed services." According to Burke, the Battle of Guadalcanal, as well as the preceding battles, "were fought with 5"/.38 guns, with time fuzes, with peace-time torpedoes, and with fire control systems which had been developed around '36 and '37." In addition, he asserted that the Japanese were driven from the Solomon Islands, New Guinea, the Marshalls, and the Gilberts with "old weapons." While these assertions might appear to be evidence that the older weapons would have resulted in a Pacific War victory for the United States anyway, Burke nevertheless painted a picture in which weapons were only effective enough to hold off the Japanese and buy time until new "weapons and ideas" were developed. If the United States had waited for the new weapons, "there would never have been an opportunity to use those weapons or ideas. We would have been destroyed first." All the more reason, to Burke, to have a cutting-edge postwar research program so that the Navy would be ready to deploy anywhere in the world on a moment's notice with the weapons necessary for victory already on hand. To Burke, this conception was particularly important in an atomic age.[33]

Forrestal employed Pacific War history again when he testified before the House Appropriations Committee in March 1946. When asked by Representative Thomas about placing too much emphasis on the maintenance of shore stations and not enough on active fleet operations, Forrestal told Thomas that the two "marched" together. Pointing out that the whole "spirit" of the Navy was to keep shore stations to a minimum, he also asserted that these bases were necessary to a certain point. "The success of the American Fleet compared with what the British Fleet could have done in the Western Pacific was largely determined by the fact that . . . [the American] fleet was backed up by a tremendous amount of stuff on shore." Forrestal continued that the British Fleet was "pinned" to its bases because of the British naval philosophy of never being more than 1,000 miles from a base. According to Forrestal, the US Pacific Fleet had to operate over 6,000 miles from its bases in some cases, and in one instance it had a task force at sea for ninety days. Asked rhetorically by Thomas if the Navy essentially carried its own bases with it, Forrestal answered in the affirmative and then elaborated on how vital mobile logistics trains had been. In addition, Forrestal thought that the Navy's system of maintaining a "pipeline" of materials to its ships had revolutionized naval warfare. "This war would still be going on if we had not developed what you might call . . . mobile logistics—the supply, the removal of the wounded, the transfer of ammunition and personnel at sea, going 15 to 16 knots."[34]

In a fashion very similar to Forrestal's, Commander Russell Smith, Seventh Fleet Flag Secretary, talked in an April 1946 *Proceedings* article about American carriers performing a new and unique role in the history of modern war—namely, "that of bombarding the enemy coast line and destroying his industries." The Navy's ability to do this apparently convinced Smith "that the Navy is not a static force any more than are the Army and the Air Forces." Smith also paid close attention to bases in the Pacific and the lessons that he thought should have been learned from the interwar and early wartime years. According to Smith, Japan's control of island chains such as Micronesia allowed it to launch its early attacks against the United States and its allies, as well as put up an effective defense against the US advance until the Battle of Guadalcanal. According to Smith, "the greater portion of our Pacific effort was spent in the slow but steady process of regaining by combat those island bastions so long renounced and lost by a foolish diplomacy." Continuing this criticism of the McKinley, Wilson, and Harding Administrations' foreign policies vis-à-vis the US control of Micronesia, Smith went on to criticize the United States' failure to more closely supervise the Japanese "fortification" of Micronesia in the interwar period. In addition, he found fault with Congressional reluctance to more adequately fortify US bases such as Guam. This led to "an inevitable result—a fundamentally weak Pacific tenure which should have been fundamentally strong and secure." Moreover, he thought that such a "basic misconception" of national defense should never again be allowed to happen. To Smith, the methods of future warfare dictated US control over advanced base locations so that any enemy force could be detected early on. He also thought that these advanced regions should be patrolled by "seagoing naval groups." This combination of bases and mobile forces in places like the postwar Pacific would supposedly "make our national defense problems of the future much easier."[35]

The Pacific War was also employed as a useable history by the Navy's ranking officer in late May 1946 Congressional hearings. Testifying before the Subcommittee to the Senate Appropriations Committee for the FY 1947 budget, Fleet Admiral Nimitz, CNO, brought up wartime Pacific operations in order to justify current naval-force funding levels. Asked what the future role of naval forces would be, he asserted that carrier air forces were the only means of providing a "highly effective and mobile" tactical air force at sea. Nimitz also stated that the carrier task forces were the only forces able to provide this tactical air force in coastal areas "distant from our own prepared air bases," and that these carrier forces could "serve as a striking force for the destruction of Pacific targets."[36] In the same vein of mobile forces and base development in the postwar Pacific, Captain John Kennaday, Fifth Naval District Director of Welfare, asserted in a June 1946 *Proceedings* article that Pacific War history demonstrated how the Navy should view shore bases versus mobile forces. According to Kennaday, a "great truth demonstrated again and again by the war in the Pacific is that bases by themselves—without mobile, aggressive forces operating from them—might just as well be the barren atolls which many of them once were." Kennaday thought it vital that the general public understand that bases such as Singapore, Pearl Harbor, Manila, or Truk were quite easily bypassed by mobile forces. He also thought it was important to understand that those locations lost to enemy forces were not conquered because of the weaknesses of the bases themselves, but because of the weaknesses of the mobile forces operating from them. According to Kennaday, the key defense was a mobile fleet, with an emphasis on a mobile train and floating facilities that could supply the fleet adequately enough so that it would not have to depend too heavily on shore installations. Kennaday saw Pacific War operations justifying a reconception of advanced bases from shore facilities to floating facilities. He asserted that shore-based facilities were not only too vulnerable to attack, but that they had also too often been left behind by rapidly advancing American forces during the war. Moreover, he asserted that shore-based facilities contributed to what he called "dead time," or time that naval forces had to spend far from the theater of operations just transiting to and from the shore bases. Citing fleet operations with floating facilities in battles around Ulithi Atoll and Okinawa as his evidence, Kennaday said that the Navy's next war, especially in an area as vast as the Western Pacific, should focus on a mobile fleet with a large afloat train and minimal shore facilities. In his view, properly advanced bases were those that were afloat and mobile, and these had contributed "indispensably" to the United States winning the Pacific War. In conclusion, he thought that the Pacific War should have made the idea of a fleet that was largely autonomous from shore establishments "axiomatic."[37]

John Sullivan, now Under Secretary of the Navy, returned in late October 1946 to some of his earlier themes about the central role of sea power at a Navy League dinner in Cleveland, Ohio. Considering his audience, Sullivan—not surprisingly—again placed the Navy in such a central wartime role as to nearly exclude the Army and AAF. For instance, in praising the American people for the hard work they did in the war, Sullivan asserted that "without them, the Navy would not have been able to come back to win mastery of all the seas and eventually force the unconditional surrender of our final enemy aboard the mighty *Missouri* in Tokyo Bay." Continuing with earlier themes about the United States concluding the "greatest" naval struggle in the history of mankind, Sullivan talked about the contributions of the officers and men to this "biggest and . . . best concentration of air-sea power the world has ever known." Briefly talking about how the victory was one of combined arms, and devoting a couple of paragraphs to the Army, Sullivan nevertheless came back to the idea that sea power "alone opens the door to mobile strategy which . . . made possible our assaults in the South Pacific . . . [and] in the Philippines." Sullivan denied that atomic bombs had made American naval forces obsolete. He talked about the need for changes, but still insisted that "security and protection . . . can be guaranteed only by air-sea power competent to control our adjacent oceans." In addition, he thought that sea power was especially critical whenever supplies had to be "seaborne." As historical evidence for the future, Sullivan cited the past, particularly the Navy's interception of essential raw materials going to Japanese military forces in the Pacific, and to Japan itself. He continued this theme of giving the major credit for victory to the Navy, alleging that the flexibility of General MacArthur's island-hopping operations in New Guinea, Borneo, and the Philippines were due solely to American naval power. According to Sullivan, it was "sea-power which brought them [MacArthur's forces] respectively across each ocean, and it was sea-power which made the same American armies effective against wholly different and immobile enemy forces."[38]

Vice Admiral Forrest Sherman, DCNO for Operations and Nimitz's strategic brain trust when it came to postwar naval policy, also employed the Pacific War as useable history in an address to the National War College in late February 1947. In the address, entitled "Problems of Unified Command," Sherman not only discussed the main topic, but how he thought it was demonstrated during the Pacific War. First, Sherman warned against too strict boundaries being drawn between the newly created Pacific and Far East Commands. According to him, "lines drawn in the ocean by the Combined Chiefs of Staff sitting in Washington in January 1943 were fine as guides but they had to be varied when it came to actual operations." Given this need for flexibility during war, he found that in "peacetime there is no point at all in trying to draw precise lines in the ocean." When discussing what these newly unified commands were really supposed to do from a naval perspective, Sherman noted Admiral Towers's Pacific Command as an example of a joint staff patterned on that of the JCS, having Towers as the nominal chair with air, ground, and naval commanders under him. Sherman also pointed to Major General Howard Craig, now the

Commander-in-Chief of the Alaskan Command (CINCAL), who developed a "fully integrated" joint staff, including a naval officer as his deputy. Sherman said that General MacArthur, as CINCFE, was, for the most part, continuing his wartime organization in occupied Japan since he had primarily ground forces under him. But Sherman also pointed out that MacArthur had a "Joint Planning Group" with representation from both naval and air forces. Sherman argued that the more closely integrated a joint staff was, the better suited it was for operations.[39]

Noting that none of the unified commands was yet approaching this level of expertise, Sherman also asserted that one matter being widely discussed was at what level of command unification ought to take place. Citing MacArthur's wartime Southwest Pacific Area command, Sherman thought that MacArthur himself had been the truly integrating factor, and that the Central Pacific had predominantly been a naval operation. According to Sherman, this lack of unified command had serious implications for the command and control of US forces during the Japanese attacks on US forces at Guadalcanal in late 1942. He thought that problems of a unified command at Guadalcanal influenced Admiral Nimitz so strongly that Nimitz subsequently created a "very tightly" integrated command structure for the invasion of the Gilberts. This organization apparently entailed a particularly "well-organized" local command arrangement so that all parties knew who was in charge if there were enemy counterattacks. Moreover, Sherman asserted that this type of highly integrated command structure, with Nimitz at the top, was repeated effectively in the invasion of the Marshall Islands, and that these integrated commands were only "loosened" once forces were ashore and the local Japanese presence had significantly subsided.[40]

Sherman was convinced that MacArthur's organization of separate ground, naval, and air forces reporting to him but not commanded by him in any great detail was well suited to the offense. Because of his own Central Pacific experiences, however, Sherman was concerned that local command had to be unified for defensive purposes. Ultimately, in a remark clearly meant for the AAF, he said he did not think it was sufficient to decide on one solution for all strategic and tactical situations. In his mind, "one of the problems of unified command is how to reconcile those two conflicting considerations and to be sure of the flexibility that is necessary." Sherman also noted grievances during the Pacific War when officers claimed that the flow of necessary supplies and the method of operations in unified commands might have gone faster or been more effective if the overall command in question had been led by an officer from the parent service. Sherman thought the war demonstrated that what was really needed was good leadership. By good leadership, he meant an officer who could not just command, but discuss, persuade, and lead by example, much as Sherman saw the JCS operating during the war. To Sherman—and to a significant part of the Navy—true unification was not something that could be legislated or ordered: it had to come from coordination, cooperation, and professional leadership, and that is what he thought had happened in the late war. Sherman concluded by re-iterating that such leadership had to start at the JCS level, and that the wartime JCS organization had to be copied in all of the newly created unified commands.[41]

However, not every officer in the Navy subscribed to these ideas of interservice coordination or naval predominance. One account provides historians with an important example of how the Navy leadership's perspective was not internalized at all levels by all personnel. In early July 1947, there was a fascinating and seemingly out-of-place call by a career naval aviator for the creation of a separate United States air force, and for that service's control of all US military-aviation assets. Commander Allen Shinn, Commander of Carrier Air Groups, Hampton Roads, Virginia, and the Atlantic Fleet's Fleet Airborne Electronics Training Unit, claimed that he spoke for a large number of junior and mid-level naval aviators in calling for the separation of all aviation assets from the Army and Navy, and their inclusion in a new US Air Force. While most of Shinn's essay dealt with what he saw as the prejudice and ignorance of the surface Navy toward naval aviation, he employed the Pacific War as evidence to justify his ideas. Specifically, Shinn focused on the conduct of Japanese aviation forces in the Pacific War. Arguing that the unification of aviation into one service did not necessarily mean the death of naval aviation, Shinn asked what might have happened if the Japanese Army Air Force (JAAF) and the Japanese Naval Air Force (JNAF) had concentrated their assets into carrier airpower. Answering his own rhetorical question, Shinn asserted that Japanese carrier air assets would have been sufficient to "wipe out" the United States' "slender margin" in carrier airpower in the Pacific in 1942. Shinn acknowledged the negative impact on morale and effectiveness that the postwar unification fight between the US Army and Navy was having on the services, but he again did this in a unique way. Arguing that competition could become rivalry, he warned about a "healthy competition" between the Army and Navy "degenerating" into unhealthy rivalry. He saw just such a rivalry impeding Japanese airpower during the war when the Japanese Army and Navy each controlled separate and competing assets and were infamous for their lack of cooperation. Shinn then asserted that postwar research indicated that the Japanese never had the military assets to beat the United States. Acknowledging that this "semi-industrialized" island nation could not have won the war, he still saw the interservice rivalry between the Japanese Army and Navy as the plague on Japanese strategy from the beginning of the war. According to him, "[the] Japs never could have won the Pacific War." He thought, however, that "they could have made it much more difficult for us to win had they operated an integrated air force managed by professional aviators." Instead of an integrated force, Shinn thought that the Japanese operated "two air forces separately mismanaged by army and navy officers in the partisan interests" of their parent services.[42]

Continuing with this theme and touching on very sensitive interservice issues, such as the control of land-based naval reconnaissance and anti-submarine warfare

(ASW) assets, Shinn again saw lessons in the Japanese war effort. He admitted that the Japanese case demonstrated that integrating air and sea assets into one organization did not ensure "successful cooperation" or successful operations in areas such as amphibious or anti-submarine warfare. According to Shinn, these operations by the Japanese Army and Navy were "notorious." Yet he also argued that the Japanese military demonstrated how poorly it performed, not because of the consolidation of air assets into one organization, but because of the two rival services controlling their own air assets. Shinn thought that it was necessary for the United States to create separate air, ground, and naval organizations staffed by professionals in their own military specialties. Shinn also thought that the American public would eventually realize what he saw as a grossly inefficient use of scarce national-security assets. He thought that naval aviation would be safe for a "few more" years in terms of its public support and funding as long as the "magnificent" achievements of carrier aviation in the Pacific War could be recalled by the public. But he thought this could only be done by the Navy for so long. After that, appropriations for naval aviation would come less often and require more effort. Then, when the nation reached that point, the United States' "naval aeronautical organization" would wither away at great cost to future American national security. Again with the Pacific War in mind, he asserted that the future strategic value of the aircraft carrier was difficult to assess. While its value in the Pacific War was "forcefully" demonstrated, he thought it "hard to imagine, within the foreseeable future, a war in which the carrier could be again the prime instrument that it was fore-destined to be in the Pacific War." Continuing with the idea that Pacific Island bases had actually become the "first priority prizes" of the war, Shinn asserted that the "aircraft carrier is inherently limited by its size and the consequent restrictions on aircraft servicing and operating capacity. Moreover, the aircraft carrier is a very expensive type of landing field."[43]

In complete contrast to Shinn's ideas, and not surprisingly, now Secretary of the Navy Sullivan returned to his earlier themes of Pacific War history in a December 1947 statement to the President's Air Policy Commission. In reference to his previous statements concerning the defensive nature of "sea-air power" Sullivan was now asked about the "offensive side of the house." He answered that in "any war we can now envisage, it would be quite likely that we would face a repetition of the task that was assigned to us in the Pacific on an even greater scale." Sullivan stated that in the Pacific War, the United States was lucky to have "a series of stepping stones . . . which enabled US forces to proceed from one part of the Pacific to another." Similarly, in a future war, "the probabilities are that the initial landings, the battle for the toe-holds, the battle for seaside airstrips, would follow the same pattern that was followed in the Pacific." Thus, to Sullivan, "the chances of success without highly developed carrier task forces, without most proficient amphibious forces, would be very, very negligible in my opinion."[44]

■ Mobile Forces versus Static Bases: The Navy Conception of Postwar Pacific Defense

Like the AAF, the Navy also started to make its position on force deployments in the postwar Pacific, and the composition of those forces, clear before the war was even over. In November 1944, in a position paper entitled "Post-War Naval Bases in the Pacific," Admirals Edwards and Duncan assumed that the control of the Pacific was "primarily a naval problem." Therefore, they also assumed that base locations had to be selected that would best suit naval needs and that would meet "strategic requirements from the Naval viewpoint." While the Admirals contradicted themselves on the next page by asserting that "[P]ost-war military problems should be studied as an integrated whole rather than as separate problems for the ground, naval and air forces," their original assumption was reiterated in the conclusion, where they asserted that "the future U.S. Naval Base system in the Pacific to support the Fleet in exercising control of the Pacific should be determined without delay." Their conclusion was obviously made without any final mention of US forces in the Pacific other than those of the US Navy.[45] In the January 1945 memo cited above, Admiral Horne, VCNO, also established what would be a major tenet of immediate postwar naval policy, that is, an emphasis on a highly mobile fleet with a minimal base system in the postwar Pacific. Horne began by pointing out that naval shore establishments were not necessarily needed at all base site locations requested by the Navy since these would consume personnel and resources that should go to "our main requirement, i.e., a powerful, mobile fleet and an adequate train." Horne saw overdependence on bases to be a "dangerous" concept, since too many advanced bases became a source of weakness unless there was a large, mobile fleet to defend them. Horne wanted US control over vast numbers of islands in the Western Pacific so as to deny them to other nations. While he also wanted international political recognition of the United States' sole right to develop bases at these locations, he thought that the actual number of bases that were to eventually be developed should be kept to a minimum, and that the majority of the Pacific Fleet's needs should be met by mobile fleet trains. Much of this also depended, according to Horne, on the final outcome of the war, and the attitude of Congress and the public toward large outlays of postwar appropriations for the Navy.[46]

Forrestal's formula for postwar Pacific defense came out most clearly in exchanges with Representative Walter Ploesser of Missouri during appropriations hearings in April 1945. Asked what the Navy might require in terms of control over the Pacific Islands, Forrestal confirmed that the Navy thought it absolutely necessary to develop islands such as Guam and Saipan into postwar bases. More importantly, he thought that the key force that could guarantee US defense of the postwar Pacific was the Navy, since this service, "with its sea power and its air power, should form a great, permanent, defensive wedge in the Pacific that will guarantee the freedom of the Pacific and guarantee us against any attack from that source in the future." Fleet Admiral Ernest King, wartime Commander-in-Chief of the US Fleet and Chief of Naval Operations (COMINCH-CNO), also spoke in the same month to the same Senate committee about these matters. King saw the Navy in the key role of maintaining US control over advanced island bases in the Pacific. When asked to describe the role of advanced bases in the Pacific, King asserted that the system of bases that the United States built up during the war was the "bone structure" of US power in the Pacific, whereas the fuel, ammunition, food, repair facilities, hospitals, and recreation facilities at these bases were the "sinews" of war. While King's statement was somewhat contradictory to ideas voiced by Forrestal and other Navy leaders about the efficacy of mobile forces over stationary bases, he made it clear that he thought the Pacific Basin was indeed a naval theater to be defended in the postwar period by American naval forces.[47]

Individual naval officers also communicated ideas which indicated similar postwar conceptions for the United States' defense of the Pacific Basin. While the views of aggressive officers such as Admiral Halsey cannot be taken as typical, neither can they be discounted, given Halsey's solid reputation with Congress, the American public, and large segments of the naval officer corps. In late May 1945, Halsey wrote a long reply to Representative Clifton Woodrum of Virginia, Chairman of the House Select Committee on Post-War Military Policy, who asked for the Admiral's views on postwar American military organization. Halsey not only addressed various aspects of what he thought should be postwar naval policy and force deployment, but indulged in a useable history of his own about postwar Pacific Basin security. Halsey began by asserting that the purpose of war was to secure what he called "decent" peacetime or postwar conditions. However, he complained that the United States had attempted a misplaced experiment in "altruism" after World War I that failed to change human nature. Halsey thought the United States had tried to prevent peace between a "have" nation and a "have-not" nation during the interwar period. No doubt referring to the Washington Treaty System and its alleged failure to prevent war between the United States and Japan, Halsey went on to argue that postwar national military forces had to be strong enough to "preserve our tangible and intangible treasures." This postwar preparation for war included carrying any future war to the enemy's territory. Thus, a navy was needed that was strong enough to "strike and disrupt any enemy sea-air plan before it can be executed." In addition, Halsey saw the need for a US Marine Corps that was strong enough to "spearhead" an "inevitable" US overseas attack. In addition to adequate amphibious forces and a strong aviation component to the Navy, sufficient sea transportation and merchant shipping were also needed. While Halsey also talked about universal military training and a fully equipped Army that was ready to invade enemy territory upon the initiation of hostilities, his plan was primarily naval, and it was overwhelmingly oriented toward the Pacific. Halsey placed great importance on international recognition of US primacy in Pacific affairs. In addition, he wanted the United States to have full and absolute control, i.e., annexation, of any bases in the Pacific it might need, and he did not want the United States to sign a peace treaty with Japan until that nation had learned to play by "decent" international rules. Until then, he saw the need for the United States to keep a "terrier force" at the "rat hole" to keep the Japanese in line! Surprisingly, he saw the need for unified operational control, not just coordination, between the services, even as the Navy called for coordination throughout its inter-service fight with the Army. However, Halsey also thought that unified control had to be in the hands of an American naval officer if US policy in a future war was to carry the conflict overseas to an enemy! Halsey concluded by stating that the nation also needed men with character, wisdom, and training in international political and military affairs to carry out its postwar policy. In conclusion, he thought that if the United States did not have such men, the current expenditure of blood and treasure might be in vain.[48]

Echoing what naval officials and officers were saying, the members of the House Committee on Naval Affairs' Subcommittee on Pacific Bases talked in August 1945 about the United States' need to retain sole control over the Pacific Islands because of its postwar mission of policing the Pacific. Committee members also talked about the necessity of defending the postwar Pacific with mobile carrier forces due to the nature of the region's geography. Pacific geography, as well as the lack of ability to "adequately" defend Pacific atolls with air and ground power be-cause of the small size of the atolls, was emphasized on at least two occasions in the report. These latter points were, of course, outstanding political support for the Navy's position vis-à-vis the AAF.[49] Documents from the Navy's Strategic Plans Di-vision also indicate the service's positions about Pacific Basin deployments and is-sues. In an April 1946 memo to Vice Admiral Sherman, Captain Ephraim McLean, OINC of the Sea Frontiers, Naval Districts, and Bases Sub-Section, discussed the need for the Navy to retain Alaskan bases in Adak, Attu, Kodiak, and Dutch Harbor. McLean was most interested in these bases because of their value as western out-posts vis-à-vis the Soviets, and because of the value of Dutch Harbor as a subma-rine base. McLean then went on to suggest via Rear Admiral Ralph Wood, former Commandant of the Seventeenth Naval District, Commander of the Alaskan Sea Frontier (COMALSEAFRON), and Commander of the Northern Pacific (COMNOR-PAC), that if the Coast Guard could be convinced to take over air-sea rescue in the area, it would be able to utilize Attu and Dutch Harbor for the Navy. McLean admit-ted that JCS approval would be needed for this, but he also claimed that there was a law currently before Congress that would clarify the Coast Guard's role in terms of air-sea rescue operations. Interservice issues also came into play to some degree. McLean stated, for instance, that if the law passed, "the Navy and Coast position will be legally sound vis-a-vis [sic] the Army and Army Air Force."[50] Deployments also figured in late July 1946 in a long analysis of the Soviet threat, conducted by

Nimitz for Truman, entitled "Facts and Information Desired by the President regarding the Soviet Union." Given worsening relations with the USSR, Nimitz thought that it would be prudent to keep US naval forces forward-deployed in both the Atlantic and Pacific. In the Pacific, he thought it to be "essential" in the "present strategic situation" that the United States "maintain an effective carrier striking force in the Western Pacific, capable of early reinforcement and prepared to render direct support to our forces on shore in that region and to cover their evacuation, if required." Nimitz went on to state that adequate "amphibious lift and supporting combatant units for possible evacuation, reinforcement or redeployment of these troops are essential." In addition, claiming that the naval-base system in the Pacific required for these types of operations was already in existence, Nimitz mentioned the necessity of effective "sea-air" anti-submarine operations, since the Navy saw the major Soviet naval threat at this time to be its submarine force. Finally, he saw the need for coordination between the US Navy and the Royal Navy, specifically referring to American use of British naval facilities in the Mediterranean in return for British use of American naval facilities in the Western and South Pacific.[51]

In September 1946, Admiral Towers, CINCPAC-CINCPOA, gave his recommendations to Nimitz for postwar Pacific bases, outlining not only his personal views on the subject but also his philosophy for naval security in the region. Starting with the notion that bases other than Midway, Hawaii, Kodiak, and Guam were of a temporary wartime nature, Towers talked of how expensive these installations were, and how expensive they would be to repair or maintain. Given his ideas that American naval forces in the postwar Pacific should be primarily focused on mobile forces like carrier groups, Towers thought that base requirements boiled down to Pearl Harbor in the Central Pacific, Guam and Saipan in the Western Pacific, and Adak in the Northern Pacific. Towers also thought that the Navy ought to abandon its facilities in the Philippines, with the exception of Subic Bay and Sangley Point. In a diary entry dated the day before the report to Nimitz, Towers wrote of "advanced bases" in the Philippines that were of a temporary nature and deteriorating rapidly, and that would be in need of significant expenditure in the near future. These were funds that Towers thought would be "foolish" to expend. In light of limited funds for base development, he suggested that the entire Leyte-Samar base be abandoned as a signal that the Navy had more bases in the Pacific than it needed, and that it could not afford this base system. Towers then went on to assert that only one base in the Marshall Islands, Kwajalein Atoll, should be maintained, and that only the Okinawa base in the Ryukyus need be retained. In fact, he even thought that non-aviation facilities on Okinawa could be reduced or inactivated. He envisioned the abandonment of Manus Island in the Admiralties as soon as problems with surplus materials had been solved, and he saw the same "closing out" of naval installations at Iwo Jima, Marcus Island, Canton Island, and Palmyra. Midway and Johnston he thought should be in a status the Navy called "reduced operational," while Wake, American

Samoa, Truk, and Palau would be classified as "caretaker status." He further thought that the last two locations should be fleet anchorages in waiting, but with minimal shore facilities. While Towers saw that most of these locations would need American Naval Military Government units for an "indefinite" period of time, he clearly planned on a very stripped-down naval-base and shore-facility system in the Pacific, no doubt so as to give maximum resources to carrier-force deployments.[52] Towers was able to enunciate these ideas to President Truman in a meeting he had with the Chief Executive and Forrestal later that same month when he was in Washington, D.C. Towers used a large globe in Truman's office to point out what he thought US principal and secondary bases in the postwar Pacific ought to be. Including Alaska and the Aleutians in the discussion, and asked by Truman what he thought about the issue of sovereignty over Micronesia and the Ryukyus, Towers spoke of the difficulties the United States had had in "breaking through" those islands to bring the war to the Japanese Home Islands. Pointing out that these islands were of very little economic value, Towers nevertheless reminded Truman that it would be dangerous for the United States to allow any other power to again develop naval or air bases in these island groups. Towers also asserted that it was only the Navy that had objected to Micronesia being "turned over" to the Japanese after World War I. Accordingly, he thought that US acquiescence to the Japanese in 1919 and 1922 was a major factor in Japan deciding to go to war in 1941.[53]

In the same month, another memo from Captain McLean to Rear Admiral Cato Glover, Assistant Chief of Naval Operations (ACNO) for Strategic Plans, indicated some differing ideas between Admiral Towers and the Strategic Plans officers over the Pacific bases that should be retained and the means by which scarce budgetary resources should be spent on base development. Admiral Nimitz gave his approval for a naval withdrawal from all of the installations in the Philippines except for Subic Bay and Sangley Point. However, there was disagreement as to whether Kwajalein or Eniwetok, both in the Marshalls, should be developed. There was also disagreement over the fate of naval installations on another base in the Marshalls, Majuro Atoll, and whether or not the Navy concurred that the AAF should be allowed to operate a base on Johnston Island.[54] Vice Admiral Sherman commented on some of these locations in a memo to Nimitz in late October 1946. Sherman stated that he generally concurred with Towers about Pacific strategic deployments, but he thought there might be a need for certain changes. First, he told Nimitz that non-aviation facilities at Okinawa should be placed in a low readiness status entitled "maintenance" in order to meet Towers's recommendation of "caretaker" status for these facilities. Sherman agreed with Towers's recommendation that Kwajalein be the focus of US Navy postwar activities in the Marshalls, but he wanted Majuro retained as an alternate seadrome and airdrome site. Moreover, Towers had recommended that Johnston Island be retained in "reduced operational" status. Sherman, however, seemed to go further, suggesting that Johnston's Naval Air Station (NAS) be reduced to a Naval Air Facility (NAF), and that the AAF be allowed to operate its units from the island after the necessary construction. Sherman ended the memo by stating that Towers's recommendations—with Sherman's changes noted above—could be implemented as soon as the entire deployment plan received JCS approval.[55] In early November 1946, Towers returned to his idea about a limited base system in the Pacific. Specifically, Towers discussed with Assistant Secretary of the Navy John Kenney and Vice Admiral Robert Carney, DCNO for Logistics, the need to abandon bases in the Philippines such as Leyte-Samar, Mactan, and Puerto Princesa. The main issue was where to base staging points for aircraft of the Naval Air Transport Service (NATS). Towers had wanted to use Kwajalein in the Marshalls, but the Navy went with Majuro Atoll instead. Towers now proposed other arrangements so that these transportation aircraft were only used between Alameda, California, and Honolulu, Hawaii. Towers thought this would allow the Navy to demobilize current operating units at Majuro, Tanapag, and Sangley Point, and effect additional savings in funding.[56]

The Navy's role was also the subject of a conversation between General MacArthur and Admiral Carney in late November 1946. Carney asked MacArthur about the effectiveness of postwar American air, ground, and naval forces in the Western Pacific. Apparently, MacArthur replied that air- and ground-force effectiveness had deteriorated so badly as to make the Navy "the principal armed element of national policy in the Western Pacific," and that the Navy was of great importance to the success of the Japanese Occupation and the diplomatic situation in East Asia. Given MacArthur's strong views on the efficacy of land-based airpower, the General could have been placating Carney with information he thought Carney wanted to hear. MacArthur nevertheless went on to assert that in the event of "trouble" with Russia, he would have to rely on the Navy to "support, reinforce, or extricate forces as might be necessary," since he thought that the Navy would be the "paramount" service in East Asia.[57] A few days later, Carney also wrote to Nimitz about his ideas concerning US naval deployments and base sites in the postwar Pacific. He started out by clearly stating that since V-J Day, the United States' only clear maritime rival in the Pacific had been eliminated. He also said that no single power or combination of powers in the Pacific could exert maritime pressure on the United States except by air operations, submarine operations, or infiltration of a nature that "could scarcely be of major character." The main maritime threat Carney envisioned was pressure "radiating" from Northeast Asia in the form of air and submarine operations against "US holdings" or the Philippines. Carney, however, did not think that this pressure would materialize into a threat of territorial seizure in the immediate future, at least not until the Soviet Union became a maritime power. Therefore, according to Carney, the missions of the Navy boiled down to attacks on selected targets by means of strategic bombing. In addition, Carney thought it would be necessary to provide forces for "minimal" amphibious lift, evacuation, shore bombardment, and air attack. US submarine operations would take place, but also in a limited fashion because of the scarcity of targets and the "non-maritime" nature of the Asian "political entities."[58]

Carney went on to explain the need for the Navy to help in the suppression of "fifth column" activities, to conduct ASW, to provide for the air defense of US territory, and to police occupied areas and trusteeships. Strangely not emphasizing the mobile forces so prevalent in the assessments of other officers such as Towers, Carney devoted most of his analysis to outlining the base network he thought would be necessary to carry out Navy responsibilities in the Western Pacific and East Asia. Carney talked about the United States needing "adequate" holdings and rights to maintain essential "air movement" in the Pacific. This statement no doubt referred to the US military's ideas of annexing Micronesia, the Bonins, the Volcanoes, Marcus Island, and the Ryukyus in order to create an integrated strategic physical complex out of those locations. Pearl Harbor was mentioned early on in the report, but Carney talked about the possibility of reducing the facilities there. He was convinced that there would never again be wartime operations in the area on the scale of the Pacific War that would require the Navy to use Pearl Harbor as it had been employed between 1941 and 1945. The Philippines, however, was to be a major base complex. Still, Carney wanted to consolidate naval facilities around Subic Bay, retain Sangley Point for transient aircraft only, retain Samar and Tawi-Tawi for anchorage rights only, and merely retain construction rights at Mactan in the event of future hostilities.[59]

In Okinawa, Carney sought the cooperative use of Army and AAF facilities in order to practice strict economy, and he thought that the US Seventh Fleet should continue to be forward-based at Tsingtao, China, for "as long as possible." He also thought that the Navy should retain a presence in Shanghai, but on a minimal scale, and he thought it vital that the Navy stay in Yokosuka, Japan, in order to avoid what he thought would be a dangerous military and political vacuum. In addition, Carney thought that a large US naval base in Yokosuka would assist SCAP in terms of keeping large numbers of Japanese gainfully employed. Carney next asserted that the present facilities in Alaska appeared adequate and not too "plush." With regard to the Carolines and Marshalls, he thought these islands should be occupied by US Naval Military Government units and "token" naval forces on a continuing basis. To Carney, an American presence was required in these islands so as to ensure the United States would be able to continue deployments in those waters and not be "placed in the future in any such position as confronted us in 1941." He focused on Truk in particular as an ideal location because of its large landmass for shore installations, as well as its anchorage of "sufficient size" for egress of large mobile forces. These were factors that he thought should not be ignored in future planning. Carney wanted Nimitz to consider Truk as a replacement for Guam. While earlier in the report, Carney had mentioned Guam as a major base site, he did not think that Guam lent itself as a "haven" for mobile forces. He reminded Nimitz that this was why the Navy had had to employ Ulithi Atoll in the Carolines as an anchorage during the war. In addition, Carney focused on what he saw as a future need to disperse American naval forces because of the operational impact of the atomic bomb. Acknowledging that Truk was "somewhat further removed from any likely scene of operations," he still thought Truk should be kept in mind as a potential replacement for Guam because of its distance, and the advantage of that distance in terms of "passive defense" against atomic weapons.[60]

The idea of abandoning US naval bases at numerous locations throughout the Pacific Basin, however, did not always go over well with civilian officials. Towers had to defend his idea of a reduced postwar Pacific naval-base system to Representative Edouard Izac of California, Chairman of the House Naval Affairs Committee's Subcommittee on Pacific Bases. Izac "deplored" the idea of the Navy abandoning so many of the bases. Towers, however, pointed out the problem of finding personnel and funds for all of those bases, and he asked Izac to be specific about the various locations that concerned him. Apparently, Izac was under the false impression that the Navy was abandoning the base at Subic Bay—which Towers corrected him on—and even Izac did not think the Navy should retain bases in the Leyte-Samar area. Izac also thought little of developing bases in areas like Tawi-Tawi. Towers emphasized to Izac that the Navy had reserved rights in the Philippines for various base locations, but that for now these bases were unneeded and the Navy thought the scarce funds would be better spent elsewhere. When Izac reported on the dilapidated condition of the temporary bases on Okinawa and the fact that the Army was beginning a permanent construction program at its facilities there, Towers replied that the issue of sovereignty over Okinawa had to be determined first. Even then, Towers did not think the United States needed a long-term base there. In response to one of Izac's questions about the base at Midway, Towers thought it would be "of little strategic value" as long as the United States held the Marianas. In addition, Towers said that he was not prepared to put any of his limited funds there, and he did not think the Navy should subsidize the building of commercial airfields in locations such as Midway. Izac agreed with the Admiral on that last point. Towers next cleared up another misunderstanding of Izac's, this one concerning mid-Pacific military air routes. Izac had asked Towers about other Navy bases that he thought should be developed but that the Navy planned to abandon, specifically Majuro Atoll. Towers answered that the Navy was not abandoning Majuro, but that it was withdrawing the seaplane service unit. In addition, he told Izac that NATS was limiting its operations to the San Francisco–Honolulu run so that it could demobilize its seaplane units at Majuro, Saipan, and Sangley Point.[61] Not stated, but clearly implied, was the fact that fiscal savings realized from these demobilized units would allow more funding for the Pacific Fleet itself.

Some of the previous points made about base locations and deployments were reiterated by Admiral Louis Denfield, Towers's successor as Commander-in-Chief of the US Pacific Command and US Pacific Fleet (CINCPAC-CINCPACFLT), in letters to other admirals in late April and early May of 1947. In the first letter, to Vice Admiral William Fechteler, DCNO for Personnel, Denfield was highly impressed by Truk and was surprised "that the Japs did not have more installations on those islands. They certainly fooled us for years into thinking that Truk was their Pearl Harbor of the Pacific."[62] In the second letter, to Fleet Admiral Leahy, Denfield reported what he thought were cordial, cooperative, and successful new arrangements with the post–January 1, 1947, unified commands in the Pacific. He also repeated to Leahy his statements to Fechteler. Specifically, Denfield was surprised that the Japanese had not built more fleet installations on Truk, given the island's size. He did discuss using the location as a staging area for amphibious forces or as a fleet anchorage under certain conditions. Later in the letter he expressed misgivings similar to Carney's when he voiced his concern that Guam's harbor was too small and constricted for the US Pacific Fleet "in the event that the atomic bomb was used against us." Thus, he thought that future war plans should entertain the possibility of either Truk or the Palaus as the main fleet anchorage in the "Far Pacific" in case of this atomic contingency, since he saw the latter locations as allowing the fleet to be safely in one location and still well dispersed.[63]

In early June 1947, it was again demonstrated that postwar naval dispositions in the Pacific were sometimes arrived at for reasons of economy, convenience, or safety. This situation can be seen in elaborations from the Joint Marianas Board on deployments to Guam and Saipan. The Board determined fairly easily that Guam would be the location of a "Major Naval Operating Base" since Apra Harbor had been developed as a naval base. Naval installations at Tanapag Harbor on Saipan, on the other hand, would include a seaplane facility, a depot, and a supply annex that would comprise a "Minor Naval Operating Base." In addition, the Board asserted that the deployment of naval air units on Guam and Saipan was also dictated largely by the location of existing facilities. Aircraft-repair facilities and an aviation supply depot were placed at NAS Orote, Guam, for instance, because of the air station's proximity to the harbor, the availability of deep-water berthing and ship-repair facilities, and the location of the Naval Supply Center. Marine Corps air units were also stationed on Guam as part of the deployment of Fleet Marine Forces (FMF) units to the island. In addition, the Board did not think it efficient or safe to operate light and heavy planes from the same airdrome. For this reason, NAS Agana, Guam, was designated the location for heavy-plane units, including NATS and civil air transportation planes. Carrier air groups, whether temporarily or intermittently ashore, were going to be based at Isley Field on Saipan. This latter deployment was necessitated by the lack of space on Guam, including the lack of air space for aerial gunnery training because of transport operations that were being conducted from the island. Finally, the seaplane facility being located at NAS Tanapag, Saipan, was arrived at because Tanapag Harbor provided the only sheltered body of water in the Marianas that was suitable for seaplane operations. According to the Board, Apra Harbor was too congested and had poor approaches.[64]

In late July 1947, Admiral Charles Cooke, Commander of US Naval Forces, Western Pacific (COMNAVFORWESPAC), also communicated a number of ideas about forward-deployed American naval forces to Army Lieutenant General Albert Wedemeyer, Special Presidential Envoy, prior to the latter's fact-finding mission in China. While Cooke's views may not have been mainstream for the United States naval officer corps, they are certainly illuminating about the concept of employing American naval power in the Western Pacific and East Asia in the first few years after the Pacific War. Cooke spent most of the document on a long discourse to Wedemeyer about the "flawed" interwar Washington Treaty System, the "failures" of appeasement, and the recent threat of Soviet expansionism that had supposedly replaced the specter of Japanese militarism. To deter another war, Cooke thought it vital that "diplomatic strength and strategic potential . . . [rest] on the ability to carry on a total war." Cooke thought that for the United States, this meant the ability of the nation to project "effective" armed force onto the landmasses of East Asia. He saw this power-projection capability consisting of naval power to control the sea lanes through which this strength would be projected, the actual ground- and airpower to be projected, and beachheads upon which to project this military force. According to Cooke, the United States still possessed the potential "beachheads" and still had the naval power and other "major elements" of sea power, but it did not have an adequate base nearer than Guam. To him, this put US land- and airpower projection capabilities "in a perilous condition." Cooke believed that the American air base in Okinawa, and the naval anchorage and other minor facilities in Tsingtao, China, "constitute our immediate steps to occupy by the American Navy the naval vacuum in this critical area, created by the elimination of the Japanese Navy." However, he was not counting on the long-term availability of American naval bases in Japan or China, because of the instability in China and the uncertainty of Japanese bases "15 years from now."[65]

Similar ideas about a relatively short US occupation of Japan, and thus concern about American naval access to Japanese bases, was the subject of a memo from Admiral Nimitz to Vice Admiral Robert Griffin, Commander-in-Chief of US Naval Forces, Far East (CINCNAVFE), in late October 1947. Nimitz wanted Griffin to be clear that Navy policy concerning US facilities in Japan was to retain the equipment, dry docks, and facilities equivalent to those normally required of a US Naval Operating Base at Yokosuka. Essentially, he wanted a base that could fulfill Navy requirements in Japan after the withdrawal of the "Army of Occupation." Nimitz's reasoning was his assumption, similar to Eisenhower's and MacArthur's, that the US Army's occupation of Japan would be relatively short, and that a US-Japan peace treaty would soon be signed. In fact, like Cooke, it seems Nimitz assumed a fairly fast withdrawal of US ground forces from all of its East Asian positions. He also thought that a US-Japan treaty might only allow for some sort of "coast guard–type" of Japanese maritime police force. Nimitz probably feared a situation in which the Japanese did not have military forces sufficient to defend their nation against Soviet expansion. Therefore, he wanted "full freedom of action" in regard to US naval-base interests. Specifically, he desired a US naval base at Yokosuka in order to retain an American presence in the region and, most likely, retain some capability of projecting American power toward the Asian mainland.[66]

■ Unity of Command

Much as with the AAF's deployment plans for the postwar Pacific, Navy issues of unity of command also came into consideration in its dispositions. Forrestal's diary again speaks to this issue even before the war ended. In a March 1945 entry, Forrestal was concerned about command issues over Vice Admiral Thomas Kinkaid's Seventh Fleet, which was assigned to General MacArthur's SWPA forces for operations in the Philippines. Apparently, two of the six prewar battleships assigned to Kinkaid were in serious need of overhaul and repair at Pearl Harbor. MacArthur, however, was refusing to release the ships back to Admiral Nimitz, then CINC-PAC-CINCPOA, because of operations in Lingayen Gulf. To Forrestal, MacArthur's refusal epitomized the problems with the wartime command arrangements in the Pacific, since MacArthur obviously needed to complete his mission but should not have in any way "overstepped" his authority into Nimitz's purview. Unity of command in the Pacific between MacArthur and Nimitz again came into play in a conversation that same month between Forrestal and Admiral Leahy. Specifically, the issue was the Navy's idea that admirals such as Nimitz should be in charge of ships and naval operations on the water, literally, and that the Army should only take over operations once landmasses were reached.[67] In addition, Forrestal brought up the issue of the Twenty-First Bomber Command, the Marianas-based AAF unit of B-29 Superfortress bombers that started striking Japanese cities in 1944. To Forrestal, the command arrangements made for this unit epitomized the problems with wartime command arrangements in the Pacific Basin. The decision to put the Twenty-First Bomber Command directly under JCS direction from Washington, D.C., with General Arnold acting as the JCS's Executive Agent and having day-to-day authority over the unit,[68] meant that an AAF unit was operating as an independent force in the midst of the Navy-dominated Western Pacific. As Forrestal put it to Leahy, the unit was "operating almost entirely on their own without reference to any other military efforts in the Pacific and it seemed obvious to me that they should be brought into the pattern if full advantage was to be taken of their capabilities." While Forrestal was probably exaggerating the Twenty-First Bomber

Command's actual autonomy, he was by this time quite serious about "clearly set-tling" the entire matter of postwar command arrangements.[69]

Some of the difficulties of command relationships, which were created at higher levels but had to be dealt with by mid-level commanders, also came up in Admiral Towers's diary. Concerning a mid-July 1946 meeting with Lieutenant General Hull, Towers recorded that Hull thought present command relationships were unsatis-factory, but that they might be improved by mutual agreements between the two officers. Towers pointed out—and Hull admitted—that the Army commander was "handicapped" by certain directives from General MacArthur. Towers also claimed that Hull was in favor of a supreme commander in the Pacific, with ground, naval, and air subdivisions of forces, and that the mid-Pacific commander thought this arrangement should be established as soon as "occupation duties in the Western Pacific have fallen off." Towers and Hull were also apparently in agreement that General Eisenhower was in favor of this idea.[70]

Unity-of-command issues between the Army and Navy in the context of the Navy's role in an East Asian or Pacific conflict with the Soviet Union also became a little clearer in a November 1946 memo from Captain Richard Phillips, OINC of the Strategic Plans Division's Pacific Sub-Section, to Rear Admiral Glover, ACNO for Strategic Plans. Phillips was certain that a major mission for the US Pacific Fleet in the event of a Soviet invasion of Southern Korea would be to withdraw Marine forces from Tsingtao, China. In addition, he was sure the Navy would be responsible for the evacuation of all US forces from Korea and Northern China, for establishing control over the Yellow Sea and the Sea of Japan, and for assisting Allied forces in the defense of the Japanese Home Islands. The specific command problem came about because General MacArthur thought it necessary that he command all forces that would be responsible for carrying out these tasks, including naval units. MacArthur also claimed that SCAP had developed a plan that covered this kind of command arrangement, and that he had submitted it to the War Department. He therefore thought that the JCS should reach an agreement on command structure in case of an emergency in Asia. Admiral Towers, however, was only prepared to have his command carry out the tasks given to him by Nimitz. Only then was he willing to "discuss" the Army and Navy plans with MacArthur in order to reach "working agreements." Phillips was under the impression that the JCS was going to meet in a few days to make final decisions on the question of unity of command between MacArthur and Towers. Phillips recommended to Glover that no action be taken by the Navy until the JCS made its final decision, as he thought an early action might weaken the Navy's stand in the unity-of-command controversy. More specifi-cally, Phillips was thinking of a recent dispatch by Lieutenant General John Hodge, Commanding General of US Army Forces in Korea (USAFIK). In the dispatch, Hodge emphasized the need for unity of command in case of a Soviet invasion. Hodge probably meant unity of command under MacArthur. Phillips, however, cited

Hodge and the report from the Congressional Joint Committee on the Investigation of the Pearl Harbor attack as evidence for the Navy's case. The report recommended that unity of command be "imposed" on all American military and naval outposts. Phillips thought that Hodge's statement and the Pearl Harbor report gave the Navy a strong argument for its position in the unity-of-command controversy. More exactly, Phillips thought that all of these factors taken together gave the Navy good ground for insisting that the Army be required to come to a "speedy" agreement with the Navy on unity of command in the region.[71]

■ Conclusion

Clearly, as has been shown in the previous two chapters of this study, the unity of command controversy did not end with Captain Phillips's memo or even with the creation of the nominally unified commands in January 1947. In fact, the controversy to a great extent continued into the 1980s at least. This chapter, however, has demonstrated certain aspects about the US Navy's conception of its role in the postwar Pacific. While the Navy was far from monolithic in terms of strategic thought concerning the postwar defense of the Pacific Basin, it did, between 1945 and 1947, determine the rough outline for a regional defense of the area. More specifically, the Navy used the history of the Pacific War—not to mention the geography of the Pacific Basin—to assert that carrier airpower was the centerpiece of postwar Pacific defense. To the officials and officers who controlled the early postwar Navy, and to most historians since 1945, the war itself was overwhelming evidence of the ascendancy of naval aviation as the main arm of the postwar Navy. In particular, wartime operations demonstrated to naval officials and officers that aircraft carriers were the best means of mobile force by which to control and patrol the vast Pacific. Equally important, however, was the idea that mobile forces, rather than stationary bases, were the key to the actual postwar defense of the region. While numerous documents cited above indicate that officers still placed great stress on the United States obtaining postwar control of strategic locations in the Pacific, they were now much less interested in planting bases on each of these locations. In fact, none of the documents cited by 1946 and 1947 claimed that the United States needed large numbers of bases. While a few officers thought so during and immediately after the war, a majority of senior naval officers by 1946 were convinced that static bases were a waste of scarce resources and a tactical drag on mobile forces.[72]

This argument was also a key ingredient in the conflict with the AAF. The Navy had to convince Congress and the public that it had adopted airpower over battleships. However, it also had to ensure that lawmakers and the public were convinced that carrier airpower was emphasized over static naval bases. The emphasis on keeping the number of bases small became ammunition against the AAF, which was obviously so dependent on stationary bases in regions like the Pacific Basin. Also, once the clear postwar enemy became the Soviet Union rather than a resurgent Japan, the Navy had to demonstrate how it could be employed against a continental enemy with a minimal naval force. Here, it was relatively easy for the AAF to argue its case. For the Navy, it was more difficult. Thus, it was vital to demonstrate that the Navy had not only given up its fascination with battleships, but that it fully understood how to exploit the real and imagined potential of carrier airpower, with all of its mobility, in the far reaches of the Pacific Basin. It should also be pointed out, however, that the Navy's arguments were just as disingenuous as the Army Air Force's. The AAF obviously ignored operational realities from the Pacific War, such as the contributions of the Army Ground and Service Forces, the amphibious assault capabilities of the Marine Corps, and the strategic and tactical potential of the Navy's carrier forces. Yet the Navy also ignored or de-emphasized the interservice and combined-arms nature of US victory in the Pacific War. In addition, it de-emphasized significant proportions of its own forces' contribution to that victory. For instance, none of the primary sources noted above, either classified planning documents or public addresses, gave much credit to the Navy's battleship forces as anti-aircraft escorts for the carriers or gunfire support for the amphibious forces. Similarly, very little, if anything, was said about the need for naval surface forces, especially in the Solomons and Philippines campaigns.[73] Nor did I find many references to the efforts of the Navy's service forces, the contributions of the motor torpedo boat (MTB) squadrons, or even the contributions made by land-based naval reconnaissance forces. Most egregiously, all of the documentation that spoke to carrier forces destroying Japanese industrial capability failed to take into account that it was the Navy's submarine blockade that really crippled Japan industrially, rather than either the Navy's carrier strike forces or the AAF's strategic bombers.[74] Certainly, none of the other participants subscribed to Admiral Spruance's wartime assertion that the Pacific War was really an amphibious conflict in which all other forces were merely support.[75] All of this, of course, speaks to the highly political nature of defense planning, especially planning that takes place under slim budgetary and personnel conditions as well as a political context clouded by Pearl Harbor. The lesson for historians—if there is one—is not that politics entered the postwar strategic-planning process, or even that history was used and abused in this process. The lesson is to note the twists and turns which the American national-security establishment took when it had to analyze a previous war to plan for the nation's future security under resource constraints placed on it by politicians looking after the country's political and fiscal well-being.

CHAPTER 4

Trusteeship versus Annexation

The State Department and US Strategic Security in the Pacific Basin

The postwar State Department position on the Pacific Basin provides another key aspect of US policy toward the region during the transition between the end of the war and the beginning formulation of Containment as the mainstay of American foreign policy. The State Department had a particularly difficult job when it came to the disposition of the former Japanese territories. It first had to provide a formula for US control that satisfied the American military's desire for "absolute control" of the Pacific Islands taken from Japan, a term usually used by the Army and Navy to mean sovereign control or annexation. At the same time, the State Department had to satisfy American and international public opinion that the United States would not violate President Franklin Roosevelt's wartime assurances that the United States would not indulge in territorial acquisitions. If the US military was not sensitive to this dilemma, President Truman was attuned to it. He was convinced that US control had to be complete, but also had to be carried out through some form of UN administration. State Department officers had to balance these sometimes contradictory goals. Particularly interesting, however, is that the documents cited below indicate that the State Department was not necessarily opposed to an American imperialism that asserted US hegemony over the Pacific Basin. The State Department's main concern, instead, was that American hegemony not be perceived as traditional Great Power imperialism.

■ Wartime Concerns

In late February 1945, Assistant Secretary of State James Dunn, Chairman of the State-War-Navy Coordinating Committee (SWNCC), sent a memo to Secretary of State Edward Stettinius about international trusteeships over wartime colonized and conquered areas. As it had throughout the war, the JCS was again expressing the view that any discussions or negotiations about trusteeships should wait until after the war was over, as these negotiations could adversely affect US relations with the Soviet Union. Dunn was now proposing that preparations be made to discuss the general principles of international trusteeship, as well as the institutional machinery for those trusteeships at the upcoming inaugural UN Conference in San Francisco. No doubt in order to placate the military, Dunn thought that the principles and machinery could be negotiated without discussing trusteeships over specific territories. More specifically, he told Stettinius that the Soviets, the British, and the Chinese would desire and press for these discussions, and that these questions would come up at the Conference, but that the matter of specific territories could be left for later determination.[1] The JCS was aware of these facts and did not object to discussions as long as the discussions did not in any way prejudice US defense requirements in the region, especially the military's desired future control of the former Japanese Mandated Islands or "any other territories" the JCS thought might be needed for the future defense of the United States. Dunn suggested to Stettinius that at some point, the United States would have to negotiate about these occupied territories with the other Dumbarton Oaks powers,[2] that some of these territories were strategic in nature, and that some proposals for a special kind of security trusteeship should be developed. Dunn reiterated how important it was for the concerned agencies within the US Government to explore this subject thoroughly before having to do so with other nations. Accordingly, he hoped this type of planning would proceed "expeditiously," and that the War and Navy Departments would be ready to take part. Dunn concluded his communication to Stettinius with the idea that it was premature to enter into any discussions with any other governments on this matter until the planning had reached a stage where it was possible to say that the US Government had its own position worked out in "reasonable detail." If or when the US Government reached this position, however, he thought the Secretaries of War and the Navy would want those discussions limited to the powers taking direct part in the Dumbarton Oaks talks. Dunn continued, saying that only after full discussions with those powers about trusteeship matters would the War and Navy Departments want a general UN discussion on the subject. Given the conditions being set by the Army and Navy, Dunn suggested that State begin a draft paper on territorial trusteeships as soon as possible, and that it be "promptly circulated" to Secretary of War Henry Stimson and Secretary of the Navy James Forrestal as well as to the JCS.[3]

The State Department had Roosevelt's support for its idea of an international trusteeship for the former Japanese Mandates. In mid-March 1945, Charles Taussig, Chairman of the United States Section on the Anglo-American Caribbean Commission, briefed Roosevelt on disagreements between military-service and State Department representatives on the interdepartmental Committee on Dependent Area Aspects of International Organizations. Taussig claimed that there had been general agreement on categories of strategic areas, but that the military wanted entire groups of islands in the Pacific north of the equator to come under US administration. Taussig told the President that this kind of control would entail entire island groups in Micronesia, whether or not they had been fortified by the Japanese, coming under unilateral US administration and being exempt from any international agreements pertaining to civilian populations. He also said that the military had been unwilling to divide the strategic areas into categories of closed and open. Roosevelt favored the two-area concept, wanting the open areas to be subject to international agreements, and saying that the military could merely ask the UN Security Council to change an open area to a closed area if it needed that change. He then asked Taussig if the Navy was just trying to "grab" everything in the area as a territorial policy. Taussig replied that the services did not have much confidence in civilian controls, and Roosevelt agreed with him about that lack of military confidence in civilian administration. Taussig also emphasized to the President that the military had no confidence in the UN in general, or even the State Department, by citing a letter from Vice Admiral Russell Willson, Navy Member of the Joint Strategic Survey Committee, to Secretary Forrestal in which Willson referred to the need for the Navy to send representatives to San Francisco in order to protect Navy interests from the "international welfare boys." Roosevelt answered Taussig's observation with a statement that neither the Army nor the Navy had any business administering civilian populations, since they had no competence in this matter. He was, however, "interested" in a bill introduced by Representative William Cole of New York that would have all US territories turned over to the Navy. He was even more interested by a suggestion from Under Secretary of the Interior Abe Fortas that the United States voluntarily have its administered territories report to the UN and respond to UN requests for specific information. Roosevelt said he would approve of this latter idea, and that it might provide a "useful trading point" in San Francisco.[4]

Additional difficulties were recorded by Stettinius in early April. By that time, it had become obvious to him that the War and Navy Departments desired to annex the Pacific Islands won in the campaigns against Japan, instead of turning them into trusteeships. While Stettinius was going to send President Roosevelt a memo outlining both sides of this disagreement, Roosevelt sent him information from Secretary of the Interior Harold Ickes saying that the United States should be the "administering power" of the former Japanese Mandates, but should not insist on "complete sovereignty" over them. Ickes was fearful that if the United States insisted on sovereign control over Micronesia, as the military wanted, the British could claim sovereign control over its trusteeships, including those in the Middle East that would allow the British complete control over Middle Eastern oil in a way that would damage postwar US security interests.[5]

These basic differences between the military services and the State Department were again apparent in a communication from Stettinius to Roosevelt just three days before the President died. Stettinius reminded Roosevelt about one of the agreements from the Yalta Conference in which it was decided that representatives of the five Permanent Members of the UN Security Council would discuss trusteeship matters before the machinery was actually worked out at the San Francisco Conference. It had also been decided that these preliminary discussions would not include specific territories. Stettinius further told the President that State had been working "diligently" with the War, Navy, and Interior Departments to develop a US position regarding these matters, and that a draft plan had been written. However, he said that this draft plan had not yet been approved by either Secretary Stimson or Secretary Forrestal.

Stettinius went on to say that he thought minor changes to the draft plan would bring consensus, yet he also thought that Stimson and Forrestal would separately communicate their trusteeship ideas to Roosevelt. Again, the major issue was that War and Navy thought the United States should retain "complete control," i.e., sovereignty, over the strategic islands in the Pacific, and make this form of control known to other nations unequivocally before it entered into any discussions about trusteeship matters. While Stimson and Forrestal were claiming opposition to any "imperialistic" annexation of territory, they thought that US policy should be based on the idea of the United States having "exclusive" strategic rights over various areas of the Pacific in the cause of international peace and freedom. Stettinius argued to Roosevelt that the State Department was fully in accord with US retention of strategic positions in the Pacific, but State thought its current plan provided for that security within a system of international trusteeship. He added that the Interior Department agreed with the State Department's position. If the current plan were not used within a clear trusteeship system, he feared it might prejudice all possibility of international trusteeship and result in large portions of the American public denouncing the United States for violating its own wartime promises of abstaining from territorial aggrandizement. Accordingly, Stettinius was now recommending to the President that no official US position on the matter be enunciated until the War, Navy, and State Departments "thrashed" the matter out, preferably with Roosevelt present. While War and Navy still did not want any specific territories discussed until after the end of the war, Stettinius recommended to Roosevelt that the matter be resolved now. The Secretary of State's reasoning was that the United States had taken the lead during the war in these trusteeship matters, the public was in favor of a trusteeship system, and failure to solve the issue in favor of international trusteeship would seriously harm US political interests. Stettinius concluded the memo by apologizing for interrupting Roosevelt's vacation, but also asked if departmental representatives could come down to Warm Springs for a "short discussion" on the matter.[6]

Two days after Roosevelt's death, Stettinius was again expressing these concerns. At the railroad station, even as Roosevelt's body arrived, he held a private talk with Forrestal, General Marshall, and Admiral King. He told them that a solution to the trusteeship issue had to be found before the San Francisco Conference took place, but that it was impossible to do so with the policy of annexation that the armed forces had advocated. He also said that the State Department was willing to meet the military "half way," but that his Department could never agree to a policy of annexation. He then suggested another meeting between representatives to iron out this issue before the UN Conference started. He thought that all three men had listened "sympathetically" and with appreciation, asserting that Forrestal even claimed he had drafted a memo on the subject.[7] Without fully agreeing on a trusteeship policy, State and the military departments apparently came to some agreement a few days later for purposes of the initial UN Conference. In a memo to Under Secretary of State Joseph Grew, Stettinius related a meeting he, Stimson, and Forrestal had with President Truman. Stettinius opened the meeting by telling Truman how the three departments had been working for many months to find a satisfactory solution to the question of trusteeships. He handed Truman papers that proposed policies that would maintain the United States' strategic position in the Pacific without the United States being charged with annexation. He also said that this policy was the result of much labor and had been endorsed by all three Secretaries.[8] The specific policy was included as an annex to the memo provided to Truman. Contrary to Stettinius's statement about interdepartmental agreements, however, the only thing actually agreed upon was to discuss the possible machinery for a trusteeship system without proposing specific territories. The position paper also spoke to discussing this trusteeship system only for territories that were currently held under mandate, territories that could be detached from enemy states after the war, or territories voluntarily placed under trusteeship by the states administering them. The policy was then to suggest that specific territories only be agreed upon at subsequent meetings. Still, according to the three Secretaries, this system would provide for the maintenance of US military and strategic rights so as to ensure "general peace and security" in the Pacific and allow for an administration that would ensure the "social, economic, and political welfare of the inhabitants of the dependent territories."[9] Truman responded that the paper gave him a good understanding of the policy, and that he wanted US policy clear in his mind since he had just been asked about trusteeship at his last press conference. However, Stimson and Forrestal were still not entirely satisfied. Stimson, for instance, wanted it emphasized that now was not the time for the United States to give up bases and its protective position in the Pacific. Forrestal supported Stimson's position.[10]

■ The Postwar Position

The differences between the War and Navy Departments on the one hand and the State Department on the other continued for the rest of the war without resolution. In fact, differences over annexation versus trusteeship were not settled until the winter of 1946–1947. Part and parcel of this interdepartmental disagreement were issues over defining which nations should be involved in the negotiations over the various territorial trusteeships. What began in September 1945, then, were a series of intradepartmental, interdepartmental, and international deliberations that sought to define which nations should be labeled as "states directly concerned" in trusteeship matters and therefore able to play direct roles in these negotiations. In the process of these talks, there were all kinds of linkages made by American and foreign officials concerning US trusteeship goals in the Pacific Basin vis-à-vis other issues in other areas of the world. Similar to the linkage made by Ickes concerning Middle Eastern oil, the negotiations within the State Department and then between the Great Powers brought the former Japanese Mandates and other Pacific territories into focus for quite a bit of attention.[11] For instance, in a Memorandum of Record by Charles Bohlen, Special Assistant to the Secretary of State, it became clear that the Soviet Union wanted to participate in some sort of trusteeship in Tripolitania, or at least gain some sort of concession for not doing so that might satisfy some other Soviet interest. When Soviet Foreign Minister Vyacheslav Molotov suggested to James Byrnes, Stettinius's successor as Secretary of State, that the United States, Great Britain, and the Soviet Union all share in the postwar administration of the Italian colonies, Byrnes replied that the United States did not wish to undertake such a burden, but that it would participate in the UN Trusteeship Council. Probably on an exploratory expedition, Molotov inquired about the United States' role in the Philippines as a colonial burden that the United States had taken on in the past. Byrnes replied that the United States had acquired the Philippines as a result of the Spanish-American War, but he also argued that the United States had not voluntarily assumed such burdens in other colonial areas and was even in the process of granting independence to the Philippines.[12]

Under some pressure to devise a policy on the issue, Truman made a statement about the former Japanese territories in mid-January 1946. At a press conference on 15 January, Truman was quoted as saying that the United States would place any islands it did not need for military security under UN trusteeship, but that it would retain those islands it did need for military purposes. When he was asked if the islands retained would be under the "individual" trusteeship of the United

States, Truman replied in the affirmative. Asked if the United States would be seeking UN approval for those individual trusteeships, he also replied in the affirmative.[13] In spite of the apparent solution put forth by Truman, there were still problems, since Byrnes voiced concerns the next day that the issue might come up while he was at the first session of the UN General Assembly in London. Cabling Acting Secretary of State Acheson from London, Byrnes even asked Acheson to find out if the War, Navy, or State Departments had initiated studies that would result in some sort of position on the former Japanese Mandates as either strategic trusteeships or ordinary ones. Byrnes then instructed Acheson that he should do so immediately for the State Department if no one had been assigned to this task. Byrnes also told Acheson that he should suggest the same thing to the Army and the Navy or have this done through SWNCC. Byrnes was most concerned that the issue might arise at the next meeting of the General Assembly without the United States being prepared.[14]

In fact, the issue of "states directly concerned" and linkages to the Pacific Islands came up again the very next day. John Dulles, a Representative on the US Delegation to the General Assembly, made it clear that the United States wanted to limit the number of states directly concerned in trusteeship matters to a minimum, depending on the territory in question. However, according to Andrei Gromyko, Soviet Ambassador to the United States and Soviet Delegate to the General Assembly, the USSR wanted to maximize the number so as to be able to participate in all of these negotiations. Gromyko asked Dulles his views about states directly concerned vis-à-vis the mandated territories of the defeated Axis nations, territories that included the former Japanese Mandate over Micronesia. Dulles replied that the State Department view of the matter was that only the United States, Great Britain, and France were the states directly concerned with the mandated territories, since those three powers were the residual Allied and Associated Powers under the Treaty of Versailles. He went on to say that the State Department did not consider a state directly concerned merely because of geographic proximity to the territory in question. Gromyko pointed out the absence of the Soviet Union in that grouping of nations and said that the Soviet Government was a state directly concerned in all trust-territory questions. When Dulles asked Gromyko the basis of that view, Gromyko answered that the Soviet Union was concerned with all major economic, political, and geographic questions everywhere on the globe![15]

This issue of states directly concerned continued when Acting Secretary of State Acheson gave a long statement about the Japanese Islands in a press conference on 22 January 1946. In a previous press conference, Acheson had been asked if the requirement of unanimity among the five Permanent Members of the Security Council impeded the creation of an individual trusteeship by which the United States could fortify specific geographic areas it needed for its defense. Acheson now answered the question, but not directly. Instead, he outlined a procedure by which

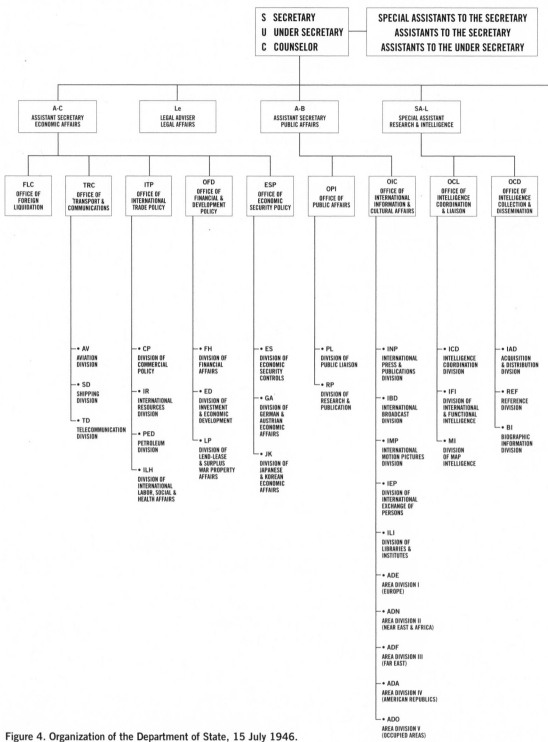

Figure 4. Organization of the Department of State, 15 July 1946.

(Courtesy of the National Archives, College Park, Maryland.)

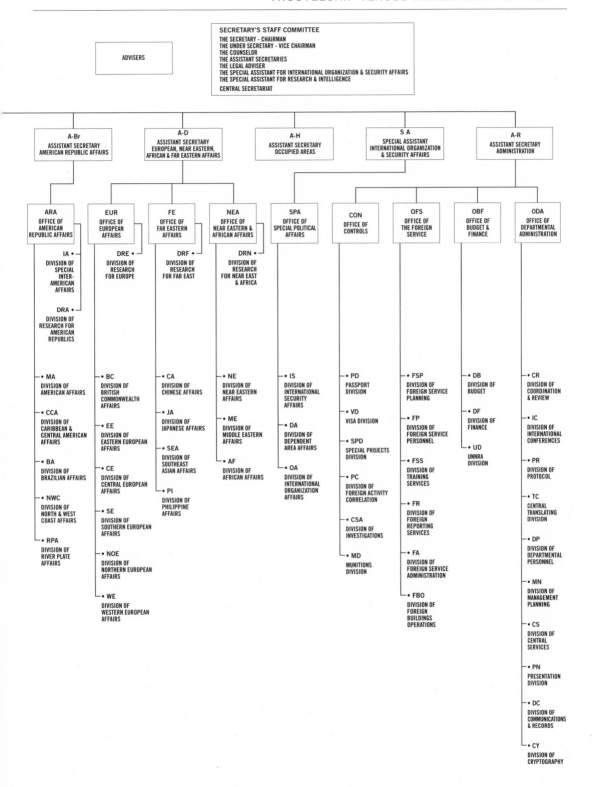

SECRETARY'S STAFF COMMITTEE

THE SECRETARY - CHAIRMAN
THE UNDER SECRETARY - VICE CHAIRMAN
THE COUNSELOR
THE ASSISTANT SECRETARIES
THE LEGAL ADVISER
THE SPECIAL ASSISTANT FOR INTERNATIONAL ORGANIZATION & SECURITY AFFAIRS
THE SPECIAL ASSISTANT FOR RESEARCH & INTELLIGENCE

CENTRAL SECRETARIAT

ADVISERS

A-Br
ASSISTANT SECRETARY
AMERICAN REPUBLIC AFFAIRS

A-D
ASSISTANT SECRETARY
EUROPEAN, NEAR EASTERN,
AFRICAN & FAR EASTERN AFFAIRS

A-H
ASSISTANT SECRETARY
OCCUPIED AREAS

S A
SPECIAL ASSISTANT
INTERNATIONAL ORGANIZATION
& SECURITY AFFAIRS

A-R
ASSISTANT SECRETARY
ADMINISTRATION

ARA
OFFICE OF
AMERICAN
REPUBLIC AFFAIRS

EUR
OFFICE OF
EUROPEAN
AFFAIRS

FE
OFFICE OF
FAR EASTERN
AFFAIRS

NEA
OFFICE OF
NEAR EASTERN &
AFRICAN AFFAIRS

SPA
OFFICE OF
SPECIAL POLITICAL
AFFAIRS

CON
OFFICE OF
CONTROLS

OFS
OFFICE OF
THE FOREIGN
SERVICE

OBF
OFFICE OF
BUDGET &
FINANCE

ODA
OFFICE OF
DEPARTMENTAL
ADMINISTRATION

IA •
DIVISION OF
SPECIAL
INTER-
AMERICAN
AFFAIRS

DRA •
DIVISION OF
RESEARCH FOR
AMERICAN
REPUBLICS

DRE •
DIVISION OF
RESEARCH
FOR EUROPE

DRF •
DIVISION OF
RESEARCH
FOR FAR EAST

DRN •
DIVISION OF
RESEARCH
FOR NEAR EAST
& AFRICA

• MA
DIVISION OF
AMERICAN AFFAIRS

• CCA
DIVISION OF
CARIBBEAN &
CENTRAL AMERICAN
AFFAIRS

• BA
DIVISION OF
BRAZILIAN AFFAIRS

• NWC
DIVISION OF
NORTH & WEST
COAST AFFAIRS

• RPA
DIVISION OF
RIVER PLATE
AFFAIRS

• BC
DIVISION OF
BRITISH
COMMONWEALTH
AFFAIRS

• EE
DIVISION OF
EASTERN EUROPEAN
AFFAIRS

• CE
DIVISION OF
CENTRAL EUROPEAN
AFFAIRS

• SE
DIVISION OF
SOUTHERN EUROPEAN
AFFAIRS

• NOE
DIVISION OF
NORTHERN EUROPEAN
AFFAIRS

• WE
DIVISION OF
WESTERN EUROPEAN
AFFAIRS

• CA
DIVISION OF
CHINESE AFFAIRS

• JA
DIVISION OF
JAPANESE AFFAIRS

• SEA
DIVISION OF
SOUTHEAST
ASIAN AFFAIRS

• PI
DIVISION OF
PHILIPPINE
AFFAIRS

• NE
DIVISION OF
NEAR EASTERN
AFFAIRS

• ME
DIVISION OF
MIDDLE EASTERN
AFFAIRS

• AF
DIVISION OF
AFRICAN AFFAIRS

• IS
DIVISION OF
INTERNATIONAL
SECURITY
AFFAIRS

• DA
DIVISION OF
DEPENDENT
AREA AFFAIRS

• OA
DIVISION OF
INTERNATIONAL
ORGANIZATION
AFFAIRS

• PD
PASSPORT
DIVISION

• VD
VISA DIVISION

• SPD
SPECIAL PROJECTS
DIVISION

• PC
DIVISION OF
FOREIGN ACTIVITY
CORRELATION

• CSA
DIVISION OF
INVESTIGATIONS

• MD
MUNITIONS
DIVISION

• FSP
DIVISION OF
FOREIGN SERVICE
PLANNING

• FP
DIVISION OF
FOREIGN SERVICE
PERSONNEL

• FSS
DIVISION OF
TRAINING
SERVICES

• FR
DIVISION OF
FOREIGN
REPORTING
SERVICES

• FA
DIVISION OF
FOREIGN SERVICE
ADMINISTRATION

• FBO
DIVISION OF
FOREIGN
BUILDINGS
OPERATIONS

• DB
DIVISION OF
BUDGET

• DF
DIVISION OF
FINANCE

• UD
UNNRA
DIVISION

• CR
DIVISION OF
COORDINATION
& REVIEW

• IC
DIVISION OF
INTERNATIONAL
CONFERENCES

• PR
DIVISION OF
PROTOCOL

• TC
CENTRAL
TRANSLATING
DIVISION

• DP
DIVISION OF
DEPARTMENTAL
PERSONNEL

• MN
DIVISION OF
MANAGEMENT
PLANNING

• CS
DIVISION OF
CENTRAL
SERVICES

• PN
PRESENTATION
DIVISION

• DC
DIVISION OF
COMMUNICATIONS
& RECORDS

• CY
DIVISION OF
CRYPTOGRAPHY

a nation that was "principally concerned" in a particular area could propose that area as a strategic trusteeship to the Security Council, and negotiate with the Council. He also said that in certain cases, a nation that was in possession of an area because it was the mandate power or because it had militarily conquered the area would be the principal leader in those negotiations.

Acheson continued by saying that any one of the five Permanent Members could refuse to agree to the negotiations with a Security Council veto. However, he also said that such a situation would leave things as they had been. In other words, a nation in possession of some area would simply remain in control if the Permanent Members could not agree on a trusteeship solution. If the Permanent Members could agree, then there would be a trusteeship established. He further stated that once an area had been entered into as a "strategic area," it could not be changed without the consent of the Security Council. Acheson therefore concluded that in the case of the former Japanese Mandates, Micronesia could not be re-designated without US consent. Acheson said he favored the negotiations between the five powers in spite of the fact that he thought these negotiations would take more time. Essentially, he thought that the lengthier negotiations would be more final once they had been conducted in this more thorough manner. He emphasized, however, that if there was no agreement, the United States would simply stay in control where it had been before the negotiations had even begun. When he was asked if the United States needed to be awarded an area at a peace conference prior to trusteeship decisions being made, Acheson answered that he did not think that was necessary, and that the nations could proceed in any order they thought best. Asked if he thought the formula for trusteeship protected the interests of the United States, he said he thought that sound agreements had been carefully worked out at the San Francisco Conference that protected the interests of the powers.[16] In essence, Acheson was telling the reporters that the United States was offering the former Japanese Mandates to the UN Security Council for deliberation. He was making it clear, however, that the United States was the principal nation with an interest in this strategic area, and that if unanimity could not be obtained, the United States would simply keep these island groups under its unilateral control. To be sure, the United States wanted a UN blessing, but it would remain in Micronesia and the other Japanese territories even without that blessing.

This position was also reiterated some years later by Donald Blaisdell, who was from 1945 to 1947 the Associate Chief for Military Aspects of Security in the State Department's Division of International Security Affairs (IS). Blaisdell told an interviewer that the United States at that time had a certain "mental picture" of what international security in the postwar world should entail. He specified that the United States had the largest navy in the world, the atomic bomb, an admittedly small army, but also an air force that would make the bomb "useable" in any part of the world. He said further that the United States had decided, as postwar policy, to maintain its wartime strategy of placing American military forces anywhere in the world that it felt necessary for its security. In fact, he suggested that the United States was just continuing its wartime strategy by envisioning UN-organized military forces as mere extensions of US military forces. This situation, he argued, is what brought the United States into conflict with the USSR, since the Soviets did not want the United States to be able to place its military forces anywhere in the world. Blaisdell went into further detail by asserting that there were certain areas of the world the Soviets wanted under their control, and that one issue related to these matters of Soviet control was trusteeship over islands in the "Southwest Pacific." He thought it interesting, however, that even though the Soviets did not want the United States to be the trustee power in the former Japanese Mandates, they did not use their veto in the Security Council to prevent US control. He assumed that the Soviets did not exercise this right because the United States had made it clear that it was staying in these Pacific Islands and would administer them even without UN approval. Blaisdell was convinced that the United States had taken the "high" position in this confrontation. He thought it was essential for American security that the US control the Pacific Islands. Moreover, he was convinced that "we were just going to stay there, were going to use those islands as we saw fit." This was probably why he thought the islands had been kept separate from other negotiations within the UN Security Council's Military Staff Committee. His bottom line was that the issue of nations looking for staging areas for UN forces so that those forces could be present and operate anywhere in the world "got pretty deeply into the whole strategic philosophy of the United States itself."[17] In other words, the UN becoming essentially an extension of US strategy was fine, but that organization using the United States as an extension of its own international security strategy was completely unacceptable to the United States.

The issue of states directly concerned again came to the fore in a message from John Hickerson, Deputy Director of the State Department's Office of European Affairs (EUR), to Byrnes in late February 1946. Hickerson had a problem with the United States claming to be a state directly concerned in the approval of the proposed British trusteeship over Tanganyika. He asked Byrnes to consider whether or not the United States really wanted to assert itself as a state directly concerned in this trusteeship. In particular, he argued that if the United States took this position regarding Tanganyika, then Great Britain and France could definitely take the same position regarding UN approval of an American trusteeship over the former Japanese Mandates. He further argued that this might strengthen the Soviet Union's case as a state directly concerned in the Pacific Islands. Hickerson said he had no final views on this matter. From the viewpoint of US national interests in the Pacific, however, he thought Byrnes should consider the proposal that the United States, Australia, and New Zealand be declared as the states directly concerned when it came to the disposition of the Pacific Islands, since in his view these Pacific states had borne the brunt of the war against Japan.[18]

This line of thought continued in early April. At that time, the Secretary's Staff Committee said that there was disagreement within the State Department about the United States being declared a state directly concerned in the disposition of British and Belgian trusteeships in Africa since the United States doing so might bring about similar British and Soviet assertions vis-à-vis the Pacific Islands. Adding to this was Secretary Forrestal's letter earlier in the same month urging that the number of states directly concerned with Pacific Island trusteeships be kept to a minimum, and cautioning that US assertion of rights regarding the African trusteeships could have a detrimental impact on US interests in the Pacific. The members of the Committee, representing the various offices of the State Department, thought instead that the term "states directly concerned" should probably apply to the five Permanent Members of the UN as the successor nations of the Allied and Associated Powers of the Treaty of Versailles. Moreover, they thought that trying to obtain a more restrictive definition than this would be difficult to secure, and that a broader definition would be "undesirable." The Committee also argued that since nations such as Great Britain, the Soviet Union, and even China were acceptors of the Japanese surrender, it was doubtful that the United States could succeed in excluding them from the negotiations having to do with the disposition of the former Japanese territories. In addition, the Committee asserted that including the other four Great Powers as states directly concerned would not at all jeopardize US control in Micronesia. As Acheson stated to the press earlier in the year, even if one of the five powers were excluded from the Micronesian trusteeship negotiations, it could still veto any strategic-area agreements on the UN Security Council. Similarly, if the five states were all included but could not come to an agreement, the Committee argued that "the United States will remain in *de facto* control of the islands." The Committee apparently thought it best, therefore, that the other states be included, and that the United States' position be known as promptly as possible. The Committee then argued that as soon as a departmental policy had been achieved, that policy should be recommended to the President and, if approved by the President, communicated to the Secretary of War, the Secretary of the Navy, and the JCS through SWNCC. The object here was to establish a universal policy within the US Government that called for including all of the other four Permanent Members of the UN Security Council, but conducting particularly close consultations with Great Britain and France as the two remaining Principal Allied and Associative Powers from 1919. As regarded the issue of states directly concerned, the Committee stated that only the five Permanent Members should be counted as such, and that the five should have to consult with each other if other states were to be included in the trusteeship negotiations.[19]

These same issues came up again, however, a few days later when the Committee reconvened. This time, Alger Hiss, Director of the State Department's Office of Special Political Affairs (SPA), not only gave a brief history on this issue but recommended specific policies for the United States to follow. Hiss began by informing the Committee that the British and the Belgians had submitted draft trusteeship agreements for their African territories, and that the French were planning to as well. He said that an important factor in the problem was whether or not the United States would claim to be a state directly concerned in all mandated territorial issues, and the impact that claim would have on the former Japanese Mandates question. He reminded the Committee of the Secretary's opposition to this latter position because of the potential for British and Soviet insistence on similar rights. Hiss went on to say that it had been the understanding in San Francisco in 1945 that the mandatory power of a trusteeship was obviously a state directly concerned, while the others would be determined by diplomatic negotiations. This was important, he pointed out, since it meant no change could be made to a trusteeship agreement without the consent of the state directly concerned. He also pointed out that since 1921, the US position had been that titles to mandates resided with the Principal Allied and Associated Powers, that the United States had entered into treaties with mandatory powers since that time, and that it was therefore impossible to modify the present mandates without US assent.[20]

Hiss then asserted that in San Francisco, the United States informally took the position that it would be a state directly concerned in all mandate matters. However, he said that the War and Navy Departments were now taking the position that the United States should not assert itself as a state directly concerned in the African territories, so that it could limit the number of states directly concerned with the Pacific territories. Hiss argued that the United States practice of "self-restraint" when it came to staying out of the African negotiations did not mean other nations would do the same when it came to the Pacific Islands. Moreover, he said that the British had already foreclosed this question by sending draft trusteeship copies to the United States, the USSR, and China, thus inviting those powers to be states directly concerned. Hiss was also concerned that if the United States actually renounced any claims to be a negotiating power in the African territories, it would be like foregoing its rights in those areas of the world. This, in turn, might bring up questions as to why the United States, after helping formulate the current trusteeship system, was renouncing its treaty rights within that system. Hiss said that Congress might ask about this, especially since foregoing negotiating status meant giving up treaty rights in those areas of the world. Hiss also said that the Army's and Navy's ideas about limiting the number of states directly concerned with Pacific Basin strategic trusteeships would not prevent interference in those matters by other powers, since the trusteeship agreements would have to be approved by the UN Security Council members, even if they had been excluded as states directly concerned. Hiss suggested that the United States consult with the British and French as to the definition of the term "states directly concerned" and keep an open mind as to their suggestions.[21]

Hiss then introduced the following plan of action. First, he thought it best that all five nations be considered states directly concerned when it came to the mandated territories because the United States, Great Britain, and France were the remaining Principal Allied and Associated Powers from the First World War, while the Soviet Union and China were Principal Allied and Associated Powers when it came to the surrender of Italy and Japan in the Second World War. Further, Hiss thought some "trading" could go on. Specifically, he asserted that the United States, Great Britain, France, and the Soviet Union, as parties to the Italian Armistice, could be declared as the states directly concerned in the disposition of the Italian colonies. As far as non-mandated Pacific territories went, the states directly concerned would be the acceptors of the Japanese surrender—namely, the United States, Great Britain, the Soviet Union, and China.

Next, Hiss thought that the five powers would consult on an ad hoc basis to determine whether or not any other states were directly concerned, or if any other states had to be consulted. Under Secretary of State Acheson then asked Hiss if the United States' position would be prejudiced if the Soviet Union and China were admitted as states directly concerned, since the United States had veto power in the Security Council over strategic trusteeship agreements anyway. Hiss responded that the legal right of those two states to be directly concerned had to be acknowledged, or the United States would be basing its position solely on the right of conquest.

Byrnes then asked about the status of non-mandated Japanese Islands such as Okinawa. He wanted to know what would happen if the Security Council did not approve of the United States' proposed trusteeship agreement. Benjamin Cohen, Counselor of the Department, responded that there would be a step preceding this: the disposition of those islands in a peace treaty with Japan. In the event that the peace treaty was not made, the United States would still be in possession of those non-mandated islands. Cohen emphasized that the really important matter was the status of a state directly concerned, and that there must be agreement on what this meant before a trusteeship agreement could be submitted to either the Security Council or the Trusteeship Council. He assumed that the more narrowly the United States construed the term the better, since other states would then just have to be consulted, but he wanted those other states to be "broadly" consulted. Cohen continued that he thought it was legitimate that the states directly concerned be only the immediate administering or controlling power, and that if the United States wanted to be a state directly concerned in all mandates, it could hardly argue for the Soviets to be excluded. He also pointed out that the UN Charter referred to states directly concerned in the plural, and that agreement between these states was to be reached. Hiss added that the Charter specifically talked about the trusteeship terms being agreed upon by the states directly concerned, including the mandatory power.[22]

Byrnes then asked how this agreement was to be obtained. Hickerson replied that the Charter was ambiguous on this point, and that he thought some sort of mistake had been made. He agreed that the Army and Navy wanted all of the Japanese Islands to be strategic areas, and that all "Big Five" states would have a veto. But he now thought that the best thing to do was consult with the British and the French to see what they had in mind, before the United States took any kind of formal position. He reminded his colleagues that the British had submitted their draft agreement for the African mandates for information only, and without prejudice to the definition of "states directly concerned." He also pointed out that these African mandates were for non-strategic areas and that if the United States took the position that all of the Big Five were directly concerned about them, the United States would be extending veto power to the UN General Assembly since it had authority over non-strategic areas. Hickerson therefore supported Cohen's position. Hiss disagreed, pointing out that veto power would not be for the Big Five, but would accrue to whichever states were deemed directly concerned. However, he also thought that the veto power was in no one's interest except that of the mandatory power. Cohen was not sure about that. He thought Hiss was assuming that the United States could veto an agreement even before it reached either the Trusteeship Council or the Security Council, and that the veto would give the United States great influence. On the contrary, Cohen thought this would entail the US position being on record early in the process, and therefore compromised if it had to negotiate some sort of agreement before trusteeship treaties went to a UN organ.[23]

Hiss now suggested that the United States waive its rights at an early stage, in the interest of reaching an agreement for the higher body to consider. Cohen thought it would be easier to reach a mutual agreement if the states directly concerned were kept to a minimum and the others merely consulted. He thought that the mandatory power could introduce the draft agreement. However, he also thought that the United States should be careful about drawing sharp lines between the legal right of a state to participate in the drafting and approval of a trusteeship agreement on the one hand, and consultations prior to its submission to the Security Council or General Assembly on the other. Hiss repeated that his proposal was designed to restrict the number of states directly concerned as much as possible, but he thought that there would have to be four or five in each case. He also disagreed with the idea that other states would give up their claims just because the United States did. He agreed with Hickerson that this could be determined by consultation with nations like Great Britain and France, but he also thought that the term "states directly concerned" would have to be precisely determined by the United States prior to such consultations. Hiss went on to explain to the Committee that timing was a further consideration in the formulation of US policy. He reminded the other Committee members about how difficult it would be to get approval for a trusteeship agreement from the other fifty members of the General Assembly, something

Hickerson had also mentioned at the same meeting. At this point, Cohen was asked if "states directly concerned" really implied a plurality of states involved. Cohen answered that while it seemed to, the same language could also apply to one colonial power voluntarily placing its colonies under trusteeship. He thought it would be "strange" for a plurality of states to be required in this case. Cohen then stated that the United States should obtain concurrence from the other nations involved that the trusteeship agreements would be submitted to certain groups of "interested states" for their views. Under Secretary of State Acheson then asked if there was any difference, insofar as the term "states directly concerned" applied, between the Japanese Mandates and the other Japanese territories separated from Japan at the end of the war. Hickerson thought there might be, and Cohen asserted that while the Mandates went back to the Treaty of Versailles, the other Japanese territories' disposition would need a new treaty since there were no specific references to them in the terms of the Japanese surrender. Acheson then said that he assumed that the Russians would not advance claims to these other non-mandated territories, since they now held the Kuriles. Cohen asked if the Yalta Agreement confirmed that the Kuriles was the only territory the Russians would obtain from Japan. Byrnes responded that the Yalta Agreement merely stated that the Kuriles would be "handed over" to the Soviets. The only argument that he said could be derived from this situation was that no additional claims had yet been made by the USSR.[24]

Hickerson then brought up the issue of the best tactics to employ in terms of the United States proposing a strategic trusteeship over the former Japanese Mandates. The question was whether to propose the strategic trusteeship to the other states directly concerned in the negotiations, or take the matter directly to the UN Security Council. Hickerson said that the State Department's Russian specialists thought that the United States would be in a better position tactically if it took the issue to the Security Council. If it was blocked there, no doubt by the Soviet Union, the United States could then loudly protest the Soviet action. Byrnes agreed with the line of thinking that the sooner the matter went to the Security Council, the better. Hickerson, however, had a different approach to suggest. He favored consulting with the British and the French. More specifically, he wanted to see if those two countries wanted to "dodge" the whole issue of states directly concerned and go directly to the Security Council with a trusteeship proposal for the Japanese Mandates. He argued that the United States could then assert it was doing this so as not to prejudice the whole process vis-à-vis the states-directly-concerned issue. He further asserted that all of the states directly concerned were on the Security Council anyway, with the exception of New Zealand. He thought that New Zealand could be separately consulted, and then the whole issue would be open in the Security Council. Byrnes now decided that Hiss's method should be tried first, but that if delays in negotiations were encountered, the United States should announce that it would take its own trusteeship agreement directly to the Security Council, giving something like a thirty-day notice first. He was clear now, however, that he wanted to try to get an agreement on the trusteeship issue before going to the Security Council.[25]

Acheson again asked whether or not the United States' future position was prejudiced if it recognized the legal rights of "certain other states" in the mandated areas as states directly concerned. He thought that if an agreement was vetoed in the Security Council, the United States would simply take into account that it had recognized the other state's interests in the territory. Hiss replied that if the United States based its claim solely on right of conquest and the trusteeship agreement was not approved, it would have no legal claim. Hickerson, however, was not certain about the latter statement. He referred to the Marianas as an example where Germany actually had the last clear-cut title of sovereignty since Japan had a mandate after the First World War, but not sovereignty. The United States had now driven Japan out and had possession of those islands, but he admitted that the issue of which nation had title was "cloudy." He hoped this could be solved with the Japanese Peace Treaty, but if not, the United States would still be in de facto control of the area. Cohen now chimed in that he thought that the United States should avoid asserting the right of conquest over the area. Hiss asserted that the United States would have to admit Japan had some sort of title over its mandates if the United States was to base its claim solely on conquest. Of immediate concern to him, however, was a US reply to the British, the Belgians, and the French about US status as a state directly concerned in their mandates. He assumed from the discussion that the State Department was not prepared to assert itself as a state directly concerned in all of the mandates on a legal basis. But he wanted to know if the United States could say this had been the US position, even though it was now refraining from asserting that position. Hiss also wanted to know if the United States could comment on the proposed trusteeship agreements without asserting the prior position.[26]

Acheson was unclear why the United States had to say this had been its position without asserting that position. Hiss replied that the United States had taken this legal position for more than twenty years, and that it should not waive this position in the hope other nations would do so as well. Hickerson added as an example that the United States could assert a right under existing treaties as a state directly concerned in Tanganyika, but he did not think the USSR or China could assert a legal claim there or in the former Japanese Mandates. He thought their claims would have to be based on agreements yet to be negotiated, and that the United States could waive its rights with respect to Tanganyika and rely on expressing its views in the General Assembly. Acheson replied that he would prefer the United States neither waive nor claim rights, but just say that it had been consulted. Cohen answered that the United States, in its reply to the European mandatory powers, propose that on the trusteeship agreements the United States should reserve its legal right under existing treaties, and that its observations on the trusteeship agreements should be without prejudice to its claims as a state directly concerned. He further proposed that the United States discuss the problem of defining that status with the British and the French, and that it take the position that the conclusion of the trusteeship agreements would be facilitated by narrowly defining that status. Cohen thought that if the British and French would agree to it, the United States would propose consultation with the states having "legitimate" interests in any particular trusteeship agreement. Byrnes said he thought this might take care of the immediate situation, and Hiss suggested that the War and Navy Departments be consulted regarding their views. In particular, he thought the military departments needed to be shown how their ideas about this matter were invalid, though Acheson replied that he thought that the military views on this situation were quite valid. If, however, there was a failure to reach agreement on these matters, the Secretary's Staff Committee would meet again.[27]

Late in May, Hickerson was visited by George Middleton, First Secretary of the British Embassy in Washington, D.C. Middleton handed Hickerson a note, dated that day, that responded to the United States' position on the African trust-territory negotiations and its stance on waiving its status as a state directly concerned. Middleton was looking for Hickerson's immediate response. Hickerson read the note and said the United States would have several comments on it. He indicated that the British Government must have misunderstood the US policy, so he reiterated that US policy was not to press its claim as a state directly concerned when it came to the trusteeships over Tanganyika, the Cameroons, and Togoland, even though it could under "certain circumstances." While Hickerson did not outline what these circumstances were, he emphasized to Middleton that the whole purpose of the US policy was to reduce to a minimum the states actually signing the trusteeship agreements, and thus holding veto power over them in the UN. Probably referring to the United States' ideas about the Japanese territories, he said that the United States' position was that it hoped the British and French could agree to be "consulted" in these matters rather than insisting on being officially recognized as states directly concerned. Hickerson then became even more explicit. He said that the United States expected Great Britain to refrain from pressing its claim as a state directly concerned with the disposition of the former Japanese Mandates if the United States did not press its claim as a state directly concerned with the three British mandates in Africa. The United States also expected Great Britain to hold to a minimum the number of states signing the three African trusteeship agreements, no doubt so that the United States could do the same with its Micronesian trusteeship. He further said that if Great Britain recognized states as directly concerned that the United States did not, the United States would then assert itself as a state directly concerned in the African trusteeships. Middleton claimed he understood the US policy in this sense, and that he thought the British Government did as well. He said, however, that the whole difficulty lay in the fact that the British

Government had not yet decided whether or not to waive its claim as a state directly concerned when it came to Micronesia. The meeting ended inconclusively, but with Hickerson stating that the United States might have other comments to make on the British note.[28]

The US position became even clearer a few days later. The United States had written a note in response to the British communication of 24 May. Benjamin Gerig, Chief of the State Department's Division of Dependent Area Affairs (DA), circulated the US note to the other concerned divisions within the State Department. The note specifically said that if the United States and Great Britain could not agree not to press their claims as states directly concerned in the specific trusteeship agreements, the United States would feel obligated to reconsider its position as to when it would want to be considered a state directly concerned, and even when it wanted to be considered a signatory power to trusteeship agreements. The memo made it clear that the United States was not, in fact, waiving its right to be considered a state directly concerned, or even waiving its right to press that claim, but that it was merely waiving its right to sign these specific trusteeship agreements.[29]

Part of the problem, however, stemmed from the fact that there was still internal disagreement within the US Government as to what the policy on the Micronesian trusteeship should be, and how detailed the United States should be in communicating its ideas in the UN. In a memo two days later to Hiss and Blaisdell, Gerig discussed the special treatment of trust territories referred to in Article 43 of the UN Charter. In particular, Gerig was concerned that SWNCC's Ad Hoc Subcommittee of Security Functions of the United Nations was going to insert too many detailed provisions into a proposed "Standard Agreement" on the issue that was being prepared.

Gerig was particularly concerned that if SWNCC delved too deeply into the issues of trusteeship, it would "probably open up the prior questions of the disposition and form of administration of the Japanese Mandated Islands and other Japanese territories, which remain for determination." He reminded Hiss and Blaisdell that a paper was being prepared for SWNCC on this matter. In the meantime, he did not want the issue being "indirectly" introduced to SWNCC because of the vital importance of the issue. He also thought that there was need for a final decision from the White House on the exact form of trusteeship administration that was to be proposed. Accordingly, he was requesting that the formation of a Working Group, proposed by Hiss, be postponed until a final decision on the form of administration had actually been decided within SWNCC.[30] Clearly, State and the military services were still arguing over trusteeship versus annexation.

"States directly concerned" was again the object of a long set of instructions in early June 1946 from Acheson to Gerig in regard to negotiating with Great Britain, France, and Belgium over the issue of the African trusteeships and their relationship to the Japanese territories. First, Gerig was instructed to attempt to gain acceptance of the United States' position during the previous twenty-five years.

Specifically, he was to assert that the United States, as a signatory state of the Treaty of Versailles and as a party to bilateral treaties with Great Britain, had special and specific rights concerning mandated territories. These rights included being counted as a state directly concerned in all mandate matters. However, Acheson then directed Gerig to emphasize that the United States, in the interest of expediting the conclusion of the trusteeship agreements, thought it best to limit the number of states directly concerned to a minimum. Specifically, the United States was now suggesting that the present mandatory powers draft the trusteeship agreements, and that the other "particularly interested" powers be "consulted" before the draft agreements were submitted to the General Assembly. Acheson said that this latter condition was dependent on the other powers refraining from pressing their claims as states directly concerned in regard to the African territories, just as the United States had done.

Gerig was then instructed to explain to the other powers that the United States was taking this action in order to facilitate the conclusion of the trusteeship agreements. Acheson thought that prior consultation with the other interested powers would obviate the need for "prolonged discussion and perhaps extensive revision of the terms of trusteeship by the General Assembly." Gerig was also given specific instructions about how to reply if he was asked what the phrase "particularly interested powers" meant. The phrase was meant to suggest the inclusion in the trusteeship negotiations of all nations with special treaty rights, all of the remaining powers of the Security Council and the Trusteeship Council, and any states in the region of the trusteeship that had special interests in the specific territory. Acheson also told Gerig to ensure that the other powers understood that the United States, by waiving its right to be a signatory power to the initial trusteeship drafts, was not waiving any of its rights with respect to any alterations or amendments that might be subsequently proposed.[31]

Further, Acheson wanted Gerig to make sure that the other powers understood that the states directly concerned in the mandated territories were to have legal rights in those territories. Acheson additionally wanted Gerig to confirm that the other powers understood that the United States was entitled to be a state directly concerned in all mandated territories because of its treaty rights, but that it simply did not desire to be a signatory power to the African draft trusteeships as long as the other powers were similarly willing to refrain. Gerig was also instructed that he did not need to obtain British and French concurrence in this US position as long as they agreed to the consultation process outlined above. If geographic proximity was employed as a justification for involvement in a trusteeship negotiation, Gerig was to reject any such interpretation as a reason for a nation being a state directly concerned. Acheson also warned about the British, the French, and the Belgians insisting that states other than the mandatory power be considered as states directly concerned and as signatories to the trusteeship agreements. In this case, Gerig was to reserve his position and seek further instructions from the State Department. Regarding the former Japanese Mandates, Gerig was to state that it was the intention of the United States to place these islands under trusteeship. However, he was also to communicate that it was the United States' position that in regard to the Japanese Mandates and all other Japanese territories, the number of states directly concerned was to be kept to an "absolute minimum." Further, he was to communicate that the United States really preferred to submit the draft agreements to the General Assembly or the Security Council as the sole state "directly concerned" in the former Japanese Mandates, but only after "consultation" with the other "interested states." Finally, Acheson made it clear to Gerig that every decision the Division Chief took in regard to the draft trusteeship agreements for the African territories concerning states directly concerned and the terms of trusteeship "may set a precedent which may affect the trusteeship agreements for territories in the Pacific."[32]

Acheson also gave instructions on this topic in late August 1946 to John Minter, US Chargé d'Affaires to Australia. The State Department authorized Minter to discuss the Australian Draft Trusteeship Agreement over New Guinea with the Australian Government. Minter was told, however, that the defense and security aspects of the Australian Draft, especially the issue of US base rights in the Admiralty Islands, were still being discussed in Washington. He was also told that the State Department's views on these matters would be cabled to him later. Repeated to Minter at this point were the same instructions that had been given to Gerig. Minter was instructed, for instance, that if the question of the former Japanese Mandates came up, he was to inform the Australians that the US Government intended to place the islands under trusteeship. He was then to inform the Australians that in regard to the former Japanese Mandates and all other Japanese territories, the United States wanted the number of states directly concerned to be kept to an absolute minimum. This situation meant that the United States preferred to be the sole state directly concerned, as it submitted its draft to the General Assembly or Security Council after it had consulted with the other interested states.[33]

In early October 1946, these matters again were discussed and repeated by Dulles to Byrnes concerning conversations he had with Hiss and Gerig regarding the preparation of the United States' trusteeship position for the first session of the General Assembly meeting. Dulles was trying to get a clearer picture of the State Department's position on trusteeships before he lunched with Truman and then Forrestal. When he met with the President, Dulles told Truman that at the General Assembly meeting, the President should make an authoritative and definitive statement regarding US intentions vis-à-vis the former Japanese Mandates. Truman responded that he would be discussing this with Byrnes as soon as the Secretary of State returned to Washington. In his conversation with Forrestal, Dulles repeated the importance of the United States clearly stating its intentions at the next General

Assembly meeting. He reminded Forrestal that there had been indecision for about a year and a half, and the United States now needed to demonstrate to the rest of the world that it had the ability to act decisively in international affairs. There were, he continued, a number of countries that doubted that the United States had this capacity, and these nations wondered whether it was safe for them to associate with the United States. Indecision in relation to the US position on the former Japanese Mandates would, if prolonged, weaken the United States' position in the world, especially since the differences between the War, Navy, and State Departments were well known. If these departmental differences continued, Dulles asserted, it would give the world the impression that in such matters, the US Government was unable to make up its mind and come to a decision. While Dulles argued that some decision had to be made, irrespective of what it was, he also said he thought it was important that the decision be in favor of strategic trusteeship, not annexation. There was, he insisted, a long history, beginning with the Atlantic Charter, that gave other nations the idea that the United States would not annex any territories. If the United States did annex these territories, he told Forrestal, it might make such a negative example as to cause the whole trusteeship system to collapse. Forrestal said he was impressed and asked Dulles to speak with Admirals Nimitz and Sherman about this matter. In later conversations with those two key officers, Dulles repeated the reasons for strategic trusteeship, and said that he thought it was possible and proper to obtain the military rights the Navy felt it needed in these largely uninhabited islands. He pointed out, for instance, that the United States had not annexed territory in the Panama Canal Zone, but had a lease in perpetuity. He answered further questions from both Admirals and told Byrnes that he thought they were "fairly satisfied" by his answers. He also told Byrnes that he thought the Navy was by no means unalterably opposed to strategic trusteeship for the former Japanese Mandates. Nimitz had even asked Dulles to look over a draft paper that had been written to cover this contingency.[34]

Connections between the former Japanese Mandates and other territorial issues came up again later that month during a meeting of the US Delegation to the UN. The issue, according to Gerig, who was also an Adviser to the US Delegation, was what stance the United States would take in regard to South Africa's desire to annex South West Africa, or at least what attitude the United States would take if South Africa unilaterally submitted a draft trusteeship to the General Assembly. Ambassador Warren Austin, Senior US Representative on the US Delegation, told Gerig that it might be "unwise" for the United States to take a position on the annexation of South West Africa since the United States might be "forced" into annexing some of the former Japanese Mandates. At this point, Eleanor Roosevelt, another of the Representatives on the US Delegation, asked about the policy of annexation in the Pacific that was being contemplated. She wanted to know why members of the Delegation feared connections between South West Africa and the former Japanese Mandates. She reminded the other members that although the War and Navy Departments could offer advice about policy, it was still up to the State Department and the President to make final decisions about matters such as annexation. Dulles came back to the issue of the United States lacking concrete policies in regard to the former Japanese Mandates. He reminded those present that the Delegation would be in an embarrassing position unless it declared some US intention for the Japanese Mandates. He recounted the history of dissension between the concerned Executive Departments even before the Dumbarton Oaks Conference, and he urged Austin, as Chairman of the US Delegation, to again confer with Truman and Byrnes on the urgent necessity of declaring US intentions vis-à-vis the former Japanese Mandates. In the meantime, the Delegation decided to defer the South West Africa question until that nation could be consulted on "technical" matters.[35]

A few days later, not surprisingly, there was still no declaration of intention by the United States. Another Representative on the Delegation, Congressional Representative Sol Bloom of New York, Chairman of the House Committee on Foreign Affairs, reported that the Delegation's Trusteeship Committee had discussed the issue for quite some time, but had not come to any conclusion. Bloom also said that the Trusteeship Council could not come to a conclusion about the matter until there was some US declaration of intention. He therefore requested that the Delegation send another message to Washington asking for further instructions on what he called the "Pacific problem." Dulles concurred and again noted the South African question. He said the Delegation could not have a decision on the question regarding UN inspections of an annexed South West Africa because there would be a precedent for UN inspections of US positions in the former Japanese Mandates if the United States decided to annex the Pacific Islands. He rhetorically asked how the Navy would like Soviet representatives inspecting Pacific Island bases! He also said that another question to be resolved was trade monopolies in the former Japanese Mandates. Apparently, the Navy wanted to establish trade monopolies for Americans in Micronesia so that foreign intelligence personnel posing as traders could not gain access to the island bases. Dulles then asked how the United States could oppose similar proposals from the British for its Tanganyika trusteeship, and how it could take any kind of a trusteeship position until the "American Pacific Islands position" was defined. He agreed with Bloom that the United States had to abstain from these questions until a decision from Washington was obtained. John Ross, Deputy Director of State's Office of Special Political Affairs and a Senior Adviser to the US Delegation, then reported to the Delegation that a message to this effect had been sent to higher authorities. He said that the matter was being discussed between Secretary Byrnes, Secretary Forrestal, and the President, but that no final decision had yet been reached. Ross therefore suggested that another message be sent so that the President and his Cabinet members understood that the Delegation could not do any work on the trusteeship issue until the United States' position had been completely defined. In addition, Ambassador Austin wanted to know if the Navy's position had changed at all.[36]

In a related context, Bloom inquired about the chairmen of the concerned committees in the House and Senate. Several of these members of Congress, he pointed out, had significant interests in the Pacific questions, and they needed to be consulted, at least informally, before any decisions were made. If these consultations did not take place, Bloom thought that there would be "considerable difficulty." In particular, he thought that the military committees needed to be brought into this. Austin suggested that these members be contacted by phone over the next few days. Charles Fahy, State Department Legal Adviser and another Senior Adviser to the US Delegation, then suggested to the Delegation that there was a difference between annexation of territory for military bases as provided for in a peace treaty, and annexation of a mandated territory as South Africa was planning. Dulles pointed out that the Delegation only needed clearance on the mandate territorial issue in this case. When Senator Thomas Connally of Texas, Chairman of the Senate Foreign Relations Committee as well as another Representative on the US Delegation, asked if this was because other nations had interests in the Pacific Islands, Dulles replied that that was the case, and also because the League of Nations was being replaced by the UN. Dulles pointed out that if there was an agreement on a strategic trusteeship, as he hoped there would be, the Navy would be very "stringent" on what it would accept. He did not want the Delegation to be in a position of opposing some part of another nation's trusteeship agreement if that aspect was going to be insisted upon by the American military for the United States' agreement. He reiterated his concurrence with Bloom about the need for further instructions and clarifications on the US position.[37]

Regarding states directly concerned, a telephone conversation a few days later between Dulles, Hiss, and Ross made Dulles's position a little clearer. The conversation was related in a memo by Hiss, who was certain that if a number of states, including the Soviet Union, were included in trusteeship negotiations as states directly concerned, there would probably not be any agreements approved at the next General Assembly meeting, and the trusteeship system would be "indefinitely" delayed. Dulles, however, said that he was substantially in agreement with the State Department's position. Therefore, he thought that if the United States' proposals about states directly concerned were not adopted, the United States should propose that the General Assembly refuse to designate any powers as states directly concerned except the respective mandatory states. Dulles went on to say that he felt the Russians were planning a campaign of obstructionism in regard to the proposed agreements. He pointed out that the USSR wanted provisions in the agreements for early independence of the trusteeships, something that would be unacceptable to the mandatory powers. He also pointed out that if the Russians had veto power, they could prevent the establishment of the trusteeship system.

Dulles stated that although he thought establishment of the trusteeship system was important, it was less important than the propaganda issue the Russians were raising about which nations were the true defenders of dependent peoples. Dulles continued with the idea that once the trusteeship agreements were approved, there would be little of substance for the Trusteeship Council to accomplish, and the administering powers would really be the ones responsible for what occurred in their respective territories, just as had happened with the League of Nations Mandates. He thought the really important issue here was Chapter 11 of the UN Charter, which related to dependent territories generally and thus to a larger proportion of the world's population and the Earth's surface than the trusteeships ever would. He was apparently anxious that the United States not be in a position of appearing to "rush" the trusteeship agreements through the General Assembly when those agreements were satisfactory to the colonial powers but not to the Russians. Still, he also thought the Russians were going to try to identify the United States with the colonial powers.[38]

Dulles next asserted that, as a lawyer, he could not conscientiously argue very strongly for the State Department's interpretation of the UN Charter. In his opinion, using the phrase "states directly concerned" meant a group larger than just the respective mandatory states. However, for practical reasons he agreed with the Department's position to urge the General Assembly to avoid determining that any state other than the mandatory power was the state directly concerned. He also wanted to talk promptly with the Russians and the other mandatory powers about the Department's interpretation and then discuss the whole matter with the Department's officers themselves. Hiss also said that Gerig told him that in recent talks, the British had begun to indicate more sympathy with the United States' suggestion that the UN Charter be interpreted so that only the mandatory power of each territory was considered the state directly concerned. Hiss said Gerig therefore thought it might be possible to get the British to "go along with us." Dulles doubted this, however, and was not at all sure the United States could avoid having a number of states designated as directly concerned. He was sure the Russians and the Arab states would oppose the US position, and that Chile and some of the other Latin American nations would do so as well. He thought that if the mandatory powers also opposed the United States on this point, the possibilities for action contrary to US views would be "considerable." Moreover, he pointed out that it only took one-third of the General Assembly plus one vote to block the approval of a trusteeship agreement in the UN.[39]

■ Truman Makes a Decision

In November 1946, because of Truman's concerns about American policy in the Pacific and the United States' international image, the United States submitted a

Draft Trusteeship Agreement to the UN. State Department concern over Soviet reaction to and propaganda about the Draft Trusteeship Agreement can be seen sur-
facing at about that same time. More specifically, Elbridge Dubrow, US Chargé to the
Soviet Union, sent Byrnes comments from the Special TASS Correspondent in New
York about US actions. The account, of course, painted US actions as imperialistic
behavior. What is interesting, however, is that the Soviet accounts were not all that
inaccurate. The Soviet correspondent writing this article first talked about the US
Government making decisions about the future of the former Japanese Mandates
and the other Japanese territories "over the heads of its allies" who were also responsible for the peaceful settlement of Japan. The author also talked about the
broad scope of American plans—plans that envisioned the United States taking
control of the former Japanese Mandates and any other island taken from Japan
that the United States desired! The article further criticized US attempts to turn a
"considerable" part of the Pacific Ocean into an exclusive US strategic zone. The
Soviet piece even quoted a 7 November *New York Herald Tribune* article that talked
about the United States turning the Pacific into an American lake from San Francisco to the Philippines. The article further emphasized US planning that focused
on satisfying the needs of the US military services for air and sea bases in the region, especially the provisions for "exceptional and secret" base rights. The Soviet
correspondent also cited an 8 November *New York Herald Tribune* editorial that, if
accurate, confirmed the idea that if any other power used the veto in the UN to reject the US draft agreement, the United States would merely retain "ownership" of
the territories by right of conquest![40]

A few days later, another piece, entitled "USA and Japanese Mandated Islands"
and written by a correspondent named Ocherski in the Soviet newspaper *Red Fleet*,
was sent by Army Lieutenant General Walter Smith, US Ambassador to the Soviet
Union, to Byrnes. Ocherski talked about US intentions to retain Pacific Island bases
so as to maintain a very strong Pacific Fleet. Ocherski also reported that American
military leaders explained this in defensive terms, but that only "simpletons" would
accept the defensive explanation. Ocherski even cited an alleged quote by Vice Admiral Sherman about the United States needing control of its "ocean frontier" so
that it could attack targets along those frontiers! Ocherski went on to assert that
US Pacific policy clearly reflected the influential business and military circles that
preferred power politics, militarism, and imperialism to international collaboration.
The author also argued that the US Draft Trusteeship Agreement for the former
Japanese Mandates was only one part of US plans for the Pacific, and that American
designs for the postwar Pacific were in "flagrant violation" of international law and
the UN Charter. Ocherski also quoted "conservative" US newspapers and commen-
tators saying that the Draft Trusteeship called for annexing 15,000 Pacific Islands
under the guise of trusteeship! The author then concluded by asserting that US actions represented an aggressive utilization of these islands that was aimed at the

USSR, that the United States sought to ignore international cooperation, and that it hoped to impose its will on others.[41]

On the same day, the US Delegation met again to further discuss several issues relating to the Pacific Islands Draft Agreement. Dulles wanted the Agreement to include a statement that the administering authority was governing the territory on behalf of the UN. However, he also wanted that announcement to state that the administering power would have the authority to govern the Trust Territory of the Pacific Islands "as if it were an integral part" of the administering power, rather than simply "as an integral part." The latter phrase was preferred by the Navy because it gave the United States greater leeway in its governance of the Japanese Islands. Accordingly, the Navy was opposed to Dulles's suggestion for change. Dulles assumed, however, that the Navy's preference was too aggressive a stance for the United States to take, and that the United States should not press for any agreement provisions to be applied to other powers that the United States was not willing to have in its own agreements. At this point, Mrs. Roosevelt asserted that the Delegation had a responsibility to press for anything that it thought might improve matters for other nations or should be included in agreements. She was hoping for some sort of US gesture through unilateral disarmament, and she thought that the Delegation should ensure that the military was not perceived as controlling policymaking within the US Government. She also thought that the best way to communicate this last notion was through the trusteeship system. Another Representative on the Delegation, Congressional Representative Helen Douglas of California, a member of the House Committee on Foreign Affairs, supported Roosevelt's views, arguing that if the Delegation held back on these trusteeship matters, its actions could "wreck" the UN. Gerig then suggested that perhaps the issue was the difference between declared strategic and non-strategic areas. He asserted that these areas were so different that certain provisions could be made for the non-strategic trusteeships, such as measures against trade monopolies. The United States would not be at all embarrassed if it supported those measures, but it could prevent them from taking effect in the strategic trusteeships, such as the US trusteeship in Micronesia. He thought, however, that the provision for conducting trusteeship administration in the name of the UN was a secondary matter, and that it could be dropped.[42]

Dulles disagreed with Gerig. He understood that the Delegation's hands were tied because the Navy refused to agree to any changes, but he thought it was fundamental that the Draft Trusteeship Agreement include clauses about the United States administering the former Japanese Mandates in the name of the UN. Roosevelt asserted that the Navy was only thinking of Navy interests here, and that the Delegation had to take into account how the US population felt about these issues. Ambassador Austin then suggested that it might help to air the idea that the United States was only going to administer the area in this strategic manner until the UN's security system had been established. Dulles agreed that the latter statement might help, but thought that this idea would have to be cleared with Washington first. He also thought that it would be more effective if Austin suggested the idea. Austin then gave more details about conversations he had had with at least one Filipino general about the United States' position. According to Austin, the Philippines was "violently opposed" to the United States' position on the Japanese Islands, but they were more accepting of US strategic trusteeships in the area if these only existed until the UN was fully established. Austin said he would make a special effort to get this idea cleared in Washington, even though Dulles pointed out that the Navy would be opposed on the grounds that it was a dilution of the United States' current position on strategic trusteeships in the Pacific. Dulles was further worried that this issue aligned the United States with imperial powers such as Great Britain, France, Belgium, and South Africa. Specifically, Dulles was concerned about the foreign-policy implications if the United States was identified on "this side of the fence" in international affairs. Douglas added that there would be domestic problems as well.[43]

Four days later, the Delegation heard about the trusteeship issues from Charles Noyes, Assistant to the Secretary of State, Special Assistant to the US Representative on the US Delegation, and Adviser on Security Council Matters to the US Delegation. Noyes told the Delegation about a meeting he had with several State Department members who were organized into a Working Group to deal with the US Draft Trusteeship Agreement. This Working Group went through the Draft article by article in an attempt to raise any "delicate" questions that might arise in Security Council deliberations. Specifically, the Group sought to determine the authority by which the United States was proposing the Draft Trusteeship Agreement. The Group also attempted to determine if it was possible for the United States to contend that it was the only state directly concerned. In addition, the Group explored what US reaction would be to Soviet demands that the USSR be treated as a state directly concerned before the Draft Trusteeship Agreement was submitted to the Security Council. Noyes said that his Group agreed that as the military occupant of the Japanese Islands, the United States was within its rights to propose a trust agreement to the Council. However, the Group also agreed that the United States had to overcome the charge that it could not propose a trust agreement until a Japanese peace treaty had been signed. Once this matter was settled, James Green, Associate Chief for Trusteeship Administration in State's Division of Dependent Area Affairs, dealt with the question of the United States being the sole state directly concerned. Green stated that the United States' position caused difficulties for itself in the General Assembly because the United States could not contend that it was similar in situation to a mandatory power under the League system. Green said that the best position for the United States to take, given its present circumstances, would be to argue that the United States had done the appropriate thing by presenting the Draft Trusteeship Agreement to the UN unilaterally, since the other powers on the Security Council had a veto. He then thought the United States should argue that an additional system was not necessary, and that the final decision could be left up to the General Assembly rather than allowing the USSR to be labeled a "state directly concerned."[44]

In regard to the third question, the Working Group said that further instructions could be obtained from the State Department if the Russians really insisted on being considered a state directly concerned with signatory power. In addition, the Group stated that it was in no hurry to have the Security Council accept the United States' proposed agreement just to make known the United States' intentions that it was not going to annex the former Japanese Mandates! Since US intentions not to annex had been made by the President's actions, the main goal was to obtain Security Council approval of a trusteeship that was satisfactory to the United States. It was argued that if the Security Council was not satisfied with the Draft Trusteeship Agreement, the United States could simply postpone its consideration until a peace treaty had been signed with Japan. It was assumed that a Japanese peace treaty would solve these Pacific Basin strategic problems for the United States. As to the issue of stating that the Japanese Islands were to be governed as an integral part of the administering power, Noyes reiterated Navy resistance to any change in the language as well as Dulles's concerns about that resistance. Noyes's Working Group was certain the United States would be confronted with this issue, even though he stated that the United States did not intend to imply sovereign control by this phrase. Regarding the whole issue of annexation, Hugh Borton, Chief of the State Department's Division of Japanese Affairs (JA), repeated Truman's decision that there would be no annexation of any of the Japanese Islands or Mandates. Borton also related Truman's statement that the United States would later submit a draft trusteeship agreement for the Bonin and Volcano Islands along the lines of the present one, but that no decision would be made at this point about the Ryukyu Islands. It was here that the Army and Navy said that the United States should be able to submit proposed trusteeship agreements for either of the two latter island groups before a Japanese peace treaty was signed.[45]

On 30 November, Dulles recorded conversations he and Gerig had with Gromyko and Kirill Novikov, Secretary General of the Soviet Delegation, about creating a formula for the establishment of the UN Trusteeship Council. The two Soviet diplomats discussed the difficulty of the "states directly concerned" issue, as well as the issue of fortified trust areas needing Security Council approval. Dulles said the Soviet view seemed to be that all five Permanent Members would not have to be considered states directly concerned in all trust-territory matters, and that there could be "prior agreements" as to which states were deemed as such in regard to each set of territories. Dulles said the Soviets intimated that the USSR was not very interested in being a state directly concerned with the African mandated territories, but that they were interested in such status concerning the territories of enemy nations such as Italy and Japan. However, they also offered that if the United States accepted this position, the USSR might not press its claim in regard to Western Samoa and New Guinea. Dulles and Gerig replied that if the USSR did not claim to be a state directly concerned in regard to the African territories, its position would be the same as the United States' regarding the African mandates. However, the Soviets were not prepared to concede their claim as long as it was "part and parcel" of an agreement linked to the Pacific Islands. Dulles and Gerig asked the Soviets directly what the USSR might obtain from being considered a state directly concerned in regard to the Pacific Islands. Gromyko and Novikov answered that their particular interest was in military fortifications. They stated that their understanding of the UN Charter meant that there was no right to fortify these territories for national purposes. They therefore stated that there should be no fortification in the Pacific Islands—other than for local defense—that was not approved by the Security Council after special arrangements had been negotiated there. They also saw no great difference between strategic and non-strategic areas, and they alluded to a continuing right of the Security Council to inspect fortified areas.[46]

Dulles and Gerig responded that they could not agree to this interpretation of the Charter. Moreover, they suggested that the Soviet diplomats look at the matter "practically." If the Soviet interpretation of the Charter were taken into account, it would allow the USSR to prevent US maintenance of bases in the Pacific Islands except where the USSR specifically authorized these bases. This situation was totally unacceptable to the United States, and it would never agree to such a situation. Insinuating that such a situation might lead the United States to annex the former Japanese Mandates, Dulles related that the US preferred trusteeship to annexation or de facto possession since trusteeship would give island inhabitants the benefit of UN Charter provisions. He also thought trusteeship would make the internationalization of military establishments easier, if or when the Security Council demonstrated competence in this area. Dulles was quick to point out, however, that this competence by the UN had not yet been demonstrated, and that until it was, the United States would want the same rights in Micronesia and the other Japanese territories as the USSR had in the Kurile Islands. Dulles and Gerig pointed out to Gromyko and Novikov that the USSR had shown no disposition to accept a regime in the Kuriles similar to what it was now trying to impose on the United States in the former Japanese territories. Gromyko and Novikov, however, argued that this was a different case, since it had been agreed between the United States and the USSR that the Soviet Union could annex the Kuriles. Dulles and Gerig answered that the latter had been an informal agreement that had not been ratified by a peace treaty, and that other nations, such as China, were concerned in these matters. Dulles then stated that it was his hope that neither the United States nor the Soviet Union would have advanced military bases or zones that would menace each other or other friendly nations. He stated, however, that the United States would not agree to a double standard in which it was subjected to Soviet control and inspection in a vital strategic area, even through the Security Council, when the Soviets did not have to reciprocate. Gromyko and Novikov replied that they would fight the issue through to the floor of the General Assembly, and that they were confident they could defeat the Draft Trusteeship Agreement provisions as they related to things such as bases. Interestingly, Dulles noted in his report that in spite of such frank discussion, the atmosphere was still friendly and cordial, and each side pledged to think the matter over to see if some possible basis could be found for proceeding further on the issue.[47]

In early December, according to Hiss in a memo he sent to Acheson, Dulles and Novikov were chosen by the UN as a "committee of two" to try to resolve the remaining differences about the subject of states directly concerned. Dulles said that it might be possible to solve the issue by having the General Assembly direct those nations submitting trusteeship agreements to first consult with the Permanent Members of the Trusteeship Council, and with the other members of the UN that expressed interests in particular territories. Dulles said that the Soviets' main concern was that there not be a repetition of the procedure the United States had followed in respect to the former Japanese Mandates. Specifically, the Soviets were concerned that the United States had published its proposed agreement without prior consultation or invitation of any consultation before submitting the Draft Trusteeship Agreement to the Security Council. In particular, Dulles said the Soviets did not want the United States to propose a trusteeship over other Pacific Islands, such as Okinawa, without prior consultation. Dulles also said the Soviets told him they were sincere about consultation, and were not demanding the right to veto or that an agreement had to be reached between parties before a state actually submitted its trusteeship agreement. Dulles had discussed this with Byrnes, who was anxious about the Navy's reaction. Byrnes's fear was that the Navy would think this practice might commit the United States to discussions in which the United States' ability to resist suggestions from other states might be less than if it had simply published its intentions. Hiss told Dulles that the latter's proposal seemed entirely consistent with the theory and practice that the State Department had advocated to the mandatory powers in the past when consultation, rather than formal agreements, were emphasized by the United States. Hiss had also discussed these matters with Captain Robert Dennison, ACNO for Politico-Military Affairs. Dennison claimed that there would be a favorable response from the Navy if it could be agreed that "states directly concerned" status was not a condition for actually submitting a trusteeship agreement, just a commitment to consult beforehand. Dennison even thought there was some advantage to prior consultations, since "dirty laundry" or controversial points could be solved in the process of the consultations rather than aired in public. He did say he assumed the consultations would not involve organized meetings or votes. Hiss responded that consultations would be by "diplomatic means," but that group discussions might be held by assigned representatives of the states concerned. He assured Dennison, however, that there would not be any organized voting. Dennison seemed satisfied with this, and Dulles requested Byrnes's approval on a draft of an enclosed proposal along these lines before forwarding it to Novikov.[48]

The British, however, were not very satisfied with this situation. In a memo dated the next day, Gerig related a meeting he and Dulles had with British Parliamentary Secretary Ivor Thomas. The meeting dealt with the proposed draft that had been given to Novikov and the representatives of several other states. Thomas told Dulles and Gerig that British Foreign Minister Ernest Bevin had also seen the draft and did not think it wise to give any private assurances to the Soviet Delegation. Bevin was mainly concerned about policy implications toward the former Italian Mandates. Thomas also told Dulles and Gerig that Australia and South Africa were "very much concerned" about a procedure that might require them to consult in advance with the Soviet Union and China over territories about which the British Commonwealth had special concerns. Thomas specifically said that South Africa might even initiate a trusteeship agreement for South West Africa if it was now no longer necessary to consult with the USSR. Dulles, however, had previously said that this new procedure was not an outline to determine which states were directly concerned, but rather a way to avoid a precise attempt to define this status. Thomas seemed satisfied with this as long as the procedure did not allow for private assurances not covered by written agreement. More to the point, Dulles dictated a memo for Austin in front of Thomas stating that the United States would not give any private assurances or commitments to the Soviet Delegation about supporting a Soviet claim to be a state directly concerned vis-à-vis the disposition of the former Italian Mandates. Dulles said, however, that he did not know what the US attitude would be toward a Soviet request about the Japanese Islands—especially the Ryukyus, which he thought was the main Soviet concern. He thought this issue would arise in the process of negotiating the Japanese Peace Treaty, and that in the meantime the Soviets were trying to get some sort of agreement with the other Great Powers about the Japanese Islands. In addition, Dulles and Thomas both had information that China was "very much concerned" about possible claims on the Ryukyus. The conversation ended with assurances by both parties that the requisite votes on the Security Council were now secured for this draft proposal, even if the Soviets voted against it. The two diplomats thought, however, that the proposal ought to be made available to the General Assembly so that its members understood the effort that went into this matter, in case the Soviets did vote against this agreement.[49]

The latter proposal, however, did not solve all of the issues between the United States and the USSR over the disposition of the former Japanese territories. This became apparent a few days later when Forrestal recorded in his diary a conversation he had with Byrnes about the Pacific Islands. Earlier that day, Forrestal had discussed with Dulles the latter's idea of traveling out to the Pacific to look at the

Japanese Mandates and the other areas of the region that were going to be involved in trusteeship talks. Byrnes, however, saw no reason for Dulles to do this, since he thought Dulles's work was finished. Still, Byrnes informed Forrestal of a conversation he had had with Soviet Foreign Minister Molotov about the Pacific Islands that suggested that there was more work to do between the two governments. Molotov told Byrnes that the Soviet Union would insist that the phrase "directly concerned" was applicable to all five of the Great Powers. Molotov also said that Russia would have to be involved in any decisions that concerned fortifications in the Pacific Islands, and that he wanted to know exactly what the United States proposed to do with the former Japanese Mandates. Byrnes responded that he wanted to know what the Russians proposed to do with the Kuriles and Sakhalin Island! Molotov argued that the latter groups could not be included in the discussions, since they were the subjects of previous agreements. Byrnes then retorted that he considered nothing as being subject to previous agreements, and that the Kuriles and Sakhalin would have to be brought into the discussions. Molotov, according to Byrnes, returned a number of times to the issue of US plans for Micronesia. Each time, Byrnes asked about Soviet plans for the Kuriles and Sakhalin. Byrnes confirmed for Forrestal what Dulles had said earlier: that the Russian attitude was that any trusteeship agreement concerning the Pacific Islands would have to be referred to the Security Council, where the Russians could exercise their veto power. Byrnes then concluded that he saw a "long road" of argument ahead on the trusteeships. However, he also said that he was not in a "rush" to have any trusteeship agreement made definitive. In addition, Byrnes did not see any great harm coming to the world if the trusteeship agreements were never consummated! Forrestal told Byrnes that he fully concurred with this attitude.[50]

Unfortunately for the United States, other nations were not satisfied with this situation. In late January 1947, Norman Makin, Australian Ambassador to the United States, sent a communication to George Marshall, Byrnes's successor as Secretary of State. Makin told Marshall that the Australian Government believed that the ultimate solution for the disposition of the former Japanese Mandates was their control by the United States, but that his government did not consider the disposition of the Mandates as a separate question to be isolated from a comprehensive settlement for the entire Pacific Ocean area. In fact, Makin argued that to isolate the disposition of the Japanese Mandates from that of other Pacific Basin questions, as the United States was doing with its unilateral submission of the Draft Trusteeship Agreement, was "untenable" both politically and legally. Makin went on to state that his government thought the timing and the procedure the United States had chosen was erroneous and would add to the difficulties of achieving a comprehensive settlement of Pacific matters. Makin was especially confused because the United States had just taken the position of supporting Australia's claim to be a "principal party" in the negotiation of a Japanese settlement. He found the United States' unilateral actions in regard to the former Japanese Mandates to be confusing since these actions disregarded Australia's vital interests concerning those territories.[51]

Great Britain also protested to the Americans about the United States' unilateral submission of the Draft Trusteeship Agreement since there had not yet been a negotiation of a Japanese peace treaty. In a communication in early February, Marshall wrote to the British Ambassador to the United States, Lord Inverchapel, that the United States regretted that the United Kingdom Government did not share the US view that the former Japanese Mandates could be placed under trusteeship before the negotiation of a treaty. More exactly, Marshall argued that there was nothing in the UN Charter preventing the United States from doing this, especially since the former Mandates never belonged to Japan, and since it had been reaffirmed at Cairo and Potsdam that Japan would be deprived of these territories. In addition, Marshall asserted that practically all of the states with any interests in the former Japanese Mandates were either on the Security Council or had been provided with information on the situation by the United States. For these reasons, he continued, the United States considered that the issue could be dealt with by the Security Council now, and did not need to await the Japanese Peace Treaty. Furthermore, Marshall stated that it was the United States' position that these types of proposals ought to be placed formally before the Security Council at an early date, something he claimed Article 77 of the UN Charter talked about in regard to former League of Nations Mandates. He also cited a February 1946 resolution from the General Assembly inviting the administering authorities of mandated territories to place their territories under trusteeship. While he was willing to admit that the United States was not the mandatory power over the Japanese Islands, he argued that it was the de facto administrator of those islands and therefore should perform its duty in accordance with the General Assembly resolution. He also asserted that these actions were taken with the inhabitants' interests in mind, and that US delay at this point in time would cause "misunderstandings" since President Truman had already announced what the United States was going to do in early November 1946. Marshall then stated that the United States noted Great Britain's concern that its actions might "confuse" the issue about trusteeship over the former Italian colonies, but that the United States had no intention of contributing to such confusion. The United States, he said, did not see any direct connection between the two categories of territories in question. Although both were under military occupation, the Japanese Islands were in a totally different category, since they had been under international mandate for years. Marshall did concede that after the United States' proposal had been formally placed before the Security Council, it would be willing to consider a reasonable postponement until a comprehensive Japanese peace treaty had been negotiated, if the other members of the Security Council desired. He said, however, that the United States did not think this was necessary. Accordingly, Marshall stated that the US Government hoped the UK Government was convinced of the desirability of this course of action, since the United States did not think that there would be any serious objection to its plan of early formal submission.[52]

In late March, the Australians again made a statement about this very matter. Paul Hasluck, the Australian Delegate to the Security Council, was instructed to communicate to the United States that since the issue of the Japanese Mandates first arose, both the UK and Australia had wanted to make certain that the United States' proposal to assume strategic trusteeship over the area was endorsed by those nations that had made substantial contributions to the victory over Japan. Hasluck was instructed to ensure that the United States understood that Australia had always supported the United States becoming the sole and exclusive trustee over the island territories gained at such sacrifice by the United States. Australia also warmly supported US control and administration of the former Japanese Mandates in the interests of peace and security. Hasluck stated, however, that the method of securing the US objective of being the sole trustee was supposed to be by postponing the process until the "successful" belligerent nations had formally met to create a peace settlement with Japan. The United Kingdom and Australia supported this position because they felt it necessary that all nations that had had a part in militarily defeating Japan also needed to be part of the peace-settlement process with that nation. The Security Council had even approved the Australian idea that the nations that fought against Japan should be considered part of the Security Council itself for purposes of negotiating the Japanese Peace Treaty. Interestingly enough, however, Australia's position on postponing negotiations had now changed. For some reason, both Australia and the United Kingdom decided not to press for a formal postponement of the United States' submission of the Draft Trusteeship Agreement. The change in position may have come about because the Security Council had approved a wider group of nations participating in the negotiation of a final settlement with Japan. In addition, Britain and Australia might have changed their position because the other belligerents now supported US actions. Since a large group of nations was apparently prepared to support the United States' unilateral actions, Australia was as well.[53] Of course, it could also be that Australia, the UK, and the other nations involved had simply recognized US intransigence on this issue or had greater issues to deal with.

That close allies such as the United Kingdom and Australia would acquiesce to US demands is quite understandable, but why the Soviet Union gave in to these demands in February 1947 is not entirely clear. In a previous study, I pointed out that the War Department General Staff Directorate of Intelligence speculated that the Soviets "sacrificed" their claims to a voice in Pacific trusteeships in order to gain US support for Soviet claims in Eastern Europe and East Asia. In addition, I speculated that the Soviets gave in because of their recognition of US power in the UN, and because the Soviets might have had greater objectives to pursue. It is also possible that the Soviets ceased their resistance because they could then suggest changes to the Draft Trusteeship Agreement that, if rebuffed, would give them a significant propaganda opportunity to paint the United States as an imperialistic nation.[54] An even more concrete reason, however, may have been Soviet fears that significant interference by the USSR in the United States' sphere in Micronesia might endanger a Soviet free hand in the Kuriles and Sakhalin. In early August 1947, Charles Bohlen, now the Counselor of the State Department, sent a memo to Robert Lovett, Acheson's successor as Under Secretary of State, commenting on a Soviet note objecting to the idea of an eleven-power conference to negotiate a Japanese peace treaty. Bohlen thought that the Soviets were objecting to such a large conference out of fear that the Yalta Agreement would be reopened and that it would be abrogated, thus causing Soviet loss of control over the Kuriles and Sakhalin. While Bohlen was ordered to reassure the Soviets that these were not the United States' intentions, the Soviets would have been suspicious of any potential actions along these lines.[55] Perhaps acquiescence over the former Japanese Mandates was the price the USSR thought it had to pay for continued international recognition of Soviet control over the Kuriles and Sakhalin.

■ The Policy Planning Staff, the "Reverse Course," and the American Lake

Taking the Japanese Home Islands into account as part of the Pacific Basin entails exploring the State Department's position there as well. George Kennan's Policy Planning Staff (PPS), so central to other aspects of early Containment formulation, enunciated some of the earliest ideas about Japan, its former territories, and their role in postwar American strategy and foreign policy. These ideas encapsulated much of the "Reverse Course" of American policy in 1947 as US policymakers ceased New Deal–style reforms in Japan and instead began to assist the Japanese in creating a reconstructed nation around their prewar industrial conglomerates or *zaibatsu*.[56] In mid-October 1947, for instance, PPS wrote "Results of Planning Staff Study of Questions Involved in the Japanese Peace Settlement." In this study, Kennan and his assistants saw "great risks" involved in an early relinquishment of Allied control over Japan. PPS saw no "satisfactory" evidence that Japanese society would be politically or economically stable if "turned loose" and left to its own devices at this point in time. Furthermore, the Policy Planning Staff thought that if Japan were politically or economically unstable at the time of a Japanese peace settlement, it would be difficult for the United States to prevent Communist penetration. PPS, however, saw some problems with continued occupation. It thought that the Occupation was at the point of "diminishing returns," and that the United States had already committed itself to the commencement of peace negotiations because of its invitations to other governments on this matter. The Policy Planning

Staff therefore thought that negotiations had to proceed, but they also thought that any talks ought to remain exploratory and non-binding. In addition, Kennan's staff wanted to hold open a possibility of further postponement of final decisions until the United States had a firm judgment on the basic questions involved. Accordingly, PPS thought that "discussions of substance" should begin before January, but should not be completed before June. The PPS staffers also thought that the USSR should be included in the negotiations. They were definitely concerned that if the Soviets were to exclude themselves, it should be on more substantive issues than things like procedural voting. PPS further thought that for the benefit of the Japanese, it would be best if the other powers involved agreed on a two-thirds vote. Finally, they thought that the United States should let the whole matter carry over to the next spring before even proceeding with the talks! Moreover, PPS did not think that the United States would get an agreement that satisfied its minimum requirements right away. Should the United States fail to obtain an agreement that met its requirements, the Policy Planning Staff thought it had the option of unilaterally introducing a virtual peacetime status to Japan based on US occupation of the country. In other words, the United States might achieve something approaching a peacetime status without any treaty at all! This alternative, PPS argued, was the United States' main bargaining position in the ensuing negotiations. If this negotiating position was to be fully effective, however, PPS thought that the United States needed to shift its occupational policy in the near future. The Policy Planning Staff argued that if the United States did this, it could convince the other powers of its seriousness, and be able to proceed unilaterally if the negotiations actually failed.

PPS also laid out certain territorial-status issues that it thought the United States should press for in the negotiations. These territorial issues included Japan retaining the southernmost of the Kurile Islands. In addition, PPS thought that the Bonins, the Volcanoes, and Marcus Island should be detached from Japan and placed under a US strategic trusteeship. It also wanted a final decision on the disposition of the Ryukyu Islands to be postponed. More specifically, PPS thought that the southern portion of this chain should be either a US strategic trusteeship or a US military-base system leased on a long-term basis from Japan, which would hold "nominal" sovereignty. In fact, at this point the Policy Planning Staff advised that the United States proceed in the negotiations on the assumption that it would hold a strategic trusteeship over the Bonins, the Volcanoes, and Marcus Island. It further advised that the United States proceed on the assumption that it would definitely require military facilities in Okinawa. It did, however, want a special study conducted about the potential cost and burden to the United States of keeping military facilities in the Ryukyus, especially costs related to civil administration—irregardless of US treaty rights to fortify that island chain. As to the United States requiring military-base facilities in the Japanese Home Islands, PPS claimed it did not yet have a firm-enough basis on which to make such a judgment. It did not, however, think that facilities for ground or air forces would serve any useful purpose. Therefore, the matter came down to whether or not the US Navy needed a base, with supporting air facilities, at Yokosuka. This was a question that PPS thought had far-reaching implications for Japanese and international politics. Because of these long-term implications, PPS wanted to see this question postponed, if possible, until the next spring. As to the future defense of the Japanese Home Islands, PPS stated that the United States was already committed to the demilitarization of Japan. While it thought that the Japanese Peace Treaty ought to include provisions for complete Japanese disarmament, PPS also thought that any four-power agreement on Japanese militarization should be abandoned. It also wanted the Japanese to have the right to create and maintain a civil police force and a coast guard at strengths to be initially defined by SCAP. A "council of ambassadors" could then be charged with the continued supervision of demilitarization and disarmament. PPS admitted that this situation left Japan without means of self-defense against foreign aggression, but the staffers saw no way of avoiding this result. They thought that in the ensuing time period, Japanese military security had to primarily depend either on the proximity to Japan of "adequate" US forces, or on US forces actually present in Japan during "extreme events." The Policy Planning Staff therefore thought that it should be a principle of American defense policy to retain sufficient armed force in the Pacific Basin in order to make US interests in Japanese security clear to other nations, and to prevent any other military power from establishing itself in the Japanese Home Islands.[57]

Continuing on, the Policy Planning Staff did not think there should be any formal Allied control or supervision of Japan's political life following the signing of a peace treaty. It thought a peace treaty would have a highly beneficial psychological impact on the Japanese that would be lost if formal political controls were retained. If the United States thought it had to retain political control, Kennan's staff thought that it would be better not to have a peace treaty at all. PPS pointed out that the former situation meant that when American occupation forces left Japan, Japan would be on its own politically. PPS was sure that "Moscow-controlled Communists" would attempt to penetrate and dominate Japanese political life. Japan's future would then hinge on the dependability of its internal political stability. This stability would be partially dependent on the political structures inherited from the Occupation. PPS also thought that this stability would be dependent on how well the Japanese themselves "adjusted" to those structures. The success of this situation further hinged, PPS claimed, on how "tolerable" economic conditions in Japan were, and how confident the Japanese were about their national future. If harsh economic conditions continued, the Policy Planning Staff thought that Japanese resistance to Communism would be weaker. PPS continued with its economic analysis by stating that Japan could lose a certain portion of its "economic substance" if its markets and sources of raw materials on the Asian mainland were controlled by the Soviets. The Policy Planning Staff feared that with much of Asia in chaos, and with no certain exports to the dollar area of the world, Japan faced an "extremely serious" economic situation even in the best of circumstances. PPS also asserted that the United States could never be certain of the depths of this problem, even though various elements of the State Department were conducting further studies of the situation. This potential future situation in Japan is why PPS had come to its earlier conclusion that Japan could not survive if "turned loose." The Policy Planning Staff wanted to more fully determine, in conjunction with further study by SCAP, whether or not Japan could actually stand on its feet economically and politically after a period of US aid. PPS thought that if the Japanese could not, then the United States might have to rethink its basic approach to the country, even at the possible cost of abandoning a peace treaty at this time. If, however, it was determined that Japan could stand on its own, then Kennan and his staff thought that the United States should try to prepare Japan for this newly independent environment to the greatest degree possible before the Occupation ended. Regardless of which approach the United States would have to take, PPS wanted to determine if SCAP's operating instructions were actually preparing Japan for future economic and political independence. So far, the Policy Planning Staff had information from some SCAP personnel that the purging and decartelization of Japan ran counter to Japan's future needs. SCAP, however, officially denied such claims, and PPS was not able at this time to reconcile the differences of opinion. It therefore called for additional discussions with SCAP on the issue.[58]

In a cover letter to a study completed just a day later, Kennan suggested to Under Secretary of State Lovett that SWNCC's successor, the State-Army-Navy-Air Force Coordinating Committee (SANACC), further explore the problem of the "disposal" of the Ryukyus. The enclosed study started out by stating that both the JCS and MacArthur thought it was essential to US security that the United States retain "effective control" over the Ryukyu Islands. The Policy Planning Staff had been told by Army and Navy sources that the latest thinking on this issue was that US control had to be exercised over the islands south of latitude 29 degrees, and that such control should be in the form of a strategic trusteeship. PPS accepted the principle of US control over the Southern Ryukyus. It was not convinced, however, that a strategic trusteeship would be the most effective means of US control. Instead, the Policy Planning Staff wanted a different option explored. Specifically, PPS thought that the United States should continue the military occupation of Okinawa and the other islands in the Southern Ryukyus by means of long-term leases of twenty-five to fifty years or more, with Japan itself retaining sovereign control. The Policy Planning Staff's thinking on this issue was that a strategic trusteeship over any significant portion of the Ryukyus would probably involve a financial burden on the United States. The staffers pointed out that before the war, the islands were dependent on

Japan for making up deficiencies in their economy. In addition, they cited tentative JCS financial estimates for the Ryukyus in FY 1948 alone to be 28–30 million dollars. The bottom-line analysis, not surprisingly, was that the Ryukyus were a "deficit area." PPS had not yet seen any firm estimate of the civil-administration costs if the United States assumed strategic trusteeship over the Ryukyus. Given this lack of information, it could not make any firm recommendations concerning a strategic trusteeship without first knowing if the Ryukyus could attain a balanced economy and what it would cost the United States if the islands had to be subsidized. Since it thought the latter situation was likely, the Policy Planning Staff wanted this information on hand if Congress was asked to support a US strategic trusteeship there. Accordingly, PPS wanted a thorough analysis completed of the several forms that US control of the Southern Ryukyus might take, so that it could recommend a formula that would both satisfy US military needs and minimize disadvantages for the US Government.[59]

■ Conclusion

Trends noted above in State Department policy include a general desire to see US hegemony established in the territories taken from Japan, but not in any way that could be seen as aggressive or imperialistic. Unlike the US military, the State Department was quite sensitive to both American public and international opinion about the United States and its actions. This sensitivity was particularly acute in light of rising tensions with the USSR and the possibility of Soviet exploitation of propaganda opportunities. However, it is also quite clear that State Department officials and officers could be quite imperialistic in their own right. As one would expect, these politicians and diplomats scrutinized documentation in as legalistic a manner as possible in order to define terms such as "states directly concerned" in ways that would be as advantageous to the United States' position as possible. Though not admitting that US actions constituted imperialism per se, they were nevertheless highly conscious of the impression the United States was making upon the rest of the world by its actions in the Western Pacific. In fact, it can be said that State Department officials and officers were aware enough of this charge of imperialism to be focused on marketing a positive American image to the rest of the world even as the United States was establishing its hegemony over the postwar Pacific Basin.

CHAPTER 5

Letting Go Is Hard to Do

The State Department and the Philippine Islands

Another Pacific Island group that was a vital part of the United States' planned postwar strategic-defense complex for the Pacific Basin was the Philippine Islands. As related in earlier chapters, US plans for the postwar defense of the Pacific entailed establishing forward-deployed combat units and strategic facilities in "frontline" areas such as Alaska, the Aleutians, Japan and the Ryukyus, and the Philippines, with secondary lines of defense and support in island groups such as Micronesia and Hawaii. Given the emphasis of this defense system on mobile air and naval striking units rather than static bases, base complexes like the Philippines were key links to the system, though still secondary to the mobile forces themselves.[1] At the same time, US policy toward the archipelago was significant to postwar American foreign policy since the United States had been stressing its support for decolonization throughout the war and had been pressing decolonization on its closest allies.[2] Therefore, while obtaining base facilities in the postwar Philippines, the United States also had to illustrate that its granting of Philippine independence was a showcase of decolonization in order to dispel criticism by its allies that the United States was hedging on its wartime pledges. Moreover, any delay in the granting of Philippine independence or any doubt that the new republic's independence was complete would bring about significant Soviet criticism. The State Department had a major role to play in ensuring that the United States' granting of independence to the Philippines was total and sincere, or at least had the image of being so, while the United States retained its prewar strategic position into the postwar period. All of this occurred in a political environment in which US diplomatic and military officials and officers had to reorient themselves vis-à-vis the Philippines and begin treating a former colonial subject as, at least, a junior strategic partner. The primary sources cited below suggest how difficult this was at times for US personnel.

■ US Difficulties in the New Pacific Republic

Some issues about the pending decolonization had to do with bureaucratic boundaries and the administration of American foreign policy toward the newly independent nation. For example, there was a concern about the State Department's jurisdiction over US policy as the new republic gained its independence in early July 1946. This issue can be seen in a memo from Ellsworth Carlson, State Department Country Specialist, to Woodbury Willoughby, Associate Chief of the State Department's Division of Commercial Policy (CP), in late June 1946. The specific issue was the establishment of a unified US policy toward the Philippines, which was to be administered by the State Department once Philippine independence took effect. Carlson first talked about how disturbed he was at the lack of such a unified policy. As an example of this bureaucratic confusion, he related that State, Interior, Commerce, Treasury, the Reconstruction Finance Corporation (RFC), the United States Commercial Company (USCC), War, Navy, Agriculture, the Civilian Conservation Corps (CCC), and the High Commissioner's Office all had a "hand" in Philippine affairs. In light of the Philippines gaining its independence in the next few days, Carlson thought that this was the right time to suggest the formulation of a solid policy, especially since he thought that future US-Philippine relations should be under State's jurisdiction. Carlson also thought that the State Department should prepare something beyond its recent "problem and policy" statements. He was thinking of prepared policy positions that covered more long-range policy objectives as well as immediate questions. To Carlson, these policy positions would also include solving issues with representatives of the other departments and agencies concerned.[3]

Another issue that worried State's officers was that of Filipinos accused of being Japanese collaborators spreading "anti-American ideology." The concern about these collaborators by one State Department officer illustrates not only the racial context in which policy was being made in the US Government in the late 1940s but also the residue of colonial mentality that was still highly evident in US policy toward the Philippines in this time period. In an early September 1946 memo from Edward Mill, Acting Assistant Chief of the State Department's Division of Philippine Affairs (PI), to Frank Lockhart, Chief of the Division, Mill brought to Lockhart's attention the "anti-US" remarks by Jose Laurel, an alleged collaborator, in a recent *New York Times* article. Mill asserted that "puppet leaders" such as Laurel had conspired to bring about the defeat of the United States during the war, thus not only committing treason against the United States but against the Philippines as well, and he was fearful that the former collaborators would become rallying points for anti-American ideologies in the Philippines. Mill thought that Roosevelt's wartime policy of removing collaborators was still in force and was still US policy, and he was quick to point out that the Philippine Government's alleged failure to remove all of the collaborators and prosecute them might cause significant harm to the United States sometime in the future. Mill pointed out that if Laurel and other collaborators sensed weakness on the part of the Philippine Government, they might be encouraged to rally for "anti-Americanism and anti-white propaganda in the Philippines." According to Mill, anti-American groups had already found a way to discredit the United States in its relations with the Philippines over issues such as military-base rights. Mill was willing to admit that criticism was healthy in a democracy, but he thought that these "anti-American" groups were simply being malicious toward the United States. Mill was fearful that these groups might attempt to spread these ideas throughout Asia "wherever the colonial powers have imposed their rule upon subject peoples. The result may be to give rebirth to the old idea of the Greater East Asia sphere so recently espoused by Japan." Mill thought these matters were concerns for "thinking Americans," but that the Philippine Government, under the impression that the United States had lost interest in the collaboration issue, wanted to "whitewash" things. While Mill said he knew that the United States could not "interfere" in the internal affairs of the new republic any longer, he thought it was imperative that the United States make it clear to the Filipinos that the United States still stood for Roosevelt's policy in regard to collaborators. Not to do so, he thought, would encourage the former collaborators to become active again in Philippine political life. To Mill, this result "will be calculated to bring only harm to the United States."[4]

An even more pressing issue was the opposition of Philippine public opinion to the United States' proposed Military Bases Agreement. The United States wanted to reopen several prewar military installations for air and ground forces around Manila, but the atrocious conduct of US military personnel toward Filipinos in 1946 created a grass-roots and media opposition to that notion. At least one historian has demonstrated from Philippine Government documents that some of this "anti-Americanism" was actually orchestrated by Filipino political elites in order to obtain political concessions from the United States in the base negotiations.[5] However, the increasing anti-American attitude in the Philippine press was taken quite seriously by American diplomatic personnel, and it was the topic of one September 1946 memo to Secretary of State Byrnes by Naval Reserve Commander Julius Edelstein, Acting Director of Information and Cultural Relations at the US Embassy in Manila. Edelstein began by telling Byrnes that there had been an increasing number of "anti-American" comments in the Philippine press in the last fortnight, with special emphasis on the proposed Military Bases Agreement. These reports about "deadlocked" negotiations had, according to Edelstein, aroused "tremendous interest" in the Philippines. Specifically, Edelstein claimed the Philippine press was charging the United States with trying to force the Philippines into granting base rights that the Philippine Government was not willing to grant. Edelstein asserted that the result had been a "field day" for the expression of anti-American sentiment. Supposedly, the Philippine press corps even alleged that American journalists "threatened" Filipino journalists with reports to their US newspapers about the Philippine press corps stirring up an increasing amount of anti-Americanism. According to Edelstein, the Philippine reporters were quite concerned about these charges by their American counterparts. One reporter apparently even went to the length of writing an entire column to the effect that he was not anti-American, but that the proposed Military Bases Agreement exemplified a type of American imperialism that was a threat to Philippine sovereignty. Edelstein asserted that the tone of the press reports had disturbed Manuel Roxas, President of the Philippine Republic, and that the reporting had given an "unfavorable background" to other pieces of legislation under consideration by the Philippine Congress that had an impact on US-Philippine relations.[6]

In another communication between Paul McNutt, US Ambassador to the Philippines, and Byrnes in late September, McNutt detailed some of the issues that had arisen between Filipinos and US military personnel, especially misconduct by American Military Police (MP). McNutt admitted that a "number" of excesses by US personnel did occur, but he claimed they were mostly before 4 July 1946, the day the Philippines was granted independence from the United States. These excesses consisted of raids on private homes, supposedly in search of stolen goods. In addition, there were charges against American military personnel about seizing, manhandling, and holding Filipino civilians. McNutt was willing to admit that there was a complete disregard for Philippine civilian authority on the part of some American military personnel. However, according to McNutt, part of the problem was a lack of liaison between the US Army and Philippine Army MPs, though he claimed that there had been some recent improvement in cooperation along these lines. Another issue was the town of Puerta Princesa, Palawan, being put off limits to American GIs for the last two months because of an anti-prostitution drive by the US Army. Supposedly, this led to disgruntled Filipino businessmen, civil unrest, and then reprisals by the American MPs, at least as Filipino authorities saw the matter. McNutt, however, was quick to point out that there had not been any complaints brought against the US Navy. He also did not think that there was "any basis" for the highly publicized charge that reprisals were taken by the US Army against civilians who signed complaint petitions against American soldiers. Furthermore, he asserted that while the US Army cited an Executive Order as its authority for its various actions, he admitted that the Army was liberally interpreting this authorization in its favor. He also pointed out that President Roxas had indicated that the Executive Order in question was only a gentleman's agreement that was no longer in force. McNutt ended the report to Byrnes by stating that the Filipino judge assigned to investigate these matters, Roberto Regala, had been instructed by Roxas to make an interim report, and then a final report once the US Board of Investigation submitted its findings. Roxas supposedly wanted full publicity given to the US report, including subsequent action taken by the US Government. McNutt also said that Major General Eugene Eubank, COMAF 13, desired that all of the pertinent facts be made known, and that matters be adjusted "amicably."[7]

A few days later, Nathaniel Davis, McNutt's Minister-Counselor, sent a communication to Byrnes in which he illustrated what he thought were dangerous xenophobic tendencies on the part of the Filipinos that would have obvious implications for the ongoing military-base rights negotiations. Davis started by pointing out the number of bills that were going before the Philippine Congress that had to do with the employment of aliens in the new republic, and what he thought indicated a "definite" trend of public sentiment against foreigners. Davis recounted to Byrnes what he also saw as a long history of the Filipinos trying to restrict the number of Chinese nationals engaged in the retail trade, and he mentioned previous attempts to turn historical xenophobia into anti-foreign legislation. To Davis, it was fortunate that the US High Commissioner had been able to veto these bills before Philippine independence in July 1946, but with the coming of independence, the "brake" had apparently been released. Thus, a number of bills were supposedly being introduced to bar Chinese from filling positions such as accountants, foreign-service officers, and retail-stall operators. Davis also talked about the necessity for US representatives to convince the Philippine Government to change the rulings about disbarring American lawyers who had been practicing law in the Philippines. Davis still saw most Filipinos as "happy-go-lucky" and "cheerful" individuals, loyal to all friends of any nationality. He thought, therefore, that part of this xenophobia might be the nationalistic "growing pains" of a new nation, or that it might be some manifestation of an "inferiority complex" induced by the colonial past. The real crux of the matter to Davis, however, was that this anti-foreign feeling was manifesting itself in "vocal" but "uninformed" commentary in the press on US-Philippine negotiations over the United States' military-base rights. Davis thought that the press espoused a certain "tenor" concerning US "special rights" for American military personnel. He reported, for instance, that the Philippine press had charged the US Army and the US Navy with efforts to gain "exclusive jurisdiction" over "vast areas" of Philippine territory, including an alleged attempt by the Army to gain control of the "entire" Manila waterfront. In addition, Davis reported that the press was talking about American military requests that had "little" to do with defense and that were making a "mockery" of Philippine independence. He said that the press was "ignoring" the idea that these diplomatic agreements were "mutual" defense treaties, and he was sure that the ideas enunciated in the press struck responsive chords in "youthful intellectual" circles, the

Philippine Congress, and even the Roxas Administration. He also asserted that anyone reading the Philippine newspapers as a sole source of information would be convinced that just one American soldier on Filipino soil would be a derogation of Philippine sovereignty! Davis went on to assert that there were officials in the Philippine Government, including Vice President and Secretary of Foreign Affairs Elpidio Quirino, who recognized the value of the American bases for "mutual" protection. Davis thought that these officials wanted the bases segregated from major population centers, however, because of their recognition of Filipino xenophobia. In conclusion, Davis argued that there were certain "indices" to the "national temper." He thought that time could "dry up" these undercurrents of anti-foreign feeling, but that both American and Philippine leaders had to recognize and deal with them in all matters. He also thought that the Roxas Administration was cognizant of this anti-foreign feeling, as was evident in the President's role in supposedly toning down some of the more nationalistic activities that had occurred. However, Davis warned Byrnes that this xenophobia might split Philippine political parties to the detriment of the Roxas Administration, and that only an "upsurge" in prosperity, business activities, visible reconstruction, and an absence of incidents could reverse the trend.[8]

Adding to US problems was Soviet propaganda about US-Philippine relations. In an 11 October telegram, Elbridge Durbrow, US Chargé in Moscow, told Byrnes about a *Pravda* article written by one O. Zabozlaeva the day before that included Soviet interpretations of Philippine-American negotiations. Zabozlaeva accused US officials of seeing the Philippines as an "ideal" example of colonial settlement that all imperial powers should strive to meet. Zabozlaeva also accused the United States of absolutely dominating the newly independent republic in political, economic, and military contexts. Zabozlaeva went on to assert that trade between the two nations was being established on a so-called free-trade basis, but that this trade arrangement actually gave economic preference to the United States, established the Philippines as a supplier of raw materials to the United States, and made the archipelago a "monopolistic" consumer market for American goods. Zabozlaeva further accused the United States of creating a compensation situation for war losses that indemnified American and Filipino companies at the expense of "simple" Filipino individuals. According to Zabozlaeva, even the Philippine press recognized the continued colonial aspect of this situation. Zabozlaeva thought that this latter situation was evident from various articles that appeared on 4 July 1946, which asserted that it would take years for the Philippines to be truly independent. Zabozlaeva then accused the United States of attempting to retain its hegemony over the Philippines after driving out the Japanese, in contravention of US promises to grant true independence. Zabozlaeva asserted that this situation was an inconsistency that was known and felt by most Filipinos. Zabozlaeva additionally depicted MacArthur as a "landlord" in the Philippines who had taken collaborators like

Roxas under his protection. Zabozlaeva further claimed that the US Government had used military forces on various occasions to break up Philippine political activity while it reinstated known collaborators. In the end, Zabozlaeva argued that the Philippines were "independent" in name only.[9]

Another notice from Durbrow in late October indicated that the Soviet newspaper *Red Fleet* had printed an editorial by an M. Mirski on US-Philippine relations that portrayed a thoroughly traditional colonial relationship between the United States and the Philippines. According to Mirski, the Roxas Government, in its three months in power, had been attempting to suppress national democratic opinion on the orders of "reactionary" American leaders. Evidence for this assertion included the Philippine Government's recent actions against the Hukbalahap guerrillas, when, supposedly, American MPs participated in these operations against the guerrilla group. Mirski went on to assert that these activities by the Philippine Government were fully in accord with American "colonial" interests. Part of this colonialism was apparently the Philippine pre-independence right to import some commodities duty-free to the United States. This situation prompted Mirski to argue that American "business circles" had started an "independence movement" that had the trappings of national self-determination while preserving American economic domination of the archipelago. Mirski continued with the idea that the Philippines had therefore been granted its independence, but with laws and provisos such as the Bell Act that preserved the United States' position in the new republic.[10] Mirski claimed that there were 90,000 American military personnel in the Philippines, that they were part of an occupational regime, and that they were not leaving any time soon. Mirski also asserted that Roxas was more concerned with defending American colonial interests than with Philippine independence. Again, Mirski's evidence for this charge was the economic concessions the Philippines had supposedly given the United States in limiting the amount of commodities sent to the United States on an annual basis. As further "evidence" of US domination, Mirski pointed out that the United States was able to retain naval bases and forces in the new republic, train the Philippine Army, and conduct negotiations for new US military base sites in the archipelago.[11]

On the same day as the Mirski article, Edelstein sent Byrnes a statement from Roxas concerning the Philippine President's reaction to Zabozlaeva's piece. Roxas stated that the charge that the Philippines had a "depreciated" independence and was dominated by US military and economic interests had come to his attention. He said that he thought these were irresponsible accusations, and even alluded to similar ones being enunciated by "self-serving interests" in the United States. He denied each of Zabozlaeva's accusations as falsehoods without any credibility, and he criticized *Pravda* for devoting so much time and space to these issues when there were so many other "world concerns." More specifically, Roxas denied the charge that the US Government had reinstated collaborators after the liberation.

In addition, he denied that US troops, including tanks, had been used to disperse political meetings. He further denied that US troops had been used to determine the outcome of the presidential elections, or that his government had pursued "cruel persecution" of partisan opponents. He ended with asserting that it was his desire that the Filipino people understand how false the charges were, and how politically irresponsible they were. He also wanted the world community to understand how much the Philippines cherished its hard-won independence. Accordingly, in the final part of his statement, he said that the Filipino people would protect that independence with all means at their command and would resist "any attempt by any nation to threaten or curtail that independence."[12]

This problem of relations between Filipino civilians and US military personnel was also the subject of a communication by McNutt to Byrnes in late October 1946. McNutt told Byrnes that a "Federal Council of United States Agencies" had been established in the Philippines. This Council consisted of the chiefs of the US agencies in the new republic, including the Army and Navy, and it had begun meeting in order to stem the "misunderstandings" and anti-American expressions circulating about the US Army's activities. The Council, by a motion from Major General Christiansen, Acting Commanding General of AFWESPAC, designated a "Technical Coordinating Committee" to consist of public-relations representatives from all of these agencies. Commander Edelstein was to be both McNutt's representative on the Committee and its Chairman. McNutt also told Byrnes that the Committee was meeting daily and the Council was meeting weekly, with the Committee recommending that each US agency in the Philippines hire a Filipino public-relations assistant. The Committee also suggested that a series of stories be prepared on Army-Navy jurisdictional procedures, and that these stories be offered to the local press. The Committee further recommended that a study be done of a more comprehensive procedure of orientation and indoctrination for US personnel assigned to the Philippines, and that Filipino correspondents assigned to cover US agencies in the Philippines be accredited with the "freest possible basis" to cover US activities. The rest of the message included a verbatim press release about the new public-relations procedures that the Embassy was proposing. This release emphasized the "open door" nature of American activities and the broad US contacts with both the Philippine press and public.[13]

Negative press coverage was the object of an additional message from Edelstein to Byrnes dated the same day. The *Philippine Free Press*, which Edelstein classified as the most influential publication in the new republic, printed its lead editorial with an article entitled "Driving the Wedge." The article, about relations between the United States and the Philippines, had an attached cartoon consisting of an American GI as the driver of the wedge, and the American public slumbering in ignorance about what their own government was doing in the Philippines. Edelstein pointed out that the *Philippine Free Press* had the widest circulation of any publication in the Philippines, especially in the provinces; that it was British-owned; and that it had a reputation for being both pro-Filipino and pro-American. To Edelstein, the fact that this "usually sober" weekly was now taking such an anti-American "line" indicated to him that negative viewpoints about the United States had been widely spread among the "articulate" classes. He also reported that the anti-American reporting by this paper seemed to have started about two weeks before. At that time, the newspaper ran a lead article with a picture of signs supposedly erected by American soldiers at US Army installations on Leyte that read "Filipinos keep out." According to Edelstein, this story did much to focus gathering sentiment against the US Army in particular and the United States in general.[14]

Just a few days later, however, Edelstein reported to Byrnes that some progress was being made in changing the tone of the Philippine press. Edelstein thought that the situation was changing mainly because of the efforts of the Federal Council of United States Agencies. According to Edelstein, AFWESPAC was showing a "new consciousness" in its public-relations responsibilities. Apparently the command was fully publicizing a new safe-driving campaign that was being instituted for GI drivers around Manila, since unsafe driving practices by American soldiers in the cities was one of the major issues for the Philippine population. The Philippine press also gave considerable attention to an order circulated to the command by General Christiansen about soldiers' proper conduct toward the Philippine public. Edelstein also claimed that a statement sent from Tokyo by General MacArthur had a similarly positive impact on the situation. Not surprisingly, MacArthur's statement was carried in a number of the major Philippine newspapers. One paper, the *Evening Herald*, which Edelstein claimed was "sensationally minded," interpreted MacArthur's remarks as blaming the Filipinos for the deterioration in US-Philippine relations. Several others, however, including the *Manila Tribune* and *Manila Bulletin*, gave this issue front-page treatment and even had "carefully worded" editorials that called on the Filipino people to "do their part." The last paper, Edelstein noted, had been "consistently anti-Army" up to this point in time. Edelstein further thought that the newly coordinated policy among the US agencies in the Philippines was helping gain a more "favorable position" in the Philippine press and radio. In addition, Radio Station WVTM, operated by the US Army, was the designated armed-forces radio station in the Philippines and was cooperating closely with the Council. The station made recordings of Navy Day broadcasts available to the other radio stations in the archipelago and participated in a nationwide Philippine Red Cross blood drive. Edelstein did say that the Army was "hesitant" in submitting some of its public-relations activities to the deliberations of the Technical Coordinating Committee, but he thought that there was every reason to expect the new procedures would work out. He also pointed out that the Philippine press was wary of the sudden friendliness on the part of the Army and the other agencies. He thought that they were maintaining a "tongue in cheek attitude," but he was also certain that this could be "easily overcome." Finally, Edelstein speculated that MacArthur's interest in the situation was a factor in improved relations. He claimed that several representatives from MacArthur's GHQ had been sent to Manila to consult with AFWESPAC officials and make reports back to him. Part of this newly favorable attitude on the part of the Army may also have been because of "prominent attention" in the press to a directive from General Eisenhower to MacArthur for a report on the conditions in the Philippines. This directive from Eisenhower was apparently based on a dispatch by Richard Johnston, the *New York Times* Correspondent in the Philippines.[15] Of note in all of this controversy, however, is that Edelstein never even speculated that the negative press coverage of US forces, while based on instances of poor conduct by American military forces, may indeed have been at least partially orchestrated by a Philippine Government intent on obtaining concessions from the United States in return for the Military Base Agreement.[16] The lack of speculation about even the improvement of relations was evident about a week later when Edelstein again reported to Byrnes that there was "noticeable progress" being made in changing the tone of the Philippine press about American GIs in the Islands. He once again attributed this changing tone to the efforts of the Technical Coordinating Committee, as well as to AFWESPAC's efforts to "'clean house,' improve the discipline of its personnel, enforce traffic regulations, and smarten up generally." The Embassy, in turn, had been making suggestions for specific actions and programs to the Army, as well as encouraging it in the other endeavors, and Edelstein thought that these efforts also had an impact.[17]

Whatever the cause, one piece of evidence of this more positive tone was headline treatment of a statement by Philippine Vice President Quirino about a "marked improvement" in GI conduct. Ample attention had also been given, according to Edelstein, to additional MP traffic patrols to apprehend GI violators, traffic-discipline efforts among GIs stationed at Clark Field, and an intensified orientation program for AFWESPAC's Information and Education Section.

However, Edelstein was quick to point out that the Philippine press was still giving quite a bit of attention to "scattered reports" of GI misconduct. He also asserted that there had been a particular round of "anti-Army" editorial comment after Judge Regala, Philippine Observer of the Palawan Board of Investigation, indicated considerable discrepancies between the Army Board report on GI misconduct in Puerta Princesa and the Philippine investigators' findings. Edelstein further reported "sensational and irresponsible" stories from the *Philippines Liberty News* that US Marines were being accused of "terrorizing" Filipinos on Olongapo. Without giving any details about the conclusion of this latter affair, Edelstein reported that the Navy had immediately sent an investigator, a fact that was quickly announced to the newspapers. In addition, the Technical Coordinating Committee decided to send "selected" newspapermen to Olongapo so that the journalists could investigate for themselves. Edelstein concluded his report by stating that at this point in time, no revolutionary change had occurred, but he thought that there had been a noticeable change in the press's tone. He recommended that the public-relations efforts should be continued, especially quick action by US agencies following any "adverse developments." He also thought it important that sufficient announcements be made of all actions taken by the US Government. As indicated above, Edelstein told Byrnes that Judge Regala's report on Thirteenth Air Force MP excesses in Puerta Princesa had been released. Regala's report apparently came "close on the heels" of that of the Thirteenth Air Force itself, and it supposedly praised the impartiality and fairness of the Army's conduct of the investigation. According to Edelstein, however, it differed in a number of respects, citing a number of Army abuses that were not contained in the Army report. According to a Filipino contact, Edelstein told Byrnes that Roxas was studying the report and would make known his official action, if any, in a few days. Roxas apparently stated that he was going to try to reconcile the two reports, and if Regala's was accurate, he might announce a course of action.[18]

Puerta Princesa incidents aside, other defense issues between the two nations were clear in documents from February 1947. In a telegram from McNutt to Secretary of State Marshall, the Ambassador asked that Under Secretary of State for Economic Affairs William Clayton inquire to Secretary of War Patterson about the American military's proposal for the size of the Philippine Army. McNutt was also interested in knowing how a Philippine national defense program would fit into a US plan for defense of the area, if the United States had any such plans.[19] In addition, McNutt asked for an estimate as to the expense of such forces as soon as possible, deeming it "essential" to get these figures at the earliest possible moment because of the potential magnitude of these expenditures for the Philippine Government. Though this author has not seen the actual estimate, a reply a few days later from the War Department acknowledged the message and promised a statement in two weeks with estimates for the years 1946 through 1950.[20] About two months later, McNutt finally received the reply from Acting Secretary of State Dean Acheson. This message gave some budgetary information on the pay of US troops in the Philippines, that of the Philippine Scouts, and the pay and back pay of the Philippine Army itself.[21] It also gave some budgetary information on various engineering projects to be pursued. However, Acheson was quick to point out that the figures for 1946 through 1950 were not final. In addition, he said that current War Department plans were based on the curtailment of US operations in the Philippines. This last statement by Acheson relates to General Eisenhower determining in late 1946 that the Philippines were too difficult to defend in wartime and too expensive to maintain in peacetime since the US Army had more pressing defense and occupation duties in Germany, Japan, and Korea. In addition, Eisenhower thought there had been too many problems related to stationing American soldiers in and around Manila. As related in chapter 1 of this study, since American air and naval bases were being retained in the Philippines, Eisenhower was suggesting by this time that Army forces be slowly and gradually withdrawn from the Philippine Republic. However, since this decision had only recently been made, Acheson told McNutt that there were no details available yet. He could tell the Ambassador that the JCS and the War Department had not yet integrated their defense plans for the Philippines with the Philippine Army, though they had agreed on the size of the Philippine Army. Acheson also told McNutt that the budget estimates were not to be taken as indicative of War Department polices regarding troop strength, or as limitations regarding the War Department budget. Finally, he told McNutt that the State Department would press the War Department to expedite clearance of the final budgetary figures and have that information presented to the Ambassador by the newly formed Philippines-Ryukyus Command (PHILRYCOM), the unified command successor of AFWESPAC.[22]

Collaboration issues returned in late April 1947 in a memo from Edward Mill, Acting Assistant Chief of the Division of Philippine Affairs, to John Vincent, Director of the State Department's Office of Far Eastern Affairs (FE). Mill and Richard Ely, Acting Chief of the Division of Philippine Affairs, had had a luncheon with two staff officers from the War Department General Staff's Directorate of Intelligence, Colonels Stephen Mellnick and George Chester. The issue discussed at the luncheon was the Philippine public's view of the collaboration issue. According to the information the State Department had been receiving, the collaboration trials were breaking down because of lack of public support for them. However, Colonel Chester had quite the opposite picture to paint. According to Chester, the general Filipino population wanted the collaboration trials to proceed, but he claimed that a "small but powerful Government group in Manila" was trying to create the impression that the issue was dead. Chester went on to assert that when one left the vicinity of Manila, the "great mass" of the population was actually quite anti-collaborationist and wanted to see the collaborators punished, since almost every family in the country had been touched in some way by the war, the Japanese occupation, and collaboration assistance to the Japanese. Chester argued that if a plebiscite were held that day in the Philippines, the Filipinos would vote three to one in favor of continuing the prosecutions. Mellnick agreed with him, and both officers urged a strong American stand on the issue. Mellnick specifically said that Joaquin Elizalde, Philippine Ambassador to the United States, was telling Roxas that the United States was no longer interested in the collaboration question. Mellnick also accused Elizalde of trying to convince the US Government that no one in the Philippines was interested in the issue either. Both officers therefore suggested that the United States take a more active stand on the issue if the opportunity presented itself.[23]

In early May, Ely communicated to Vincent further findings about this issue and suggestions for a final policy on the collaboration question. Mellnick had apparently called Ely a few days earlier with a complaint that Roxas had appointed a

collaborator, Rafael Alunan, to be the Director of Land Settlement Administration
in the Philippines. Mellnick thought this was "very bad" and asked what the State
Department proposed to do about it. Ely told Vincent that he had to remind Mellnick
that President Truman had issued a directive on these kinds of issues. More specifically, Truman wanted it known that collaboration issues like this were up to the
Philippine Government. In this case, Philippine courts had acquitted Alunan. Mellnick said he was afraid of criticism coming from men like former Secretary of the
Interior Ickes. He thought that the War and State Departments ought to "join hands"
in communicating to Roxas that the United States did not look with favor on the
Philippine Government's policy of reinstating collaborators to public office, even if
they had been acquitted. He said he was going to try to raise this issue with Secretary of War Patterson every time the Philippines asked for US assistance, and he
wanted Ely to do the same. Ely, however, was convinced that nothing satisfactory
could come of this, since he believed trying to force Roxas's hand would just give
ammunition to "anti-American" leaders who argued that the Philippine Government was a puppet regime of the United States. For better or worse, Ely thought
that the issue should be decided by the Filipinos.[24]

■ McNutt's Report

At this time, Ambassador McNutt submitted a long report to Marshall about Asian
and European reactions to US policy toward the Philippines that he had encountered during his travel back to the United States after the end of his tour of duty.
McNutt completed negotiating some agreements with the Philippines in late March
1947, including the Military Assistance Agreement, which was signed on 21 March.
He decided to return to the United States by the western route and stopped at a
number of countries in Asia and Europe. Assisted by the Embassy staff, he under-
took studies in each country to observe the impact of the United States' Philippine
policy. In addition, he sought to find out the amount and type of information that
people in these countries had about the Philippines and US-Philippine relations.
He claimed that much "incidental intelligence" was gained en route.[25]

McNutt first told Marshall that he had been assisted in these studies by Commander Edelstein, whom McNutt credited with supervising the US informational
program in the Philippines for the previous two years. McNutt also mentioned AAF
Colonel Millard Libby, an intelligence officer who had been assigned to the Embassy
for the last two years. In addition, he told Marshall that he had visited Siam, India,
Iraq, Egypt, Greece, Italy, Switzerland, Germany, Denmark, Sweden, England,
France, Spain, and Portugal. In a number of these countries, he held press conferences at the request of local American diplomatic missions in order to discuss US-
Philippine relations and the significance of those relations for American foreign

policy. Continuing his introduction to the report, McNutt told Marshall that the body of the paper included his general observations and recommendations regarding the effect of US Philippine policy in some of these countries. McNutt's introduction also included his observations about general reactions to US policies, and a more detailed breakdown of those observations vis-à-vis each nation. Although this travel was unofficial, McNutt claimed that he was provided with every courtesy by the American diplomatic missions in each nation; that he had an excellent opportunity to canvass matters with statesmen, journalists, and private citizens in each country; and that the members of his staff had similar opportunities.[26]

In the main body of his report, McNutt claimed that in the "entire world" west of the China Sea, there was a "startling" lack of "accurate" information about recent developments in the Philippines. In spite of this lack of information, he had witnessed an "avid and exciting" interest with regard to the new Philippine Republic. He stated that the "bare facts" about Philippine independence had been reported and translated to the leaders and "common citizens" of almost all of the countries he had visited. Certain topics, such as the Military Bases Agreement and the "excitement" over it in the Philippines, were also known. He did not think, however, that there was any "broad comprehension" of the Philippine situation or "true understanding" of the mutual basis of Philippine-American relations. Thus, he was faced with a situation in which he thought most of the populations exhibited a lively interest in what was taking place in the Philippines, but lacked "factual information" to satisfy that interest. The result, he thought, was a crystallization of "mistaken impressions" and "misinformation" based on scattered news dispatches and "unfriendly" editorial comments appearing in both Asian and European newspapers. More to the point, McNutt thought that unfriendly presses had cited the Philippines as an example of American imperialism, and that there had not been any successful rebuttal of this impression. To McNutt, this perception of the United States in countries such as India, Iraq, Egypt, Greece, and Spain deprived the United States of the "acclaim" that he thought was its due, given its policies toward the Philippines. McNutt thought that if interest about the Philippines in these countries could be "properly satisfied," attitudes could satisfactorily rebound to the United States' benefit. These changed attitudes, in turn, could be used to advance and "rationalize" American foreign policy. More specifically, he thought that US information-service outlets in these nations were necessary so that American policy toward the Philippines could be "exploited" as a "pure form" of America's international program.[27]

He reported, for instance, that in India, even among those "well informed," there was a widespread impression that the United States had granted the Philippines its independence unwillingly and "painfully." In addition, the Indians thought that the United States had placed so many military and economic restrictions and qualifications on Philippine independence that the "helpless" Filipino people considered their independence meaningless. He further asserted that there were numerous references in Indian newspaper columns and speeches to the Philippines as a "horrible" example of "false" independence. Apparently at the suggestion of the US Embassy in New Delhi, McNutt held a press conference on the Philippines that drew almost one hundred Indian correspondents. Based on this turnout, he reported that interest in the subject matter was "intense," and that he had done his best to dispel the false impression that was held. He further reported that he found the same situation in Iraq and Egypt. He asserted that journalists in these countries were not aware that the Philippine Senate had unanimously approved the Military Bases Agreement, or that the Filipino population voted eight to one in a "free" election in favor of special economic rights for American citizens in the Philippines. In fact, he found these pieces of information to be "complete news" and a sort of revelation to the Iraqis and Egyptians! He additionally said that these journalists were largely unaware of the "reciprocal" nature of US-Philippine relations, or the extent to which the United States had gone in trying to rehabilitate the country. McNutt saw the press and public leaders greet these remarks with great interest, but also "wonder." Coming from the Philippines, where American prestige was supposedly at an all-time high, McNutt was even more astounded to be faced with suspicions of American imperialism and selfishness by "many citizens" in Asia and the Middle East. In Egypt, he saw little perception on the part of the populace that the United States was any different from Great Britain. He also claimed that there had been attacks on the American flag and on American citizens, and that these attacks were more than just rare occurrences. He found the same attitude in India: that the United States had similar motives as Great Britain. While he thought that the British grant of independence to India had halted the overt acts of "anti-Caucasianism," he reported the basic attitude as still being present, and he thought the attitude belittled the "supportive" role the United States had taken in the achievement of Indian independence. He thought that there was a greater amount of goodwill toward the United States among the "more educated" and "enlightened" in Egypt and India, but he did not think those groups were being "tapped" to "properly" explain American foreign policy to the masses. McNutt also told Marshall that while he and his aides were in India, the Pan-Asian Conference was in progress. He said that the Conference was attended by unofficial delegates from most of the nations in Asia, including the Philippines. Indian Prime Minister Jawarharlal Nehru was the clear leader at the proceedings, but the Philippines Delegation, which he claimed was lionized, had members from the anti-Roxas opposition. According to McNutt, even Roxas's opponents surprised the Indian press when they claimed that Philippine-American relations were on a good footing, and that there was complete freedom of opposition and expression in the new republic. There was even what appeared to McNutt to be positive interest in Roxas's land reform and organized-labor policies, something that came as a great surprise to the Ambassador.[28]

In Europe, McNutt found most of the continent to be "very little aware" of the Philippines because of European problems. There were exceptions, however. Mc-Nutt found Greece to be very similar to the Asian nations in terms of the Greeks exhibiting "vital" local interest in the Philippines but having few "accurate" facts or information on the subject. Sweden was another exception to this European ignorance, since he found the press there showing an "outstanding curiosity" about the new republic. He also found Spain to be greatly interested, though he thought the official attitude was to "slur" over American influence there. Most Spanish he encountered, both officially and privately, did express sympathetic interest in the Philippines and a sense of appreciation for what the United States had "achieved" there. He declined to make any official statements about US policy in the Philippines while in Spain, however, because of what he took to be the "completely unreliable" Spanish press. Overall, McNutt was concerned and astounded that the "Communist Party line" on the Philippines had "thoroughly" filtered into both Asian and European countries where only small Communist minorities supposedly existed. Citing Siam, India, Egypt, Iraq, and Sweden, he said he repeatedly encountered statements about Roxas being a collaborator and the Philippines being a fascist regime. He also said that he was questioned a number of times about these matters, and that surprise was registered whenever he denied them.[29]

The Ambassador concluded the main body of his report with some general recommendations for American foreign policy in the region. He thought that in cooperation and coordination with the Philippine Government, the United States ought to use all available means to create and project a "concerted" program of information about the Philippines. He further thought that such a program would result in heightened prestige for both countries since it would include "factual" information on how the United States granted independence to the new republic, and on the aid the United States was giving the Philippines to help it achieve economic autonomy and stability. As well, he thought this information program should stress the reciprocal nature of US-Philippine relations. McNutt further reported on the "great interest" in the countries he had toured concerning the economic- and social-reform programs being undertaken in the Philippines, though he did not think that very much was known about these programs. As he saw it, the potential interest in the development of a "Western democracy" in Asia was practically unlimited, and that kind of support would go far in restoring the United States' reputation as an "unselfish" force in world affairs. In that way, Communist propaganda could be countered, since its facts would be replaced with the "real situation," at least in "impartial" quarters. McNutt concluded the report with a statement to Marshall that he could begin conferring with Philippine officials and consult with State Department officials who specialized in these areas so as to present a more specific program.[30] Though the result of McNutt's suggestions are unknown by this author, his perceptions and misperceptions about Philippine-American relations and the

United States' image in the international world warrant notice in the context of de-colonization, the rise of American global power, and the beginning of the Cold War.

■ Issues with the Philippine Press

In a similar vein of perceptions and misperceptions between the US and the Philip-pines at the dawn of Philippine independence, the Philippine press reacted to slights from certain American politicians about the alleged transparency concern-ing the new republic's independence. Fayette Flexer, First Secretary of the US Em-bassy in Manila, reported to Marshall in late May 1947 about this press reaction. According to Flexer, Representative Fred Crawford of Michigan, Chairman of the Territorial and Insular Subcommittee on the House Public Lands Committee, had belittled the quality of Philippine independence during hearings on a bill proposing to have the Governor of Puerto Rico elected instead of appointed. Supposedly, Crawford said that the Philippines did not have "complete" independence, and would not as long as the United States "mothered" and "protected" it. He apparently also complained about the amount of money the Philippines was requesting from the United States. In addition, Crawford asserted that the Philippines would not be able to "stand alone," and that the other peoples of the world knew it. Crawford was also quoted as saying that if the Philippines could stand on its own, it would "thumb" its nose at the United States. Apparently, Crawford then continued that "as long as the taxpayers and bondholders of Michigan and the 47 other states foot the bills of the Filipinos, we are going to have something to say about what goes on there."[31]

Flexer reported varied press reaction in Manila. One editorial in the *Manila Tribune* agreed with Crawford and thought that serious Filipino respect for Amer-ican public opinion was in the best interests of the new republic. The *Manila Post* similarly talked about the Philippines' need to solve its own problems with Philip-pine resources and not rely on the "public solicitation" of aid from the United States by Philippine leaders, if the island archipelago did not want to be classified as a puppet regime or a "Yankee version" of the Japanese Co-Prosperity Sphere! Flexer, however, also related to Marshall that the editor of the *Manila Chronicle* printed a "tirade" that laid the whole problem at the doorstep of the United States. The editor asserted that the Philippines had been dragged into the Pacific War, had not re-ceived war-damage compensation except for "surplus junk," and was forced to tie its economy to the United States by virtue of the Bell Trade Act. This author also as-serted that Philippine defense against aggression came at the expense of surren-dering certain portions of sovereign territory to the United States, and that the United States was not even paying Filipino soldiers' pay and benefits. The editor ended by asserting that if Crawford's statements were representative of US opinion, American concern about Emperor Hirohito and the "Japs" was a greater issue to the United States than was Philippine welfare. A fourth article, by one Juan Villas-anta, came out in the *Manila Post* asserting that the Philippines had given their "ut-most" to the United States, even "mutilating" its Constitution to allow the United States to help itself to Philippine natural resources. Villasanta also argued that the Filipinos were not dealing with the United States as beggars, but as old friends. He even asked if Crawford had "something" to say about what went on in China, France, Russia, Great Britain, or any of the other nations that had received substantial US assistance during and after the war! Perhaps not surprisingly, Flexer seemed to take Crawford's side in this dispute, since he ended his report by noting to Marshall that the Philippine press's reaction to Crawford's statement "has been neither po-litically constructive nor conducive to mutual understanding."[32]

■ Conclusion

The issues brought up in US Government documents and the Philippine press in-dicate that the State Department's mission vis-à-vis US strategic interest in the Philippines in 1946 and 1947 was highly complex. The Philippines was valued as a potential future base complex in case of a war with the Soviet Union, the with-drawal of US forces from the Japanese Home Islands and Korea, or the "Commu-nization" of those forward areas. The bottom line was that access to the Philippines —as well as to Hawaii, Micronesia, the Aleutians, and the Ryukyus—was needed in the future, just in case. It was the State Department's role to ensure that the United States had access to those strategic base sites and facilities. Carrying out this role in the Philippines, however, was more difficult than it was in places like Micronesia. To be sure, the United States had to contend with other Great Powers' resistance to US hegemony in Micronesia and the other former Japanese territories, especially Soviet resistance. But the United States could always, as a last resort, claim interwar and wartime events, as well as the right of conquest, as reasons for unilateral US ac-tions.[33] The same could not be done in the Philippines. That nation was a newly in-dependent republic whose independence came after many years of US preparations and promises. Moreover, the American public's knowledge about Fil-ipino suffering under Japanese conquest was widespread. While the Filipinos very much welcomed US liberation, it was a liberation based on the notion that quick in-dependence from the United States would follow once the war was over. Nor did the State Department officers seem at all acclimated to the fact that the Philippines was no longer an American colony, territory, or commonwealth, but an independent nation in its own right. In addition, American and global public opinion concerning the United States' seriousness about anticolonialism had to be taken into account in any policies that were constructed. There had to be at least the appearance that US policy toward the Philippines was sincerely linked to the United States' calls for dismantling European colonial regimes. Moreover, the machinations of some Filipino elites who were vying for military, political, and economic concessions from the United States were a phenomenon that had to be dealt with. Interestingly, the primary sources clearly suggest that State's officers in both Manila and Washington did not perceive this element of the diplomatic equation very well at all. Their seeming ignorance of the Philippine Government's potential deception is perhaps a testament to their continued colonial mentality about the newly independent archipelago, and their inability to see the "other side" in these diplomatic contexts.

CHAPTER 6

Civil versus Military Administration

The Interior Department and US Pacific Territories

The Interior Department was faced with a dilemma over the postwar Pacific Basin that was similar to the State Department's. In fact, Interior was even more distressed than the State Department by the military services' ideas about annexing the Pacific Islands and governing their civilian populations. For reasons cited below, Interior thought it absolutely necessary that the civilian populations of island groups such as Micronesia be administered by a civilian agency. Yet at the same time, the Interior Department had to deal with the concern that if the Pacific Islands were base facilities needed for postwar US strategic security, then a civilian administration might interfere with the military's defense of the area in time of war or other national emergencies. Therefore, Interior not only had to clearly enunciate its position on this subject, but it also had to meet these concerns from the War and Navy Departments, and even from the State Department. As the other Executive Departments did concerning their purviews, Interior employed a fascinating, though at times highly inaccurate, useable history of US territorial administration as a way to argue its position.

■ Interior's Case for Pacific Island Civil Administration

The Interior Department's position on the disposition of the Japanese territories, as well as prewar American possessions in the Pacific, started to become clear at least as early as November 1944. On the first of that month, Secretary of the Interior Ickes sent a short note to Forrestal saying that he had received word from a "reliable" source that the Navy was working on a bill to transfer jurisdiction of "the islands" from Interior to the Navy Department. Ickes did not specify whether the islands in question were prewar American possessions or the newly conquered territories in Micronesia, but he did remind Forrestal that he had mentioned the matter to President Roosevelt. He also told Forrestal that Roosevelt had expressed his opposition to the Navy having jurisdiction over any of the Pacific Islands. Ickes reiterated that he was "virtually certain" that work was being done on this—without Forrestal's knowledge—by a Captain Ramsey in the Navy's Judge Advocate General's (JAG) Office. Ickes finished by asking Forrestal that he take immediate steps to put a stop to this "enterprise."[1]

A few days before Roosevelt died in April 1945, Ickes also sent the President a memorandum about issues that had come up with the Army and the Navy with regard to what he called the "international trusteeship problem." Ickes began by telling Roosevelt that he was particularly disturbed about some reports concerning the military services' attitude toward trusteeship. He was informed of these attitudes by Under Secretary of the Interior Abe Fortas, who told him that the Army and the Navy wanted the United States to insist on complete sovereignty over the former Japanese Mandates. Ickes also reported that the two services were urging that the matter of international trusteeship not be discussed at the UN Conference in San Francisco. At the very least, he told the President that the War and Navy Departments did not want international-trusteeship issues discussed there until the United States had a "firm agreement" about US jurisdiction over Micronesia. Ickes further told Roosevelt that he agreed the United States should be the administering power of the former Japanese Mandates, and that the "arrangement" worked out by the interdepartmental State-War-Navy-Interior Committee should assure for the US Government all of the rights it could possibly desire for security purposes. He was concerned, however, that the arrangement had gone too far in providing a "scheme" by which those areas were now exempted from international accountability. Ickes, whose concerns were also recounted to Roosevelt by Secretary of State Stettinius at this same time, was fearful that if the United States insisted on complete sovereignty, an "international grab-bag" would result that would end in "serious prejudice" to the interests of the United States and to the idea of a peaceful world organization. As an example, Ickes argued that the British might respond to US sovereignty over Micronesia by claiming "absolute title" to certain areas of the Middle East that reflected their security interests but would interfere with US strategic interests in Middle Eastern oil. He also thought it would be a mistake to fail to reach agreement on the subject of mandated territories at the San Francisco Conference. He said that the elimination of the topic would arouse suspicion and be a continuing source of hostility and distrust, and he did not think the new international organization—or any international organization—could be successfully launched until these vital issues had been "boldly confronted" and dealt with by way of "practical idealism." In conclusion, he urged to Roosevelt that the mandated territories and any other territories separated from Japan be placed under the trusteeship system, with only such safeguards as might be necessary for US national security. He further thought that the US Government should make a prompt decision as to policy on the matter, and engage in "vigorous" efforts to gain acceptance for that policy in San Francisco.[2]

Many of Ickes's ideas about the Pacific can also be seen in an article manuscript entitled "The Philippines Come Of Age," which he was preparing for the 24 July 1945 issue of *Liberty* magazine. Ickes began the piece by informing his readers that the Philippines were to become independent on 4 July 1946, and that at that point the archipelago would have no more political ties with the United States than Great Britain, Canada, or Mexico. Ickes wrote that this was a goal that the Filipinos had been working toward for years, and that many in the United States looked on the granting of Philippine independence with pride. According to Ickes, many Americans thought that this independence meant the United States would be relieved of "paying attention" or having any connections to the new republic. To Ickes, however, Philippine independence meant the United States had made good on a promise. He compared the situation to a parent who raises a child and then sends the child into the world when the child reaches its majority. Ickes paternalistically thought the United States had been a good parent, providing the Philippines with a "better education" than most colonies and seeing to it that the Filipinos were "healthy." In addition, he pointed out the significant amount of trade preferences and governmental expenditures the Filipinos had been the benefactors of. In fact, Ickes thought that Filipino resistance to Japanese conquest, and their loyalty to the United States during the war were proof that the Filipinos thought the United States was a good parent. Ickes also thought that looking at the Philippines as a growing young man was the more reasonable viewpoint. Yet he asserted that Pearl Harbor should have taught the Americans that raising a boy to take a man's place in the world was far different from training a country to take its place in a community of nations. The basic difference, to Ickes, was that in the United States, equality before the law protected the weak from the strong. Yet he saw no parallel in the community of nations. Thus, in international relations, small nations chose protectors, and this would probably remain the mode of practice until there was a firm and strong international organization that could provide an equal law of nations.[3]

Ickes now claimed that the United States had overlooked this fact when it authorized the granting of Philippine independence in the 1930s. He thought the Filipinos overlooked it as well, and said that both Americans and Filipinos were merely thinking of independence in the simple terms of family life! Now, however, he claimed that both nations had come to grips with reality and recognized the differences. Therefore, by an Act of Congress, the United States was authorized to acquire and retain such land, sea, and air bases as might be deemed necessary for the mutual protection of the United States and the Philippines. Ickes believed it probable that the War and Navy Departments would take full advantage of the Congressional authorization. Even now, he argued, the Philippines were being used as a base of operations against Japanese targets in Southeast Asia, China, and the Japanese Home Islands. It was not only obvious to him that military and naval authorities would make full use of the Philippines for future operations against Japan, but that American retention of these bases after the war would be "vital" to keeping the peace in the Pacific. "Without the presence of the military forces of the United States in this area, it is more than reasonable to assume that the Philippines within a comparatively few years will again be subject to invasion." Ickes told his readers that the retention of these military bases meant more than just the installation of armaments and the staffing of forts and fleets. These bases also had to be supplied with foodstuffs and other materials. It was also clear to him that military operations in the Philippines would be hampered unless there was "genuine" law and order—meaning law and order not enforced by bayonets, but which came from a people enjoying a stable government providing the necessities of life. Ickes thought a stable economy for the Philippines was also necessary because US prestige in the Pacific and East Asia not only depended on the presence of American military forces but also on Philippine independence working out to the best advantage of the new republic. Granting Philippine independence only to have that independence result in the "decay" of the archipelago's economy would seriously impair the United States' prestige in the region.[4]

Ickes then gave specifics on Philippine economic conditions. He related how the private economy had been disrupted by the Japanese occupation and "wanton destruction." He also claimed that every local bank, insurance company, and building-and-loan society was bankrupt. He said the same was true for wholesale and retail stores, shops, utilities, sawmills, mines, and light industries. Since the sources from which the government had derived its revenue were "dried up," the basis for taxation could not be restored, he thought, in less than three years, and the Philippine Commonwealth only had enough funds on hand to operate normal government with strict economy for less than a year. In addition, the Commonwealth had been able to pay interest on the national debt, but not the legally required contribution. Ickes also reported that the island nation was in "bad physical shape." Much of Manila had been reduced to rubble, Zanboanga had been leveled, and a large portion of Cebu and Iloilo had been destroyed in 1942. Furthermore, he reported that the Japanese were razing cities and market towns as they retreated. Ickes also noted that the Philippines had been highly dependent on inter-island shipping, since the archipelago consisted of over one hundred islands. Ickes's estimates were that over 90 percent of inter-island shipping was destroyed, and that most of the important bridges had been blown up. In addition, he said that most of the railroad locomotives and rolling stock had been destroyed, and that the highways had been churned to mud in the battles. Moreover, he asserted that it had been necessary to destroy many public buildings, as they had been turned into strongholds by the Japanese during the liberation. Ickes further claimed that for nearly three years, Filipino children had been deprived of schooling, and that illiteracy could rise by the next census. Education, he argued, would consume most of the entire general tax fund and probable tax collections for one year. The wartime losses that he had outlined above apparently did not take into account the terrific toll on housing, sanitation, and public health.[5]

Ickes next talked about the Philippines' most important economic base being trade with the United States. He claimed that the standard of living in the Philippines was higher than in most "Asiatic" countries because of this trade, and that governmental revenue was tied to it. This trade had supposedly given the Philippines a higher prewar level of prosperity, but had been completely severed by the war. Even before the Japanese invasion, however, Ickes claimed that the United States had been preparing to curb the trade between the two nations through the Tydings-McDuffie Act of 1934. The Tydings-McDuffie Act had established a Commonwealth Government in 1936. This government was to last for ten years before national independence was granted by the United States. During the last five years before independence, it was hoped that the Philippine economy would be "weaned" from the US economy. Starting in 1940 and increasing each year, American tariffs were to slowly rise against Philippine goods being exported to the United States. By 1946, the tariffs were to amount to 25 percent. With independence looming by July 1945, the full force of the tariffs was about to be brought to bear on Philippine goods. Although later amendments modified the percentages, the effects of the Japanese occupation, according to Ickes, nullified those adjustments, and the Philippine economy was about to undergo a significant shock. According to Ickes, free trade with the United States was the "lifeline" of the Philippine economy. Without free trade, he claimed the island nation could not sustain its heavy Pacific shipping costs. With the new tariffs, he thought it might even be cheaper for the United States to find suppliers of certain goods nearer to home. In fact, Ickes focused on sugar as his main example. Ickes argued that Philippine exports of sugar to the United States accounted for about one-eighth of the Philippine national income. He argued that the US tariffs would end the Philippine sugar trade completely. In a crossed-out section of the manuscript, he even asserted that the tariff legislation was worded in such a way as to create a free-trade sugar situation with Cuba, and that Cuba would have the advantage of proximity to the United States. Ickes pointed out that sugar was only one of the economic items affected by independence. Another loss would be revenue from the coconut-oil trade, a trade on which the United States had traditionally collected a three-cent tax per pound of oil, which was then remitted to the Philippine Commonwealth. Under Tydings-McDuffie, the Philippines would lose this tax and have to raise a tax of five cents. A result of this increased tax would be palm-kernel oil derived from British colonies in Africa becoming cheaper for Filipino soap manufacturers to use. Ickes also argued that the Filipino tobacco and mineral industries would be "wiped out," since even as the United States worked the Filipinos toward political independence, the new republic was being tied economically to the United States with "bonds so strong that they could not exist without us." Worse than this economic situation and its aggravation by the war, Ickes thought the United States had made its foreign policy toward the Philippines the basis of US "propaganda" in East Asia. As Ickes pointed out, the United States had boasted about its granting independence to the Philippines as an example of what Asians could expect after the war. He claimed, however, that no one had taken into account the propaganda advantage to the "enemy" of an economic collapse in the Philippines. Nor did he think that anyone had analyzed the difficulties of establishing American military and naval installations in an economically devastated country. He also noted the humanitarian problems of such an economic collapse.[6]

Ickes said that the Philippines had been warned about the economic dangers inherent in independence. Specifically, he mentioned warnings put out by Senator Millard Tydings himself in the 1930s, just before the legislation that bore the Senator's name went into effect. Paul McNutt, US High Commissioner to the Philippines in the 1930s, even called for a reexamination of Philippine independence at that time because of the economic situation. Still, Ickes said that the Filipinos chose independence in the 1930s since they could not foresee the havoc of the coming war. Ickes also said that several suggestions for solutions for these problems had been presented since the beginning of the war. Supposedly, members of the postwar Filipino Rehabilitation Commission proposed that the Philippines be granted its independence, plus twenty years of free trade, war-damage compensation, rehabilitation of the financial system, and grants-in-aid. In addition, Ickes said that Senator Robert Taft of Ohio had already suggested increasing the amounts of war-damage compensation, a bill that Ickes thought would pass. There was, however, no system of financial rehabilitation that had yet been worked out, and he foresaw serious resistance to the free-trade proposal. Another possible solution put forth had been to postpone independence, but Ickes thought this was doubtful, and any such proposal had to come from the Philippines, not the United States. He said another idea was to make the Philippines the forty-ninth state within the United States, but he also said there were a number of considerations that would mitigate against such an idea. The Philippines had a population of about 18 million people. This number was equivalent, in July 1945, to the populations of New York and New Jersey combined! Since these two states enjoyed fifty-nine members in the US House of Representatives, Ickes pointed out the clear domestic political problems that would ensue from instituting such a change. It was also suggested that the Philippines be given dominion status, similar to that of Canada within the British Commonwealth. However, Ickes stated to the readers that there were political considerations in the

Philippines that made it unwise to predict this or any other solution to the archipelago's problems. These political considerations were especially complicated by Filipinos who had resisted the Japanese during the war and were now demanding a greater say in their own government. Ickes concluded by telling his readers that Filipino voices should be heard, but that he did not think their problems were peculiar to the Philippines. He noted similar political issues in the United States, especially played out by "short-sighted" and "selfish" interests, which had operated in the politics of granting Philippine independence. Referring to the lobbyists for the sugar, dairy, and other industries, Ickes told his readers that these parties would have to be contended with in any solutions worked out for the Philippine's problems. While he foresaw no easy solutions to these problems, he argued that the solutions had to be found or the United States would be under threat of having "[won] the war in the Pacific and of losing the fruits of peace in that area."[7]

By the fall of 1945, Ickes was back to his primary issue: the postwar civil administration of the former Japanese territories. Despite the President's undoubted preoccupation with rising tensions with the Soviet Union, Ickes nevertheless sent Truman a letter on the subject of postwar civil administration in the Pacific Islands about a week and a half after the Japanese surrender in September 1945. Ickes began the letter by asserting his belief that immediate attention should be given to the question of civil administration in the former Japanese territories. He then claimed that it would be in keeping with American tradition to devise "suitable" means by which a civil administration of the islands could be established that also provided for the security interests of the nation. Ickes understood that some time would pass before decisions would be made about the disposition of the former Japanese Mandates, but he had asked the Interior Department's Division of Territories and Island Possessions to make a general study of Pacific Island issues and be prepared to make more detailed plans. He argued to Truman that full use should be made of the "expert" opinion in the Interior Department, the Federal agency he claimed had long been responsible for the "well-being" of indigenous peoples in US territories. Ickes then provided Truman with a historical lesson about the Federal administration of these indigenous peoples. Reiterating that military administration of civil affairs had prevailed at various times in the Philippines, Alaska, Puerto Rico, and the Virgin Islands, he argued that in all cases, civil administration had later been transferred to the Interior Department. Only Guam and American Samoa remained under military administration. In addition, the Interior Department was administering Baker, Howland, Jarvis, Canton, and Enderbury Islands in the Pacific Ocean; the War Department's Bureau of Insular Affairs had become part of Interior's Division of Territories and Island Possessions; and Interior had been "guiding" the Philippines toward independence since the 1930s. Ickes therefore thought that there was every reason to believe that the "sound" conduct of civil administration in inhabited areas adjacent to strategic bases would support, not handicap, the military services. He argued that neither US security nor prestige would be served by a policy of military rule in the former Japanese Mandates, since such a policy would appear to be akin to the "militaristic policies" of the old colonial powers. He further thought that such an administration might even appear more militaristic than that of the Japanese, who at least had staffed their South Seas Bureau with civilians. He pointed out to Truman that the British Army and Navy had worked closely with civilian administrators and tolerated local "self-rule" in such vital outposts as Ceylon, Singapore, the Fiji Islands, and the Northwest Frontier Province of India. Ickes admitted that differences of opinion between military and civilian personnel could arise in such situations, but he thought that adequate safeguards could be made for military and policing functions. He also thought that joint administrative efforts could work if the military services were given strict control of the actual base areas in these territories—just as they were in the mainland United States—and if the military and civilian departments maintained close liaisons. Ickes was, accordingly, going to ask the Division of Territories and Possessions to draft a detailed report along these lines, and he thought that the War, Navy, and State Departments should be consulted.[8] What was also clear at this time, however, was that Truman was not prepared to discuss this issue with him. The President returned a quick note the next day, saying that he had read Ickes's letter with great interest, but that it was too early to discuss this subject and that he would be "glad" to talk it over with Ickes at a later date.[9]

Later in the same month, Abe Fortas, at this time the Acting Secretary of the Interior, came back to Truman on this subject of Pacific Island administration. Apparently, Truman had by this time referred the subject to the War, Navy, and State Departments. Fortas stated to Truman that he was sure the President intended to draw upon the Interior Department's long experience in "handling" the problems of indigenous peoples. Accordingly, Fortas cited how the Interior Department had "handled" Indian affairs for over one hundred years, as well as the civil administration in nearly all US possessions. Fortas also pointed out to Truman that by having the Navy continue to administer Guam and American Samoa, the United States took on the "dubious" distinction of being the only Pacific power that governed an inhabited colonial area as if it were a military base. He did not think this was a status that could be justified or would be welcomed by the American people in lieu of "enlightened" opinion about the administration of dependent peoples. Fortas said he recognized the vital interests of the State Department and the military services in determining the policies and methods of administration of these strategic areas. In fact, he thought it best to treat the issue as a single US problem, and he realized that world attention would be focused on what the United States did vis-à-vis the administration of the Pacific Islands. Fortas thought that if the United States committed itself to Civil Government, this position would actually strengthen its case before the world for exclusive American retention and control of strategic areas

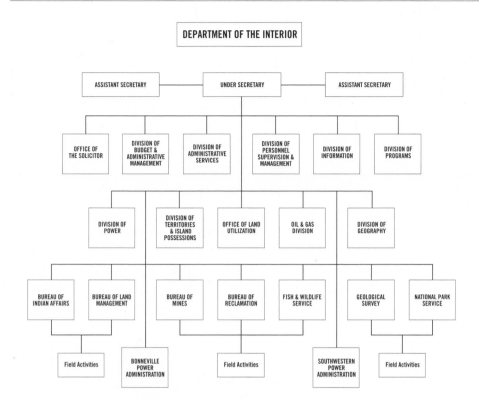

Figure 5. The Department of the Interior, 1948. (Reprinted from the *US Government Manual, 1948,* courtesy of the US Government Printing Office, Washington, D.C.)

such as Micronesia. Fortas then told Truman that the Interior Department would like to assist in this process by providing "expert" opinion on Civil Government aimed toward the ultimate attainment of democratic institutions and economic stability in these areas. In addition, he thought Interior's experiences in these areas would help in creating an organization to administer the islands that met both US security needs and UN obligations. He ended the letter by asking Truman to advise the other departments about Interior's obvious role in the deliberations.[10] Truman responded, this time to Ickes, that final decisions would again be a long time in coming, but that solving the administrative problems should begin at once. Accordingly, Truman invited the Interior Department to take part in the administrative plans for the Pacific territories in light of its long association with the administration of dependent peoples and territories.[11]

By October 1945, Truman had established what has been variously called the Cabinet Committee, the Committee of Four Secretaries, and the Quadripartite Committee. This body was comprised of the Secretaries from the War, Navy, State, and Interior Departments or their representatives, and it was tasked with discussing the issue of Pacific Island administration.[12] Though the four Secretaries apparently did not meet at this time, they did start exchanging ideas about how US security and political interests in the Pacific could be met. One example of these exchanges was a late December 1945 letter from Ickes to Forrestal. Ickes began the letter by stating that the administrative problems in the Pacific Islands were not hypothetical future ones to solve, but immediate ones arising from US control of the area. He assumed that interim measures taken in this first period of governance would go far in determining the administration, trade, and relations with the indigenous peoples of the region for some time to come. He was also sure that awaiting a formal international agreement about the disposition of the former Japanese territories without providing for orderly administration would probably not serve the United States' best interests. Ickes also told Forrestal that he was unclear as to why disputes over trusteeship or sovereign control had any bearing on the problem. According to Ickes, the United States had assumed actual governing responsibility for the area for the time being. Even if the island groups such as Micronesia were eventually assigned to another power, Ickes maintained that the United States still had the current responsibility for the inhabitants' welfare. He also assumed that these islands would be under continuous international scrutiny, and that US actions had acquired an importance out of proportion to the islands' small size and population. He therefore thought that it was in the United States' interests to "assist the natives of the islands toward a better way of life within the limits of their capabilities and the potentialities of their environment." Additionally, Ickes thought that in "terms of ultimate economy and goodwill, such a policy would benefit our relations with peoples far beyond the limits of the island area." Ickes was similarly sure that the American people would favor Civil Government of the Pacific Islands in order to achieve these goals. Not only did he think American traditions were opposed to military rule, but he argued, as he had to Truman a few months before, that even colonial powers like Japan had "outgrown" it. He was certain that Forrestal must be worried that so many people at home and abroad believed that the US military saw its strategic interests in the Pacific Islands superseding concern for the inhabitants' civil rights and economic welfare. Ickes said that the strategic position of the island groups was just as significant from a political as a military point of view, since he thought that the United States could "gain a great advantage if we can go to the peace table with a record of interim civilian administration that clearly demonstrates the democratic, non-imperialistic attitude of this Government toward the island peoples." Ickes concluded the letter by claiming that he could not understand why attention should only be focused on the United States acquiring its bases in the region when "local human problems" also constituted an immediate and pressing responsibility of the US Government. He even reminded Forrestal that Truman's memos on this subject referred to "islands" not "bases." He therefore thought the four departments needed to begin work on these immediate and long-term issues in a similar kind of context, and he requested that Forrestal have the Committee of Four Secretaries draft an interim report for the President by 1 February 1947. He added that he was sending a copy of his letter to Truman.[13]

It is unclear if such a report from the four Secretaries ever got to Truman by February. However, it was apparently clear enough to Wesley Clark, Assistant to the Secretary of the Interior, that the State Department agreed with the idea of civil administration in the Pacific Islands, but that the military services still desired these "bases" to be under their control. In this vein of military versus civil control, Clark had also been supplied by Eric Beecroft, Special Assistant to the Secretary of the Interior, with information about these territories that was intended for Ickes in his conflict with the military services.[14] Beecroft made the argument that the United States should carry out its responsibilities in the former Japanese Mandates in accordance with the "basic objectives" of the trusteeship system outlined in the UN Charter. To him, this meant that Military Government should be replaced by Civil Government as soon as possible so that economic, educational, and public-health measures could be provided to the local inhabitants. He further thought this replacement of Military Government with Civil Government should also take place in Guam and American Samoa, and that these latter two locations should have organic acts of legislation, with standards consistent with other American territories. Beecroft, claiming that he was taking information from military officers who had served in Micronesia, thought that the local inhabitants' abilities and intelligence meant that they could "progress" rapidly, as he thought the Hawaiian people had, toward self-government. Not surprisingly, he also believed that the Interior Department, through the Division of Territories and Island Possessions, should be the agency to conduct the American supervision of the island territories. Citing Interior's one-hundred-plus years of experience in US territorial administration, he thought it was the agency that was best suited to meeting the international standards of the UN. Again citing Fortas's earlier statement about the United States being the only Pacific power to govern civilian populations as if they were part of a military base, Beecroft said that he was sure American opinion would not justify the continuation of a policy that even the Japanese had avoided.[15]

The Interior Department continued to call for civil administration of the former Japanese Mandates by its Division of Territories and Island Possessions, even as the War, Navy, and State Departments agreed on deferring the question until the status of Micronesia had been determined by the UN. In meetings of the Ad Hoc Subcommittee of the Cabinet Committee, Edwin Arnold, Director of Interior's Division of Territories and Island Possessions, was the only one of the four representatives to disagree with the decision to defer Micronesian status. Nevertheless, the majority decision was submitted to Truman in heavily revised form by Secretary of State Byrnes, Chairman of the Cabinet Committee.[16] Arnold, however, wrote a position paper on the subject. In the paper, he proposed that Military Government be replaced by Civil Government in all of the Pacific Islands under control of the US armed services, except those islands or parts of islands that had been designated as military reservations. Arnold meant the proposal to apply to Guam and American Samoa, as well as to the Pacific Islands already under US control. He also meant the proposal to apply to all of the Micronesian Islands formerly under Japanese mandate, as well as to the Ryukyus, the Bonins, and the Volcanoes. Furthermore, Arnold thought that this policy should apply to any Pacific Islands that might come under US administration "from time to time." Of course, the administrative agency was to be Interior's Division of Territories and Island Possessions. Arnold's memo further spoke to the Interior Department's administration of the Philippine Islands as that archipelago prepared for independence. In addition, he cited Interior's efforts toward Hawaiian and Alaskan preparations for statehood, the Department's assistance to Puerto Rico as that island territory set about determining its future status in the US polity, and Interior's role in the Virgin Islands' "increasing" amount of self-government. He repeated the need for the United States to avoid being the only Pacific power that governed civilian populations as if they were part of military bases. Arnold then argued that even if there was some delay in transferring the eventual jurisdiction of the Pacific Islands, the United States should immediately make and announce the decision to employ civil administration in the Pacific. He argued, again, that this action would strengthen US claims for military and administrative supervision of the region, allay beliefs that US interest in the region was narrowly military, and allow the United States to insist on "proper standards" of civil administration by other powers over their territories. Arnold admitted that even an immediate interim civil administration might be subject to change because of later international agreements, but that sound military use could still be provided for in current civil administration or future trusteeship regimes. In addition, Arnold asserted that an immediate change to civil administration would ease the necessary adjustments that would have to be made by the Executive Departments when the final disposition of the Pacific territories was determined. Arnold argued that this change would alleviate the problem of civil-affairs personnel thinking that the current administration was only a temporary one. In addition, he asserted that such a change would provide for a continuity of responsibility among those carrying out island administration. Finally, Arnold suggested that American experience in Micronesia already indicated that any division of these territories for administrative purposes would multiply problems of administration. Therefore, Arnold thought that if American taxpayers were to be relieved of the cost of island administration, and if the island populations were to enjoy adequate conditions, all of Micronesia, including Guam, should be under a single administrative unit. He additionally thought that treating the entire region as a single administrative entity would allow for a more economical management of problems such as transportation, communication, food distribution, public health, and public finance.[17]

■ Interior's Plans for Pacific Island Civil Administration

Another Interior Department position paper from this time period also outlined the issues between the Interior Department on the one hand, and the State, War, and Navy Departments on the other, over the administration of the former Japanese Mandates. These differences, in turn, give the reader a fairly detailed picture of Interior's position on the whole issue. The proposal began by calling for Civil Governments of civilian populations under the American flag in time of peace. Such Civil Governments were to be founded in organic legislation or constitutions wherein the US Congress actually prescribed the form of government over the area concerned. The paper also called for that type of government to be democratic in form so that the local population might participate to the fullest degree possible, or at least to the "fullest capability" of the people in question. Organic acts, in turn, needed to contain a bill of rights whereby Congress extended guarantees against the infringement of basic liberties to the local population. Furthermore, these organic acts were to also guarantee personal freedoms that were consistent with those enjoyed by US citizens and inhabitants of US territories. It was also argued that these Civil Governments should be "reasonably true" to American political traditions, i.e., a checks-and-balances system of executive, legislative, and judicial branches that were free and equal to each other. The position paper did talk, however, about the right and power of the US military to take, use, and exclusively occupy such land areas and harbor and anchorage facilities as were needed for the national defense. Moreover, these military rights were to be "confirmed and safeguarded." Administrative responsibility was to be centralized in one office or agency of the US Government, and that agency had to be given a status of "sufficient importance" in the structure of government and enough access to the highest councils of government in order to give power and effectiveness to its policies. The author of the position paper, therefore, assumed that the agency in question needed some access to the President at the Cabinet level and would treat with the other departments on an equal basis. This independence in position would supposedly allow the agency in question to "effectively" look after the interests of the people under its charge. The position paper reiterated many of the points put forth earlier by Ickes, Fortas, and Beecroft. Since the Interior Department had such long experience and working knowledge of US dependent areas, it was the agency of choice. The position paper also called for the Department's Division of Territories and Island Possessions to be combined with an entirely new office for territorial administration if Guam, American Samoa, and the Trust Territory of the Pacific Islands (TTPI) were not put under Interior Department jurisdiction. The author preferred, however, that because of the Division's long record of territorial administration and its small budget, all matters having to do with the civil administration of the Pacific territories should be placed with the Division rather than in some newly created agency.[18]

Several points were also made in detail about the organic legislation in question. There was a call, for instance, for separate pieces of organic legislation for Guam and American Samoa. Guam was seen as "more advanced" economically, politically, and socially than was American Samoa. In addition, the Guamanians were supposedly more familiar with American political structures and philosophies because of contact, training, and association with Americans. Finally, Guam's Spanish-Filipino-Chamorro population allegedly had a closer affinity "to western (modern) civilization than do the native (Polynesian) Samoans." It was also thought that the organic legislation should grant US citizenship to both the Guamanians and the American Samoans without any kind of test or naturalization proceedings. Moreover, the idea was enunciated that a bill of rights be made very explicit in terms of the right of trial by jury if the defendant wanted to be tried in such a manner. The author of the position paper was not so concerned about whether locally elected legislatures were one- or two-house chambers, since Guam had a two-house body and American Samoa had a one-house body, but was more concerned that members of these bodies be locally elected. Samoa's legislature, or Fono, was largely composed of hereditary chiefs—something the author attributed to American Samoa's lack of concepts of Jeffersonian democracy, Western suffrage, or democratic election processes. It was thought that the answer to a legislature for American Samoa was quite difficult because of this, but that having a two-house body with one being hereditary and one being elective might be the most viable solution. Legislation that set up an independent judiciary, including a system of local courts and a separate Federal court or a right of appeal to the Federal courts, was also considered necessary.[19]

Interestingly, the author was prepared to see the organic act for American Samoa be drafted by the Navy Department, but not the legislation for Guam—in part because several bills on Guam had already been introduced in Congress, and the author felt that it would be easier to get one of these passed and propose changes where desirable. The author did not, however, think that the State Department should be solely responsible for drafting the organic legislation for the TTPI. Interior's thinking on this matter was that the TTPI should not be regarded as "foreign affairs," and therefore should not be placed solely in the purview of the State Department. The paper argued, however, that Interior and "other interested departments" should have a hand in drafting such legislation, but that the legislation should follow the basic premises mentioned earlier in the paper. The Interior memo also wanted the organic legislation to authorize the President to determine which US governmental agency should have permanent administrative responsibility, and wanted the President to have all of the Interior Department's points before him when he made this decision. Interior was willing to see the Navy have interim responsibility for the TTPI pending determination of a permanent agency for such administration as long as "interim" was clearly spelled out in terms of the number of years it would entail. Interior specifically did not want "interim" on Guam and American Samoa to be more than one year since these islands had already been US possessions for more than fifty years. Along these lines, Interior agreed with the other departments that an Executive Order be issued with Congressional approval that terminated Military Government in the Trust Territory and instituted a clearly defined interim Naval Civil Administration.[20]

Even as the United States sought approval in the UN into 1947 for its Draft Trusteeship Agreement, this line of thinking about Pacific Island civil administration was continued by one official outside of the Interior Department. In early April 1947, Emil Sady, State Department Assistant on Dependent Area Affairs, put forth a position paper for SWNCC in which he recounted the history of dependent territorial administration by the United States. In addition, Sady related the history and issues between the War, Navy, State, and Interior Departments concerning the civil administration of the former Japanese Mandates. Finally, he outlined in fairly specific detail what he thought the administrative organization of postwar US Pacific Island civil governance ought to be. In the introduction to this long draft paper, Sady stated that there was a need to determine the "essential principles" on which any future plan of territorial administration rested, and that there was a need to determine how to adopt such steps. Sady assumed that Congress would authorize the President to approve the Draft Trusteeship Agreement for the former Japanese Mandates, and that Congress would also authorize the President to administer the Trust Territory in accordance with the terms of Agreement and the UN Charter. He further assumed that the TTPI Government, as well as the civil rights and status of the inhabitants, should be established by Act of Congress. Sady went on to say that responsibility for administration should be vested in a civilian agency, with the exception of military and naval reservations. He thought that the latter should be designated by the President and placed under the appropriate military agency. Sady also stated that in time of war, civilian authority would be subordinated as might be necessary to the senior military or naval commander in the area by order of the President. In addition, he called for the newly created Subcommittee on Non-Self-Governing Territories of the US Government's Interdepartmental Committee on International Social Policy, or a new committee consisting of representatives of the "interested departments," to coordinate the policies of the various agencies that were to have significant responsibilities in the TTPI. Sady further called for the administrative union of the TTPI with Guam, and argued that a decision on the most "suitable" form of administration was urgent from a legal viewpoint, as well as to demonstrate to national and international opinion that the United States was undertaking its trusteeship responsibilities in good faith. Sady continued by recommending that the concurrences of the other interested departments should be sought in this matter so that a consensus paper could be submitted to the President to seek authority to draft such legislation and executive orders as might be necessary.[21]

Sady then went into great detail in his appendices about the history of US territorial administration, as well as background information on the interdepartmental conflict over TTPI administration. He noted that on 20 October 1945, President Truman had created the Interdepartmental Committee on International Social Policy so that the War, Navy, State, and Interior Departments could make recommendations about the administration of the Pacific Islands. He also noted that an Ad Hoc Subcommittee of representatives from those four departments had been subsequently created, and that it had recommended to Truman in February 1946 that no action be taken about the type of Pacific Island administration until the future status of the islands had been determined. Interior, of course, had dissented from this viewpoint since it had recommended in the same report that War and Navy Department Military Government be replaced by Interior Department Civil Government, with the exception of islands or parts of islands designated as military reservations. Sady recounted how interim authority over the former Japanese Mandates had been delegated to the Secretary of the Navy, then the CNO, and finally to CINCPAC-CINCPOA with the concurrence of the JCS. He pointed out that by April 1947, the UN Security Council had approved the United States' proposed Draft Trusteeship Agreement for the Pacific Islands, and that the Agreement would enter into force as soon as it was approved by the US Government. Sady did not think such an agreement would have to await the Japanese Peace Treaty, and he said that the Department of State was drafting a Joint Resolution to this effect for the President to sign.[22]

Sady went into further detail on the non-self-governing territories being administered by the United States, including a breakdown of the Federal agencies administering each territory. The War Department by this time was administering the Panama Canal, while the Navy was administering Guam, American Samoa, Midway, Kure, Wake, Johnston, Kingman, and Palmyra. The Interior Department was administering Puerto Rico and the US Virgin Islands, as well as Alaska and Hawaii. In addition, Interior was administering Baker, Howland, and Jarvis Islands, as well as Canton and Enderbury Islands, the latter two in a joint status with the British. The list of territories that was provided by Sady clearly demonstrated that the Interior Department was administering the larger number of territories, with the greatest concentrations of civilian populations. Sady also related the legislative history for War and Navy Department authority over the Panama Canal, Pacific Island territories such as Guam and American Samoa, and now the former Japanese Mandates. However, he went into even greater detail on the history of the Interior Department's legislative authority in territorial administration. He demonstrated that the Interior Department had had Congressional authority since 1873 to exercise administration in all of the United States' territories that had previously been administered by the Department of State. This meant that Interior took over the administration of the Territory of Alaska in 1884 after the War, Treasury, and Navy

Departments had been in charge since 1867. In addition, he pointed out that Hawaii was made a US territory in 1900, and that the legislation provided for a territorial government. While Sady admitted that no specific Executive agency had been determined at that time, Interior was so designated in 1907 because of the 1873 legislation. Sady continued by describing the evolution of territorial administration in Puerto Rico from the War and State Departments to Interior in 1907. In addition, he noted that the US Virgin Islands was transferred from the Navy to Interior in 1931, and that the Philippines had been under the War Department's Bureau of Insular Affairs until taken over by the Interior Department's Division of Territories and Island Possessions in 1939. In the Interior Department's view, this last administrative transfer finally provided for the consolidation of all US territories under one Federal agency, though it failed to mention the territories still under War and Navy Department jurisdictions. Sady also asserted that although several Federal agencies had responsibilities in these various territories, they were all coordinated by the governors of each territory, who in turn reported to the President through the Secretary of the Interior.[23]

Sady summarized the various bills that had been introduced into Congress concerning the future administration of Guam, American Samoa, and the TTPI. One set of House and Senate bills called for transferring these territories from the Navy to Interior, while one Senate bill called for the Navy and Interior to divide the administration. Sady also noted that hearings could begin on these various bills at any time. He therefore thought it best that the interested departments reach agreement on the outstanding issues as soon as possible. Sady also outlined the geographical statistics on the size of Micronesia, the number of islands, the population of the various groups, and the economy of the islands. He especially focused on Guam, and paid particular attention to the linguistic and cultural groupings of Micronesia's population. He further summarized the Navy's removal of all Japanese, Ryukyuans, and Koreans after the 1945 surrender, and the problems of "educational advancement" of the Micronesians because of "the successive efforts of Germans, Spaniards, Japanese and Americans to introduce their own language, religion and culture into the area." Since Military Government per se was to be terminated as soon as the Trusteeship Agreement entered into force, Sady thought it necessary to decide as soon as possible which Federal agency was going to administer the TTPI. He then put forth a number of principles upon which Interior thought the TTPI administration should be based.[24]

Sady thought that the form of government established in the TTPI would have a direct bearing on US foreign policy. Since the United States had once been a colony itself, he reasoned that it was now a significant symbol of freedom and democratic principles for peoples of non-self-governing territories. Sady thought that the United States had also upheld the rights of people throughout the world to govern themselves. He further saw the United States as historically insisting on international guarantees of political, economic, and social rights for dependent peoples. In fact, he reminded his superiors that the United States had been instrumental in getting such standards written into the UN Charter. He also assumed that the extent to which the United States now practiced these principles with the people it was governing in the territories would be subject to examination and judgment by the UN. Therefore, he thought that the US record of administration would greatly determine its political and moral authority to speak on behalf of hundreds of millions of people who did not yet govern themselves. At the same time, Sady was clear that the form of administration must allow the United States to exercise its security prerogatives in the region. Bases in areas such as Micronesia should be established wherever the US military determined they needed to be, and the military should have authority over entire areas such as Micronesia in time of national emergency. Accordingly, it was thought that a form of government needed to be devised that would fulfill the United States' international obligations to the UN, contribute to the international prestige of the country, and provide for US security needs.[25]

With these considerations in mind, as well as those of a "practical, efficient, and economical" administration, Sady went into detail on the principles he had devised. Like his colleagues in the Interior Department, he thought that Congress should adopt organic legislation that provided for the TTPI Government as well as defined the inhabitants' civil rights and status. Reiterating the previous section of his report, Sady again called for all administrative responsibility to be vested in one agency. While specialized agencies might be needed to provide for certain services such as transportation, Sady thought it would be "unfortunate" if the TTPI were geographically or functionally divided. If other agencies, such as the Army or Navy, had to provide specialized services, he thought that they should be reimbursed on a contractual basis and coordinated through the agency governing the area. Along the same lines, Sady called for creating an administrative union of the former Japanese Mandates with Guam—something also called for by Article 9 of the Trusteeship Agreement, and something that Sady claimed would not affect the American island possession status of Guam. In addition, Sady asserted that military and naval reservations in the TTPI should be designated by the President as closed areas and placed under the authority of the military service requiring the territory. He further called for the US Government to have authorization to remove civilian inhabitants from these areas if need be, a process he claimed was already in operation in the Continental United States. As in other reports cited above, Sady reiterated that in the event of a national emergency, civil authority would be subordinated by specific order of the President to the supreme American military commander in the region. He pointed out that this pattern was consistent with the administration of the other US territories and possessions. Still, it was believed that in peacetime, at least, primary responsibility and authority for Civil Government should be vested in civilians, both in Washington and in the field. Sady thought that any plan that placed military officers in the line of civil authority would face severe criticism at home and abroad. He was convinced that separation of military and civilian authority would be more in keeping with American traditions of fostering self-government and fulfilling the political and social objectives of the UN Charter.[26]

The fact that the United States was the only power administering its dependent territories with military agencies or a military chain of command was again pointed out. As an example of the civil-military cooperation that he hoped to see in the future in the Pacific territories, Sady talked about cooperative agreements between the Interior Department, the Coast Guard, and the Army Transportation Service (ATS) in Alaska over issues such as the transportation of civilians. He made the important distinction that no civilians had been placed under a military chain of command in these cooperative agreements. He further claimed that military security would not be endangered by civil administration, even in such strategic outposts as Hawaii and the Aleutian Islands. Sady even reminded his readers that Interior had administered strategic locations such as these in the past without the impairment of national security. Additionally, Sady did not think that currently existing agencies should be diverted from their primary responsibilities in the Pacific territories by the assumption of civil-administration duties. Since personnel and budget cuts could impair the ability of an agency to carry out these Pacific Island administrative duties, he pondered several ideas about how best to implement TTPI administration. One idea was to establish a new civilian agency reporting directly to the President. While Sady thought this was a "highly desirable" idea, it could only be carried out if all other non-self-governing US territories were transferred to the new agency. He thought that such a new agency would be "closer" administratively to the President, would somehow enhance the prestige of both the President and the peoples being governed, and would provide for "more effective" cooperation between agencies. One disadvantage, however, included the perception that the United States was creating some sort of "colonial office" to govern its territories. In addition, Sady thought that there might be opposition in the older territories such as Hawaii and Puerto Rico, where the populations might object to being placed under a new administrative arrangement.[27]

Another option, of course, was to place the TTPI in an existing agency. Since Interior was already responsible for "all" of the other territories except for Guam and American Samoa, it was assumed to be "logical" for Interior to administer the TTPI. While the Trust Territory and the other territorial responsibilities could be transferred to another existing agency, Sady found such a possibility "difficult to justify since no other existing civilian agency is more suitable or qualified for this task than the Department of the Interior." He even suggested raising the Division of Territories and Island Possessions to. bureau status in order to enhance its prestige and influence. Another alternative was to establish a purely civilian-staffed administration under the Secretary of the Navy or the newly proposed Secretary of Defense. This alternative was considered because Guam, American Samoa, and the TTPI had heretofore been administered by the Navy Department. Yet he argued that this alternative could not be justified on grounds of military security without implying that all US territories of strategic importance should be put under military administration. Claiming that military and civilian officials had worked side by side in Hawaii, Alaska, and other areas for many years without "serious" controversy, Sady asserted that the latter alternative would not bring any advantages in terms of interagency cooperation. In addition, Sady argued that the principal functions of government, such as education, public health, social welfare, agriculture, and industrial development, were outside of the special competence and primary interest of the military services. No matter how the military services staffed their agencies, those civil-affairs units would "suffer" from being "extraneous" to the primary purpose of the military service. Also, a large number of persons would have to be brought into the areas to fulfill the needs of administration until more local inhabitants could be trained, and the armed services would not be able to provide these personnel or properly supervise them. As an example, Sady argued that about three hundred teachers would be needed for the TTPI's educational needs alone, and that the military services would not be able to supply these teachers from their base personnel, nor direct and supervise such teachers.[28]

Sady then went into further detail by discussing the number of hospitals that would be needed in the TTPI, as well as the number of doctors, dentists, and nurses needed to staff these facilities. While the Micronesians near large bases such as Kwajalein could be medically served by military personnel, more populated islands such as Guam and Saipan would need larger medical staffs than the military services could provide. While military and civilian medical personnel could cooperate in areas such as the exchange of information on various tropical diseases, he clearly saw the need for medical administration for the majority of Micronesians to be under Interior Department control. In other areas such as farming, fisheries, and industrial development, Sady claimed that there would not be any savings involved in the consolidation of services with the military and naval branches. In addition, he thought that a civilian-staffed administration under the military services would come in for the same type of political criticism that the present state of affairs entailed. Therefore, he returned to the idea of a civilian agency, either one in existence or one that was to be newly created, as the TTPI administering authority. He also claimed that SWNCC was now no longer very concerned about this situation as long as the administrative arrangement provided for safeguards by which the United States could fulfill its international and national security requirements in the region.[29]

Sady next outlined the number of government agencies that would have an interest in the TTPI, demonstrating to this author the potential complexity of this "new imperial management" that the United States was undertaking at the dawn of global decolonization. In particular, Sady saw the State Department having an interest since TTPI administration concerned US relations with international organizations. The War and Navy Departments were seen as key to air transportation, health, construction, and communication on certain islands. Sady argued that reclamation, fisheries, conservation, mineral development, and public land administration were the Interior Department's purview. The Department of Agriculture had an obvious role, in his opinion, but so did the Federal Security Agency in terms of public health and education. Commerce would be involved in terms of trading practices and commercial development, while Treasury would be advising on tariffs, customs collection, and Coast Guard transportation. The Justice Department, in turn, would provide various internal security services, as well as services in regard to civil rights, immigration, and judicial matters. Sady also saw involvement by the US Post Office, and even the Department of Labor. Sady obviously thought it necessary, in light of this administrative involvement, for some mechanism to be established in order to provide for interdepartmental consultation and use of facilities. While the governor of a territory might have to institute independent staffing by the overall agency in some of the areas mentioned above, Sady thought it best if interdepartmental machinery were constructed that would allow for cooperation and coordination rather than the actual formulation of policy. The latter was seen by him as too cumbersome, expensive, and prone to delay. This interdepartmental cooperation could be achieved, Sady thought, through the US Government's Interdepartmental Subcommittee on Non-Self-Governing Territories, or a new committee established for this purpose. Sady thought that the former would have the advantage of coordinating TTPI administration with the conduct of US foreign policy by securing a uniformity of policies with the widest number of departments in the field. The existing Subcommittee or a new one would have to have the power to make recommendations to the head of the agency administering the TTPI, and when necessary, to the President himself. Sady then suggested that on the day the President signed the Trusteeship Agreement, it would be appropriate for him to terminate Military Government, establish the form of administration as illustrated in the report, or direct the Secretary of the Navy to administer the TTPI on an interim basis if agreement between the interested departments could not be reached by the time the Trusteeship Agreement went into force. While Sady thought that the termination of Military Government was most desirable from a legal point of view, he really thought it highly desirable as well to establish the "most suitable" form of administration at the outset of the trusteeship. This transfer of responsibility, he thought, should be gradual so as not to impair the health and welfare of the island inhabitants. He also wanted to see Congress enact the organic legislation mentioned above in "due course." As he said in the introduction of the report, concurrence of all the concerned departments was necessary, including Interior, and he thought that a copy of his paper should be forwarded to the President.[30]

Finally, Sady outlined how he envisioned this new TTPI administrative organization. His plan called for the appointment of a Governor of Guam and the TTPI, with headquarters on Guam and accountability to the civilian agency in Washington, D.C. The Washington Office would have responsibility for broad policies and general results of insular administration. It would be responsible for the appointment and training of personnel, budget review, prior approval of field policies, and post-audit of those field operations. The Washington Office of this Federal agency would also be responsible for the required reports to the UN, for designating a Special Representative to the UN Trusteeship Council, and for cooperating with the other departments in the Subcommittee on Non-Self-Governing Territories of the Committee on International Social Policy. Additionally, the Washington Office was to prepare legislation and reports related to the Civil Government of the islands, approve the organization and incorporation of local communities for self-government, and ensure that the laws and codes being enforced in the TTPI were consistent with those of the Trusteeship Agreement and the UN Charter. Only a small staff, however, was envisioned in Washington for these purposes. Subordinate to the Washington Office would be a Territorial Administration, in which the Governor of Guam and the Trust Territory would have a functional staff consisting of specialists in public health, education, public safety, agriculture and fishing, and public finance. These specialists would work in close cooperation with other specialists on the district level and perform any functions not performed by the District Administration. Along these lines, it was envisioned that Congress would create a District Federal Court for the islands south of Hawaii, and that this district court would supervise local courts, establish courts of appeal, and exercise original jurisdiction over certain major crimes beyond the jurisdiction of the local courts. Next, a District Administration was seen as necessary, whereby the Governor would appoint District Administrators for the West Carolines District, the Central Carolines, the East Carolines, and the Marshalls. The size of each District Administrator's staff would depend on the population of each district and the nature of the administrative problems therein. Even the smallest districts and sub-districts, however, would have specialists in health, education, public safety, and economic development. In a related manner, the Governor, with the assistance of a Deputy Governor, would serve as the District Administrator for the Marianas, including Guam. The Guamanians would also elect a Chief Commissioner, who would be responsible to the administrative branch of the Guam Government. It was also planned that the Guamanians would elect representatives to a Legislative Council, a body that would have legislative powers subject to veto by the Governor, but with the right of appeal to the President. Since the Guamanians, in effect, were to have their own local government, the Governor's functional staff would serve as their technical advisers, just as the functional staff in the other districts did for the District Administrators.[31]

Since all "Orientals" had by this time been evacuated from the TTPI, Sady now saw the entire civilian population there as indigenous. Since "these people" were primarily organized into sociopolitical tribal or community organizations, he thought that those indigenous organizations should be used for the development of democratic self-government in the area. Along these lines, Sady thought that the largest number of persons having "common" political and social affinities should be included in each corporate unit, and that allowance should be made for the extension or grouping of incorporated communities as the cultural basis for community development. Eventually, it was hoped such groupings would encompass an entire district or more. Also, both the administering agency and the people of such incorporated governmental bodies would approve the charters of incorporation. Additionally, certain powers of self-government would be granted to the corporate group, and the charter would set forth the organization of local government and define the relationship of the corporate group to the Island Administration. Sady saw this entire plan for development as subject to broad, enabling legislation. Even if formal incorporation was not developed, Sady thought that certain powers of self-government should be granted to the local communities, and that it should be an essential aim of the administering agency to increase those powers until the local communities were entirely in charge of their own domestic affairs. While a District Council was to be established in each of the planned districts, it was thought possible later on to have a popularly elected Assembly to represent people throughout the area. At the very least, however, it was deemed the administering agency's responsibility to consult with representatives of the people at all levels of administration and work toward the development of local executive and legislative machinery so that local affairs could be delegated.[32]

■ Krug's Report

Julius Krug became Secretary of the Interior in the spring of 1946, following Ickes's February resignation from Truman's Cabinet. Accordingly, Krug inherited the problem of interdepartmental rivalry between War, Navy, State, and Interior over Pacific Island civil administration. These interdepartmental conflicts continued throughout 1946 and into the next year, even as the United States submitted its Draft Trusteeship Agreement to the UN and that body deliberated on the US proposal. The continued interdepartmental conflicts were marked, however, by at least one attempt on the part of the Interior Department to build coalitions with certain State Department personnel over the issue of UN trusteeship. For instance, in mid-April 1947, Assistant Secretary of the Interior Girard Davidson wrote a quick note to Krug, reminding him to talk to Under Secretary of State Acheson about the civilian administration of the island possessions. Davidson

thought that the "lower echelons" of the State Department favored civil administration as the Interior Department did, but he also thought that the intermediate
group of State Department personnel and the Secretariat were opposed to this,
and "rather friendly" to military control. Still, Davidson assumed that Acheson favored civilian administration, but thought the latter would want to have the Interior Department "carry the ball" on that point.[33] In addition, Krug had his own
views about what the United States should do concerning Pacific Island civil administration. In May 1947, he submitted a fairly detailed report to Truman about
his ideas on the subject after he had visited Guam, American Samoa, the former
Japanese Mandates, and Okinawa. The report was sent to Truman at the same
time that a Navy report on these territories was being released to the public. Krug
hoped that both reports would go far in maintaining and "arousing" American
public interest in the governance of the Pacific Islands. Whatever the impact in
1947, the report provides today's reader with a good summation of Krug's views
on governing the islands. In addition, the report conveys some key Interior Department notions about Pacific Basin territories and how it thought the United
States should govern those territories.[34]

Krug began his report by stating that it was his firm belief that the United
States had to practice democracy in the Pacific as it practiced it at home. Moreover,
he thought that the United States had to practice democracy as a clear aspect of the
American way of life, as it had promised the world it was going to do. He further
stated that if the United States was to stand before the world as a champion of free
and representative government, it had to practice democracy in its own dependent
areas just as it was "preaching" for other countries to do in other areas of the world.
Krug complained that the United States was currently imposing a form of government on the Guamanians, the American Samoans, and the Micronesians that
Americans would not stand for on the mainland, and for which the United States
would probably criticize any other government. He further complained that all
power was held by the American military governors in these areas, and that the islanders were being denied such basic civil rights as trial by jury, right of appeal,
and taxation with representation. He asserted that since the military governors
held all executive, legislative, and judicial power in their hands, the islanders had
no voice in matters such as education, public health, or the economic aspects of
their communities' lives.[35]

Krug's answer was to establish Civil Government for all civilian populations
under the US flag in time of peace. He was therefore asking Truman to seek legislation from Congress to establish local self-government in Guam and American
Samoa, provide for civilian governors on those islands, and extend US citizenship
and other basic civil rights to the islanders as was afforded to mainlanders by the
US Constitution. In addition, Krug recommended that the United States declare its
intent to administer the TTPI through civil administration at the earliest possible

moment. Generally, he wanted Congress to grant the Pacific Islanders the maximum degree of political rights. More specifically, he wanted Congress to define just what "civil rights" would mean for the Pacific Islanders in the TTPI, and what political status they would have. Clearly, he wanted civilian administrators to replace the military governors, civil courts to take the place of the military provost courts, and local municipal bodies to become legislative assemblies. Krug thought that it was equally important that these political changes be accompanied by a program of economic reconstruction and development. He thought it was vital that the inhabitants of the former Japanese Mandates in particular receive economic assistance in the form of trade-good programs and the development of local markets for products such as copra. Since their economic ties with Japan had been completely severed but those with the United States had not yet been established, Krug thought that there should be an economic program tied in with the political one that would be geared to the well-being of the Micronesians. In addition, Krug saw an American political and economic development program being supplemented by an educational one that would be "designed to assist these island peoples in raising themselves to a reasonably modern social and cultural level." Krug admitted there were many aspects of indigenous culture that should be preserved, but he thought that the United States had more responsibility than just "preserving" the Pacific Islanders as an "exhibit" of "bygone" culture. Krug pointed out to Truman that this program would require a great deal of cooperation from many specialized Federal agencies. The central administering agency would have to have the coordinating authority to ensure that Federal agencies specializing in education, public health, agriculture, and fisheries were cooperating and performing. Therefore, he thought that a "fully coordinated" organization was necessary for reasons of economy, sound administration, the islands' needs for development, and the United States' special responsibilities under the Trusteeship Agreement.[36]

Krug told Truman that there was no doubt in his mind about the strategic importance of these islands and their value to the United States as forward outposts of defense. He knew the military services had to be afforded free access to all of these locations at all times. Moreover, he understood that the military had to be allowed to set aside and exclusively control islands or parts of islands and their surrounding waters as was necessary for the establishment and maintenance of military bases. Additionally, he knew that the military services needed to have exclusive jurisdiction over these bases and reservations. He did not think, however, that civilian administration of these islands' nonmilitary areas was incompatible with an effective national defense. As evidence for his claim, Krug pointed out that military and naval "mastery" of the Civil Governments of Puerto Rico, Alaska, and the US Virgin Islands had not been necessary during the war. Moreover, he thought that the emergency in Hawaii demonstrated that military control could be extended to an entire strategic area when necessary, and then withdrawn to the military reservations once the emergency had passed. He also argued that the war had provided many examples of close cooperation between civilian and military agencies for the good of the nation. In his view, to keep the Pacific Islands under permanent military administration would admit a basic weakness in American governmental principles. He thought that instituting Civil Government in the Pacific Islands as soon as possible and "practicing democracy" there would be the best way for the United States to "overcome the non-democratic philosophies of government which today are bidding for control of the whole of Asia."[37]

Krug then went into more detailed observations about various Pacific Islands that he had visited. On Guam, he found a people who "appear to be cheerful and well-fed but somewhat impatient with the lag in the rebuilding of their communities and in the reconstruction of their economy." In addition, he found that their recent experiences had caused the Guamanians to develop a "political consciousness" that was "far beyond" that which had existed on the island before the war. He specifically said that Guamanian political leaders wanted Guam's political status and civil rights guaranteed by Congress, a pledge made by the United States as far back as 1898! Krug also discussed the destruction on the island, especially from the American naval and air bombardment as well as the ground fighting needed to liberate Guam from Japanese control. Structures of all kinds, as well as breadfruit, coconut, and timber trees, were down; devastation was highly evident everywhere he went, livestock was largely gone, and permanent housing construction had not yet begun. Krug told Truman that the island had never been economically self-sufficient in its modern history, and that there was no industry. He pointed out to Truman, however, that in peacetime the soil had at least been fertile and the livestock plentiful. Now, he reminded Truman, about 50 percent of the island was to be military reservations, making many of these formerly successful Guamanian farmers landless. Moreover, many Guamanians had been forced into temporary refugee camps that were operated by the Naval Military Government (MG).[38]

Krug again criticized the present situation in which neither the 23,000 Guamanians nor the American civilians on the island had an effective part in enacting the laws that governed them, since all power was vested in the US Naval Governor, Rear Admiral Charles Pownall. Krug admitted that Admiral Pownall occasionally sought advice from an "effective" local Congress, but the Secretary of the Interior also told Truman that the local body was without authority. He went into detail about Pownall's powers, including the authority to tax, the appointment and removal of judges who presided without juries, and the ability to sit in review of the judges and their decisions. There was apparently no right of appeal for either local inhabitants or American citizens residing on Guam other than Pownall's decision to submit capital cases to the Secretary of the Navy for review. In addition, Pownall was obviously in control of the Navy and Marine Corps personnel, as well as the Guamanian policemen who enforced the laws. While Krug said he was not trying to imply that Pownall had been out of line in his actions, he thought that any system that vested so much power in one person was intolerable and completely out of character for people living under the American flag.[39]

Krug then returned to the economic needs of the island, in particular the fact that so much taxable property, such as buildings, had been destroyed; that so much land was reserved for the military; and that all of the island's financial needs had to be met from Federal funds and local taxes levied by the Navy. Krug saw a definite need to change this situation so that private businesses would be revived and supply the food, clothing, and other needs of the local economy. He also reported that the Bank of Guam, owned and operated by the Navy, was the only institution of commercial credit on the island, but that this institution did not take the risks normally associated with private banking ventures. On a related matter, Krug informed Truman that the Navy and a shipping firm known as American President Lines supplied most of the local freight-transportation needs. In addition, the shipping firm had taken care of some postal business until the reestablishment of the US Post Office on Guam. The Post Office now shipped much of the light consumer goods that came to Guam. However, Krug thought that passenger service to and from the island was inadequate. Pan American World Airways had recently reestablished its facilities on Guam. This new Pan Am facility would connect Guam with the Philippines, China, Japan, Hawaii, and the mainland United States, as had been the case before the war. Shipping for civilian passengers, however, was not adequate, as American President Lines was soon to end service and military craft could not accommodate much civilian traffic. Nonetheless, Krug saw a positive development in the establishment of a trans-Pacific commercial cable relay station, since this at least gave the civilian population access to communication facilities at commercial rates. While he thought the Navy was extending adequate health care to local American civilians and the Guamanians, Krug asserted to Truman that these were functions normally carried out by local governments or the medical profession in most American communities of Guam's size. He did have praise for both the Army and Navy in ensuring sanitation, pest control, and medical education, but he thought that the Guamanians should take over these functions from Navy personnel as soon as possible. Krug also had praise for the state of education on Guam. Apparently, the Naval Government prescribed the curriculum, selected the teachers, spent a considerable portion of its funds on education, and had done quite a bit to "raise the cultural level of the people and to teach them the general principles of the American way of life." He remarked on the prolific use of the English language and the general "progress" that had been made in this area.[40]

In summation, Krug thought that the people of Guam were ready for autonomy in their local affairs under a civilian governor. According to Krug, the Guamanians "have made remarkable progress under American sovereignty. They speak our language with facility; they understand our political philosophy and have the same social organization and institutions on the island." Moreover, Krug praised the Guamanians for being devout Christians for generations, and for demonstrating their loyalty to the United States during the war. Because the Guam Congress had been in operation since 1931, he thought it was well qualified to assume legislative powers, and that the people of Guam were ready to enact local laws and have a voice in determining how their tax dollars were spent. As a final point, Krug reiterated to Truman that he thought the Guamanians were entitled to these rights, especially to the right to have a role in creating the laws under which they lived. For this reason, he wanted the Marines withdrawn as village policemen, he wanted the local courts freed of the "heavy hand" of executive control, and he wanted the Guamanians and local Americans to have the right of appeal to the US Federal court system.[41]

His thoughts about American Samoa were different. As with the Guamanians, Krug saw the American Samoans as healthy, well fed, and "adequately housed according to native standards," but he was also convinced that the American Samoans had had less contact with mainland Americans. He admitted that the Samoans who lived and worked around the American naval base at Pago Pago spoke English, practiced American religious and social forms, and had a "good understanding" of American political philosophy. Samoans of the "back country," however, still lived in a "native" society of handicraft production and the cultivation of tropical crops, and he found that they still retained their tribal customs and only spoke "our language" with difficulty. Krug also reported that the laws of American Samoa, like those on Guam, were promulgated by the Naval Governor, in this case Captain Vernon Huber, who had absolute and final authority. As on Guam, Huber had control of the court system, though he too referred capital cases to the Secretary of the Navy if this was requested by the defendant. There was no right of appeal to the US court system, and Huber had complete authority in local matters, including taxation. Failure to pay the poll tax levied by the Naval Government was punishable by imprisonment, and the Naval Government also had control over customs funds, which were levied on all food and clothes imported into the island. Imports and exports were regulated by a Commodity Administrator who was appointed by Huber. Moreover, Huber had complete authority over a six-person Department of Samoan Industry, a governmental cooperative marketing agent for Samoan products that oversaw fair trade practices. An example of Huber's control was also seen in the copra industry. Copra and related palm products could not be exported unless they were consigned to persons in the United States, except upon specific authority of the Naval Governor. According to Krug, profits from these activities were deposited to the credit of the Naval Government of American Samoa. Krug also described the Bank of American Samoa in terms similar to those of the Bank of Guam. However, non-Samoans could not extend credit to Samoans in excess of $25 without Huber's permission, something Krug did not mention vis-à-vis the Bank of Guam. He pointed out another difference from Guam: a complete lack of civilian communication facilities, though Navy radio facilities were sometimes made available to the Samoans. In addition, a passenger service called the Matson Line carried civilian passengers and mail, and took care of freight needs on an unscheduled basis. An inter-island freight and passenger service that had been privately owned before the war was now operated by the Naval Government—and, according to Krug, at a substantial profit. He understood, however, that the Naval Government meant to return this line to private ownership in the near future.[42]

Krug also related, without any editorial comment, that health and sanitation in Samoa were the responsibility of the Naval Government, and that naval medical personnel were providing care at a newly completed hospital. In addition, he related how the Naval Government maintained and operated the school system, and that there were a number of church schools on the island. He found the schools in Pago Pago to be sufficient, but thought that those in the rural areas were "somewhat primitive" and needed higher physical-plant and teaching standards. While he favored the American Samoans providing some of the funding for their school system through local taxation, he thought the United States would have to continue shouldering some of this cost itself. Krug then returned to indigenous politics. The only "semblance" of a legislative body that he found was the annual "Fono," or general meeting of chiefs and native officials. This body was presided over by Huber, but it was no more than an advisory council. Although he thought the Samoans should be given a greater role in making the laws they lived under, he was convinced that the Fono, as presently constituted, could not be transformed into a democratically elected legislative body since he thought the chiefs and family heads would be able to "unduly" influence any voting by members of their clans. Yet at the same time, Krug did not think that the American Samoans should be governed by executive fiat. He wanted to establish an elective legislature "without delay," and without regard for the present-day "hierarchy," even though he thought that the new assembly would be dominated by bloc voting under the family heads for a time. With experience in the use of the voting franchise, he was convinced that the American Samoans "would soon adapt themselves to democratic institutions." Krug wanted to afford full protection of civil liberties to the American Samoans as on Guam. This meant having local courts freed of the Naval Governor, extending the US Constitution and laws to the American Samoans "so far as they can possibly be made applicable," and divorcing local executive power from local legislative and judicial functions. Krug thought that all of these changes needed to be legislatively enacted and limited by an Act of Congress. Finally, he wanted a civilian governor appointed by the President with the advice and consent of the Senate.[43]

As regarded the former Japanese Mandates, Krug admitted to Truman that his visit was brief, and limited to visiting Kwajalein. While he said he did not have an opportunity to converse with the local inhabitants, he was informed that they were glad to be rid of their Japanese masters, and that they were quite friendly to the United States. He was also informed that the Micronesians were law-abiding to a "remarkable degree," although military provost courts tried the more serious criminal cases in the islands. He had further been told that while Micronesian affairs were being administered by Naval Military Government, local government was largely through local chiefs. Additionally, Krug told Truman that he had been informed that the island economies had been completely disrupted and were in a "chaotic" condition. Accordingly, he thought that action to improve these economic circumstances was long overdue. As an example, he described a situation in which prewar Japanese sources of consumer goods and prewar Japanese markets for Micronesian goods no longer existed, and communication and inter-island shipping were largely unavailable. Because of this, he thought it was necessary that the US Government continue to assist the Micronesians in procuring trade goods and in disposing of copra, shells, handicrafts, and other local products. However, he also thought that this aid should be gradually withdrawn and replaced by forms of private enterprise in which the local population acted as owners and operators. In the interim, he thought that "reasonable" regulation of non-Micronesians needed to take place so as to prevent exploitation, but he did not think the area should be kept permanently closed to "legitimate" traders and commercial enterprises, as the military wanted.[44]

Krug then provided a historical lesson to Truman about the civilian administration of Micronesia by relating that the Japanese naval squadron commander who took possession of Micronesia from the Germans in 1914 established a military administration as part of the garrison force. However, the military administration was transferred to a civilian administration in July 1918. Although this civilian administration remained under the authority of the local Japanese naval garrison commander, the naval garrison was abolished in 1922 upon Japan's award as administering power of the League of Nations Mandate. A civilian agency, the South Seas Bureau, then presided over Micronesia until just a few years before the outbreak of the Pacific War. Krug used this example of Japanese administration to argue that while Micronesia clearly had to be kept under US control for purposes of American national security, it did not follow that this governance had to be by way of military administration. He thought that the civilian populations of the islands were entitled to civilian government, and a type of government in which they were encouraged to participate. He thought it best if the Micronesians were given a "maximum measure" of local self-government. He envisioned this self-government not necessarily as the imposition of American political processes and institutions in all cases, but the continuance of indigenous customs on some islands. The bottom line for him, however, was the establishment of local municipal councils based on a democratic franchise. He also wanted a situation in which TTPI administration was subject at all times to public criticism and responsible to the "democratically expressed" needs of the people. According to Krug, Article 11 of the Draft Trustee-ship Agreement granted the Micronesians the status of TTPI citizens and afforded them diplomatic and consular protection when they were outside of Micronesia or the United States. Thus Krug assumed that there was nothing in the proposed Agreement that prevented the United States from extending all of the rights and protections afforded to US citizens to the Micronesians as well. He thought that their rights should be guaranteed by an Act of Congress, and that they should be given a system of civil courts to replace the military ones. Finally, he thought that all of these measures could be realized without danger to US military security. In his view, a local society of "self-respecting" human beings in the Pacific Basin, imbued with the love of democracy, could be the greatest asset to US national security, and a "forward bulwark" of the American way of life in Asia![45]

Krug concluded his report with some comments on Okinawa. He reminded Tru-man that the island was part of sovereign Japanese territory, along with the rest of the Ryukyus, and that it was also under US military administration, in this case an administration being carried out by the Army. He also reported that much of the is-land was "utterly" devastated, that the population had suffered a great deal of phys-ical hardship and complete economic destruction, and that they were in such a pitiful state that they could use whatever economic aid the United States could pro-vide. Krug saw the Army's Military Government as quite able, especially in regard to returning the Okinawans to their lands. In turn, he thought that the Okinawans were quite adept at restoring these lands, sometimes even without the benefit of draft animals, and that the islanders, with the Army's assistance, were providing themselves with temporary housing. Schools had also been started and he thought that, with the guidance of the Army's Military Government officers, "these industri-ous people are learning the ways of democracy and are participating to a limited ex-tent to their own government." Krug concluded his lengthy report with the assertion that General MacArthur supported his idea that Military Government should be withdrawn as the Okinawans proceeded down the road to democracy. To Krug, an early withdrawal of Military Government would entail its replacement by a civil ad-ministration in which the Okinawans would be given more responsibility in the conduct of their own affairs. "We must be prepared to permit these people to prac-tice the democracy we preach." Krug thought that the "form" and not only the words of "our way of life" must be established in Okinawa as proof to the people of East Asia "that democracy is suited to oriental peoples living in an oriental economy. A truly democratic Okinawa and Japan, lying as they do off the mainland of Asia, can serve as a spearhead of our way of life."[46]

While it is unclear to what extent Krug's report was disseminated throughout the US Government or if it had any kind of public disclosure or impact, it was taken to have at least some value by some of Truman's advisers. In fact, eventual civil ad-ministration was assumed by certain officials in the Truman Administration by this time. A memo later the same month from John Kingsley, White House Office Program Coordinator, to John Steelman, the Assistant to the President, talked about Krug's report as an "interesting and valuable" one that was arguing for "probably the only sound policy in the long run." It seemed to Kingsley that the only question about military versus civilian control over the Pacific Islands was the matter of timing the transfer of control from the military services to the Interior Department. While he did not think that Civil Government should be instituted at the present, Kingsley believed that there would be an advantage in at least publicizing the fact that the Truman Administration was considering the possibility. Accordingly, he favored the publication of Krug's report.[47]

■ Conclusion

The Interior Department's case for administering the postwar Pacific Basin territories is a fascinating study of useable history. In addition, Interior's arguments are a case study in bureaucratic assumptions about the Department's past successes. Furthermore, Interior Department officials were making strong assumptions about the failures that other Executive Departments would encounter in administering the Pacific Basin territories. However—and most intriguing from this author's perspective—is that the Interior Department, contrary to views held by War, Navy, and State Department officials, did not ignore domestic and international political realities when devising their policies for the postwar Pacific. Interior Department officials, in fact, used anticolonial thought in American and international public opinion as evidence for their assertion that Interior should administer the new territories. More importantly, in their own imperialistic way, Interior Department officials created an original justification for the civil administration of the Pacific Islands. Military opposition to Interior Department governance focused on the idea that civil administration was dangerous to US national security because it removed the military services from administrative control over the Pacific territories. Interior, however, countered this line of thinking by asserting that civil administration could succeed in coupling and integrating these territories more significantly into the American polity than War and Navy Department administration ever could, thereby creating an even greater degree of control and security in the region for the United States. Interior, in other words, argued for a civil administration that heavily integrated Pacific Islanders into the American polity not as a way to lessen US control over the area but as the best way to ensure long-term US control over the postwar Pacific.

The Importance of a "Backwater"

The Pacific Basin as an Aspect of
Early Cold War US Strategic Policy

An examination of the United States' early postwar plans for the defense and administration of its Pacific Basin territories reveals a number of phenomena of interest to students of American foreign-relations history. First, it quickly becomes clear that the major participants in each of the Executive Departments employed a "useable history" to argue and justify their bureaucratic positions on the defense and administration of both the prewar territories and those acquired during the Pacific War. Second, the Pacific Basin has been a significant and heretofore vastly understudied arena of not only interservice but interdepartmental rivalry. A great deal of the existing literature on the US Government in the late 1940s focuses on the interservice rivalry between the War and Navy Departments over the future Department of Defense (DOD). While the main focus of this study was not departmental rivalry per se, a study of US Pacific policy in the first two years after the end of the war suggests that many policy debates at this time not only took place between the military services, but between both civilian and military departments over central aspects of US foreign and defense policies.

For example, policymakers and planners had to determine which of the military services was going to be designated the nation's "first line of defense" in the postwar period. That competition between the War and Navy Departments was a domestic political conflict that impacted US military forces wherever they were stationed in the world. The Pacific, however, was a microcosm of interservice rivalry in a region that Cabinet officers and the JCS thought was vital to future US security because of the fears of another Pearl Harbor. Moreover, US policy toward the Pacific Basin in the immediate postwar period has rarely been studied in the context of interdepartmental rivalry. Yet the conflict between the War and Navy Departments on the one hand and the State and Interior Departments on the other over the control of Pacific policy was a serious issue for the Truman Administration.

Thus, it is possible that although the Pacific Basin was a Cold War "backwater," it was nevertheless an important region of the world to the United States. Interwar misperceptions of Japanese fortification in Micronesia, the trauma of Pearl Harbor, the horrors of the Pacific War campaigns, and the fears of a future global war with the USSR in which the Soviet Union might enjoy early victories in Eurasia were paramount to American policymakers, planners, and strategic thinkers at this time. These individuals, both military and civilian, were concerned enough about the United States' future position in the Pacific Basin to be willing to weaken the United States' commitment to UN principles and argue for predominant US control in the area, whether by strategic trusteeship or annexation. Tertiary theater or not, the Pacific Basin was a region that the United States felt it needed secured before it could pursue its other strategic interests in the early Cold War.

Notes

■ Introduction

1. For some of these perceptions, see William Roger Louis, *Imperialism at Bay: The United States and the Decolonization of the British Empire, 1941–1945* (Oxford: The Clarendon Press, 1977).

2. For the misperceptions that Japan had fortified Micronesia prior to 1934, see Earl Pomeroy, *Pacific Outpost: American Strategy in Guam and Micronesia* (Stanford, Calif.: Stanford University Press, 1951), 74–180. The reader should understand, however, that declassified documentation from both the US and Japanese Governments that was not available to Professor Pomeroy now clearly demonstrates that US fears about Japanese violation of the League of Nations agreements were unfounded. This documentation shows that Japan did not begin to fortify Micronesia until after it had left the League in 1934, that the fortification of Micronesia did not begin in a serious manner until after 1939, and that in some cases fortification was still underway in 1943. See Mark Peattie, *Nanyo: The Rise and Fall of the Japanese in Micronesia, 1885–1945* (Honolulu: University of Hawaii Press, 1988), 230–256; and Hal Friedman, *Creating an American Lake: United States Imperialism and Strategic Security, 1945–1947* (Westport, Conn.: Greenwood Press, 2001), 13–16.

3. Melvin Leffler, *A Preponderance of Power: National Security, the Truman Administration, and the Cold War* (Stanford, Calif.: Stanford University Press, 1992), 1–181.

4. For this idea of "Red Fascism," see Les Adler and Thomas Paterson, "Red Fascism: The Merger of Nazi Germany and Soviet Russia in the American Image of Totalitarianism, 1930s–1950s," *American Historical Review* 75 (April 1970): 1046–1064.

5. For an excellent secondary account of this geostrategic prioritization, see Michael

Palmer, *Origins of the Maritime Strategy: The Development of American Naval Strategy, 1945–1955* (Annapolis, Md.: Naval Institute Press, 1990), 16–39. For one primary account, see Annex B to Appendix C, "Size of Forces and Availability of Funds for Overseas Bases," 29, Joint Staff Planners (hereafter cited as JPS) 684/31, "Over-All Examination of U.S. Requirements for Military Bases and Base Rights," 24 June 1947, Joint Chiefs of Staff (hereafter cited as JCS) Central Decimal File, 1946–1947, Records of the Combined and Joint Chiefs of Staff (hereafter cited as CCS), Record Group (hereafter cited as RG) 218, National Archives, College Park, Maryland (hereafter cited as NA II). Here, the JPS talked about US bases in Hawaii and the Caribbean being "relatively" advanced compared to other primary base areas. Thus, they wanted funding allocated first to "those areas vital to the defense of the U.S. such as the northern, northeastern and northwestern approaches, and secondarily to those essential to the projection of early offensive operations such as the Azores, Ryukyus, and Marianas."

6. For the key focus of the Navy on the Pacific War, see Vincent Davis, *Postwar Defense Policy and the U.S. Navy, 1943–1946* (Chapel Hill: University of North Carolina Press, 1966). For one of numerous books demonstrating that the Marines perceived the Pacific War as a largely Marine Corps operation, see Allan Millett, *In Many a Strife: General Gerald C. Thomas and the U.S. Marine Corps, 1917–1956* (Annapolis, Md.: Naval Institute Press, 1993). For the American public's concentration on Japan as the primary enemy in the Second World War, see John Dower, *War Without Mercy: Race and Power in the Pacific War* (New York: Pantheon Books, 1986).

7. Louis, *Imperialism at Bay*, 121–460; see also Eleanor Lattimore, "Pacific Ocean or American Lake?" *Far Eastern Survey* 14 (7 November 1945): 313–316.

8. Friedman, *Creating an American Lake*, passim.

9. Because of the distance to Guam from Southeast Asia, B-52 bases in Thailand were more valuable to the United States during the Vietnam War. Guam, however, remained important because it was a US Territory from which American forces could operate without any political or diplomatic difficulties. Wayne Thompson, *To Hanoi and Back: The U.S. Air Force and North Vietnam, 1966–1973* (Washington, D.C.: Smithsonian Institution Press, 2000), 9, 23, 223–224, 255, 264, 271–274, 275, 277–278, and 280.

10. Carol Reardon, *Soldiers and Scholars: The U.S. Army and the Uses of Military History, 1865–1920* (Lawrence: University Press of Kansas, 1990); idem., *Pickett's Charge in History and Memory* (Chapel Hill: University of North Carolina Press, 1997); David Hanlon, *Remaking Micronesia: Discourses over Development in a Pacific Territory, 1944–1982* (Honolulu: University of Hawaii Press, 1998).

11. The literature on post–World War II interservice rivalry is voluminous, but rarely takes into account the Army Ground Forces. One rare example is Richard Haynes, "The Defense Unification Battle, 1947–1950: The Army," *Prologue: The Journal of the National Archives* 7 (Spring 1975): 27–31.

12. Examples of previous accounts include Inis Claude, *Swords Into Plowshares: The Problems and Progress of International Organizations* (New York: Random House, 1984), 357–

376; and William Roger Louis, ed., *National Security and International Trusteeship in the Pacific* (Annapolis, Md.: Naval Institute Press, 1972).

■ Chapter 1. Ground Power in Paradise

1. Marshall to MacArthur, 21 September 1945, Record Group 9 (hereafter cited as RG 9): Radiograms, Blue Binders, Troop Deployment File, Douglas MacArthur Memorial Archives and Library, Norfolk, Virginia (hereafter cited as MacArthur Memorial Archives).

2. MacArthur to Marshall, 21 September 1945, RG 9: Radiograms, Blue Binders, Troop Deployment File, MacArthur Memorial Archives.

3. For more on the JCS having a similar viewpoint as late as the summer of 1947, see Friedman, *Creating an American Lake*, 33–34.

4. MacArthur to Marshall, 1 November 1945, folder October 1944–February 1951, Ennis Whitehead Collection (hereafter cited as the Whitehead Collection), 168.6008-3, Air Force Historical Research Agency, Maxwell Air Force Base, Montgomery, Alabama (hereafter cited as AFHRA), 1–2.

5. Major General Marshall to MacArthur, 28 November 1945 cover letter; and General Headquarters, U.S. Army Forces in the Pacific, "Staff Study Relevant: Post War Development Plan for Philippines and Okinawa," 1–22. Both in Record Group 4: Records of the General Headquarters, US Army Forces, Pacific (hereafter cited as RG 4: AFPAC), Operations, MacArthur Memorial Archives.

6. Eisenhower, "Appearance before House of Representatives Committee on Military Affairs for Hearings on Demobilization of the Army," 22 January 1946, *Hearings, Volume No. 2*, January 1946–June 1946, in box 144, Pre-Presidential Papers, Dwight D. Eisenhower Library, Abilene, Kansas (hereafter cited as DDEL), 183, 304, and 325–328.

7. Eisenhower to MacArthur, 28 January 1946, Douglas MacArthur File, folder March 1945–January 1952, box 74, Pre-Presidential Papers, DDEL.

8. Eisenhower, "Outline Notes Used for Talk to Women Magazine Writers," 5 June 1946, 2 and 4, Speeches, May 1946–December 1946 (3), box 192, Pre-Presidential Papers, DDEL.

9. Hull to MacArthur, 12 July 1946, RG 9: Radiograms, US Army Forces, Middle Pacific (hereafter cited as AFMIDPAC), MacArthur Memorial Archives, 1–3.

10. MacArthur to Whitehead, Hull, and Christiansen, 25 July 1946, RG 9: Radiograms, AFMIDPAC, MacArthur Memorial Archives, 1–6. See chapter 2 of this volume for details about PACUSA deployments planned in conjunction with "Arouse."

11. Cover letter by Witsell, 6 August 1946, and "War Department Plan for Overseas Bases (Post Occupation Period)," Record Group 5: Records of the Supreme Commander for the Allied Powers in Japan (hereafter cited as RG 5: SCAP), General File, MacArthur Memorial Archives. SCAP was MacArthur's other area of responsibility in the postwar period, along with that of CINCAFPAC.

12. Ibid., 1–7, 17–56, and 10–11.

13. Ibid., 11–13.

14. Ibid., 13–14.

15. Ibid., 14–16.

16. Norstad, Map Attachments to "Presentation Given to President by Major General Lauris Norstad on 29 October 1946, 'Postwar Military Establishment,'" folder Speeches 1946 (2), box 26, Papers of Lauris Norstad (hereafter cited as the Norstad Papers), DDEL.

17. MacArthur to Eisenhower, 25 November 1946, RG 9: Radiograms, AFMIDPAC, MacArthur Memorial Archives, 1–3.

18. Hull to MacArthur, 4 December 1946, RG 9: Radiograms, AFMIDPAC, MacArthur Memorial Archives.

19. Hull to MacArthur, 17 December 1946, RG 9: Radiograms, AFMIDPAC, MacArthur Memorial Archives.

20. Griswold to MacArthur, 8 February 1947, RG 9: Radiograms, Marianas-Bonins Command (hereafter cited as MARBO), MacArthur Memorial Archives.

21. Griswold to MacArthur, 14 February 1947, RG 9: Radiograms, MARBO, MacArthur Memorial Archives.

22. MacArthur to Griswold, 15 February 1947, RG 9: Radiograms, MARBO, MacArthur Memorial Archives.

23. Eisenhower, "Remarks before House Subcommittee on Military Appropriations," 19 February 1947, House Subcommittee on Military Appropriations File, box 194, Pre-Presidential Papers, DDEL, 2.

24. Eisenhower, "Address at Civic Reception, St. Louis, Missouri," 24 February 1947, folder Speeches, January 1947–October 1947 (3), box 192, Pre-Presidential Papers, DDEL, 5.

25. MacArthur to Griswold, 26 May 1947, RG 9: Radiograms, MARBO, MacArthur Memorial Archives.

26. Barbey and Gardner, cover letter to Eisenhower and Nimitz, "Survey for Military Development of Marianas," 1 June 1947, *Report of the Joint Marianas On-Site Board for the Military Development of the Marianas* (hereafter cited as the *Joint Marianas Report*), 178.2917-1, AFRHA.

27. Appendix A, Forces: The Problem, *Joint Marianas Report*, 178.2917-1, AFRHA, 55 and 57.

28. Ibid., 57. For the concern about Saipan as an enemy target for invasion, see Rear Admiral William Smith, Navy Bureau of Yards and Docks, Assistant Chief for Plans and Research, and Major General Pedro del Valle, Marine Corps Director of Personnel, to Vice Admiral Barbey, "Minority Report to the Joint Marianas On-Site Board," 33–36; and Nimitz to Eisenhower, 11 March 1947, Tab A-5 to Appendix A, both in *Joint Marianas Report*, 178.2917-1, AFHRA, 75.

29. Appendix A, *Joint Marianas Report*, 178.2917-1, AFHRA, 57.

30. "Statement of General of the Army Dwight D. Eisenhower, Chief of Staff," US Congress, Senate Committee on Foreign Relations, *Hearings before the Committee on Foreign Relations*, United States Senate, 80th Congress, 1st session, 7 July 1947, 18.

31. Pomeroy, *Pacific Outpost*, 3–115.

32. Friedman, *Creating an American Lake*, 12–16.

33. Christiansen to MacArthur, 17 October 1946, RG 9: Radiograms, US Army Forces, Western Pacific (hereafter cited as AFWESPAC), MacArthur Memorial Archives, 1–2. For US military conduct in Manila and the resulting problems, see Nick Cullather, *Illusions of Influence: The Political Economy of United States–Philippines Relations, 1942–1960* (Stanford, Calif.: Stanford University Press, 1994), 49.

34. Christiansen to MacArthur, 17 October 1946, RG 9: Radiograms, AFWESPAC, MacArthur Memorial Archives, 2–4.

35. Norstad to Lincoln, 7 November 1946, folder Official-Classified, 1946–47 (1), box 22, Norstad Papers, DDEL.

36. Eisenhower to MacArthur, 8 November 1946, Douglas MacArthur File, folder March 1945–January 1952, box 74, Pre-Presidential Papers, DDEL, 1–2.

37. Nimitz to Eisenhower, 12 November 1946, folder State Department, 1946–1947, box 38, White House Central Files (hereafter cited as WHCF), Harry S. Truman Library, Independence, Missouri (hereafter cited as HSTL).

38. Eisenhower to the JCS, 23 November 1946, "War Department Requirements for Military Bases and Rights in the Philippine Islands," folder State Department, 1946–1947, box 38, WHCF, HSTL, 1–2.

39. Patterson to Byrnes, 29 November 1946, folder State Department, 1946–1947, box 38, WHCF, HSTL, 1–2 .

40. Byrnes to Acheson, 1 December 1946, folder State Department, 1946–1947, box 38, WHCF, HSTL. Acheson was Acting Secretary of State whenever Byrnes was out of the country. Acheson's regular billet was Under Secretary of State.

41. Acheson to Truman, 4 December 1946, folder State Department, 1946–1947, box 38, WHCF, HSTL.

42. Handy to Eisenhower, 13 December 1946, Thomas Handy File, folder April 1945–December 1946, box 54, Pre-Presidential Papers, DDEL.

43. Handy to Leahy, 24 December 1946, folder State Department, 1946–1947, box 38, WHCF, HSTL.

44. Acheson to Truman, 24 December 1946, folder State Department, 1946–1947, box 38, WHCF, HSTL, 1–2.

45. The Philippine Scouts were an adjunct US Army organization that dated back to the Philippine War of 1899–1902, when they were known as Native Scouts. Apparently, they were still in some mode of operation in late December 1946. For pre–Pacific War background on the Philippine Scouts, see Brian Linn, *The U.S. Army and Counterinsurgency in the Philippine War, 1899–1902* (Chapel Hill: University of North Carolina Press, 1989); and idem., *Guardians of Empire: The U.S. Army and the Pacific, 1902–1940* (Chapel Hill: University of North Carolina Press, 1997). For Leahy's reference to the postwar outfit, see the memorandum by Leahy, 30 December 1946, file State Department, 1946–1947, box 38, WHCF, HSTL.

46. See Acheson to Truman, 24 December 1946, 2–3; as well as the draft memorandum for the Secretary of War and the cover letter from Leahy to Handy, 31 December 1946, all in folder State Department, 1946–1947, box 38, WHCF, HSTL.

47. Handy to Eisenhower, 2 January 1947, Thomas Handy File, folder January 1947–December 1949, box 54, Pre-Presidential Papers, DDEL, 1–2.

48. Truman to Byrnes, 6 January 1947, folder State Department, 1946–1947, box 38, WHCF, HSTL.

49. Truman to Patterson, 9 January 1947, folder State Department, 1946–1947, box 38, WHCF, HSTL. Also, see the memorandum from Acheson about Roxas's political pressures vis-à-vis public statements and Philippine Congressional resolutions, 24 December 1946, folder State Department, 1946–1947, box 38, WHCF, HSTL.

50. For a more complete analysis of these issues, see Friedman, *Creating an American Lake*, 27–36.

51. Hull to MacArthur, 3 August 1946, RG 9: Radiograms, AFMIDPAC, MacArthur Memorial Archives, 1–5.

52. Hull to Christiansen, 10 August 1946, RG 9: Radiograms, AFMIDPAC, MacArthur Memorial Archives.

53. MacArthur to Hull, 5 September 1946, RG 9: Radiograms, Outgoing Messages (hereafter cited as XTS), MacArthur Memorial Archives.

54. Hull to the Chief of the Special Purposes Garrison, US Army (hereafter cited as C SPGAR USA), 21 September 1946, RG 9: Radiograms, AFMIDPAC, MacArthur Memorial Archives, 1–3.

55. Hull to MacArthur, 16 October 1946, RG 9: Radiograms, AFMIDPAC, MacArthur Memorial Archives.

56. Hull to MacArthur, 28 October 1946, RG 9: AFMIDPAC, MacArthur Memorial Archives.

57. Hull to Harry, 11 November 1946, RG 9: Radiograms, AFMIDPAC, MacArthur Memorial Archives, 1–3. South Pacific bases were becoming a much lower priority with the JCS by this time because of the clear reorientation of US strategic planning in the Pacific toward the Soviets rather than a resurgent Japan. This reorientation meant the JCS was becoming more focused on base facilities north of the equator that could be used for offensive power projection toward Northeast Asia rather than with bases south of the equator that might have to be employed in the unlikely scenario that the Soviets conquered the Pacific Basin north of the equator. See Friedman, *Creating an American Lake*, 17–36.

58. Hull to MacArthur, 4 December 1946, RG 9: Radiograms, AFMIDPAC, MacArthur Memorial Archives.

59. Griswold to MacArthur, 24 May 1947, RG 9: Radiograms, MARBO, MacArthur Memorial Archives.

60. US relations with Australia and New Zealand over future base facilities in the South Pacific were quite strained by this time. In fact, these strained relations not only complicated US access to these bases sites, but they also helped spur the JCS to decide to

forego the bases. See Roger Bell, *Unequal Allies: Australian-American Relations and the Pacific War* (Carlton, Australia: Melbourne University Press, 1977), 144–172.

61. There is a vast historiography on this issue. For an excellent example, see Herman Wolk, *Planning and Organizing the Postwar Air Force, 1943–1947* (Washington, D.C.: Office of Air Force History, 1984), 45–223.

62. Ibid., 158.

63. Ibid., 157–158 and 160.

64. Ibid., 158 and 160.

65. See Richardson to MacArthur, 19 August 1945, RG 9: Radiograms, Blue Binders, Plans and Operations (hereafter cited as P&O) File, MacArthur Memorial Archives, 1.

66. Ibid.; and MacArthur to Marshall, 20 August 1945, RG 9: Radiograms, Blue Binders, P&O File, MacArthur Memorial Archives, 2.

67. MacArthur to Marshall, 28 August 1945, RG 9: Radiograms, Blue Binders, P&O File, MacArthur Memorial Archives, 1 and 2.

68. Wolk, *Planning and Organizing the Postwar Air Force*, 41, 158, and 160.

69. MacArthur to Marshall, 9 October 1945, RG 9: Radiograms, Blue Binders, P&O File, MacArthur Memorial Archives.

70. Patterson to MacArthur, 22 July 1946, RG 9: Radiograms, AFMIDPAC, MacArthur Memorial Archives.

71. Eisenhower to MacArthur, 30 July 1946, RG 9: Radiograms, Blue Binders, P&O File, MacArthur Memorial Archives, 1–3.

72. Ibid., 3–4.

73. MacArthur to Eisenhower, 31 July 1946, RG 9: Radiograms, Blue Binders, P&O File, MacArthur Memorial Archives, 1–3.

74. MacArthur to Patterson, 4 August 1946, RG 9: Radiograms, Blue Binders, P&O File, MacArthur Memorial Archives.

75. Eisenhower to MacArthur, 29 August 1946, RG 9: Radiograms, Blue Binders, P&O File, MacArthur Memorial Archives, 1–4.

76. MacArthur to Eisenhower, 31 August 1946, RG 9: Radiograms, Blue Binders, P&O File, MacArthur Memorial Archives, 1–3.

77. Eisenhower to MacArthur, 5 September 1946, RG 9: Radiograms, Blue Binders, P&O File, MacArthur Memorial Archives, 1–3.

78. Ibid., 3–5.

79. Ibid., 6–8.

80. See MacArthur to Eisenhower, 8 September 1946, RG 9: Radiograms, Blue Binders, P&O File, MacArthur Memorial Archives, 1–3.

81. Eisenhower to MacArthur, 25 October 1946, Douglas MacArthur File, folder March 1945–January 1952, box 74, Pre-Presidential Papers, DDEL, 2.

82. Handy to Eisenhower, 13 December 1946, Thomas Handy File, folder April 1945–December 1946, box 54, Pre-Presidential Papers, DDEL.

83. See Hull to Harry, 2 January 1947, RG 9: Radiograms, AFMIDPAC, MacArthur Memorial

Archives, 1–2.

84. Ronald Spector, *Eagle Against the Sun: The American War with Japan* (New York: The Free Press, 1985), 417–420; and Edward Marolda and Robert Schneller, *Shield and Sword: The United States Navy and the Persian Gulf War* (Annapolis, Md.: Naval Institute Press, 2001), 13–20.

85. Hull to Harry, 2 January 1947, RG 9: Radiograms, AFMIDPAC, MacArthur Memorial Archives, 3.

■ Chapter 2. Air-Power War in Paradise

1. For wartime and immediate naval planning for the postwar world, see Davis, *Postwar Defense Policy*, 3–38.

2. Perry Smith, *The Air Force Plans for Peace, 1943–1945* (Baltimore: Johns Hopkins University Press, 1970), 55–56 and 78. Herman Wolk has found AAF documents that I think could have been authored by naval officers when it came to discussing the Western Hemisphere and Pacific Ocean Areas as exclusive US responsibilities. The only difference was that AAF planners saw VHB groups as the "only" way to strategically defend and police these regions. See Wolk, *Planning and Organizing the Postwar Air Force*, 75. The reader should understand that AAF forces in the Pacific went through a number of changes in designation between the end of the war in September 1945 and the end of this study in late 1947. Until December 1945, the AAF forces in the Pacific were known as the Far East Air Forces (FEAF). FEAF then became known as PACUSA until January 1947. At that time, PACUSA was then again designated FEAF. Readers should also understand that the US Air Force's archives have gone through several changes in designation, from the Air Force Archives to the Albert F. Simpson Historical Research Center, and then to the Air Force Historical Research Agency (AFHRA). I have used the different designations depending on the particular designation used by the archive at the time the work I am citing was published.

3. Smith, *Air Force Plans for Peace*, 112–113, for AAF wartime perspectives on the USSR, especially as a nation that lacked future potential as a strategic-bombing power. For continued postwar perspectives on the Soviet Union by the AAF's Air Intelligence Division, see Friedman, *Creating an American Lake*, 38, 39, 44–45, and 55.

4. Smith, *Air Force Plans for Peace,* 51–52, 69, and 81. For Arnold's view of the Soviets' lack of potential for developing strategic aviation technology, see ibid., 81–82.

5. Smith, *Air Force Plans for Peace*, 39–53, 61–63, and 73–83; Davis, *Postwar Defense Policy*, 3–38; and Elliot Converse, "United States Plans for a Postwar Overseas Military Base System, 1942–1948," Ph.D. diss., Princeton University, 1984, 1–129.

6. For Mahanian doctrine focused around battleship fleets, see William Livezey, *Mahan on Sea Power* (Norman: University of Oklahoma Press, 1986). For the Navy's transition from battleships to aircraft carriers in the context of Mahanian doctrine, see Clark Reynolds,

The Fast Carriers: The Forging of an Air Navy (Annapolis, Md.: Naval Institute Press, 1992); and idem., *Admiral John H. Towers: The Struggle for Naval Air Supremacy* (Annapolis, Md.: Naval Institute Press, 1991).

7. Smith, *Air Force Plans for Peace*, 35–38.

8. Smith, *Air Force Plans for Peace*, 77–78 and 79.

9. Smith, *Air Force Plans for Peace*, 48–49. For an excellent analysis of American plans for a preventive war against the Soviet Union during the Early Cold War, see Russell Buhite and William Christopher Hamel, "War for Peace: The Question of an American Preventive War against the Soviet Union, 1945–1955," *Diplomatic History* 14 (Summer 1990): 367–384.

10. For AAF thinking on this subject, see Smith, *Air Force Plans for Peace*, 43 and 75. For the postwar atmosphere of fiscal conservancy, as well as the military services' resistance to and subversion of that fiscal conservancy, see Michael Hogan, *A Cross of Iron: Harry S. Truman and the Origins of the National Security State, 1945–1954* (Cambridge: Cambridge University Press, 1998).

11. Norstad to Army-Navy Staff College, 27 November 1944, folder The B-29 in the Pacific, box 26, Norstad Papers, DDEL, 1, 3, 4, 5, 7, and 9. The reality about this administrative arrangement during the war was actually a bureaucratic compromise between the services over issues the Army and Navy could not solve; see Wolk, *Planning and Organizing the Postwar Air Force*, 41. However, it should also be pointed out that because of concern over command priorities vis-à-vis the dropping of the atomic bomb, the 509th Composite Bomb Group, the AAF unit assigned the task, was directed by higher authorities in Washington, D.C. This unit was directly under the command of Major General Leslie Groves, Commanding General of the Manhattan Engineer District (MED). Groves originated all orders governing the use of the bomb, and he in turn reported directly to General Arnold. This latter arrangement was apparently approved of by General Marshall. See Norstad to Major General Curtis LeMay, Commanding General of the Twenty-First Bomber Command, 29 May 1945, microfilm M1109, RG 77, "Correspondence MED, 1942–1946," National Archives (NA), Washington, D.C., as cited in Al Christman, *Target Hiroshima: Deak Parsons and the Creation of the Atomic Bomb* (Annapolis, Md.: Naval Institute Press, 1998), 176–177.

12. Norstad to Army-Navy Staff College, 27 November 1944, folder The B-29 in the Pacific, box 26, Norstad Papers, DDEL, 11–12, 15, and 16.

13. Ibid., 17 and 22.

14. Ibid., 23–26.

15. NBC network broadcast "Pacific Story," Address by Brigadier General Lauris Norstad, 11 February 1945, folder Speeches, 1945 (1), box 26, Norstad Papers, DDEL,1–5.

16. Reynolds, *The Fast Carriers*, 380–401; and idem., *Admiral John H. Towers*, 367–511.

17. Arnold to Stimson, "Second Report of the Commanding General of the Army Air Forces to the Secretary of War," 27 February 1945, folder F3-6, box 25, Record Group 220, Records of Temporary Committees, Commissions, and Boards, President's Air Policy

Commission (hereafter cited as RG 220), HSTL, 94 and 95.

18. For additional information on Arnold, see Wolk, *Planning and Organizing the Postwar Air Force*, 6, 26, 38, 46, 89–90, 100–103, and 106; Michael Sherry, *The Rise of American Air Power: The Creation of Armageddon* (New Haven: Yale University Press, 1987), 61, 183–187, 307, and 313; and Dik Daso, *Hap Arnold and the Evolution of American Airpower* (Washington, D.C.: Smithsonian Institution Press, 2000).

19. Cover letter, "Notes for General Norstad at Aviation Writers Association Luncheon, 2 March 1945, Hotel Statler," folder Speeches, 1945 (2), box 26, Norstad Papers, DDEL.

20. Norstad, "Notes for General Norstad at Aviation Writers Association Luncheon, 2 March 1945, Hotel Statler," folder Speeches, 1945 (2), box 26, Norstad Papers, DDEL, 1–4.

21. Norstad, "Air Power and National Security," 11 August 1945, folder Speeches, 1945 (2), box 26, Norstad Papers, DDEL, 1–3.

22. Whitehead to Kenney, "Airborne Forces in the United States Post-War Military Establishment," 15 August 1945, Letters of Kenney and Whitehead, Fifth Air Force Records, 14 April 1943–1 October 1945, 730.161-3, AFHRA, 1–2. For a good account of Kenney's, and especially Whitehead's, very flexible use of tactical airpower as well as airborne and airlifted troops in the war in the Southwest Pacific, see Donald Goldstein, "Ennis C. Whitehead, Aerospace Commander and Pioneer" (Ph.D. diss., the University of Denver, 1970), 79–271.

23. Giles to Norstad, 30 October 1945, folder Personal–1945 (1), box 23, Norstad Papers, DDEL. For a thorough account of AAF arguments that land-based airpower brought about the Japanese surrender, as well as the politics surrounding that perspective, see Gian Gentile, "Shaping the Past Battlefield, 'For the Future': The United States Strategic Bombing Survey's Evaluation of the American Air War Against Japan," *Journal of Military History* 64 (October 2000): 1085–1112.

24. "Statement by General Carl Spaatz, Hearings, U.S. Senate Military Affairs Committee," 15 November 1945, Muir Fairchild Collection (hereafter cited as the Fairchild Collection), 168.7001-79, 1945–1947, AFHRA, 2–4 and 7–9.

25. "Statement by Lt. Gen. J. H. Doolittle before the Senate Military Affairs Committee," no date, Fairchild Collection, 168.7001-79, 1945–1947, AFHRA, 10. For similar perspectives put forth by other AAF officers at this same time, see Gentile, "Shaping the Past Battlefield," 1085–1112.

26. "Statement by Lt. Gen. J. H. Doolittle before the Senate Military Affairs Committee," no date, Fairchild Collection, 168.7001-79, 1945–1947, AFHRA, 11 and 13. For balanced perspectives, see Gentile, "Shaping the Past Battlefield," 1085–1112; Barton Bernstein, "The Alarming Japanese Buildup on Southern Kyushu, Growing U.S. Fears, and Counterfactual Analysis: Would the Planned November 1945 Invasion of Southern Kyushu Have Occurred?" *Pacific Historical Review* 68 (November 1999): 561–609; and Robert Pape, *Bombing to Win: Air Power and Coercion in War* (Ithaca, N.Y.: Cornell University Press, 1996), 87–136.

27. Fisher to Spaatz, 13 November 1945, Twentieth Air Force–Official File (1), box 27,

Norstad Papers, DDEL.

28. Norstad to the Aero Club of Philadelphia, Pennsylvania, 15 January 1946, folder Speeches, 1946 (1), box 26, Norstad Papers, DDEL, 8–10.

29. "General Kenney's Statement," 31 January 1946, folder Speeches, 46-04-01 to 48-24-07, George Kenney Collection (hereafter cited as the Kenney Collection), 168.7103-27, AFHRA, 1–2.

30. Kenney, "Address by General George C. Kenney to the Spokane Chamber of Commerce, 25 September 1946," folder Speeches, 46-04-01 to 48-07-24, Kenney Collection, 168.7103-27, AFHRA.

31. Bowman to Eaker, 15 November 1946, with "Statement of Army Air Forces Position regarding Pacific Island Bases" enclosed, folder Pacific (3) folder, box 262, Chief of Staff File, Papers of Carl Spaatz, Manuscript Division, Library of Congress, Washington, D.C. (hereafter cited as the Spaatz Papers), 1 and 3–4.

32. Norstad, "Vital Interests–Strategic," 22 November 1946, folder Speeches, 1946 (3), box 26, Norstad Papers, DDEL, 5–6 and 8–11.

33. Bowles to Eisenhower, "Military Communications, Related Services, and Organizational Considerations," 10 February 1947, folder 2, Correspondence, 1945–1950, box 1, Papers of Edward Bowles (hereafter cited as the Bowles Papers), HSTL, 2 and 3.

34. McDonald, Air Intelligence Report No. 100-171-34, "Soviet Military Intentions versus the United States," 8 August 1947, ACAS for Intelligence Files, 142.048-171, AFHRA, 4.

35. Harry Borowski, *A Hollow Threat: Strategic Airpower and Containment before Korea* (Westport, Conn.: Greenwood Press, 1982), 91–111.

36. For Towers's perspective on this, see Reynolds, *Admiral John H. Towers*, 512–545.

37. Borowski, *A Hollow Threat*, 32 and 38–39. For the deployments to Western Europe, see ibid., 72 and 74–75. For the deployments to Alaska, see ibid., 73 and 77–87.

38. Borowski, *A Hollow Threat*, 74.

39. John Greenwood claims that on numerous occasions the Navy requested that the AAF destroy Japanese air bases so that carrier air groups could operate safely off of hostile coasts; John Greenwood and David Rosenberg, "Additional Observations," 279, addendum to David Rosenberg, "American Postwar Air Doctrine and Organization: The Navy Experience," in Alfred Hurley and Robert Ehrhard, eds., *Air Power and Warfare: The Proceedings of the 8th Military History Symposium, United States Air Force Academy, 18–20, October 1978* (Washington, D.C.: Government Printing Office, 1979), 245–278.

40. Borowski, *A Hollow Threat*, 76 as well as 74 and 77. For background on the AAF's superb public-relations campaign in the 1940s, see Davis, *Postwar Defense Policy*, 80–81, 138, 146–148, 152–155, 237, 239, and 254; and Jeffrey Barlow, "The Revolt of the Admirals Reconsidered," *New Interpretations in Naval History: Selected Papers from the Eighth Naval History Symposium*, ed. William Cogar (Annapolis, Md.: Naval Institute Press, 1989), 226–227.

41. For the Navy perspective on these issues, see chapter 3 of this study.

42. Pape, *Bombing to Win*, 87–136.

43. Spaatz Board Report, no date, folder Atomic Bomb Projects, box 20, Norstad Papers, DDEL. Though no date was given on the document, Herman Wolk cites the Spaatz Board reporting its findings in October 1945; see Wolk, *Planning and Organizing the Postwar Air Force*, 121.

44. Whitehead to MacArthur, "Proposed Deployment of PACUSA in accordance with COMGENAIR Reduction," 30 January 1946, folder December 1945–May 1946, Whitehead Collection, 168.6008-1, AFHRA.

45. Spaatz in "Broadcast by Richard Harkness," 12 March 1946, folder Air Force Planning and Policy, box 255, Chief of Staff File, Spaatz Papers. For a geographical perspective on AAF and SAC ideas for postwar VHB deployments, particularly in the Zone of the Interior, the Caribbean, the Northern Pacific, and the Western Pacific, see "Eventual Deployment–U.S. Contribution of VHB groups to United Nations Security Air Force," no date, RG 4: USAFPAC, Printed Materials, Post-war Mission of the Air Forces, MacArthur Memorial Archives.

46. *Strategic Air Command–1946*, volume 1, exhibits 22/23, 39–41, folder 21 March 1946–31 December 1946, 416.01, AFHRA, 41.

47. Whitehead to Kenney, 16 March 1946, folder October 1944–February 1951, Whitehead Collection, 168.6008-3, AFHRA, 2.

48. Ibid., 2–3.

49. Ibid, 2–4.

50. Whitehead to Spaatz, 4 June 1946, box 262, Chief of Staff File, Spaatz Papers, 2.

51. Streett to Spaatz, "Operational Training and Strategic Employment of Units of Strategic Air Command," exhibit 23, 25 July 1946, *Strategic Air Command–1946*, volume 2, 21 March 1946–31 December 1946, 416.01, AFHRA, 1–5.

52. "Command Responsibilities," 18 July 1946, *Strategic Air Command–1946*, volume 2, 21 March 1946–31 December 1946, 416.01, AFHRA, 1 and 2; and "Organization of Units and Bases of Strategic Air Command," no date, *Strategic Air Command–1946*, volume 2, 21 March 1946–31 December 1946, 416.01, AFHRA, 1.

53. MacArthur to Whitehead, Hull, and Christiansen, 25 July 1946, RG 9: Radiograms, AFMIDPAC, MacArthur Memorial Archives, 1–3,.

54. Norstad to War Department Atomic Energy Group, "War Department Plans for the Military Use of Atomic Energy," 19 September 1946, folder Speeches, 1946 (1), box 26, Norstad Papers, DDEL, 11.

55. Kenney to Whitehead, 18 October 1946, folder October 1944–February 1951, Whitehead Collection, 168.6008-3, AFHRA.

56. Norstad, "Presentation Given to President by Major General Lauris Norstad on 29 October 1946, 'Postwar Military Establishment,'" folder Speeches, 1946 (2), box 26, Norstad Papers, DDEL.

57. McMullen to Whitehead, 13 December 1946, folder January 1945–March 1951, Whitehead Collection, 168.6008-3, AFHRA, 1–2.

58. McMullen to Whitehead, 17 April 1947, folder January 1945–March 1951, Whitehead

Collection, 168.6008-3, AFHRA.

59. Kenney to Whitehead, 2 May 1947, RG 9: Radiograms, Air Force, 1945–1951, MacArthur Memorial Archives.

60. Whitehead to Kenney, 4 May 1947, RG 9: Radiograms, Air Force, 1945–1951, MacArthur Memorial Archives.

61. Whitehead to Spaatz, "Memorandum to Chief of Staff, Subject: Outline of B-29 Group Rotation Plan," folder 23 May 1947, June 1946–December 1947, Whitehead Collection, 168.6008-1, AFHRA, 1–2.

62. Appendix A, "Forces: The Problem," *Joint Marianas Report*, 178.2917-1, AFRHA, 56.

63. Whitehead to Kenney, 16 March 1946, folder October 1944–February 1951, Whitehead Collection, 168.6008-3, AFHRA, 2.

64. Colonel Woodbury Burgess, PACUSA Assistant Chief of Staff for Intelligence, "Overall Combat Capabilities of PACUSA," 1 April 1946, part of "Estimate of Soviet Offensive Capabilities in Korea and Vicinity," attached to Whitehead to Spaatz, "Subject: Situation Summary, Pacific Air Command United States Army," PACUSA Report, PACUSA Records, 720.609-7, AFHRA, 4–8a. For poor operational conditions in the AAF caused by rapid demobilization between 1945 and 1947, see Borowski, *A Hollow Threat*, 27–111.

65. Whitehead to Kenney, 5 June 1946, folder October 1944–February 1951, Whitehead Collection, 168.6008-3, AFHRA, 2.

66. Whitehead to White, 5 June 1946, folder January 1946–February 1951, Whitehead Collection, 168.6008-3, AFHRA, 2.

67. Whitehead to Timberlake, 9 July 1946, folder June 1946–December 1947, Whitehead Collection, 168.6008-1, AFHRA.

68. Whitehead to MacArthur, 17 October 1946, RG 9: Radiograms, Air Force, MacArthur Memorial Archives, 2.

69. For incidents between US military personnel and Philippine citizens, as well as for background information on the base negotiations, see Cullather, *Illusions of Influence*, 33–71; and Friedman, *Creating an American Lake*, 128–134. See also chapter 5 of this study.

70. Whitehead to MacArthur, 17 October 1946, RG 9: Radiograms, Air Force, MacArthur Memorial Archives, 1–2.

71. Ibid., 2–3.

72. Ibid., 3–4.

73. Whitehead to Spaatz, 29 October 1946, folder Outgoing Messages, 1 October 1946–31 December 1947, PACUSA Records, 720.1623, AFHRA, 1–3. See also Whitehead to Spaatz, 31 October 1946, RG 9: Radiograms, Air Force, MacArthur Memorial Archives.

74. Whitehead to MacArthur, 30 December 1946, RG 9: Radiograms, Air Force, MacArthur Memorial Archives, 1–2.

75. Spaatz to Whitehead, 3 January 1947, folder January 1946–September 1950, Whitehead Collection, 168.6008-3, AFHRA, 1 and 2.

76. Whitehead to Spaatz, 8 March 1947, folder January 1946–September 1950, Whitehead Collection, 168.6008-3, AFHRA. For the general lack of AAF operational capability be-

tween 1945 and 1947, see Borowski, *A Hollow Threat*, 27–111.

77. Giles to Norstad, 30 October 1945, folder Personnel–1945 (1), box 23, Norstad Papers, DDEL.

78. The name of the airdrome was spelled "Mokolea" in the primary document cited below, but "Mokuleia" by the researcher at the Air Force Historical Research Agency who obtained this information for me.

79. Whitehead to MacArthur, "Use of Barbers Point Airdrome for Return of B-29 Airplane to Zone of Interior," 6 February 1946, folder December 1945–May 1946, Whitehead Collection, 168.6008-1, AFHRA, 1–2.

80. Whitehead to Kenney, 16 March 1946, folder October 1944–February 1951, Whitehead Collection, 168.6008-3, AFHRA, 1 and 2.

81. Ibid., 3.

82. Ibid., 5–6.

83. Whitehead to Spaatz, "Post War Air Stations in the Mariannas [*sic*]," 8 April 1946, folder December 1945–May 1946, Whitehead Collection, 168.6008-1, AFHRA, 1–2.

84. Burgess, "Overall Combat Capabilities of PACUSA," 1 April 1946, part of " Estimate of Soviet Offensive Capabilities in Korea and Vicinity," attached to Whitehead to Spaatz, "Subject: Situation Summary, Pacific Air Command United States Army," PACUSA Report, PACUSA Records, 720.609-7, AFHRA, 7.

85. Whitehead to MacArthur, "Pay of Philippine Air Force Pilots," no date, folder December 1945–May 1946, Whitehead Collection, 168.6008-1, AFRHA.

86. Whitehead to White, 23 July 1946, folder June 1946–December 1947, Whitehead Collection, 168.6008-1, AFHRA, 1.

87. Whitehead to Brigadier General Donald Stace, Major General Eugene Eubank, and Major General Francis Griswold, COMAFs 7, 13, and 20, respectively, 19 October 1946, RG 9: Radiograms, Air Force, MacArthur Memorial Archives; see also Langley Field, Virginia to . . . 68 AACS Tokyo . . . CINCAFPAC . . . Hickam Field [non-Pacific Basin locations in this document are not being listed by the author], 30 October 1946, RG 9: Radiograms, Air Force, MacArthur Memorial Archives.

88. McMullen to Whitehead, 13 December 1946, folder January 1945–March 1951, 168.6008-3, Whitehead Collection, AFHRA, 1.

89. Whitehead to Spaatz, no date, folder June 1946–December 1947, Whitehead Collection, 168.6008-1, AFHRA, 1. While Whitehead's statements about low-level bombing appear surprising from a postwar AAF perspective, they are not given his experiences in the Pacific War. First as Kenney's deputy and then as COMAF 5, Whitehead was a key figure in the AAF's reconfiguration of its forces to conduct low-level "skip" bombing against Japanese ships, a type of attack that was probably as effective in the Southwest Pacific as Navy dive-and-torpedo bombing was in the Central Pacific. Primary documents demonstrate that General Kenney himself, unlike many air officers, had always been open-minded about various kinds of bombing and was not just an advocate of high-level strategic bombing. He was especially open to new ideas when he commanded the Fifth

Air Force and then FEAF between 1942 and 1945. For reasons of postwar AAF political and institutional interests, however, Kenney and Whitehead both began enunciating the traditional arguments about high-level strategic bombing as soon as the war ended. For Whitehead's perspectives, see Goldstein, "Ennis C. Whitehead," 309–445; for Kenney's views, see Thomas Griffith, *MacArthur's Airman: General George C. Kenney and the War in the Southwest Pacific* (Lawrence: University Press of Kansas, 1998), 231–247.

90. Whitehead to Kenney, 7 April 1947, folder June 1946–December 1947, Whitehead Collection, 168.6008-1, AFHRA. For a very solid account arguing that it was Admiral William Halsey's Third Fleet which sank the *Haruna*, see Reynolds, *The Fast Carriers*, 372. Reynolds's source is Halsey's wartime memoir, *Admiral Halsey's Story*, which Reynolds claims is a "flimsy, journalistic" piece of work. Still, Reynolds's interpretation of Navy versus AAF action is very consistent with this author's research, and Whitehead's admission about low-level bombing would suggest a Navy operation since AAF operations against the Japanese Home Islands tended to be high-level strategic bombing against cities, tactical bombing of airfields, or mine-laying operations.

91. Whitehead to Spaatz, 8 March 1947, folder January 1946–September 1950, 168.6008-3, Whitehead Collection, AFHRA.

92. Whitehead to Spaatz, "Memorandum to Chief of Staff, Subject: Iwo Jima," 28 April 1947, folder June 1946–December 1947, Whitehead Collection, 168.6008-1, AFHRA, 4.

93. Whitehead to Spaatz, 23 May 1947, folder January 1946–September 1950, Whitehead Collection, 168.6003-8, AFHRA.

94. Spaatz to Whitehead, 11 June 1947, folder January 1946–September 1950, Whitehead Collection, 168.6003-8, AFHRA.

95. Whitehead to Spaatz, 10 June 1947, folder June 1946–December 1947, Whitehead Collection, 168.6008-1, AFHRA. Whitehead probably obtained much of his greatly exaggerated information about near-term Soviet airborne and submarine capabilities from AAF Intelligence since his information mirrored that being produced in Washington, D.C. AAF Intelligence had been quite cautious about its estimates of both near- and long-term Soviet military capabilities and intentions until the winter of 1946–1947. After that point in time, however, its estimates became quite alarmist. For citations to AAF Intelligence records and for speculation on the reasons for these changes in the intelligence estimates, see Friedman, *Creating an American Lake*, 53–56.

96. Whitehead to Kenney, 16 June 1947, folder October 1944–February 1951, 168.6008-3, Whitehead Collection, AFHRA, 1.

97. Whitehead to Spaatz, 28 July 1947, folder January 1946–September 1950, Whitehead Collection, 168.6003-8, AFHRA.

98. Spaatz to Whitehead, 28 July 1947, folder January 1946–September 1950, Whitehead Collection, 168.6003-8, AFHRA.

99. Whitehead to Kenney, 2 November 1947, 2, folder October 1944–February 1951, Whitehead Collection, 168.6003-8, AFHRA.

100. Whitehead to Spaatz, 17 April 1946, folder December 1945–May 1946, Whitehead Col-

lection, 168.6008-1, AFHRA, 2.

101. Whitehead to MacArthur, 11 July 1946, RG 9: Radiograms, Air Force, MacArthur Memorial Archives.

102. Hull to MacArthur, 23 July 1946, RG 9: Radiograms, AFMIDPAC, MacArthur Memorial Archives.

103. Christiansen to Whitehead, 27 July 1946, RG 9: Radiograms, AFWESPAC; and Christiansen to MacArthur, 30 July 1946, RG 9: Radiograms, AFWESPAC, both in the MacArthur Memorial Archives.

104. MacArthur to Whitehead, 31 July 1946, RG 9: Radiograms, Air Force, MacArthur Memorial Archives.

105. Hull to MacArthur, 11 August 1946, RG 9: Radiograms, AFMIDPAC, MacArthur Memorial Archives.

106. Hull to Whitehead, 16 August 1946, folder January 1946–September 1950, Whitehead Collection, 168.6008-1, AFHRA, 1–2.

107. Ibid., 2–3.

108. Whitehead to Hull, 29 August 1946, folder January 1946–September 1950, Whitehead Collection, 168.6008-3, AFHRA, 1–4.

109. Whitehead to Spaatz, 11 October 1946, folder January 1946–September 1950, Whitehead Collection, 168.6008-2, AFHRA, 1–2.

110. McMullen to Whitehead, 17 April 1947, folder January 1945–March 1951, Whitehead Collection, 168.6008-3, AFHRA, 2.

111. Whitehead to Spaatz, "Memorandum for the Chief of Staff, Subject: Iwo Jima," 28 April 1947, folder June 1946–December 1947, Whitehead Collection, 168.6008-1, AFHRA, 4–6.

112. "Enclosure Draft of Memorandum for the Secretary of War and the Secretary of the Navy," part of "Type of Government To Be Established on Various Pacific Islands," JCS 1524/2, 15 November 1945, file 8-21-45 sec. 1, JCS Geographic File, 1942–1945, CCS 014 Pacific Ocean Area, Records of the Combined and Joint Chiefs of Staff, RG 218, NA II.

■ Chapter 3. Sea-Air Power in Paradise

1. Thomas Etzold and John Gaddis, eds., *Containment: Documents on American Policy and Strategy, 1945–1950* (New York: Columbia University Press, 1978), 39–44.

2. "Post-War Naval Bases in the Pacific," study attached to a memorandum by Edwards and Duncan to Admiral Ernest King, COMINCH-CNO, 20 November 1944, folder Bases General, B-3, box 156, series 14, Strategic Plans Division Records. Records of the Office of the Chief of Naval Operations, 1942–1947, Record Group 38 (hereafter cited as Strategic Plans, RG 38, NA II).

3. Memorandum from Horne to Forrestal, 26 January 1945, folder Post-War Bases, January

1945–May 1945, box 193, Strategic Plans Division Records, US Naval Historical Center, Washington Navy Yard, Washington, D.C. (hereafter cited as Strategic Plans, OA, NHC).

4. Davis, *Postwar Defense Policy*, 120–134.

5. Hepburn, "Sites for Bases," Annex A to General Board No. 450, "Post-war Employment of International Police Force and Post-war Use of Air Bases," 20 March 1943, folder Post-War Bases, P-1, box 170, Strategic Plans, RG 38, NA II. See also Davis, *Postwar Defense Policy*, 3–38.

6. For Nimitz's perspective, see Naval Reserve Commander Dorothy Richard, *United States Naval Administration of the Trust Territory of the Pacific Islands*, volume 3 (Washington, D.C.: Office of the Chief of Naval Operations, 1957), 170. It should be noted, however, that naval historians differ on Nimitz's conservatism. While Clark Reynolds sees Nimitz as a naval conservative, Michael Palmer sees the "balanced" postwar surface fleet actually being constructed around a preponderance of aircraft carriers, not large gun ships. Malcolm Muir, however, sees both Representative Vinson and Secretary Forrestal supporting balanced postwar surface fleets that had significant numbers of battleships, cruisers, and destroyers in them and were not entirely focused around the carriers. For Reynolds's interpretation, see Reynolds, *The Fast Carriers*, 75–77, 103–104, and 168; and idem., *Admiral John H. Towers*, 407, 410, 411, 425, 441, 478, and 482. For Palmer's interpretation, see *Origins of the Maritime Strategy*, 51–53. For Muir's interpretation, see *Black Shoes and Blue Water: Surface Warfare in the United States Navy, 1945–1975* (Washington, D.C.: Naval Historical Center, 1996), 6–7.

7. Davis, *Postwar Defense Policy*, 100–118, 157–206, and 219–225.

8. See Friedman, *Creating an American Lake*, 1–36, for JCS plans that called for a defensive wedge of islands from the Aleutians down to the Ryukyus and the Philippines and then back to Micronesia and Hawaii, all defended by mobile air and naval power. Most likely, Forrestal obtained his arguments from the JCS and then became a powerful lobbying voice for Congressional enaction of this postwar posture in the region.

9. U.S. Congress, House Committee on Appropriations, *Navy Department Appropriation Bill For 1946: Hearings before the Subcommittee on Navy Department Appropriations*, 79th Congress, 1st session, 1945, 13, 14, and 25. See also Jeffrey Dorwart, "Forrestal and the Navy Plan of 1945: Mahanian Doctrine or Corporatist Blueprint?" in *New Interpretations in Naval History: Selected Papers from the Eighth Naval History Symposium*, ed. William Cogar (Annapolis, Md.: Naval Institute Press, 1989), 211–212. For viewpoints on how exactly carrier airpower would play a role in the postwar world, see Rosenberg, "American Postwar Air Doctrine and Organization: The Navy Experience," in Hurley and Ehrhart, eds., *Air Power and Warfare*, 247. Finally, for a wartime view that saw the United States policing the Pacific and Latin America while leaving Europe, the Middle East, Africa, and East Asia to Great Britain, the Soviet Union, and China, see David Rowe, "Collective Security in the Pacific: An American View," *Pacific Affairs* 18 (March 1945): 5–21.

10. Forrestal, "Pearl Harbor," 14 November 1944, *The Forrestal Diaries, 1944–1949*, Papers of James Forrestal (Washington, D.C.: NPPSO-Naval District Washington Microfilm

Section, 1973–1979); and U.S. Congress, Senate Committee on Appropriations, *Navy Department Appropriation Bill for 1946: Hearings before the Subcommittee on Navy Department Appropriations*, 79th Congress, 1st session, 1945, 4–5.

11. Forrestal, "Pearl Harbor," 14 November 1944, *The Forrestal Diaries*; US Congress, *Navy Department Appropriation Bill for 1946*, 4–5; Davis, *Postwar Defense Policy*, 100–120; and Reynolds, *The Fast Carriers*, 141, 211, 321, and 353.

12. Ibid., 8; see also U.S. Congress, Senate Committee on Appropriations, *Navy Department Appropriations Bill for 1946: Hearings before the Subcommittee on Navy Department Appropriations*, 79th Congress, 1st session, 4–5; Etzold and Gaddis, *Containment*, 39–44; Davis, *Postwar Defense Policy*, 148–150; and Borowski, *A Hollow Threat*, 74, 76, and 77.

13. U.S. Congress, Special Committee on Atomic Energy, *Hearings before the Special Committee on Atomic Energy,* 79th Congress, 1st session, 1946, 394. Some Congressional officials agreed wholeheartedly with the Navy on these points. See U.S. Congress, House Committee on Naval Affairs, *Study of Pacific Bases: A Report by the Subcommittee on Pacific Bases of the Committee on Naval Affairs*, 79th Congress, 1st session, 1945, 1014, 1020, and 1022–1023.

14. Carl Vinson, *Hearings on House Concurrent Resolution 80, Composition of the Postwar Navy*, part of *Study of Pacific Bases*, 79th Congress, 1st session, 1945, 1159–1162.

15. For further insight on the concept of a defensive perimeter in the postwar Pacific and East Asia, see John Gaddis, "The Strategic Perspective: The Rise and Fall of the 'Defensive Perimeter' Concept, 1947–1951," in Dorothy Borg and Waldo Heinrichs, eds., *Uncertain Years: Chinese-American Relations, 1947–1950* (New York: Columbia University Press, 1980), 61–118. The reader should understand that this author interprets George Kennan's role in the formulation of the defensive-perimeter concept much differently than does Gaddis. Gaddis strongly implies that Kennan was the originator of a "u-shaped" defensive-perimeter concept that stretched from the Aleutians to the Ryukyus, and then back toward Micronesia and Hawaii. In fact, primary documents cited in Friedman, *Creating an American Lake*, 1–36 and in this chapter, clearly demonstrate that the JCS and them Forrestal had similar plans for the postwar Pacific as early as the winter of 1945–1946, if not before.

16. For an example of the numerous documents that argue this perspective, see Assistant Secretary, United States Delegation, UN Security Council Military Staff Committee, to the President, 22 February 1947, file 12-9-42 sec. 29, JCS Central Decimal File, 1946–1947, CCS 360, RG 218, NA II. For a critique of this flawed theory, see Friedman, *Creating an American Lake*, 13–16.

17. SWNCC 59/7, "Draft Trusteeship Agreement—Pacific Islands," 19 October 1946, file 12-9-42 sec. 28, JCS Central Decimal File, 1946–1947, CCS 360, RG 218, NA II.

18. "Minutes of the Eleventh Meeting (Executive Session) of the United States Delegation [to the United Nations Conference]," 17 April 1945, U.S. Department of State, *Foreign Relations of the United States* (hereafter cited as *FRUS*) 1945, volume 1, 317 (hereafter cited as 1:317).

19. U.S. Congress, House Committee on Appropriations, *Navy Department Appropriation Bill for 1947: Hearings before the Subcommittee on Navy Department Appropriations,* 79th Congress, 2nd session, 1946, 19–20.

20. Reynolds, *Admiral John H. Towers,* 518–532.

21. Numerous postwar statements, such as those cited in this chapter, make it sound as if the Navy was perfectly willing to put its carrier forces in harm's way. In fact, the Navy during the Pacific War was very wary from Guadalcanal onward of exposing the fast carriers to Japanese land-based airpower. Accordingly, it always insisted on very limited time periods for carrying out amphibious assaults, and it lobbied for AAF units to be brought quickly into newly controlled areas so that there could be a fast turnover of local air-defense responsibilities to the AAF or land-based naval air units. In effect, in many cases the Navy was as dependent on the AAF for assistance in dealing with Japanese airpower as the AAF was on the Navy's carriers in conducting Pacific Island amphibious assaults. See Thomas Buell, *The Quiet Warrior: A Biography of Admiral Raymond A. Spruance* (Boston: Little, Brown and Company, 1974), 216 and 356–357; Griffith, *MacArthur's Airman,* 136–137, 145–146, 156, 158, 160–161, 163, and 177–230; and Jon Hoffman, *Once a Legend: "Red Mike" Edson of the Marine Raiders* (Novato, Calif.: Presidio Press, 2000), 233–258.

22. Forrestal, "Pearl Harbor," 14 November 1944, *The Forrestal Diaries.* Mitscher was Vice Admiral Marc Mitscher, Commander of the First Fast Carrier Task Force, Pacific.

23. Forrestal, "Strategy," 19 January 1945, *The Forrestal Diaries.*

24. US Congress, House Committee on Appropriations, *Navy Department Appropriation Bill for 1946,* 79th Congress, 1st session, 14.

25. US Congress, Senate Committee on Appropriations, *Navy Department Appropriation Bill for 1946,* 79th Congress, 1st session, 4–5.

26. Sullivan broadcast, 28 August 1945, folder 1, Statements and Addresses, July 1945–December 1947, box 13, Papers of John L. Sullivan (hereafter cited as the Sullivan Papers), HSTL, 1 and 2.

27. Sullivan, "A Report On Naval Aviation in the Pacific War," 22 September 1945, folder 1, Statements and Addresses, July 1945–December 1947, box 13, Sullivan Papers, HSTL, 33–35.

28. US Congress, House Committee on Naval Affairs, *Hearings on House Concurrent Resolution 80, Composition of the Postwar Navy,* part of Sub-Committee on Pacific Bases, *Study of Pacific Bases,* 1159–1160 and 1162.

29. "Statement of Hon. James Forrestal, Secretary of the Navy," part of *Study of Pacific Bases,* 1164–1166 and 1168–1169.

30. H. Gard Knox, RADM Frederic R. Harris (CEC), USN (RET), and RADM Husband E. Kimmel, USN (RET), "Naval Bases–Past and Future," *United States Naval Institute Proceedings* (hereafter cited as *USNIP*) 71 (October 1945): 1147–1153.

31. Sullivan, "Speech by Assistant Secretary of the Navy for Air John L. Sullivan," 27 October 1945, Mayflower Hotel, Washington, D.C., folder 1, tab 15, Statements and Address, July

1945–December 1947, box 13, Sullivan Papers, HSTL, 1–2 and 3–6.

32. Captain K. C. McIntosh (SC), USN (RET), "The Road Ahead," *USNIP* 71 (November 1945): 1286–1287.

33. Burke to Tuve, 29 November 1945, "Subject: Proposals for Future Technical Relationships between Universities and the Navy," folder Navy Department, 1946–1947, Curtis LeMay Collection (hereafter cited as the LeMay Collection), 168.64-14, AFHRA, 3–4.

34. US Congress, House Committee on Appropriations, *Navy Department Appropriation Bill for 1947: Hearings before the Subcommittee of the Committee on Appropriations*, 79th Congress, 2nd session, 19–20.

35. Commander Russell Smith, USN, "Notes on Our Naval Future," *USNIP* 72 (April 1946): 495 and 498–499.

36. US Senate, Senate Committee on Appropriations, *Navy Department Appropriation Bill for 1947: Hearings before the Subcommittee of the Committee on Appropriations*, 80th Congress, 1st session, 8.

37. Captain J. M. Kennaday, USN, "A Proper Conception of Advanced Bases," *USNIP* 72 (June 1946): 789–791.

38. Sullivan, "Text of Address by the Honorable John L. Sullivan, Undersecretary of the Navy, at Navy League Dinner, Cleveland, Ohio," 26 October 1946, folder 2, tab 36, Statements and Addresses, July 1945–December 1947, box 13, Sullivan Papers, HSTL, 1–3 and 5–6.

39. Sherman, "Problems of Unified Command," 27 February 1947, folder Speeches, 46-04-01 to 48-07-24, Kenney Collection, 168.7103-27, AFHRA, 1–3. For background on Sherman's career and his importance to American naval and national strategy during the origins of the Cold War, see Palmer, *Origins of the Maritime Strategy*, passim.

40. Ibid., 3–5.

41. Ibid., 5–10.

42. Commander Allen Shinn, USN, "A Discussion of Some Important Factors Which Make an All-Inclusive United States Air Force a Necessity to National Security," 4 July 1947, folder Official-Classified, 1946–1947 (3), box 22, Norstad Papers, DDEL, 1–4.

43. Ibid., 2, 9–19, 6–7, and 8–9.

44. Sullivan, "Statement of Honorable John L. Sullivan, Secretary of the Navy," 2 December 1947, *President's Air Policy Commission*, folder B26–3, box 17, President's Air Policy Commission, RG 220, HSTL.

45. Edwards and Duncan to King, 20 November 1944, attaching study "Post-War Naval Bases in the Pacific," folder Bases General, B-3, box 156, series 14, Strategic Plans, RG 38, NA II, 1, 4, and 7.

46. Horne to Forrestal, "Memorandum for the Secretary of the Navy, Subject: U.S. Post-War Naval Advance Base Requirements," 26 January 1945, folder Post-war Bases, January 1945–May 1945, box 193, Strategic Plans, OA, NHC.

47. US Congress, House Committee on Appropriations, *Navy Department Appropriation Bill for 1946*, 24, 25, and 43.

48. Halsey to Woodrum, 20 May 1945, folder Navy, 1945, box 29, WHCF, HSTL, 1–3.

49. US Congress, House Committee on Naval Affairs, *Study of Pacific Bases*, 1016 and 1115.

50. McLean to Sherman, 19 April 1946, "Subject: Missions of Alaskan Bases," folder 1, box 68, series 3, Strategic Plans, RG 38, NA II, 1–2.

51. Nimitz to Truman, 23 July 1946, "Facts and Information Desired by the President regarding the Soviet Union," folder 2a, box 63, Papers of George Elsey (hereafter cited as the Elsey Papers), HSTL, 6; see also Friedman, *Creating an American Lake*, 37–62.

52. Towers to Nimitz, 26 September 1946, folder 1, box 68, series 3, Strategic Plans, RG 38, NA II, 1; Towers, 25 September 1946, John Towers Diary, Papers of John Towers, Manuscript Division, Library of Congress, Washington, D.C. (hereafter cited as the Towers Diary); and Towers to Nimitz, 26 September 1946, folder 1, box 68, series 3, Strategic Plans, RG 38, NA II, 2–3.

53. Towers, 30 September 1946, Towers Diary.

54. Memorandum from McLean to Glover, 30 September 1946, Subject: Pacific Bases, folder 1, box 68, series 3, Strategic Plans, RG 38, NA II.

55. Sherman to Nimitz, 25 October 1946, "Subject: Strategic Estimate and Deployment in the Pacific," folder Naval Bases, November 1945–December 1945, box 200, series 14, Strategic Plans, OA, NHC.

56. Towers, 1 November 1946, Towers Diary.

57. Carney to Nimitz, 27 November 1946, folder 31, box 2, Double oo Files, RG 38, NA II, 1 and 3.

58. Carney to Nimitz, 2 December 1946, folder 31, box 2, Double oo Files, RG 38, NA II, 1.

59. Ibid., 2.

60. Ibid., 2–3.

61. Towers, 16 December 1946, Towers Diary.

62. Denfield to Fechteler, 30 April 1947, folder VADM William Fechteler, box 1, series 1, Papers of Louis Denfield (hereafter cited as the Denfield Papers), OA, NHC, 2.

63. Denfield to Leahy, 5 May 1947, folder FADM William Leahy, box 1, series 1, Denfield Papers, OA, NHC, 1–2.

64. "Appendix A, Forces: The Problem," *Joint Marianas Report*, 1 June 1947, 178.2917-1, AFHRA, 56, 58, and 59.

65. Cooke to Wedemeyer, 25 July 1947, folder Memos to/from Admiral/CNO-Personal, box 2, series 1, Double oo Files, RG 38, NA II, 1–4, especially 4.

66. Nimitz to Griffin, 24 October 1947, "Subject: Navy Policy on Naval Bases in Japan," folder EF 37 Japan, box 2, series 1, Records of the Politico-Military Affairs Division (hereafter cited as the Politico-Military Affairs Division), OA, NHC, 1–2.

67. Forrestal, "Pacific Command," 10 March 1945, *The Forrestal Diaries*.

68. Wolk, *Planning and Organizing the Postwar Air Force*, 160.

69. Forrestal, "Pacific Command," 10 March 1945, *The Forrestal Diaries*.

70. Towers, 17 July 1946, Towers Diary.

71. Phillips to Glover, 7 November 1946, "Subject: Preparation of Plans by CINCAFPAC and

CINCPAC for Action in Case of Emergency Involving the U.S.S.R.," folder 1, box 68, series 3, Strategic Plans, RG 38, NA II, 1–2.

72. Friedman, *Creating an American Lake*, 16–36.

73. Richard Frank, *Guadalcanal: The Definitive Account of the Landmark Battle* (New York: Random House, 1990), 428–518.

74. Clay Blair, *Silent Victory: The U.S. Submarine War against Japan* (Annapolis, Md.: Naval Institute Press, 2001), 816–819 and 877–885.

75. Buell, *The Quiet Warrior*, 217–218.

■ Chapter 4. Trusteeship versus Annexation

1. Dunn to Stettinius, "Memorandum by the Chairman of the State-War-Navy Coordinating Committee to the Secretary of State," 26 February 1945, *FRUS 1945*, 1:93.

2. The Dumbarton Oaks powers consisted of the United States, the UK, the USSR, and the Republic of China; see Louis, *Imperialism at Bay*, 378.

3. Dunn to Stettinius, "Memorandum by the Chairman of the State-War-Navy Coordinating Committee to the Secretary of State," 26 February 1945, *FRUS 1945*, 1:93–94.

4. Taussig to Roosevelt, "Memorandum of Conversation," 15 March 1945, *FRUS 1945*, 1:122–123.

5. Stettinius, "Extracts from the Diary of Edward R. Stettinius Jr., Secretary of State, 1 December 1944–1 July 1945," section 8, 18 March–7 April, 1945, *FRUS 1945*, 1:140–141.

6. Stettinius to Roosevelt, "The Secretary of State to Roosevelt," 9 April 1945, *FRUS 1945*, 1:211–213.

7. Stettinius, "Memorandum by the Secretary of State," 14 April 1945, *FRUS 1945*, 1:290.

8. Memorandum from Stettinius to Grew, 18 April 1945, *FRUS 1945*, 1:350.

9. See Annex to the Memorandum from Stettinius to Grew, entitled "Recommended Policy on Trusteeship," 18 April 1945, *FRUS 1945*, 1:351. The subsequent statements by Stimson and Forrestal probably had to do with continuing disagreements between the War and Navy Departments on the one hand, and the State and Interior Departments on the other, over the type of trusteeship system the United States should propose for the former Japanese Mandates. As described in the introduction to this book and in this chapter, War and Navy wanted to annex these territories, while State and Interior wanted them administered through a UN international trusteeship. Under Secretary of the Interior Abe Fortas developed a compromise. Fortas crafted a "strategic trusteeship" concept whereby the United States would virtually control Micronesia in all but name while reporting annually to the UN about the political, economic, social, and educational "progress" of the "native" populations. It should be understood, however, that while Fortas's idea had been put forth, the four departments had not yet agreed to adopt it, nor would they until the spring of 1947. See Louis, *Imperialism at Bay*, 461–573 for Fortas's

original concept. See Friedman, *Creating an American Lake*, 63–93 for the late adoption of the strategic-trusteeship concept.

10. Stettinius to Grew, 18 April 1945, *FRUS 1945*, 1:350.

11. Friedman, *Creating an American Lake*, 79–82.

12. Bohlen to Byrnes, "Memorandum of Conversation," 14 September 1945, *FRUS 1945*, 2:164–165.

13. Department of State Radio Bulletin, 15 January 1946, folder Documents on the Draft Trusteeship for the Japanese Mandated Islands, section 7, tab 1, box 13, series 4, Politico-Military Affairs Division, OA, NHC.

14. Byrnes to Acheson, 16 January 1946, *FRUS 1946*, 1:551–553.

15. "Minutes of the Informal Meeting of the United States Group on Trusteeship," London, 17 January 1946, *FRUS 1946*, 1:554–555.

16. Department of State Radio Bulletin, 22 January 1946, folder Documents on the Draft Trusteeship for the Japanese Mandated Islands, section 7, tab 3, box 13, series 4, Politico-Military Affairs Division, OA, NHC, 1–2.

17. Donald Blaisdell, "Oral Memoir with Donald C. Blaisdell," interview by Richard McKinzie, 29 October 1973, Oral History Collection, HSTL, 82–85.

18. Hickerson to Byrnes, 23 February 1946, *FRUS 1946*, 1:562–563.

19. Staff Committee Document SC-192, "Policy and Procedures Concerning the Negotiation of Trusteeship Agreements: Covering Note," 11 April 1946, *FRUS 1946*, 1:567–569. The Secretary's Staff Committee was a body comprised of key personnel from the State Department's major divisions and bureaus that were responsible for advising and assisting the Secretary of State in the formulation of current and long-range policy.

20. "Policy and Procedures Concerning the Negotiation of Trusteeship Agreements, Minutes of the One Hundred Ninety-Second Meeting of the Secretary's Staff Committee," Washington, D.C., 20 April 1946, *FRUS 1946*, 1:570–571.

21. Ibid., 571.

22. Ibid., 571–572.

23. Ibid., 572–573.

24. Ibid., 572–575.

25. Ibid., 575.

26. Ibid., 575–576.

27. Ibid., 576–577.

28. Hickerson to Middleton, "Memorandum of Conversation," 24 May 1946, box 6849, Central Decimal File, FW 826P.01/5-2446, Record Group 59, Records of the Department of State (hereafter cited as RG 59), NA II, 1–2.

29. Memo by Gerig, 29 May 1946, box 6849, Central Decimal File, FW 826P.01/5-2446, RG 59, NA II.

30. Gerig to Hiss and Blaisdell, 31 May 1946, box 6849, Central Decimal File, FW 826P.01/5-2446, RG 59, NA II.

31. Acheson to Gerig, 7 June 1946, *FRUS 1946*, 1:596–597.

32. Ibid., 596–597 and 597–598.

33. Acheson to Minter, 29 August 1946, *FRUS 1946*, 1:617.

34. Dulles to Byrnes, 9 October 1946, *FRUS 1946*, 1:637–638.

35. "Minutes of the Fourth Meeting of the United States Delegation," 21 October 1946, *FRUS 1946*, 1:657–658.

36. "Minutes of the Tenth Meeting of the United States Delegation," 25 October 1946, *FRUS 1946*, 1:661–662.

37. Ibid., 662–663.

38. Hiss, "Memorandum of Telephone Conversation," 1 November 1946, *FRUS 1946*, 1:668–669.

39. Ibid., 669–670.

40. Durbrow to Byrnes, 12 November 1946, *FRUS 1946*, 1:679–680.

41. Smith to Byrnes, 21 November 1946, *FRUS 1946*, 1:681–682.

42. "Minutes of the Twenty-Fourth Meeting of the United States Delegation," 21 November 1946, *FRUS 1946*, 1:682–684.

43. Ibid., 684–685.

44. Noyes to the US Delegation, 25 November 1946, *FRUS 1946*, 1:685–686.

45. Ibid., 687 and 689.

46. Dulles, "Memorandum by Mr. John Foster Dulles of the United States Delegation," 30 November 1946, *FRUS 1946*, 1:690–692.

47. Hiss to Acheson, 6 December 1946, *FRUS 1946*, 1:701–702.

48. Gerig, "Memorandum of Conversation," 7 December 1946, *FRUS 1946*, 1:703–704.

49. Forrestal, "Cabinet Luncheon," 16 December 1946, *The Forrestal Diaries*.

50. Makin to Marshall, 21 January 1947, *FRUS 1947*, 1:260–261.

51. Marshall to Inverchapel, 12 February 1947, *FRUS 1947*, 1:261–263.

52. "Statement To Be Made by the Australian Delegate to the Security Council at Its Next Meeting to Consider the United States Trusteeship Agreement for the Former Japanese-Mandated Islands," 28 March 1947, *FRUS 1947*, 1:272–273.

53. Friedman, *Creating an American Lake*, 88–89.

54. Bohlen to Lovett, 12 August 1947, *FRUS 1947*, 6:487.

55. For the "Reverse Course," see Michael Schaller, *The American Occupation of Japan: The Origins of the Cold War in Asia* (New York: Oxford University Press, 1987), 77–140.

56. For Policy Planning Staff views about the Japanese Peace Treaty, see Policy Planning Staff, "Results of Planning Staff Study of Questions Involved in the Japanese Peace Settlement," 14 October 1947, microfiche 9, M1171, Policy Planning Staff Numbered Papers (hereafter cited as PPS Papers), RG 59, NA II, 1–2.

57. Ibid., 2–5.

58. Ibid., 5–8.

59. Kennan to Lovett, cover letter, 15 October 1947; and Policy Planning Staff, "Disposition of the Ryukyu Islands," 15 October 1947; microfiche 10, M1171, PPS Papers, RG 59, NA II, 1–2.

■ Chapter 5. Letting Go Is Hard to Do

1. Friedman, Creating an American Lake, 1–36.
2. For excellent secondary accounts on this aspect of US wartime and immediate postwar diplomacy, see Louis, *Imperialism at Bay*; Christopher Thorne, *Allies of a Kind: The United States, Britain, and the War Against Japan, 1941–1945* (New York: Oxford University Press, 1979); and Robert McMahon, *Colonialism and Cold War: The United States and the Struggle for Indonesian Independence, 1945–49* (Ithaca, NY: Cornell University Press, 1981).
3. Carlson to Willoughby, 27 June 1946, reel 34, LM-126, Confidential U.S. State Department Central Files, The Philippine Republic: Internal and Foreign Affairs, 1945–1949, RG 59, NA II.
4. Mill to Lockhart, "Collaboration and Anti-Americanism in the Philippines," 4 September 1946, reel 1, LM-126, RG 59, NA II, 1–2.
5. Cullather, Illusions of Influence, 42–71.
6. Edelstein to Byrnes, "Recurrent Anti-American Trend in Manila Press with Emphasis on Proposed Military Bases Agreement," 14 September 1946, reel 35, LM-126, RG 59, NA II.
7. McNutt to Byrnes, 30 September 1946, reel 1, LM-126, RG 59, NA II, 1–2.
8. Davis to Byrnes, "Nationalistic Legislation," 2 October 1946, reel 6, LM-126, RG 59, NA II, 1–5.
9. Durbrow to Byrnes, 11 October 1946, reel 6, LM-126, RG 59, NA II, 1–2.
10. Durbrow to Byrnes, 21 October 1946, reel 1, LM-126, RG 59, NA II, 1–2. The Bell Trade Act, named for Representative Jasper Bell of Missouri, Chairman of the House Committee on Insular Affairs, was a compromise piece of legislation negotiated between the White House, the State and Treasury Departments, Congress, and the Philippine Government. Its main provisions called for duty-free trade between the United States and the Philippines for eight years, with duties starting in 1954 that would rise 5 percent annually over twenty years. Imports above quotas would also be subject to full duties starting in 1954. In addition, the Act placed absolute quotas on sugar and cordage for twenty-eight years. However, the legislation also included provisions for the United States to partially finance Philippine public-works reconstruction, as well as make US funds available for wartime-damage awards to individual Filipinos; see Cullather, *Illusions of Influence*, 35–38.
11. Durbrow to Byrnes, 21 October 1946, reel 1, LM-126, RG 59, NA II, 1–2.
12. Edelstein to Byrnes, "President Roxas Issues Statement Commenting on *Pravda* Article on Philippines," 21 October 1946, reel 6, LM-126, RG 59, NA II, 1–2.
13. McNutt to Byrnes, 22 October 1946, reel 35, LM-126, RG 59, NA II.
14. Edelstein to Byrnes, "Philippine Publication Attacks United States Army," 22 October 1946, reel 35, LM-126, RG 59, NA II, 1.
15. Edelstein to Byrnes, "Report on Progress of Public Relations Program," 29 October 1946, reel 35, LM-126, RG 59, NA II, 1–2.

16. Cullather, *Illusions of Influence*, 42–71.

17. Edelstein to Byrnes, "Further Improvement Noted in Philippine Press Tone," 8 November 1946, reel 35, LM-126, RG 59, NA II, 1–2.

18. Edelstein to Byrnes, "Further Report on Investigation on Conditions at Puerta Princesa, Palawan," 8 November 1946, reel 1, LM-126, RG 59, NA II.

19. McNutt to Marshall, 18 February 1947, and Edgar Crossman, American Co-Chairman of the Joint American-Philippine Finance Commission, from Norman Ness, Director of the State Department's Office of Financial and Development Policy (OFD), 27 February 1947, both in reel 6, LM-126, RG 59, NA II. For the role of the Philippines as a US-armed strategic buffer zone in American plans for the postwar defense of the Pacific Basin, see Chester Pach, *Arming the Free World: The Origins of the United States Military Assistance Program, 1945–1950* (Chapel Hill: University of North Carolina Press, 1991), 7–28.

20. McNutt to Marshall, 18 February 1947, and Crossman, 27 February 1947, both in reel 6, LM-126, RG 59, NA II.

21. For pre–Pacific War background on the Philippine Scouts, see Linn, *The U.S. Army and Counterinsurgency in the Philippine War*; and idem., *Guardians of Empire*. For the Philippine Scouts' continued existence into late 1946, see the memorandum by Admiral Leahy, 30 December 1946, file State Department, 1946–1947, box 38, WHCF, HSTL.

22. Acheson to McNutt, 18 April 1947, reel 6, LM-126, RG 59, NA II, 1–3. For Eisenhower's arguments and the final decision to withdraw the majority of US Army forces from the Philippines, see chapter 1 of this study. PHILRYCOM had been AFWESPAC. The latter command came into existence on 1 January 1947 with the creation of the unified commands; see Wolk, *Planning and Organizing the Postwar Air Force*, 155–160.

23. Mill to Vincent, "Views of Colonels Melnick [sic] and Chester, G-2, War Department, Concerning Collaboration Question, Philippine Veterans Benefits, and United States Foreign Service Personnel in Manila," 22 April 1947, reel 1, LM-126, RG 59, NA II, 1–2.

24. Ely to Vincent, "Attitude of U.S Government toward Filipinos Suspected of Having Collaborated with the Enemy," 7 May 1947, reel 1, LM-126, RG 59, NA II.

25. McNutt to Marshall, "Report on the Philippines," 6 May 1947, folder Foreign Affairs: Philippine Islands, box 162, President's Secretary's Files (hereafter cited as PSF), HSTL, 1.

26. Ibid., 1–3.

27. Ibid., 3–4.

28. Ibid., 4–8.

29. Ibid., 8–9.

30. Ibid., 9–10.

31. Flexer to Marshall, "Editorial Reaction in Manila to Remarks Made by Representative Fred L. Crawford before House Committee," 22 May 1947, reel 6, LM-126, RG 59, NA II, 1.

32. Ibid., 2–3.

33. For US unilateralism in the wartime and postwar Pacific, see Louis, *Imperialism at Bay*, 463–573; and Claude, *Swords into Plowshares*, 357–37.

■ Chapter 6. Civil versus Military Administration

1. Ickes to Forrestal, 1 November 1944, folder 16-1-18, box 50, General Correspondence 1944–1947, Records of Secretary of the Navy James Forrestal, 1940–1947, Record Group 80, General Records of the Office of the Secretary of the Navy (hereafter cited as RG 80), NA II. The officer in question was Captain Donald Ramsey, Legislative Counsel to the Navy Judge Advocate General.

2. For Ickes's concerns, see Ickes to Roosevelt, 5 April 1945, *FRUS 1945*, 1:198–199. For Stettinius's report to Roosevelt about Ickes's thoughts, see Stettinius, "Extracts from the Diary of Edward R. Stettinius Jr., Secretary of State, 1 December 1944–1 July 1945," section 8, 18 March–7 April, 1945, *FRUS 1945*, 1:140–141. The arrangement that Ickes was referring to was Fortas's March 1945 strategic trusteeship idea that is recounted in Louis, *Imperialism at Bay*, 461–573; Friedman, *Creating an American Lake*, 13–14, 21, and 72; and chapter 4, n. 16 of this study.

3. Harold Ickes, "The Philippines Comes Of Age," manuscript in folder Correspondence, April 1945–May 1945, box 117, Papers of Harold Ickes, Manuscript Division, Library of Congress, Washington, D.C. (hereafter cited as the Ickes Papers), 1–4.

4. Ibid., 4–7.

5. Ibid., 7–10.

6. Ibid., 10–14.

7. Ibid., 15–18. Of course, not stated by Ickes was what would be very clear, racially-based resistance by most Caucasian-Americans to so many Filipinos enjoying civil rights on a par with whites in the mainland United States. For Caucasian-American resistance to people in the United States' Pacific Basin territories being granted basic civil rights in the postwar period, see Roger Bell, *Last Among Equals: Hawaiian Statehood and American Politics* (Honolulu: University of Hawaii Press, 1984).

8. Ickes to Truman, 12 September 1945, folder OF 85-L, Trusteeship of the Pacific Islands, May 1945–1950, box 572, White House Official Files (hereafter cited as WHOF), HSTL, 1–2.

9. Truman to Ickes, 13 September 1945, folder OF 85-L, Trusteeship of the Pacific Islands, May 1945–1950, box 572, WHOF, HSTL.

10. Fortas to Truman, 28 September 1945, folder OF 85-L, Trusteeship of the Pacific Islands, May 1945–1950, box 572, WHOF, HSTL.

11. Truman to Ickes, no date, folder OF 85-L, Trusteeship of the Pacific Islands, May 1945–1950, box 572, WHOF, HSTL.

12. Acting Secretary of the Interior Oscar Chapman to incoming Secretary of the Interior Julius Krug, 18, 15 March 1946, folder Julius A. Krug, 1946–1947, box 401, Ickes Papers.

13. Ickes to Forrestal, 29 December 1945, folder Trusteeship of the Pacific Islands, May 1945–1950, 1 of 4, folder OF 85-L, box 572, WHOF, HSTL, 1–2.

14. Clark to Ickes, 12 February 1946, folder Pacific Islands, 1946–1948, box 407, Ickes Papers.

15. Beecroft, "The Pacific Islands," no date, folder Pacific Islands, 1946–1948, box 407, Ickes Papers, 1–2.

16. Byrnes to Truman, 6 March 1946, folder Pacific Islands Commission, box 133, PSF, HSTL, 1–2.

17. Arnold, Memorandum for Secretary of State Byrnes, Secretary of War Patterson, Secretary of the Navy Forrestal, and Acting Secretary of the Interior Chapman, 20 February 1946, folder Pacific Islands Commission, box 133, PSF, HSTL, 1–3.

18. "Suggested Position for State-War-Navy-Interior Conversations," no date, folder Pacific Islands, 1946–1948, box 76, Ickes Papers, 1–3.

19. Ibid., 3–4.

20. Ibid., 4–6.

21. Emil Sady, "Future Administration of the Trust Territory of the Pacific Islands," 8 April 1947, folder E. J. Sady, box 76, Papers of Phileo Nash (hereafter cited as the Phileo Nash Papers), HSTL, 1–3. Although a State Department officer at this time, Sady's points are analyzed here because he was very involved with dependent area affairs. He had come to the State Department after serving in the Interior Department's Office of Indian Affairs between 1939 and 1943, and then as an officer in the Navy from 1943 to 1946. After serving in the State Department as an Assistant and then Specialist on Dependent Area Affairs, he would transfer back to the Interior Department in 1948 as Chief of the Pacific Branch in the Department's Division of Territories and Island Possessions.

22. Ibid., 4–5.

23. Ibid., 6–10.

24. Ibid., 11–14.

25. Ibid., 14–15.

26. Ibid., 16–18.

27. Ibid., 18–19.

28. Ibid., 19–21.

29. Ibid., 21–23.

30. Ibid., 23–27.

31. Ibid., 28–31.

32. Ibid., 31–32.

33. Davidson to Krug, 17 April 1947, folder Civil Government in the Pacific, box 74, Papers of Julius Krug, Manuscript Division, Library of Congress, Washington, D.C. (hereafter cited as the Krug Papers).

34. Krug to Truman, 12 May 1947, folder OF 85-L, Trusteeship of the Pacific Islands, May 1945–1950, box 572, WHOF, HSTL.

35. Krug, "Report to the President, Pacific Island Inspection Tour of J. A. Krug, Secretary of the Interior, February–March 1947," folder OF 85-L, Trusteeship of the Pacific Islands, May 1945–1950, box 572, WHOF, HSTL, 1.

36. Ibid., 1–3.

37. Ibid., 3.

38. Ibid., 4.
39. Ibid., 4–5.
40. Ibid., 5–7.
41. Ibid., 7.
42. Ibid., 7–8.
43. Ibid., 8–10.
44. Ibid., 10.
45. Ibid., 10–11.
46. Ibid., 12.
47. Kingsley to Steelman, 19 May 1947, attached to the Krug Report, folder OF 85-L, Trusteeship of the Pacific Islands, May 1945–1950, box 572, WHOF, HSTL.

Bibliography

The following entries indicate the major and minor collections of archival materials that I employed to analyze War, Navy, State, and Interior Department Pacific Basin policies from 1945 to 1947. The most useful collections included the Strategic Plans Division Records at the Navy Operational Archives and the National Archives II; the Papers of Harold Ickes, Julius Krug, Carl Spaatz, and John Towers at the Library of Congress; the Pre-Presidential Papers and the Papers of Lauris Norstad at the Dwight D. Eisenhower Library; the AFPAC, SCAP, and Radiograms records at the Douglas MacArthur Memorial Archives and Library; and the Ennis Whitehead Collection and Pacific Air Command, United States Army records at the Air Force Historical Research Agency. Also heavily consulted were the designated *Foreign Relations of the United States* volumes for 1945, 1946, and 1947; the microfilm version of *The Forrestal Diaries*; the Records of the Department of State at the National Archives II; the cited House and Senate appropriations hearings; and various articles in the *United States Naval Institute Proceedings*. While not all of the primary and secondary sources listed were directly cited in this monograph, they were used to write the author's Master's thesis, Ph.D. dissertation, journal articles, and first book. I have therefore cited these sources, especially as many of them deal with the United States in the Pacific Basin, a very specialized field of scholarship. It is hoped that other researchers may find these sources valuable in their own endeavors, particularly for context on the US role in the Pacific since the 1800s.

■ Archival and Manuscript Records

Air Force Historical Research Agency, Maxwell Air Force Base, Montgomery, Alabama

Annotated Guide to Documents in the USAF Historical Research Center Relating to United States Armed Forces in the Pacific, August 1945–June 1950

Assistant Chief of Air Staff for Intelligence Files

Ennis Whitehead Collection

Muir Fairchild Collection

George Kenney Collection

Curtis LeMay Collection

Pacific Air Command, United States Army Records

Report of the Joint Board for the Military Development of the Marianas

Records on Soviet Activity in Siberia

Strategic Air Command–1946

U.S. Fifth Air Force Records

War Department *Intelligence Review*

Dwight D. Eisenhower Library, Abilene, Kansas

Pre-Presidential Papers

Papers of Lauris Norstad

War Department Operations and Plans Division Wartime Diary

Harry S. Truman Library, Independence, Missouri

Oral History Collection

Papers of Edward Bowles

Papers of George Elsey

Papers of Phileo Nash

Papers of John Sullivan

President's Secretary's Files

Record Group 220: Records of Temporary Committees, Commissions, and Boards

White House Central Files

White House Official Files

Library of Congress, Washington, D.C.

Papers of Harold Ickes

Papers of Julius Krug

Papers of William Leahy

Papers of Carl Spaatz

Papers of John Towers

Douglas MacArthur Memorial Archives and Library, Norfolk, Virginia

Record Group 4: Records of the General Headquarters, U.S. Army Forces, Pacific

Record Group 5: Records of the Supreme Commander for the Allied Powers, Japan, 1945–1951

Record Group 6: General Records of the Headquarters, U.S. Far East Command, 1947–1951

Record Group 9: Collections of Messages (Radiograms), 1945–1951

National Archives II, College Park, Maryland

Record Group 38: Records of the Office of the Chief of Naval Operations

Record Group 48: Records of the Department of the Interior

Record Group 59: Records of the Department of State

Record Group 80: General Records of the Office of the Secretary of the Navy

Record Group 126: Records of the Office of Territories

Record Group 218: Records of the Combined and Joint Chiefs of Staff

National Personnel Records Center, St. Louis, Missouri

Emil Sady File

Navy Operational Archives, Washington, D.C.

Officer Biographical Collection

Papers of Louis Denfield

Post–1 January 1946 Command File

Post–1 January 1946 Report File

Strategic Plans Division Records

Records of the Politico-Military Affairs Division

■ Microfilm Collections

The Forrestal Diaries, 1944–1949. Papers of James Forrestal. Washington, D.C.: NPPSO-Naval
  District Washington Microfilm Section, 1973–1979. Microfilm.

State-War-Navy Coordinating Committee Policy Files, 1944–1947. Papers of the State-War-Navy
  Coordinating Committee. Wilmington, Del.: Scholarly Resources, Inc., 1977. Microfilm.

■ United States Government Publications

United States Department of State. *Foreign Relations of the United States* (*FRUS*).

FRUS, 1945. Volume 1, *General: The United Nations.* Washington, D.C.: GPO, 1967.

FRUS, 1945. Volume 2, *Political and Economic Affairs.* Washington, D.C.: GPO, 1967.

FRUS, 1946. Volume 1, *General: The United Nations.* Washington, D.C.: GPO, 1972.

FRUS, 1947. Volume 1, *General: The United Nations.* Washington, D.C.: GPO, 1973.

FRUS, 1947. Volume 6, *The Far East.* Washington, D.C.: GPO, 1972.

Richard, Dorothy. *United States Naval Administration of the Trust Territory of the Pacific Islands.* Volumes 1–3. Washington, D.C.: Office of the Chief of Naval Operations, 1957–1963.

United States Congress. House. Committee on Naval Affairs. *Study of Pacific Bases: A Report by the Subcommittee on Pacific Bases.* 79th Congress, 1st session. Washington, D.C.: GPO, 1945.

United States Congress. House. Committee on Appropriations. *Navy Department Appropriation Bill for 1946: Hearings before the Subcommittee on Navy Department Appropriations.* 79th Congress, 1st session. Washington, D.C.: GPO, 1945.

United States Congress. House. Committee on Appropriations. *Navy Department Appropriation Bill for 1947: Hearings before the Subcommittee on Navy Department Appropriations.* 79th Congress, 2nd session. Washington, D.C.: GPO, 1946.

United States Congress. Senate. Committee on Appropriations. *Navy Department Appropriation Bill for 1946: Hearings before the Subcommittee on Navy Department Appropriations.* 79th Congress, 1st session. Washington, D.C.: GPO, 1945.

United States Congress. Senate. Committee on Appropriations. *Navy Department Appropriation Bill for 1947: Hearings before the Subcommittee on Appropriations.* 80th Congress, 1st session. Washington, D.C.: GPO, 1946.

United States Congress. Senate. Committee on Foreign Relations. *Trusteeship Agreement for the Territory of the Pacific Islands: Hearings before the Committee on Foreign Relations.* 80th Congress, 1st session. Washington, D.C.: GPO, 1947.

■ Published Works

Adler, Les, and Thomas Paterson. "Red Fascism: The Merger of Nazi Germany and Soviet Russia in the American Image of Totalitarianism, 1930s–1950s." *American Historical Review* 75 (April 1970): 1046–1064.

Albion, Robert. *Makers of Naval Policy, 1798–1947.* Annapolis, Md.: Naval Institute Press, 1980.

Alcalay, Glenn. "Maelstrom in the Marshall Islands: The Social Impact of Nuclear Weapons Testing." In *Micronesia as Strategic Colony: The Impact of U.S. Policy on Micronesian Health and Culture,* edited by Catherine Lutz, 25–36. Cambridge, Mass.: Cultural Survival, Inc., 1984.

Allard, Dean. "Interservice Differences in the United States, 1945–1950: A Naval Perspective." *Airpower Journal* 3 (Winter 1989): 71–85.

Bailey, Beth, and David Farber. *The First Strange Place: Race and Sex in World War II Hawaii.* Baltimore: Johns Hopkins University Press, 1992.

Ballendorf, Dirk. "Captain Samuel J. Masters, US Consul to Guam, 1854–56: Harbinger of American Pacific Expansion." *Diplomacy and Statecraft* 2 (November 1991): 306–326.

——. "A Historical Perspective on the Adaption and Addiction of Western Technology and Its Transfer in Micronesia." *Asian Culture (Asian-Pacific Culture) Quarterly* 18 (Autumn 1990): 33–44.

——. "An Historical Perspective on Economic Development in Micronesia, 1783 to 1945." *Asian Culture (Asian-Pacific Culture) Quarterly* 19 (Summer 1991): 47–58.

——. "Interpreting the Cultures of Micronesia: Three Paradigms of Pacific Historiography." *Journal of The Pacific Society* 13 (July 1990): 1–8.

——. "The Japanese and the Americans: Contrasting Historical Periods of Economic and Social Development in Palau." *Journal of The Pacific Society* 11 (October 1988): 7–13.

——. "Secrets without Substance: U.S. Intelligence in the Japanese Mandates, 1915–1945." *Journal of Pacific History* 19 (April 1984): 83–99.

Baratta, Joseph. "Was the Baruch Plan a Proposal for World Government?" *International History Review* 7 (November 1985): 592–621.

Barlow, Jeffrey. "The Revolt of the Admirals Reconsidered." In *New Interpretations in Naval History: Selected Papers from the Eighth Naval History Symposium*, edited by William Cogar, 224–243. Annapolis, Md.: Naval Institute Press, 1989.

Barnhart, Michael. *Japan Prepares for Total War: The Search for Economic Security, 1919–1941*. Ithaca, N.Y.: Cornell University Press, 1987.

Bell, Roger. *Last Among Equals: Hawaiian Statehood and American Politics*. Honolulu: University of Hawaii Press, 1984.

——. *Unequal Allies: Australian-American Relations and the Pacific War*. Melbourne: Melbourne University Press, 1977.

Bernstein, Barton. "The Alarming Japanese Buildup on Southern Kyushu, Growing U.S. Fears, and Counterfactual Analysis: Would the Planned November 1945 Invasion of Southern Kyushu Have Occurred?" *Pacific Historical Review* 68 (November 1999): 561–609.

——. "The Quest for Security: American Foreign Policy and International Control of Atomic Energy, 1942–1946." *Journal of American History* 60 (March 1974): 1003–1044.

Blackburn, Paul. "Oil To Burn?" *United States Naval Institute Proceedings* (hereafter *USNIP*) 74 (December 1948): 1487–1489.

Blair, Clay. *Silent Victory: The U.S. Submarine War against Japan*. Annapolis, Md.: Naval Institute Press, 2001.

Blandy, W. H. P. "Operation Crossroads: The Story of the Air and Underwater Tests of the Atomic Bomb at Bikini." *Army Ordnance* 31 (January–February 1947): 341–343.

Blum, Robert. *Drawing the Line: The Origin of American Containment Policy in East Asia*. New York: Norton Publishers, 1982.

Boneparth, Ellen, and M. James Wilkinson. "Terminating Trusteeship for the Federated States of Micronesia and the Republic of the Marshall Islands: Independence and Self-Sufficiency in the Post–Cold War Pacific." *Pacific Studies* 18 (June 1995): 61–77.

Borowski, Harry. "Air Force Atomic Capability from V-J Day to the Berlin Blockade—Potential or Real?" *Military Affairs* 44 (October 1980): 105–110.

———. *A Hollow Threat: Strategic Airpower and Containment before Korea.* Westport, Conn.: Greenwood Press, 1982.

Boyd, Carl, and Akihiko Yoshida. *The Japanese Submarine Force in World War II.* Annapolis, Md.: Naval Institute Press, 1995.

Braisted, William. "The Philippine Naval Base Problem, 1898–1909." *Mississippi Valley Historical Review* 41 (June 1954): 21–40.

———. *The United States Navy in the Pacific, 1897–1909.* Austin: University of Texas Press, 1958.

———. *The United States Navy in the Pacific, 1909–1922.* Austin: University of Texas Press, 1971.

Brands, H. W. *Bound to Empire: The United States and the Philippines.* New York: Oxford University Press, 1992.

Brune, Lester. "Considerations of Force in Cordell Hull's Diplomacy, July 26 to November 26, 1941." *Diplomatic History* 2 (Fall 1978): 389–405.

———. *The Origins of American National Security Policy: Sea Power, Air Power, and Foreign Policy, 1900–1941.* Manhattan, Kans.: MA/AH Publishing, Sunflower University Press, 1981.

Buell, Thomas. *Master of Sea Power: A Biography of Fleet Admiral Ernest J. King.* Boston: Little, Brown and Company, 1980.

———. *The Quiet Warrior: A Biography of Admiral Raymond A. Spruance.* Boston: Little, Brown and Company, 1974.

Buhite, Russell, and William Christopher Hamel. "War for Peace: The Question of an American Preventive War, 1945–1955." *Diplomatic History* 14 (Summer 1990): 367–384.

Burns, Richard Dean. "Inspection of the Mandates, 1919–1941." *Pacific Historical Review* 37 (November 1968): 445–462.

Campbell, I. C. *A History of the Pacific Islands.* Berkeley: University of California Press, 1989.

Caraley, Demetrios. *The Politics of Military Unification: A Study of Conflict and the Policy Process.* New York: Columbia University Press, 1966.

Carano, Paul, and Pedro Sanchez. *A Complete History of Guam.* Rutland, Vt.: Charles E. Tuttle Company, 1964.

Chambliss, W. C. "Base Nonsense." *USNIP* 71 (February 1945): 202–207.

Christman, Al. *Target Hiroshima: Deak Parsons and the Creation of the Atomic Bomb.* Annapolis, Md.: Naval Institute Press, 1998.

Clark, T. O. "The Administration of the Former Japanese Mandated Islands." *USNIP* 72 (April 1946): 511–515.

Claude, Inis. *Swords into Plowshares: The Problems and Progress of International Organizations.* New York: Random House, 1984.

Cohen, Warren. *The Cambridge History of American Foreign Relations.* Volume 4, *America in the Age of Soviet Power, 1945–1991.* Cambridge: Cambridge University Press, 1993.

Coletta, Paolo. "The Defense Unification Battle, 1947–1950: The Navy." *Prologue: The Journal of the National Archives* 7 (Spring 1975): 6–17.

———. "Rear Admiral Patrick N. L. Bellinger, Commander Patrol Wing Two, and General Frederick L. Martin, Air Commander, Hawaii." In *New Interpretations in Naval History: Selected Papers from the Eighth Naval History Symposium,* edited by William B. Cogar, 263–278. Annapolis, Md.: Naval Institute Press, 1989.

——. *The United States Navy and Defense Unification, 1947–1953.* Newark, Del.: University of Delaware Press, 1981.

Converse, Elliot. "United States Plans for a Postwar Overseas Military Base System, 1942–1948." Ph.D. diss., Princeton University, 1984.

Coox, Alvin. *The Anatomy of a Small War: The Soviet-Japanese Struggle for Changkufeng/Khasan, 1938.* Westport, Conn.: Greenwood Press, 1977.

——. *Nomonhan: Japan against Russia, 1939.* Stanford, Calif.: Stanford University Press, 1985.

Costigliola, Frank. *Awkward Dominion: American Political, Economic, and Cultural Relations with Europe, 1919–1933.* Ithaca, N.Y.: Cornell University Press, 1984.

Cranwell, John Philips. "Sea Power and the Atomic Bomb." *USNIP* 72 (October 1946): 1267–1275.

Cullather, Nick. *Illusions of Influence: The Political Economy of United States–Philippines Relations, 1942–1960.* Stanford, Calif.: Stanford University Press, 1994.

——. "The Limits of Multilateralism: Making Policy for the Philippines, 1945–1950." *International History Review* 13 (February 1991): 70–95.

Cumings, Bruce. *The Origins of the Korean War: Liberation and the Emergence of Separate Regimes, 1945–1947.* Princeton, N.J.: Princeton University Press, 1981.

——. *The Origins of the Korean War: The Roaring of the Cataract, 1947–1950.* Princeton, N.J.: Princeton University Press, 1990.

Davis, Vincent. *The Admirals' Lobby.* Chapel Hill: University of North Carolina Press, 1967.

——. *Postwar Defense Policy and the U.S. Navy, 1943–1946.* Chapel Hill: University of North Carolina Press, 1966.

Daws, Gavan. *Shoal of Time: A History of the Hawaiian Islands.* Honolulu: University of Hawaii Press, 1968.

Dedman, John. "Encounter over Manus." *Australian Outlook* 20 (August 1966): 135–153.

DeSmith, Stanley. *Microstates and Micronesia: Problems of America's Pacific Islands and Other Minute Territories.* New York: New York University Press, 1970.

Dingman, Roger. *Power in the Pacific: The Origins of Naval Arms Limitations, 1914–1922.* Chicago: University of Chicago Press, 1976.

Dorrance, John. *The United States and the Pacific Islands.* Westport, Conn.: Praeger Publishers, 1992.

Dorwart, Jeffrey. *Conflict of Duty: The U.S. Navy's Intelligence Dilemma, 1919–1945.* Annapolis, Md.: Naval Institute Press, 1983.

——. "Forrestal and the Navy Plan of 1945: Mahanian Doctrine or Corporatist Blueprint?" In *New Interpretations in Naval History: Selected Papers from the Eighth Naval History Symposium,* edited by William Cogar, 209–223. Annapolis, Md.: Naval Institute Press, 1989.

Dower, John. "Occupied Japan and the American Lake, 1945–50." In *America's Asia: Dissenting Essays on Asian-American Relations,* edited by Edward Friedman and Mark Selden, 146–206. New York: Vintage Books, 1971.

——. *War Without Mercy: Race and Power in the Pacific War.* New York: Pantheon Books, 1986.

Drake, Frederick. *The Empire of the Seas: A Biography of Rear Admiral Robert Wilson Shufeldt, USN.* Honolulu: University of Hawaii Press, 1984.

Emerson, Rupert. "American Policy toward Pacific Dependencies." *Pacific Affairs* 20 (September 1947): 259–275.

Etzold, Thomas, and John Lewis Gaddis, eds. *Containment: Documents on American Policy and Strategy, 1945–1950.* New York: Columbia University Press, 1978.

Evangelista, Matthew. "Stalin's Postwar Army Reappraised." *International Security* 7 (Winter 1982–1983): 110–138.

Evatt, Herbert. "The Future of the Pacific." *Pacific Historical Review* 14 (June 1945): 145–156.

Farrell, James. "The Crossroads of Bikini." *Journal of American Culture* 10 (Summer 1987): 55–66.

Firth, Stewart. "The Nuclear Issues in the Pacific Islands." *Journal of Pacific History* 21 (October 1986): 202–216.

Fisch, Arnold. *Military Government in the Ryukyus, 1945–1950.* Washington, D.C.: United States Army Center for Military History, 1988.

Foltos, Lester. "The New Pacific Barrier: America's Search for Security in the Pacific, 1945–1947." *Diplomatic History* 13 (Summer 1989): 317–342.

Forsyth, W. D. "Stability in the Pacific: Australia's Position." *Pacific Affairs* 16 (March 1943): 7–18.

Frank, Richard. *Guadalcanal: The Definitive Account of the Landmark Battle.* New York: Random House, 1990.

Friedman, Hal. "'Americanism' and Strategic Security: The Pacific Basin, 1943–1947." *American Diplomacy* 2, no. 3 (1997) [electronic journal, cited October–December 1997], available at http://www.unc.edu/depts/diplomat/AD_Issues/amdipl_5/friedman.html.

——. "Arguing over Empire: Interservice and Interdepartmental Rivalry over Micronesia, 1943–1947." *Journal of Pacific History* 29 (June 1994): 36–48.

——. "The 'Bear' in the Pacific? U.S. Intelligence Perceptions of Soviet Strategic Power Projection in the Pacific Basin and East Asia, 1945–1947." *Intelligence and National Security* 12 (October 1997): 75–101.

——. "The Beast in Paradise: The United States Navy in Micronesia, 1943–1947." *Pacific Historical Review* 62 (May 1993): 173–195.

——. "Civil versus Military Administration: The Interior Department's Position on US Pacific Territories, 1945–1947." *Pacific Studies* 29, no. 1/2 (March–June 2006).

——. *Creating an American Lake: United States Imperialism and Strategic Security in the Pacific Basin, 1945–1947.* Westport, Conn.: Greenwood Press, 2001.

——. "Creating an American Lake: United States Imperialism, Strategic Security, and the Pacific Basin, 1945–1947." Ph.D. diss., Michigan State University, 1996.

——. "Islands and Admirals: The United States Navy, Micronesia, and the Origins of the Cold War, 1945–1947." Master's thesis, Michigan State University, 1991.

——. "The Limitations of Collective Security: The United States and the Micronesian Trusteeship, 1945–1947." *ISLA: A Journal of Micronesia Studies* 3 (Dry Season 1995): 339–370.

——. "Modified Mahanism: Pearl Harbor, the Pacific War, and Changes to U.S. National Security Strategy in the Pacific Basin, 1945–1947." *The Hawaiian Journal of History* 31 (1997): 179–204.

———. "An Open Door in Paradise? United States Strategic Security and Economic Policy in the Pacific Islands, 1945–1947." *Pacific Studies* 20 (March 1997): 63–87.

———. "'Races Undesirable from a Military Point of View': United States Cultural Security in the Pacific Islands, 1945–1947." *Journal of Pacific History* 32 (June 1997): 49–70.

Gaddis, John Lewis. "The Strategic Perspective: The Rise and Fall of the 'Defensive Perimeter' Concept, 1947–1951." In *Uncertain Years: Chinese-American Relations, 1947–1953*, edited by Dorothy Borg and Waldo Heinrichs, 61–118. New York: Columbia University Press, 1980.

———. *The United States and the Origins of the Cold War, 1941–1947*. New York: Columbia University Press, 1972.

———. *We Now Know: Rethinking Cold War History*. New York: Oxford University Press, 1997.

Gale, Roger. *The Americanization of Micronesia: A Story of the Consolidation of U.S. Rule in the Pacific*. Washington, D.C.: University Press of America, 1979.

Gallicchio, Marc. *The Cold War Begins in Asia: American East Asian Policy and the Fall of the Japanese Empire*. New York: Columbia University Press, 1988.

———. "The U.S. and the Kuriles Controversy: Strategy and Diplomacy in the Soviet-Japan Border Dispute, 1941–1956." *Pacific Historical Review* 60 (February 1991): 69–101.

Gardner, Lloyd. *Approaching Vietnam: From World War II through Dienbienphu*. New York: W. W. Norton & Company, 1988.

Gentile, Gian. "Shaping the Past Battlefield, 'For the Future': The United States Strategic Bombing Survey's Evaluation of the American Air War against Japan." *Journal of Military History* 64 (October 2000): 1085–1112.

Gerber, Larry. "The Baruch Plan and the Origins of the Cold War." *Diplomatic History* 6 (Winter 1982): 69–95.

Gibson, Arrell, and John Whitehead. *Yankees in Paradise: The Pacific Basin Frontier*. Albuquerque: University of New Mexico Press, 1993.

Goldstein, Donald. "Ennis C. Whitehead, Aerospace Commander and Pioneer." Ph.D. diss., University of Denver, 1970.

Gordon, Leonard. "American Planning for Taiwan, 1942–1945." *Pacific Historical Review* 37 (August 1968): 201–228.

Gormly, James. *The Collapse of the Grand Alliance, 1945–1948*. Baton Rouge: Louisiana State University Press, 1987.

———. *From Potsdam to the Cold War: Big Three Diplomacy, 1945–1947*. Wilmington, Del.: Scholarly Resources, Inc., 1990.

———. "The Washington Declaration and the 'Poor Relation': Anglo-American Atomic Diplomacy, 1945–46." *Diplomatic History* 8 (Spring 1984): 125–143.

Graybar, Lloyd. "Bikini Revisited." *Military Affairs* 44 (October 1980): 118–123.

———. "The Buck Rogers of the Navy: Admiral William H. P. Blandy." In *New Interpretations in Naval History: Selected Papers from the Ninth Naval History Symposium*, edited by William Roberts and Jack Sweetman, 335–349. Annapolis, Md.: Naval Institute Press, 1991.

———. "The 1946 Atomic Bomb Tests: Atomic Diplomacy or Bureaucratic Infighting?" *Journal of American History* 72 (March 1986): 888–907.

Graybar, Lloyd, and Ruth Flint Graybar. "America Faces the Atomic Age: 1946." *Air University Review* 35 (January–February 1984): 68–77.

Greenman, William. "The Armed Services in Relation to a National Oil Policy." *USNIP* 72 (May 1946): 643–647.

Grenville, J. A. S., and George Young. *Politics, Strategy, and American Diplomacy: Studies in Foreign Policy, 1873–1917*. New Haven: Yale University Press, 1973.

Griffith, Thomas. *MacArthur's Airman: General George C. Kenney and the War in the Southwest Pacific*. Lawrence: University Press of Kansas, 1998.

Haight, John. "Franklin D. Roosevelt and a Naval Quarantine of Japan." *Pacific Historical Review* 40 (May 1971): 203–226.

Hanlon, David. *Remaking Micronesia: Discourses over Development in a Pacific Territory*. Honolulu: University of Hawaii Press, 1998.

Harrington, Daniel. "A Careless Hope: American Air Power and Japan, 1941." *Pacific Historical Review* 48 (May 1979): 217–238.

Harrison, Richard. "A Neutralization Plan for the Pacific: Roosevelt and Anglo-American Cooperation, 1934–1937." *Pacific Historical Review* 57 (February 1988): 47–72.

Haynes, Richard. "The Defense Unification Battle, 1947–1950: The Army." *Prologue: The Journal of the National Archives* 7 (Spring 1975): 27–31.

Heine, Carl. *Micronesia at the Crossroads: A Reappraisal of the Micronesian Political Dilemma*. Honolulu: University Press of Hawaii, 1974.

Heinrichs, Waldo. *Threshold of War: Franklin D. Roosevelt and American Entry into World War II*. New York: Oxford University Press, 1988.

Herken, Gregg. *The Winning Weapon: The Atomic Bomb in the Cold War, 1945–1950*. New York: Alfred A. Knopf, 1980.

Hersh, Seymour. *"The Target Is Destroyed": What Really Happened to Flight 007 and What America Knew about It*. New York: Random House, 1986.

Herzog, James. *Closing the Open Door: American-Japanese Diplomatic Negotiations, 1936–1941*. Annapolis, Md.: Naval Institute Press, 1973.

Hirama, Yoichi. "Japanese Naval Preparations for World War Two." *Naval War College Review* 44 (Spring 1991): 63–81.

Hoffman, Jon. *Once a Legend: "Red Mike" Edson of the Marine Raiders*. Novato, Calif.: Presidio Press, 2000.

Hogan, Michael. *A Cross of Iron: Harry S. Truman and the Origins of the National Security State, 1945–1954*. Cambridge: Cambridge University Press, 1998.

———. *Informal Entente: The Private Structure of Cooperation in Anglo-American Economic Diplomacy, 1918–1928*. Chicago: Imprint Publications, 1991.

———. *The Marshall Plan: America, Britain, and the Reconstruction of Europe*. Cambridge: Cambridge University Press, 1987.

Holland, W. L. "War Aims and Peace Aims in the Pacific." *Pacific Affairs* 15 (December 1942): 410–427.

Ickes, Harold. "The Navy at Its Worst." *Colliers* 117 (31 August 1946): 22–23 and 67.

——. *The Secret Diaries of Harold L. Ickes*. Volume 2, *The Inside Struggle, 1936–1939*. New York: Simon and Schuster, 1954.

——. *The Secret Diaries of Harold L. Ickes*. Volume 3, *The Lowering Clouds, 1939–1941*. New York: Simon and Schuster, 1954.

Iriye, Akira. *The Cambridge History of American Foreign Relations*. Volume 3: *The Globalizing of America, 1913–1945*. New York: Cambridge University Press, 1993.

——. *Power and Culture: The Japanese-American War, 1941–1945*. Cambridge, Mass.: Harvard University Press, 1981.

Isley, Jeter, and Philip Crowl. *The U.S. Marines and Amphibious War: Its Theory and Its Practice in the Pacific*. Princeton, N.J.: Princeton University Press, 1951.

James, Roy. "The Guam Congress." *Pacific Affairs* 19 (December 1946): 408–413.

Johnson, Franklyn. "The Military and the Cold War." *Military Affairs* 20 (Spring 1956): 35–39.

Johnson, Robert. *The Peace Progressives and American Foreign Relations*. Cambridge, Mass.: Harvard University Press, 1995.

Karnow, Stanley. *In Our Image: America's Empire in the Philippines*. New York: Ballantine Books, 1989.

Kaufman, Burton. *The Korean War: Challenges to Crisis, Credibility, and Command*. New York: Alfred A. Knopf, 1986.

Keiser, Gordon. *The US Marine Corps and Defense Unification, 1944–1947: The Politics of Survival*. Fort Lesley J. McNair, Washington, D.C.: National Defense University Press, 1982.

Kennaday, J. M. "A Proper Conception of Advanced Bases." *USNIP* 72 (June 1946): 789–791.

King, F. P. *Oceania and Beyond: Essays on the Pacific since 1945*. Westport, Conn.: Greenwood Press, 1976.

Kiste, Robert. "Termination of the U.S. Trusteeship in Micronesia." *Journal of Pacific History* 21 (October 1986): 127–138.

Knox, H. Gard, Frederic R. Harris, and Husband E. Kimmel. "Naval Bases–Past and Future." *USNIP* 71 (October 1945): 1147–1153.

Kolko, Gabriel. *The Politics of War: The World and United States Foreign Policy, 1943–1945*. New York: Pantheon Books, 1968.

Krieger, Wolfgang. "Was General Clay a Revisionist? Strategic Aspects of the United States Occupation of Germany." *Journal of Contemporary History* 18 (April 1983): 165–184.

LaFeber, Walter. *The American Age: United States Foreign Policy at Home and Abroad since 1750*. New York: W. W. Norton & Company, 1989.

——. *The Cambridge History of American Foreign Relations*. Volume 2: *The American Search for Opportunity, 1865–1913*. Cambridge: Cambridge University Press, 1993.

——. "Roosevelt, Churchill, and Indochina: 1942–45." *American Historical Review* 80 (December 1975): 1277–1295.

Lattimore, Eleanor. "Pacific Ocean or American Lake?" *Far Eastern Survey* 14 (7 November 1945): 313–316.

Leffler, Melvyn. "Adherence to Agreements: Yalta and the Experiences of the Early Cold War." *International Security* 11 (Summer 1986): 88–123.

———. "The American Conception of National Security and the Beginnings of the Cold War, 1945–1948." *American Historical Review* 89 (April 1984): 346–400.

———. *The Elusive Quest: America's Pursuit of European Stability and French Security, 1919–1933.* Chapel Hill: University of North Carolina Press, 1979.

———. *A Preponderance of Power: National Security, the Truman Administration, and the Cold War.* Stanford, Calif.: Stanford University Press, 1992.

———. *The Specter of Communism: The United States and the Origins of the Cold War, 1917–1953.* New York: Hill and Wang, 1994.

Lincoln, Ashbrook. "The United States Navy and the Rise of the Doctrine of Airpower." *Military Affairs* 15 (Fall 1951): 145–156.

Linn, Brian. *The U.S. Army and Counterinsurgency in the Philippine War, 1899–1902.* Chapel Hill: University of North Carolina Press, 1989.

———. *Guardians of Empire: The U.S. Army and the Pacific, 1902–1940.* Chapel Hill: University of North Carolina Press, 1997.

Livesey, William. *Mahon on Sea Power.* Norman: University of Oklahoma Press, 1986.

Louis, William Roger. *Imperialism at Bay: The United States and the Decolonization of the British Empire, 1941–1945.* Oxford: The Clarendon Press, 1977.

———. *National Security and International Trusteeship in the Pacific.* Annapolis, Md.: Naval Institute Press, 1972.

Maga, Timothy. "The Citizenship Movement in Guam, 1946–1950." *Pacific Historical Review* 53 (February 1984): 59–77.

———. *Defending Paradise: The United States and Guam, 1898–1950.* New York: Garland Press, 1988.

———. "Democracy and Defense: The Case of Guam, U.S.A., 1918–1941." *Journal of Pacific History* 20 (July 1985): 156–172.

———. "Prelude to War? The United States, Japan, and the Yap Crisis, 1918–1922." *Diplomatic History* 9 (Summer 1985): 215–231.

Mark, Eduard. "October or Thermidor? Interpretations of Statesmen and the Perception of Soviet Foreign Policy in the United States, 1927–1947." *American Historical Review* 94 (October 1989): 937–962.

Marolda, Edward, and Robert Schneller. *Shield and Sword: The United States Navy and the Persian Gulf War.* Annapolis, Md.: Naval Institute Press, 2001.

Mastny, Vojtech. *Russia's Road to the Cold War: Diplomacy, Strategy, and the Politics of Communism, 1941–1945.* New York: Columbia University Press, 1980.

May, Ernest. "American Policy and Japan's Entrance into World War I." *Mississippi Valley Historical Review* 40 (September 1953): 279–290.

Mayer, Arno. *Political Origins of the New Diplomacy, 1917–1918.* New Haven: Yale University Press, 1959.

——. *Politics and Diplomacy of Peacemaking: Containment and Counterrevolution at Versailles, 1918–1919.* London: Weidenfeld and Nicolson, 1967.

Mayers, David. "Containment and the Primacy of Diplomacy: George Kennan's Views, 1947–1948." *International Security* 11 (Summer 1986): 124–162.

McClintock, Robert. "The United Nations and Naval Power." *USNIP* 73 (June 1947): 637–647.

McCormick, Thomas. *America's Half-Century: United States Foreign Policy in the Cold War.* Baltimore: Johns Hopkins University Press, 1989.

McIntosh, K. C. "The Road Ahead." *USNIP* 71 (November 1945): 1283–1293.

McMahon, Robert. *Colonialism and Cold War: The United States and the Struggle for Indonesian Independence, 1945–1949.* Ithaca, N.Y.: Cornell University Press, 1981.

Miller, Aaron. *Search for Security: Saudi Arabian Oil and American Foreign Policy, 1939–1949.* Chapel Hill: University of North Carolina Press, 1980.

Miller, Edward. *War Plan Orange: The U.S. Strategy to Defeat Japan, 1897–1945.* Annapolis, Md.: Naval Institute Press, 1991.

Millet, Allan. *Semper Fidelis: The History of the United States Marine Corps.* New York: The Free Press, 1991.

Millis, Walter, and Eugene Duffield, eds. *The Forrestal Diaries.* New York: Viking Press, 1951.

Morris, Eric. *The Russian Navy: Myth and Reality.* New York: Stein and Day, 1977.

Muir, Malcolm. *Black Shoes and Blue Water: Surface Warfare in the United States Navy, 1945–1975.* Washington, D.C.: Naval Historical Center, 1996.

Nathan, R. S. "Geopolitics and Pacific Strategy." *Pacific Affairs* 15 (June 1942): 154–163.

Nevin, David. *The American Touch in Micronesia.* New York: W. W. Norton & Company, 1977.

Nufer, Harold. *Micronesia under American Rule: An Evaluation of the Strategic Trusteeship.* Hicksville, N.Y.: Exposition Press, 1978.

O'Connor, Raymond. "The 'Yardstick' and Naval Disarmament in the 1920s." *Mississippi Valley Historical Review* 45 (December 1958): 441–463.

Oliver, Douglas. *The Pacific Islands.* 3rd edition. Honolulu: University of Hawaii Press, 1989.

Pach, Chester. *Arming the Free World: The Origins of the United States Military Assistance Program, 1945–1950.* Chapel Hill: University of North Carolina Press, 1991.

Painter, David. *Oil and the American Century: The Political Economy of US Foreign Oil Policy, 1941–1954.* Baltimore: Johns Hopkins University Press, 1986.

Palmer, Michael. *Origins of the Maritime Strategy: The Development of American Naval Strategy, 1945–1955.* Annapolis, Md.: Naval Institute Press, 1990.

Pape, Robert. *Bombing to Win: Air Power and Coercion in War.* Ithaca, N.Y.: Cornell University Press, 1996.

Paterson, Thomas. *On Every Front: The Making of the Cold War.* New York: W. W. Norton & Company, 1979.

——. *Soviet-American Confrontation: Postwar Reconstruction and the Origins of the Cold War.* Baltimore: Johns Hopkins University Press, 1973.

Peattie, Mark. *Nanyo: The Rise and Fall of the Japanese in Micronesia, 1885–1945.* Honolulu: University of Hawaii Press, 1988.

Perkins, Whitney. *Denial of Empire: The United States and Its Dependencies.* Leyden, Netherlands: A. W. Sythoff-Leyden, 1962.

Pogue, Forrest. "The Military in a Democracy: A Review of American Caesar." *International Security* 3 (Spring 1979): 58–80.

Pollard, Robert. *Economic Security and the Origins of the Cold War, 1945–1950.* New York: Columbia University Press, 1985.

Pomeroy, Earl. "The Navy and Colonial Government." *USNIP* 71 (March 1945): 290–297.

———. *Pacific Outpost: American Strategy in Guam and Micronesia.* Stanford, Calif.: Stanford University Press, 1951.

———. "The Problem of American Overseas Bases: Some Reflections on Naval History." *USNIP* 73 (June 1947): 688–700.

Prange, Gordon. *At Dawn We Slept: The Untold Story of Pearl Harbor.* New York: Penguin Books, 1981.

Price, Willard. *Japan's Islands of Mystery.* New York: The John Day Company, 1944.

Puleston, W. D. "The Probable Effect on American National Defense of the United Nations and the Atomic Bomb." *USNIP* 72 (August 1946): 1017–1029.

Reardon, Carol. *Pickett's Charge in History and Memory.* Chapel Hill: University of North Carolina Press, 1997.

———. *Soldiers & Scholars: The U.S. Army and the Uses of Military History, 1865–1920.* Lawrence: University Press of Kansas, 1990.

Reynolds, Clark. *Admiral John H. Towers: The Struggle for Naval Air Supremacy.* Annapolis, Md.: Naval Institute Press, 1991.

———. *The Fast Carriers: The Forging of an Air Navy.* Annapolis, Md.: Naval Institute Press, 1992.

———. "Submarine Attacks on the Pacific Coast, 1942." *Pacific Historical Review* 33 (May 1964): 183–193.

Richards, Guy. "Pacific Briefing." *USNIP* 71 (February 1945): 156–171.

Richelson, Jeffrey. *American Espionage and the Soviet Target.* New York: William Morrow and Company, 1987.

Ries, John. "Congressman Vinson and the 'Deputy' to the JCS Chairman." *Military Affairs* 30 (Spring 1966): 16–24.

Rigby, Barry. "The Origins of American Expansion in Hawaii and Samoa, 1865–1900." *International History Review* 10 (May 1988): 221–237.

Riste, Olva. "Free Ports in North Norway: A Contribution to the Study of FDR's Wartime Policy towards the USSR." *Journal of Contemporary History* 5, no. 4 (1970): 77–95.

Rosenberg, David Alan. "American Atomic Strategy and the Hydrogen Bomb Decision." *Journal of American History* 66 (June 1979): 62–87.

———. "The Origins of Overkill: Nuclear Weapons and American Strategy, 1945–1960." *International Security* 7 (Spring 1983): 3–71.

———. "U.S. Nuclear Stockpile." *Bulletin of the Atomic Scientist* 38 (May 1982): 25–30.

Rosenberg, David, and John Greenwood. "Additional Observations," addendum to David

Rosenberg, "American Postwar Air Doctrine and Organization: The Navy Experience." In *Air Power and Warfare: The Proceedings of the 8th Military History Symposium, United States Air Force Academy, 18–20 October 1978,* edited by Alfred Hurley and Robert Ehrhard, 279. Washington, D.C.: Government Printing Office, 1979.

Rosenberg, David A., and Floyd D. Kennedy Jr. *History of the Strategic Arms Competition, 1945–1972.* Supporting Study: US Aircraft Carriers in the Strategic Role. Part 1, Naval Strategy in a Period of Change: Interservice Rivalry, Strategic Interaction, and the Development of a Nuclear-Attack Capability, 1945–1951. Falls Church, Va.: Lulejian Associates, 1975.

Rosenberg, Emily. *Spreading the American Dream: American Economic and Cultural Expansion, 1890–1945.* New York: Hill and Wang, 1982.

Rotter, Andrew. "The Triangular Route to Vietnam: The United States, Great Britain, and Southeast Asia, 1945–1950." *International History Review* 6 (August 1984): 404–423.

Rowcliff, G. J. "Guam." *USNIP* 71 (February 1945): 781–793.

Rowe, David Nelson. "Collective Security in the Pacific: An American View." *Pacific Affairs* 18 (March 1945): 5–21.

Rubenstein, Donald. "Love and Suffering: Adolescent Socialization and Suicide in Micronesia." *Contemporary Pacific* 7 (Spring 1995): 21–53.

Sbrega, John. "Determination versus Drift: The Anglo-American Debate over the Trusteeship Issue, 1941–1945." *Pacific Historical Review* 55 (May 1986): 256–280.

Schaller, Michael. *The American Occupation of Japan: The Origins of the Cold War in Asia.* New York: Oxford University Press, 1985.

——. *Douglas MacArthur: The Far Eastern General.* New York: Oxford University Press, 1989.

——. "Securing the Great Crescent: Occupied Japan and the Origins of Containment in Southeast Asia." *Journal of American History* 69 (September 1982): 392–414.

Schilling, Warner, Paul Hammond, and Glenn Snyder. *Strategy, Politics, and Defense Budgets.* New York: Columbia University Press, 1962.

Schroeder, John. *Shaping a Maritime Empire: The Commercial and Diplomatic Role of the American Navy, 1829–1861.* Westport, Conn.: Greenwood Press, 1985.

Sherry, Michael. *Preparing for the Next War: American Plans for Postwar Defense, 1941–1945.* New Haven: Yale University Press, 1977.

——. *The Rise of American Air Power: The Creation of Armageddon.* New Haven: Yale University Press, 1987.

——. *The United States Navy, the Mediterranean, and the Cold War, 1945–1947.* Westport, Conn.: Greenwood Press, 1992.

Sherwin, Martin. "The Atomic Bomb and the Origins of the Cold War: U.S. Atomic-Energy Policy and Diplomacy, 1941–1945." *American Historical Review* 78 (October 1973): 945–968.

——. *A World Destroyed: Hiroshima and the Origins of the Arms Race.* New York: Random House, 1987.

Shurcliff, William. *Bombs at Bikini: The Official Report of Operation Crossroads.* New York: W. H. Wise, 1947.

Siracusa, Joseph, and Glen St. John Barclay. "Australia, the United States, and the Cold War, 1945–51: From V-J Day to ANZUS." *Diplomatic History* 5 (Winter 1981): 39–52.

Smith, Perry. *The Air Force Plans for Peace*. Baltimore: Johns Hopkins University Press, 1970.

Smith, Russell. "Notes on Our Naval Future." *USNIP* 72 (April 1946): 489–503.

Spector, Ronald. *Eagle Against the Sun: The American War with Japan*. New York: The Free Press, 1985.

Stoler, Mark. "From Continentalism to Globalism: General Stanley D. Embick, the Joint Strategic Survey Committee, and the Military View of American National Policy during the Second World War." *Diplomatic History* 6 (Summer 1982): 303–321.

———. "The 'Pacific-First' Alternative in American World War II Strategy." *International History Review* 2 (July 1980): 432–452.

———. *The Politics of the Second Front: American Military Planning and Diplomacy in Coalition Warfare, 1941–1943*. Westport, Conn.: Greenwood Press, 1977.

Strauss, W. Patrick. *Americans in Polynesia, 1783–1842*. East Lansing: Michigan State University Press, 1963.

Strope, Walmer Elton. "The Navy and the Atomic Bomb." *USNIP* 73 (October 1947): 1221–1227.

Talbert, Roy. *Negative Intelligence: The Army and the American Left, 1917–1941*. Jackson: University Press of Mississippi, 1991.

Tate, Merze, and Doris Hull. "Effects of Nuclear Explosions on Pacific Islanders." *Pacific Historical Review* 33 (November 1964): 379–393.

Thompson, Wayne. *To Hanoi and Back: The U.S. Air Force and North Vietnam, 1966–1973*. Washington, D.C.: Smithsonian Institution Press, 2000.

Thorne, Christopher. *Allies of a Kind: The United States, Britain, and the War against Japan, 1941–1945*. Oxford: Oxford University Press, 1978.

Trachtenberg, Marc. "A 'Wasting Asset': American Strategy and the Shifting Nuclear Balance, 1949–1954." *International Security* 13 (Winter 1988–1989): 5–49.

Truman, Harry. *Memoirs*. Volume 1, *Year of Decisions*. Garden City, N.Y.: Doubleday and Company, 1955.

Underwood, Jeffrey. *The Wings of Democracy: The Influence of Air Power on the Roosevelt Administration, 1933–1941*. College Station: Texas A&M University Press, 1991.

Vinacke, Harold. "United States Far Eastern Policy." *Pacific Affairs* 19 (December 1946): 351–363.

Warnecke, G. W. "Suetsugu's Fence—Key To Pacific Strategy." *Pacific Affairs* 15 (December 1942): 430–449.

Webb, James. *Micronesia and US Pacific Strategy: A Blueprint for the 1980s*. New York: Praeger Publishers, 1974.

Weisgall, Jonathan. "Micronesia and the Nuclear Pacific since Hiroshima." *School of Advanced International Studies Review* 5 (Summer–Fall 1985): 41–55.

———. "The Nuclear Nomads of Bikini." *Foreign Policy* 39 (Summer 1980): 74–98.

———. *Operation Crossroads: The Atomic Bomb Tests at Bikini Atoll*. Annapolis, Md.: Naval Institute Press, 1994.

Wiens, Herold. *Pacific Island Bastions of the United States.* Princeton, N.J.: D. Van Nostrand
    Company, 1962.

Williams, William Appleman. *The Tragedy of American Diplomacy.* New York: W. W. Norton &
    Company, 1972.

Wolk, Herman. "The Defense Unification Battle, 1947–1950: The Air Force." *Prologue: The Jour-*
    nal of the National Archives 7 (Spring 1975): 18–26.

——. *Planning and Organizing the Postwar Air Force, 1943–1947.* Washington, D.C.: Office of Air
    Force History, 1984.

Wright, Carleton. "Trust Territory of the Pacific Islands." *USNIP* 74 (November 1948): 1333–
    1341.

Yergin, Daniel. *Shattered Peace: The Origins of the Cold War.* New York: Penguin Books, 1991.

Yerxa, Donald. *Admirals and Empire: The United States Navy and the Caribbean, 1898–1945.*
    Columbia: University of South Carolina Press, 1991.

Index